Your Study of
The
Doctrine and Covenants Made Easier

Part 2
Section 43 through Section 93

Second Edition

David J. Ridges

CFI, an imprint of

Springville, Utah

© 2020 David J. Ridges
All rights reserved.

No part of this book may be reproduced in any form whatsoever, whether by graphic, visual, electronic, film, microfilm, tape recording, or any other means, without prior written permission of the publisher, except in the case of brief passages embodied in critical reviews and articles.

This book is not an official publication of The Church of Jesus Christ of Latter-day Saints. The opinions and views expressed herein belong solely to the author and do not necessarily represent the opinions or views of Cedar Fort, Inc. Permission for the use of sources, graphics, and photos is also solely the responsibility of the author.

ISBN 13: 978-1-4621-3896-8

Published by CFI, an imprint of Cedar Fort, Inc.
2373 W. 700 S., Springville, UT, 84663
Distributed by Cedar Fort, Inc., www.cedarfort.com

Library of Congress Control Number: 2020945612

Cover design by Shawnda T. Craig
Cover design © 2020 Cedar Fort, Inc.

Printed in the United States of America

10 9 8 7 6 5 4 3 2 1

Printed on acid-free paper

Your Study of
The
Doctrine and Covenants Made Easier

Part 2
Section 43 through Section 93

Second Edition

DEDICATION

*To my wife, Janette, who
is my greatest blessing.*

Contents

Preface................................1
Introduction............................3
Sections
    43 6
    44 16
    45 17
    46 41
    47 55
    48 57
    49 58
    50 64
    51 74
    52 79
    53 88
    54 90
    55 92
    56 94
    57 99
    58 104
    59 119
    60 128
    61 133
    62 141
    63 143
    64 160
    65 171
    66 173

Sections

67	177
68	181
69	189
70	191
71	195
72	197
73	201
74	203
75	205
76	211
77	245
78	258
79	264
80	266
81	267
82	269
83	276
84	277
85	308
86	314
87	318
88	321
89	354
90	361
91	368
92	369
93	370

Sources 381
About the Author 385

Preface

The Doctrine and Covenants is the Savior's book to us in our day. In it, He personally teaches us the "doctrines" and "covenants" necessary to live a righteous, rewarding life, and to successfully walk along the covenant path toward eventual exaltation in the highest degree of glory in the celestial kingdom. In the October 1986 general conference of the Church, in reference to the importance of understanding the doctrines of the gospel, Elder Boyd K. Packer said:

> True doctrine, understood, changes attitudes and behavior. The study of the doctrines of the gospel will improve behavior quicker than a study of behavior will improve behavior. ("Little Children," *Ensign*, Nov. 1986)

Briefly put, "doctrines" are the teachings of the plan of salvation, the answers to questions about the meaning and purpose of life, instructions, rules, facts, hows, whys, and commandments that, if followed, will lead to exaltation. In D&C 10:62, the Lord tells us that He is going to "bring to light the true points" of His doctrine. The Doctrine and Covenants does this.

This study guide is a brief, to-the-point help to a better understanding of the doctrines of the gospel and the ordinances of salvation required for celestial exaltation. The style is somewhat conversational to help you feel as if you were being guided through the Doctrine and Covenants in one of my classes. It is designed, in many cases, to give you instant understanding of basic doctrines and principles, as well as to provide you with the background to apply them in your life, which, in turn, will help you develop a deeper understanding and testimony of the gospel. Remember that the Holy Ghost is THE teacher. He will enlighten your mind and warm your heart as you pray and study this, the Savior's book to us.

INTRODUCTION

I have had a number of friends who have told me that they "don't get much out of reading the Doctrine and Covenants." This study guide is intended to remedy that. Through background and setting notes for each section, plus brief in-the-verse notes, along with the help of the Holy Ghost, I hope you will be enabled to feel and relive the excitement and effects of these revelations on the Prophet Joseph Smith and the early participants in the Restoration and see how they apply to you. Indeed, a key to understanding and enjoying studying the Doctrine and Covenants is seeing the application of its doctrines and teachings in your own life and in the lives of your family and friends. There are boundless applications and blessings available to us directly from the Savior through the study of this book of scripture. This study guide points many of them out.

As was the case with the first edition, this second edition comes in three volumes. This is part two. This new three-volume set contains many updates and much additional historical information based on research made available through the Joseph Smith Papers Project. I have used the 2013 edition of the Doctrine and Covenants, as published by The Church of Jesus Christ of Latter-day Saints, as the basic text. References to the Bible come from the King James Version, as published by The Church of Jesus Christ of Latter-day Saints. JST references refer to the Joseph Smith Translation of the Bible.

Every verse of the Doctrine and Covenants from section 43 through section 93 is included in this second volume. All the remaining verses of the Doctrine and Covenants are contained in parts one and three of this three-volume study guide set. All three volumes have background and setting notes for each section, as well as brief notes of explanation between and within the verses to clarify and help you learn and grow in your appreciation and understanding of this sacred volume of scripture. The notes within the verses are printed in italics and enclosed in brackets in order to make it easy for you to distinguish between the actual scripture text and my teaching comments. Notes between the verses are indented and printed in a different font than the scripture text. **Bold** is often used to highlight things for teaching purposes.

You may be aware, as mentioned above, that, as a result of recent research for the Joseph Smith Papers Project, there are a number of changes to the section headings in the 2013 printing of the Doctrine and Covenants compared to previous editions. Such adjustments, most of them minor, have been made to 78 sections. One example of this is found in sections 39 and 40, where the name "James Covel" is now used rather than "James Covill." Another example of these Joseph Smith Papers Project research-based changes is this: If you are using an edition of the Doctrine and Covenants prior to the 2013 edition, you will see a number of corrected or added dates for the sections in this study guide. For example, prior to the 2013 edition of the Doctrine and Covenants, the date given for section 80 is March 1832. Based on recent research, the date is now given as March 7, 1832. Furthermore, at the time I wrote the first edition of this study guide, the then-current research for when living the Word of Wisdom became a temple recommend requirement was documented as being in the 1930s under President Heber J. Grant. However, current research has established it as being in 1919, shortly after President Grant became the Prophet. That fact is included in the background notes for section 89 in this second edition of this study guide. The Second Edition of *Doctrine and Covenants Made Easier* incorporates these changes as well as adding hundreds of additional helps and clarifications to assist you in your study.

This study guide is designed to be a user-friendly, "teacher in your hand" introductory study of this portion of the Doctrine and Covenants, as well as a refresher course for more advanced students of the scriptures. It is also designed to be a quick-reference resource that will enable readers to look up a particular passage or block of scripture for use in lessons, talks, or personal study as desired. It is my hope that you will incorporate some of the notes given in this study guide into your own scriptures, whether paper copy or on digital devices, to assist you in reading and studying this portion of the Doctrine and Covenants in the future. Thus, your own scriptures will become one of your best tools in your continued study of the gospel.

—David J. Ridges

NOTE

In section 10, verse 62, the Savior specifically told us that He was going to restore "the true points of my doctrine." "Doctrines" are eternal truths, facts, or things in the plan of salvation that do not change, such as:

- Faith, repentance, baptism, and the gift of the Holy Ghost.

- The Godhead consists of the Father, the Son, and the Holy Ghost.

- The members of the Godhead are three separate beings.

- There are three kingdoms of glory; namely, the telestial, terrestrial, and celestial.

- In the celestial kingdom, there are three degrees.

- The highest degree of glory in the celestial is called "exaltation."

- Those who attain exaltation will live in their own eternal family unit and ultimately become gods.

- Heavenly Father is completely fair, thus everyone will ultimately get a perfect opportunity before the final judgment to hear, understand, and then accept or reject the gospel.

- The sins we have repented of will not even be mentioned on Judgment Day.

- Little children who die before the years of accountability will receive exaltation.

- Ordinance work for the dead is part of the Father's plan of happiness for His children.

- We are spirit children of Heavenly Parents.

- The Atonement of Christ works for our shortcomings and imperfections as well as our sins.

- Baptism is required for entrance into the celestial kingdom, except in the case of little children who die before the age of accountability and the intellectually handicapped who do not have sufficient understanding to be accountable.

- God will not allow His living prophets to lead us astray.

- And many, many more wonderful doctrines that help us understand the "whats," "whys" and "hows" of the Father's plan of salvation for us, His children.

In the Doctrine and Covenants, the Lord has indeed restored many true doctrines, which, among other things, enable us to better live the gospel because we better understand it. Throughout these three volumes of study guides for the Doctrine and Covenants, I will often add extra notes to point out and summarize the many doctrines given by the Savior for us as He said He would. You will see an example of this immediately after verse 2, next.

SECTION 43

Background

This revelation was given through the Prophet Joseph Smith at Kirtland, Ohio, in February 1831. The Church, as an official organization, was less than one year old (having been organized on April 6, 1830). At this point in time, members were moving from New York and other locations to the Kirtland, Ohio, area as commanded by the Lord in D&C 37:3; see also D&C 38:31–32.

One of the extremely important messages to us in this section is that the Lord will not allow His prophet to lead us astray. This is a "law," as stated by the Lord in verses four and five. In other words, we are 100 percent safe in following the living prophet.

As with many other revelations in the Doctrine and Covenants, specific current problems or circumstances led up to the giving of this revelation. Many of these early members were converted from Christian churches of the day. In some of these churches, it was accepted as common practice that any member of a congregation could receive revelation for any other member or members. They could also proclaim doctrine for their entire church. As you can well imagine, such actions resulted in confusion and lack of doctrinal focus and clarity, and it was causing considerable trouble at the time of this revelation through Joseph Smith.

One notable example of this problem was that of a Mrs. Hubble, who claimed to be a prophetess of the Lord. She believed she was receiving revelations for the Church, including that she should become a teacher to the Church. The Prophet Joseph Smith spoke of her as follows:

"Soon after the foregoing revelation [D&C 42] was received, a woman [Mrs. Hubble] came making great pretensions of revealing commandments, laws and other curious matters; and as almost every person has advocates for both theory and practice, in the various notions and projects of the age, it became necessary to inquire of the Lord, when I received the following [D&C 43]" (*History of the Church*, 1:154).

In a footnote to the above quote, we learn that John Whitmer (the first official historian of the Church; see D&C 47:1) wrote of Mrs. Hubble. The footnote reads as follows:

"This woman's name, according to the history of the church kept by John Whitmer, was Hubble. 'She professed to be a prophetess of the Lord, and professed to have many revelations, and knew the

SECTION 43

Book of Mormon was true, and that she should become a teacher in the church of Christ. She appeared to be very sanctimonious and deceived some who were not able to detect her in her hypocrisy; others, however, had the spirit of discernment and her follies and abominations were manifest.' John Whitmer's *History of the Church*, Ch. 3." (See Joseph Smith, *History of the Church*, 1:154, footnote 12. See also *The Joseph Smith Papers, Histories, Volume 2: Assigned Histories, 1831–1847*, ed. Karen Lynn Davidson and others [2012], 29; spelling, capitalization, and punctuation standardized; see also *The Joseph Smith Papers, Documents, Volume 1: July 1828–June 1831*, 257, note 95).

Thus, it was quite common at this point in the early history of the Church for members to claim revelation for the Church and to attempt to correct the prophet. The Lord gives clear correction to this in verses 1–6.

Among other teachings and doctrines given in this section, you will find the role of councils in the Church (verse 8), the importance of covenants as we "bind" ourselves to safe behaviors (verse 9), and the necessity for us to support and sustain the living prophet if we want heaven's guidance through him (verses 12–14). Verses 15–35 contain a warning that the elders of the Church are to give to the inhabitants of the earth in the last days.

In these last twenty verses, we will learn brief details about the Second Coming, the rule of the righteous with the Savior during the Millennium, the binding of Satan and his subsequent loosing for a "little season," the end of the earth, the resurrection of the righteous, and the final fate of the wicked.

We will now proceed to study section 43, using **bold** for teaching emphasis, [*brackets with italics*] for teaching notes within the verses, and indentation in a different font for teaching notes and comments between verses. Remember, as we begin, that the first issue addressed by the Lord is the issue of having one person only, namely the living prophet, authorized to receive commandments and doctrine for the whole Church.

1 O HEARKEN, ye elders of my church, and give ear to the words which I shall speak unto you.

2 For behold, verily, verily, I say unto you, that ye have received a commandment for a law [*section 42*] unto my church, through him [*Joseph Smith*] **whom I have appointed unto you to receive commandments and revelations from my hand.**

Doctrine

Verses 3–5. The Lord will not let the prophet lead the Church astray.

3 And **this ye shall know** assuredly—that **there is none other appointed unto you to receive commandments and revelations** until he be taken, if he abide in me.

> Did you notice the last phrase of verse 3, above? It is an important part of understanding that the Lord will not allow the living prophet to lead us astray. It says, in effect, that the prophet will remain the Lord's mouthpiece to the Saints as long as he remains faithful and worthy. Verse 4, next, explains what would happen if the living prophet were to begin to stray. You will see that if this were to happen, the living prophet would have no more power except to appoint his successor—in other words, the prophet who would take his place. This is a very exact procedure and would leave no room for doubt or speculation on our part as to who our authorized prophet is. (This is one reason that it is so important for us to read and understand the Doctrine and Covenants. There is great security for us in so doing.)

4 But verily, verily, I say unto you, that **none else shall be appointed unto this gift** [*to serve as the living prophet*] **except it be through him**; for **if it** [*the office of prophet*] **be taken from him he shall not have power except to appoint another in his stead.**

> In verse 5, next, the Lord leaves absolutely no doubt in our minds that the above fail-safe guarantee is solidly in place so that we can completely trust the official words and teachings of our living prophet. Simply put, it is a law of God.

5 And **this shall be a law unto you**, that ye **receive not the teachings of any that shall come before you** [*except the living prophet*] **as revelations or commandments** [*in other words, as new doctrines or commandments to the whole Church*];

> Next, the Lord reminds us that this "law" is given to protect us from deception and confusion as to who gives us the final word of the Lord.

6 And **this I give unto you that you may not be deceived**, that you may know they [*people other than the prophet who claim to receive revelation for the whole Church*] are not of me.

> One thing before we go on. We have never had our living prophet lead us astray. The reason is simple. He can't. The Lord will not allow it. If he were to attempt to do so, the Lord would remove him from office, as explained here in section 43, after requiring one last thing of him, namely, to appoint his replacement under the Lord's specific direction. Apostates, people

who have left the Church, often claim that the current prophet is leading us astray. They obviously don't understand the "law" of the Lord given in verse 5, above. Thus, we know that we have no valid reason to believe their false claims and teachings.

Next, in verse 7, the Savior explains that He will have teachers and leaders in the Church, who are properly authorized and called of God, to teach and explain the revelations and commandments that have come through the living prophet.

7 For verily I say unto you, that **he that is ordained of me shall come in at the gate** [*come through proper channels; be properly called, authorized and sustained, and so forth*] **and be ordained** as I have told you before [*in D&C 42:11*], **to teach those revelations which you have received and shall receive through him** [*Joseph Smith; the living prophet*] whom I have appointed.

In verse 8, next, we are given a general format for councils in the Church. These can include ward councils, councils of presidencies, family councils, and so on. Perhaps you have noticed, especially in recent years, that the Brethren (General Authorities) have encouraged more use of councils in local church units in order to address local needs and concerns more effectively. One of the things they have especially emphasized is the need for each member of such councils to participate actively in the discussion and decision making for which such councils are designed by the Lord.

8 And now, behold, I give unto you a commandment, that when ye are assembled together **ye shall instruct and edify** [*build and strengthen*] **each other, that ye may know how to act and direct my church**, how to act upon the points of my law [*especially section 42; see D&C 42:2*] and commandments, which I have given.

The first two phrases of verse 9, next, explain the desired outcome of councils in the Church.

9 And **thus ye shall become instructed in the law of my church, and** be **sanctified** [*made pure, holy, fit to be in the presence of God; cleansed from sin*] by that which ye have received, and **ye shall bind yourselves** [*make covenants; compare with D&C 82:15*] **to act in all holiness before me—**

One of the important lessons we can gain from the last phrase in verse 9, above, is the symbolism involved in making covenants. When we make covenants with God, we are, in effect, "binding" ourselves to safe behaviors. In other words, we "bind" or tie ourselves to God when we are thinking rationally and wisely, so that later, when we are tempted to sin, we have extra incentive and strength to do what is right. Honest people are greatly strengthened by making covenants.

10 That inasmuch as ye do this, glory shall be added to the kingdom which ye have received [*one possible interpretation of this is "the Church will grow and prosper in your lives"*]. Inasmuch as ye do it not, it shall be taken, even that which ye have received [*perhaps meaning you will lose the blessings you have received, and possibly your membership in the Church*].

11 **Purge** [*cleanse*] **ye out the iniquity** [*the sin and evil*] **which is among you**; sanctify yourselves [*become more pure and holy*] before me;

> In verses 12–14, next, these early members of the Church are taught the necessity on their part of supporting and sustaining the living prophet—in this case the Prophet Joseph Smith. Part of this support involves praying for him. Another aspect of support consists of donating for his temporal needs. For us in our day, in addition to our prayers, this includes the payment of tithes and offerings, which sustain our prophet's travels and ministry throughout the Church and the world.

12 And **if ye desire the glories of the kingdom** [*if you want the full blessings of the gospel*], appoint [*sustain; see D&C 43:12, footnote 12a*] ye my servant Joseph Smith, Jun., and **uphold him before me by the prayer of faith**.

13 And again, I say unto you, that **if ye desire the mysteries of the kingdom** [*the basic, simple, revealed truths and doctrines of the gospel, not strange, obscure mysteries; see Bible Dictionary under "Mystery"*], **provide for him food and raiment** [*clothing*], and **whatsoever thing he needeth to accomplish the work wherewith I have commanded him**;

14 And **if ye do it not he shall remain unto them that have received him** [*you will be left out, and those who do support him will become the Lord's people*], that I may reserve unto myself a pure people before me.

> As mentioned in the introduction to this section, verses 15–35 explain the necessity of taking the gospel message to all the world. They provide brief glimpses into several doctrines of the Father's plan of salvation for His children, along with counsel to each of us as we do our part to spread the

gospel. We will continue to use **bold** to point things out as we study these verses.

At first, the **bolded** portion of verse 15, next, may seem a bit arrogant. But when you stop to think about it, if our missionaries were to take time to learn the philosophies and teachings of the people they are teaching, they would have no time to actually study and teach the simple gospel message they are to present.

15 Again I say, hearken ye elders of my church, whom I have appointed: **Ye are not sent forth to be taught, but to teach** the children of men the things which I have put into your hands by the power of my Spirit;

16 And **ye are to be taught from on high**. Sanctify yourselves [*repent as needed and work on becoming more clean and pure*] and **ye shall be endowed with power** [*you will be given power from God to preach and spread the Church*], that ye may give even as I have spoken.

17 Hearken ye, for, behold, **the great day of the Lord is nigh at hand** [*the Second Coming is getting close*].

18 For **the day cometh that the Lord shall utter his voice out of heaven** [*perhaps including the "voice" of thunderings, lightnings, tempests, and waves in the last days; see verse 21; see also D&C 88:90*]; the heavens shall shake and the earth shall tremble, and the trump of God shall sound both long and loud [*signaling the Second Coming and the resurrection of the righteous; see D&C 88:92, 96–97*], and shall say to the sleeping nations [*perhaps meaning spiritually asleep*]: Ye saints arise and live [*the resurrection of the righteous dead, at the beginning of the Millennium*]; ye sinners stay and sleep until I shall call again [*the wicked must wait until the end of the thousand-year Millennium to be resurrected; see D&C 88:100–102*].

In verse 19, next, you will see a rather common phrase in the scriptures: "gird up your loins." It can mean "get dressed," "be ready for action," "be prepared," and so forth, depending on the context. In this verse, as you can see, it means to be prepared spiritually to meet the Savior.

19 Wherefore **gird up your loins** [*prepare yourselves*] lest ye be found among the wicked.

Next, in verse 20, the Savior tells the elders to preach the gospel every chance they get, and to warn all people to prepare to meet Christ at His coming. This applies to all of us as we have opportunities to share the gospel. We must be careful and appropriate as we do this, by following the Lord's counsel in D&C 38:41 to teach with "mildness and in meekness."

20 **Lift up your voices** [*speak up*] and spare not [*don't hesitate*]. Call upon the nations to repent, both old and young, both bond [*slaves, people in bondage*] and free, **saying: Prepare yourselves for the great day of the Lord**;

> Verse 21 has a significant doctrinal statement by the Savior. We know that Jesus was resurrected and is a celestial being with a glorified, resurrected body of flesh and bones (see D&C 130:22). Most of the Christian churches teach that He is now a mysterious entity encompassed within the unfathomable Godhead, and that He is basically undefinable and incomprehensible to mortals. But, in the first line of verse 21, He clearly and simply states that He is a man. This is beautiful, clear, and understandable doctrine!

21 For if **I**, who **am a man** [*Jesus Christ; see verse 34*], do lift up my voice and call upon you to repent, **and ye hate** [*avoid, shrink away from; see* Webster's New World Dictionary, Second College Edition] **me**, what will ye say [*what excuses will you have for your wickedness*] when the day cometh when the thunders shall utter their voices from the ends of the earth [*when natural disasters, earthquakes, plagues, pestilences, and such increase in the last days; see D&C 88:89–91*], **speaking to the ears of all that live, saying—Repent, and prepare for the great day of the Lord** [*the Second Coming and beginning of the Millennium*]?

> In verses 21–27, the Lord explains why He is going to cause a great increase in frequency and intensity of natural disasters in the last days, leading up to His Second Coming, which will usher in the Millennium. These are often referred to as "signs of the times," meaning obvious signs and indicators that show us that the coming of the Lord is getting close. He explains in these verses that these signs are a wake-up call, a call to repentance, to the wicked and those who have strayed from God.

22 Yea, and again, when the **lightnings** shall streak forth from the east unto the west, and **shall utter forth their voices** unto all that live, and make the ears of all tingle that hear, **saying** these words—**Repent ye**, for the great day of the Lord is come?

23 And again, **the Lord shall utter his voice** out of heaven, saying: Hearken, O ye nations of the earth, and **hear the words of**

SECTION 43

that God who made you.

> In verses 24–25, next, the Lord explains that He has tried the gentle approach to gather His children to Him, but they have ignored those warm, gentle, pleasant invitations. Therefore, in effect, He has to raise His voice in order to get their attention. This is a demonstration of His mercy as He attempts to get more people to use their agency to choose to return to God, rather than being condemned on Judgment Day.

24 O, ye nations of the earth, **how often would I have gathered you** together as a hen gathereth her chickens under her wings [*symbolic of the warmth and security available to us in the arms of the Savior and His gospel*], but ye would not!

25 **How oft have I called upon you by** the mouth of **my servants**, and by the ministering of **angels**, and by **mine own voice**, and by the voice of **thunderings**, and by the voice of **lightnings**, and by the voice of **tempests**, and by the voice of **earthquakes**, and great **hailstorms**, and by the voice of **famines** and **pestilences** [*plagues, epidemics*] of every kind, and by the great sound of a **trump** [*including the pure, clear gospel truths*], and by the voice of **judgment**, and **by the voice of mercy** all the day long, and by the voice of **glory and honor and the riches of eternal life** [*exaltation*], and **would have saved you with an everlasting salvation, but ye would not!**

26 Behold, **the day has come, when the cup of the wrath of mine indignation** [*righteous anger*] **is full** [*the last days have arrived during which the Lord will express His righteous anger upon the wicked inhabitants of the earth via natural disasters and such, as explained in verse 25, above*].

> Having taught these elders (see verse 1) of the early Church what their basic message to the world is to be, Jesus now reaffirms that these are His words to them, and He invites them to move ahead with this vital work.

27 Behold, verily I say unto you, that **these are the words of the Lord your God.**

28 Wherefore [*therefore*], **labor ye, labor ye in my vineyard for the last time**—for the last time call upon the inhabitants of the earth.

> Do you remember hearing that this is the "last dispensation" and that the Church will never go into apostasy (fall away) again? It is true, and verse 28, above, is one of the places in scripture where we learn that this is the case. These early

missionaries are told that this is the "last time" that the gospel will be taught before the Savior comes (verse 29, next).

And, while we're on the subject of the Second Coming, it is important to note the caution, in verse 29, next, that Jesus gives concerning the timing of His coming. He will come in all His glory "in mine own due time"—in other words, when the timing is right. This makes it impossible to pin it down to a specific day, week, month, or even year. This is in complete harmony with Matthew 24:36 and Mark 13:32, where we are definitely told that no man can know the exact timing of the Second Coming.

29 For **in mine own due time** will I come upon the earth in judgment, and **my people** [*the faithful members of the Church*] **shall be redeemed and shall reign with me on earth** [*the righteous members of the Church will assist the Savior in governing the earth during the Millennium; see Revelation 20:4*].

Next, in verses 30–33, the Savior bears personal testimony to us that the Millennium will come, and He gives brief details of what will happen from that point to the end of the earth.

30 For **the great Millennium** [*the thousand years of peace*], of which I have spoken by the mouth of my servants, **shall come.**

Doctrine

Vs. 31. Satan will be bound during the Millennium and not allowed to tempt mortals then.

31 For **Satan shall be bound** [*will not be allowed to tempt people on earth during the Millennium (D&C 101:28)*], and when he is **loosed again** [*after the thousand years have ended; see D&C 88:110–11*] he shall only reign for **a little season** [*during which the final battle (the Battle of Gog and Magog) will take place; see D&C 88:111–15*], and then cometh the **end of the earth** [*meaning that the mortal earth will become a celestial planet, will be moved from this solar system back into the presence of the Father (see* Teachings of the Prophet Joseph Smith, *181) and will become the home of those who lived on it and who are judged worthy of celestial glory; see D&C 130:9–11*].

Doctrine

Vs. 32. When righteous mortals during the Millennium finish their earth life, they will die and be resurrected instantly.

Next, in verse 32, the Savior gives a detail about life for the righteous during the Millennium, which you have perhaps heard. It is that the righteous, after they have finished living out their mortal lives during the Millennium, will die and be resurrected instantly. We know from other scriptures that they will live to be one hundred years of age (Isaiah 65:20) and that they will actually die, but that they will not need to be buried in the ground because they will be resurrected immediately after they die (D&C 101:31).

32 And he that liveth in righteousness shall be changed in the twinkling of an eye, and the earth shall pass away so as by fire.

The last phrase of verse 32, above, could have dual meaning, referring both to the cleansing of the earth by fire at the time of the Savior's coming (see D&C 101:24–25; Matthew 3:12), as well as the celestialization of the earth after the Millennium and "little season" are over (see D&C 29:22–24).

Verse 33, next, could also have dual meaning, referring to the literal burning of the wicked at the Second Coming (they are burned, destroyed by His glory; see D&C 5:19, 2 Nephi 12:10, 19, 21), and their subsequently being turned over to Satan to suffer for their sins (see D&C 19:15–17). It certainly refers to the final state of sons of perdition (compare with D&C 76:44–48).

33 And the wicked shall go away into unquenchable fire, and their end [*their final situation*] no man knoweth on earth, nor ever shall know, until they come before me in judgment.

Finally, having given these early elders (and all of us) much counsel and instruction about the importance of sharing the gospel, and having explained several details about the plan of salvation that are vital for our understanding of the big picture and the purposes of life, Jesus now concludes, instructing them (and us) to take His words seriously.

We would do well to understand, from the Savior's approach in the above verses, that it is not enough simply to tell people to repent. Without a basic understanding of doctrines of the plan of salvation, people have no context in which to make repentance meaningful.

34 Hearken ye to these words. Behold, **I am Jesus Christ**, the Savior of the world. **Treasure these things up in your hearts**, and let the solemnities [*serious matters*] of eternity rest upon your minds [*take these things seriously, and keep the reality of living eternally firmly in mind*].

35 Be sober [*be serious-minded about serious things*]. **Keep all my commandments.** Even so. Amen.

SECTION 44

Background

The Joseph Smith Papers Project research gives helpful background information for section 44. We will quote from the 2018 *Doctrine and Covenants Student* Manual:

"Soon after arriving in Kirtland, Ohio, the Prophet Joseph Smith received the revelations recorded in Doctrine and Covenants 42, which outlined laws guiding the Church. Included was the commandment that the elders should 'go forth in the power of my Spirit, preaching my gospel, two by two. . . . And from this place ye shall go forth' (D&C 42:6, 8). The revelation recorded in Doctrine and Covenants 44 called for the elders of the Church to meet together before going forth to preach the gospel.

"The Prophet Joseph Smith acted on that instruction and sent a letter on February 22, 1831, to Martin Harris, who was still living in New York. The Prophet made reference to the revelation when he explained to Martin that 'the work is here breaking forth on the east, west, north, and south; you will also inform the Elders which are there that all of them who can be spared will come here without delay if possible, this by Commandment of the Lord as he has a great work for them all' (in *The Joseph Smith Papers, Documents, Volume 1: July 1828–June 1831*, 263; punctuation and spelling standardized).

"In subsequent weeks during the spring of 1831, many of the Saints from New York gathered to Kirtland, Ohio. The fourth conference of the Church was held in June 1831, and many elders participated in the meetings of this conference, which prepared them to leave afterward to preach the gospel."

Thus, the fourth general conference of the Church was held June 3–6, 1831, in a schoolhouse on the outskirts of Kirtland and was the first such conference held in Ohio. The three previous general conferences were held in Fayette, New York, beginning on June 9, 1830, September 26, 1830, and January 2, 1831, respectively. At this point in time, membership in the Church is approaching two thousand.

Among other things in this section, we will be taught many of the purposes of conferences held by the Church. If we understand these purposes, we will have an even greater desire to attend. We will point out a number of these purposes and benefits, using **(1)**, **(2)**, and so on, and using **bold**. As you will see, many of these benefits are spiritual and eternal, as much or more so than physical.

First, in verse 1, next, the Lord instructs the Prophet and Sidney Rigdon to call the missionaries in from their various fields of labor to attend this conference.

1 BEHOLD, thus saith the Lord unto you my servants, **it is expedient** [*necessary*] in me **that the elders of my church should be called together**, from the east and from the west, and from the north and from the south, by letter or some other way.

2 And it shall come to pass, that inasmuch as they are faithful, and exercise faith in me, **(1) I will pour out my Spirit upon them** in the day that they assemble themselves together [*as they meet together in this conference*].

3 And it shall come to pass that **they shall go forth into the regions round about, and preach repentance** unto the people.

4 **And many shall be converted [(2) *They will obtain greater power to spread the gospel*], insomuch** that **(3) ye shall obtain power to organize yourselves according to the laws of man** [*you will have greater power to organize Church units in various communities according to the laws of the land*];

5 That **(4) your enemies may not have power over you**; that **(5) you may be preserved in all things**; that **(6) you may be enabled to keep my laws; (7) that every bond may be broken wherewith the enemy seeketh to destroy my people.**

Verse 6, next, reminds these Saints to take care of the poor and the needy among them. The "law" spoken of would likely be section 42, in which instructions were given for the implementation of the law of consecration, which contains provisions for the care of the needy (see D&C 42:30–31).

6 Behold, I say unto you, that ye must **visit the poor and the needy and administer to their relief**, that they may be kept until all things may be done according to **my law** which ye have received. Amen.

SECTION 45

Background

This revelation was given to the Church through Joseph Smith at Kirtland, Ohio, on March 7, 1831. At this point in time, the Church is just eleven months old and there are about two thousand members, most of whom have gathered or who are on their way to gather in the Kirtland, Ohio, area. During this time, Sidney Rigdon's mother and oldest brother will join the Church (see *Doctrine and Covenants Student Manual*, 1981, 91). Joseph Smith and Sidney Rigdon continue to work on what will become the Joseph Smith Translation of the Bible (JST), as instructed by the Lord in D&C 41:7. The Prophet's wife, Emma, is expecting twins. They will be born on April 30, 1831, but will only live about three hours before they pass away.

At this time, the Saints are facing many false rumors and much bad publicity. Wild stories about them are circulating freely, adding to the difficulty of gathering and worshipping the Lord in Ohio. Local civic leaders, ministers and their congregations, newspaper editors, and others have united in a joint effort to stop their friends and neighbors from being converted to this new religion. The Prophet Joseph Smith wrote of this as follows:

"At this age of the Church [*early in the spring of 1831*] many false reports, lies, and foolish stories, were published in the newspapers, and circulated in every direction, to prevent people from investigating the work, or embracing the faith. A great earthquake in China, which destroyed from one to two thousand inhabitants, was burlesqued [*twisted*] in some papers, as '"Mormonism" in China.' But to the joy of the Saints who had to struggle against every thing that prejudice and wickedness could invent, I received the following [*Doctrine and Covenants, section 45*]." (*History of the Church,* 1:158.)

One of the major messages we learn from this revelation is the importance of perspective during times of trials, disappointments, and hardships. It is as if the Lord were lifting the minds and hearts of these struggling Saints up to a "high mountain" from which they are permitted to see things as the Lord sees them, including the great blessings that await the righteous in the future. Afterward, they are, in effect, "returned" down to earth to daily life and struggles but are much better able to cope and progress. Perhaps you have had similar experiences in which the Lord has enabled you to "see" for a brief moment as He sees, thus empowering you to submit more cheerfully to trials and to have more joy and satisfaction in daily living. This is one of the great blessings of having the gospel in our lives with the accompanying gift of the Holy Ghost.

One of the great treasures in this section is found in verses 16–59, where the Savior quotes the Olivet Discourse (Matthew 24), in which He answered questions and pointed out many signs of the times to His disciples during the last week of His mortal life as they met on the Mount of Olives (see Matthew 24:3). Matthew 24 is one of the best-known chapters in the Bible dealing with the signs of the times (prophecies that will be fulfilled shortly before the Second Coming). The great value of these verses in section 45 in the Doctrine and Covenants is that we find more than three hundred words added to this discourse that are not found in Matthew 24.

As we proceed, we will be taught gospel vocabulary and many doctrines of the gospel, including numerous details of the plan of salvation. If you understand the gospel vocabulary and doctrinal concepts given in section 45, you will find that your understanding of many other passages in the scriptures is greatly enhanced. We will add an unusually large number of notes and considerable commentary as we study this section. You may wish to make several notes in your own Doctrine and Covenants, section 45, based on what we cover now.

First of all, in verse 1, the Savior identifies Himself and introduces Himself to us as the one giving this revelation.

Doctrine

Vs. 1. Jesus Christ is the Creator of the earth and the heavens and everything in them (except people because we are "offspring" [see Acts 17:29] **of Heavenly Parents, not "creations" like rocks, trees, horses, and the like.)**

1 **HEARKEN** [listen carefully], **O ye people of my church, to whom the kingdom** [the true Church with the true gospel of Jesus Christ here on earth] **has been given; hearken ye and give ear to him** [Jesus Christ] **who laid the foundation of the earth** [who created the earth], **who made the heavens and all the hosts thereof**, and **by whom all things were made which live, and move, and have a being** [Jesus is the creator of heaven and earth and everything in them].

Next, in the first part of verse 2, Christ warns us to be prepared to meet Him since we don't know when we might die. Alma 34:33 has essentially the same message for us.

In the last part of verse 2, we are likewise counseled to be prepared to meet the Savior. In the context of this section, this part of the verse seems to imply that the Second Coming will come a bit sooner than we expect, based on the signs of the times. We need to be ready or our souls will not be saved.

2 And again I say, **hearken unto my voice, lest death shall overtake you**; in an hour **when ye think not the summer shall be past** [you don't know when you are going to die and your mortal opportunities to prepare to meet God will be over; also, the Second Coming will arrive when you don't expect it], and **the harvest ended** [the

gathering of the righteous and the destruction of the wicked will be over], and **your souls not saved** [*unless you are prepared*].

Doctrine

Verses 3–5. If we are earnestly and honestly striving to live the gospel faithfully, we can plan on a pleasant Judgment Day.

Verses 3–5, next, go together. They are a most comforting reminder of the role of the Savior and His Atonement in making it possible for us to be saved, despite our inadequacies and imperfections.

To set the stage for understanding these three verses, we will take a bit of poetic license and imagine the following scenario: Suppose that you have just died and are waiting your turn to be judged. You find yourself fretting about things you did not complete while on earth despite your good intentions and honest desires to be good.

As you wait, you review your life. Despite the fact that you attended church faithfully, paid a full tithing (except for the tithing check still in your drawer, which you forgot to turn in last month), kept the Word of Wisdom, tried to be nice, didn't swear much (you're actually progressing on this), attended the temple pretty regularly and so on, you find yourself focusing on sins and imperfections you haven't yet overcome. Just as you decide that you can't possibly make the celestial kingdom but hope to make the terrestrial, the door opens and it is your turn to be judged.

Embarrassed by your shortcomings and humbled by what you didn't get done on earth, you walk in to face the Savior to be judged, whispering with head bowed that He can save time by sending you to terrestrial glory without any further discussion. At this point, the Savior comes around the judgment bar of God, walks up to you, puts His arm around you, hugs you, and says:

3 **Listen to him** [*Jesus Christ*] **who is the advocate** [*our Mediator, "attorney," the one who wants us to win on Judgment Day*] **with the Father, who is pleading your cause before him** [*who wants you to be saved*]—

Next, still hugging you, He turns you to face the Father with Him,

4 Saying: **Father, behold the sufferings and death of him** [*Christ*] **who did no sin** [*in other words, consider My Atonement in behalf of this person (you)*], **in whom thou wast well pleased; behold the blood of thy Son which was shed**, the blood of him whom thou gavest that thyself might be glorified [*the purpose of the Atonement is to bring*

such people as you back to the Father permanently];

5 Wherefore [*therefore, because of My Atonement*], **Father, spare** [*apply the law of mercy, rather than the law of justice to*] **these my brethren** [*in our scenario, "apply my Atonement to this, my sister, or to this, my brother"*] **that believe on my name, that they may come unto me and have everlasting life** [*the term "everlasting life" always means exaltation in the highest degree of glory in the celestial kingdom*].

> Can you imagine your relief and gratitude when you realize that the Savior's Atonement applies fully to people like you! You have been honestly and sincerely striving to keep the commandments and to do good, and, as is the case with all who are accountable, you have been a bit slow on some things. Yet, at this glorious moment, you find complete fulfillment of Revelation 21:4, which says: "And God shall wipe away all tears from their eyes; and there shall be no more death, neither sorrow, nor crying, neither shall there be any more pain: for the former things [*mortal trials, sins, and so on*] are passed away." You have truly been cleansed from all your sins by the Savior's Atonement and stand pure and clean (sanctified) in His presence as He now judges you!
>
> As we continue with section 45,

the Savior uses several gospel doctrinal vocabulary words and phrases as He reviews His role and sets in perspective the stage for the teachings given in verses 16–59.

6 Hearken, O ye people of my church, and ye elders **listen together** [*listen in unity of heart and purpose*], and **hear** [*obey*] my voice **while it is called today** [*while you still have time*], and harden not your hearts [*don't become prideful and insensitive to the gospel*];

7 For verily I say unto you that I am **Alpha and Omega** [*the "A" and the "Z" of the Greek alphabet, another way of saying the beginning and the end*], **the beginning and the end** [*Jesus has been involved in saving us since the beginning (including the council in heaven, the War in Heaven, and the creation of the earth), and will be there in the end, including as our final judge (John 5:22)*], **the light and the life of the world**—a light that shineth in darkness [*spiritual darkness*] and **the darkness comprehendeth it not**.

> The word "comprehendeth," in verse 7, above, can have at least two meanings in this context. One is that those who are not spiritually sensitive do not understand the light of the gospel or even realize

that it is there for them. They do not understand or appreciate spiritual things.

Another meaning of "comprehend" is to surround and overcome. It is comforting to know that spiritual darkness cannot ultimately win over Christ and the righteous. Perhaps you've noticed that, upon opening an outside door at night, darkness does not stream into the house and obliterate the light. Light always penetrates darkness rather than the other way around. Simple, powerful symbolism is in this natural state of things. The darkness of Satan and his evil hosts cannot overcome or "comprehend" Christ, the Light and Life of the world, nor the righteous, who are honestly striving to keep their covenants and live righteous lives.

8 I [*Jesus*] **came unto mine own, and mine own received me not** [*not just the Jews, but all who reject Him; see* Teachings of the Prophet Joseph Smith, *pages 14–15*]; **but unto as many as received me gave I power to do many miracles, and to become the sons of God** [*a scriptural vocabulary phrase meaning those who attain exaltation; see D&C 76:24, Mosiah 5:7*]; and even **unto them that believed on my name gave I power to obtain eternal life** [*this phrase always means "exaltation," the highest degree of glory in the celestial kingdom—in other words, becoming gods and living in the family unit forever*].

Next, in verse 9, Jesus tells us why He restored His gospel in these last days.

9 And even so I have sent mine everlasting covenant [*the full gospel; see D&C 133:57*] **into the world, to be a light to the world,** and to be **a standard for my people** [*members of the Church*], **and for the Gentiles** [*in this context, all people who are not members of the Church*] **to seek to it, and to be a messenger before my face to prepare the way before me** [*including to prepare the way for the Second Coming*].

In verses 10–15, next, the Savior issues a wonderful invitation to all who join His Church. He says, in effect, that He will chat and reason with us, just as He did with prophets and Saints in ancient times. What an invitation! He will teach us so that the gospel makes sense and so that we can see the big picture and the reasons for keeping the commandments. We will continue to use **bold** to point things out.

10 Wherefore, come ye unto it [*the gospel of Jesus Christ*], **and with him that cometh I will reason as with men in days of old,** and I will show unto you my strong reasoning [*we will be able to see things as Christ sees them*].

SECTION 45

11 Wherefore, **hearken ye together and let me show unto you even my wisdom**—the wisdom of him whom ye say is **the God of Enoch, and his brethren** [*the City of Enoch was taken up into heaven, as recorded in Moses 7:21; see also D&C 38:4*],

12 **Who were separated from the earth** [*who were taken up off the earth*]**, and were received unto myself**—a city reserved **until a day of righteousness shall come** [*the City of Enoch will come back down to earth at the beginning of the Millennium; see Moses 7:62–63*]—**a day that was sought for by all holy men** [*many of the righteous throughout history have wished that the Millennium would come during their lifetime*]**, and they found it** [*peace and righteousness on earth*] **not because of wickedness and abominations;**

By the way, when the City of Enoch was taken up, it included the buildings, ground, gardens, and domestic animals (see *Discourses of Brigham Young*, 105). The inhabitants of the City of Enoch were translated when taken up, and they were resurrected at the time of Christ's resurrection (see D&C 133:54–55.)

Verse 13, next, expresses the sentiments occasionally felt by many of the righteous. There are times when it seems that no one else wants to live the gospel as thoroughly as they do, which leaves them feeling lonely and like strangers away from home for a season.

13 **And confessed** [*came to the conclusion*] **they were strangers and pilgrims on the earth** [*because of the wickedness on earth*];

14 **But obtained a promise that they should find it and see it in their flesh** [*as resurrected beings who will rule and reign with the Savior during the Millennium; see Revelation 20:4*].

15 Wherefore, hearken and **I will reason with you, and I will speak unto you and prophesy, as unto men in days of old** [*Jesus desires that we have the same perspective and opportunity to understand as He gave to Saints in ancient times*].

As mentioned previously, the Savior will now teach us what He taught His disciples, as recorded in Matthew, chapter 24. It was the last week of His mortal life, probably Tuesday (He will be crucified on Friday). The Savior's triumphal entry into Jerusalem two days earlier (Matthew 21) had set the entire city of Jerusalem into an uproar. City officials and priests, along with many others, were determined to destroy Jesus and His followers. (Much the same sentiments existed against the members of the Church in the hearts and efforts of residents of the Kirtland, Ohio, area at the time section 65 was given). The Master's disciples were very concerned about His safety, as well as their own future. They came to Him with two specific questions as He sat upon the Mount of Olives (Joseph Smith–Matthew 1:4):

1. When would the destruction of the temple in Jerusalem and the Jews take place?

2. What are the signs of His Second Coming and the destruction of the wicked?

We will now study His answers in verses 16–59.

16 And **I will show it plainly as I showed it unto my disciples** as I stood before them in the flesh [*on the Mount of Olives before His crucifixion and resurrection*], and spake unto them, saying: As **ye have asked of me concerning the signs of my coming**, in the day **when I shall come in my glory** in the clouds of heaven [*the Second Coming*], to fulfil the promises that I have made unto your fathers [*ancestors*],

17 For as ye have looked upon the long absence of your spirits from your bodies to be a bondage [*we will miss our physical bodies after we die and go to the spirit world*], **I will show unto you how the day of redemption shall come** [*Jesus will teach us about how we will be redeemed, including how our spirits will get our physical bodies back in the resurrection*], **and also the restoration of the scattered Israel** [*Jesus will also teach us about the gathering of Israel In the last days in these verses*].

Next, in verses 18–24, Jesus answers the question as to what will happen to the Jews and to the temple in Jerusalem after He is crucified. Most of this took place within forty years of His death and resurrection.

18 And now **ye behold** [*right now you can see*] **this temple** which is in Jerusalem, **which ye call the house of God** [*the wording "which ye call" is significant; in effect, Jesus is saying that the temple, which is still referred to by the Jews as the house of the Lord, is not the house of the Lord; it has been defiled by wickedness, money changers, and so on and has been rejected by Christ*], **and your enemies** [*the Jews, the enemies of His righteous disciples who are listening to Him as he teaches them*] **say that this house shall never fall.**

19 But, verily [*truly*] I say unto you, that **desolation** [*terrible destruction*] **shall come upon this**

generation [*the Jews then living*] as a thief in the night [*it will catch them by surprise*], and **this people** [*the Jewish nation at the time of Christ*] **shall be destroyed and scattered among all nations** [*a part of the scattering of Israel*].

20 And **this temple** [*the temple in Jerusalem*] which ye now see **shall be thrown down** that there shall not be left one stone upon another.

> In about A.D. 70, the Romans literally burned the flammable components of the temple and then tore the above-ground portion of the building apart, stone by stone. It is helpful to note that when the Romans began destroying the Jewish nation, faithful Christians of the day heeded the word of the Lord (Matthew 24:16) and fled to Pella (about eighty miles north of Jerusalem, east of the Jordan River), and were thus spared the atrocities that were heaped upon the unbelieving Jews. We will include a longer note on this after verse 21, next.

21 And it shall come to pass, that **this generation of Jews shall not pass away until every desolation which I have told you concerning them shall come to pass.**

> A brief summary of the fulfillment of the Savior's prophecy about the "desolations" (verse 21, above) that would befall the Jews of that day is found in the institute of religion *Doctrine and Covenants Student Manual*, 1981, page 93, quoting Smith and Sjodahl as follows (**bold** added for emphasis):
>
> "In the year A.D. 66, Cestus Gallus marched into Judea and threatened Jerusalem. He might have taken the City, but he retreated and met with defeat near Beth-Horon. **The Christians in the City, remembering the words of our Lord, fled to the little city of Pella**, but the Jews were fired, by their temporary success, to renewed resistance. Vespasian was then sent from Rome to crush the rebellion. He took some of the strongholds of the Country and approached Jerusalem. Internal strife prevailed there, and such horrors were perpetrated that Vespasian decided to give his army a rest, while the Jews destroyed each other. Vespasian was elevated to the throne, and his son, Titus, was left to continue the conquest. **The siege began in the year A.D. 70.** Soon famine prevailed. Citizens who ventured outside the walls to search for roots to eat, if seized, were crucified by the Roman soldiers. Sometimes hundreds in that awful position could be seen from the walls. A trench was dug around the City, in order to make its isolation complete. Prisoners of war were cut open, while alive, to enable soldiers to search their bodies for gold which they might have swallowed. Six hundred thousand persons died within the walls,

and the dead bodies, too numerous to be buried, were left in the houses. The Zealots, a fanatical sect whose members maintained that God would save them at the last moment, went about murdering and urging the people to resistance. Even Titus was sick at heart at the daily horrors he witnessed or heard of. At length **the temple became a fort**. Titus attacked it as such. **A Roman soldier**, contrary to order, **set fire to it**. After a while the scene was one of carnage and plunder. **Six thousand Jews perished in the flames**. In this awful war **more than a million and a half of the Jews perished, and many were sold into slavery, and thus 'scattered among all nations.'** (*Commentary*, 260–61.)"

As the Savior continued teaching his disciples, He confirmed their testimonies of the gospel by bearing His own to them, as recorded in verses 22–23, next.

22 **Ye say that ye know** that the end of the world cometh [*"end of the world" means "end of wickedness"; this phrase can refer to the destruction of the wicked in conjunction with the Second Coming and can also mean after the end of the Millennium and the "little season" that follows (D&C 88:110–15)*]; **ye say also that ye know** that the heavens and the earth shall pass away [*this earth will die and be resurrected (D&C 88:26) and, when it is celestialized (D&C 130:9–11), it will be moved from its current "heavens" (solar system and such) back into the presence of the Father where it was originally created. See statement by Brigham Young,* Journal of Discourses, *Vol. 17, pages 143–44, as follows: "When man fell, the earth fell into space, and took up its abode in this planetary system, and the sun became our light . . . When it (the earth) is glorified, it will return again into the presence of the Father"; see also* Teachings of the Prophet Joseph Smith, *page 181)*];

23 And **in this ye say truly, for so it is**; but these things which I have told you shall not pass away until all shall be fulfilled.

Next, in verses 24–25, we are briefly taught about the scattering and latter-day gathering of the Jews.

24 And **this I have told you concerning Jerusalem**; and when that day shall come [*the devastations upon the Jews in the years immediately following the crucifixion of Christ*], shall **a remnant** [*of the Jews*] be **scattered among all nations**;

Doctrine

Verses 25–53. The signs of the times are prophecies to be fulfilled in the last days

showing that the Second Coming of Christ is getting close.

25 But **they** [*the Jews*] **shall be gathered again** [*in the last days*]; **but** they **shall remain** [*will not be gathered to Christ*] **until the times of the Gentiles be fulfilled** [*until the Gentiles are gathered*]

> The phrase "times of the Gentiles" in verse 25, above, is a reference to the last days in which we live, at which time the gospel will be preached to the Gentiles. In this context, "Gentiles" means everyone except the Jews. According to the Savior's teaching in verse 25, in the last days, the gospel will be preached first to the Gentiles, meaning everyone except the Jews. Then, when the "times of the Gentiles" have been fulfilled—in other words, when the Gentiles have had a chance to hear the true gospel of Jesus Christ, then the Jews will get another opportunity. We are now living during the "times of the Gentiles." This is one of the "signs of the times" that is currently being fulfilled.
>
> Jesus continues now, teaching His disciples (and us) of additional signs of the times that will indicate that His Second Coming is getting close.

26 And **in that day** [*in the last days, before His coming*] shall be heard of **wars and rumors of wars** [*this sign is being fulfilled now, in our day*], and **the whole earth shall be in commotion** [*including political disasters as well as natural disasters, such as plagues and other calamities, which are now being fulfilled*], and **men's hearts shall fail them** [*people will give up hope, be depressed, and much despair will be everywhere, which is now also being fulfilled*], and **they shall say that Christ delayeth his coming until the end of the earth** [*things will get so bad that people will worry that there won't be anyone left on earth by the time the Savior comes*].

27 And **the love of men shall wax** [*grow*] **cold** [*people will not care about anyone but themselves—now being fulfilled*], and **iniquity** [*gross wickedness*] **shall abound** [*will be everywhere—now being fulfilled*].

28 And **when the times of the Gentiles is come in** [*when the time comes to preach the gospel to the Gentiles*], **a light** [*the restoration of the gospel through Joseph Smith*] **shall break forth among them that sit in darkness** [*spiritual darkness*], and it shall be **the fulness of my gospel**;

> The restoration of the gospel, spoken of in verse 28, above, is another sign of the times. It is basically fulfilled and continues to be fulfilled. The other part of verse 28, speaking of the gospel being

taken to "them that sit in darkness," is a sign of the times that is currently being fulfilled through the preaching of the gospel as we take it to all the world.

Next, in verse 29, we are told that many people will reject the gospel when it is preached to them in the last days. And, as you will see, the Savior explains why this will be the case.

29 **But they receive it not**; for they perceive not the light, and they turn their hearts from me **because of the precepts** [*the prevailing teachings, rules, laws, morals, and principles*] **of men.**

30 And **in that generation** [*the last days; the dispensation of the fullness of times*] **shall the times of the Gentiles be fulfilled.**

31 And there shall be men standing in that generation, that shall not pass [*will not die*] until they shall see an overflowing scourge; for **a desolating sickness shall cover the land.**

Many have suggested different possibilities as to what the "desolating sickness" spoken of in verse 31, above, might be. Some think it is AIDS. Some think it is antibiotic-resistant strains of germs. Yet others speculate that it could be an especially deadly form of flu, such as COVID-19, causing a worldwide plague. The most "desolating" and destructive "sickness" of all is personal wickedness, which causes moral and spiritual darkness and the destruction of individuals and nations. We are seeing this now throughout the world. While we have not been told specifically what this "desolating sickness" is, we are left to wonder if it might be more spiritual than physical.

Next, in verse 32, the Lord tells us how to avoid the "overflowing scourge" and "desolating sickness" spoken of in verse 31.

32 But **my disciples** [*true followers*] **shall stand in holy places** [*including righteous homes, temples, church meetings, family history centers, seminaries and institutes, scripture reading, Church magazines, general conferences, and so on*], **and shall not be moved** [*will not be overcome*]; but among the wicked, men shall lift up their voices and curse God and die.

Next, the Savior lists additional signs of the times and explains what the reaction of the majority of earth's inhabitants will be.

33 And there shall be **earthquakes** also in divers [*various*] places, and **many desolations** [*devastating disasters*]; **yet men will harden their hearts against me**, and they **will take up the sword, one against another,**

and **they will kill one another**.

> In verse 34, next, along with the first phrase of verse 35, the Savior stops quoting the Olivet Discourse (Matthew 24) for a moment and tells us how His disciples reacted to what He had just told them.

34 And now, when I the Lord had spoken these words unto my disciples, **they were troubled**.

> There is a major message for us in what the Master tells His disciples next as to how they should react to the signs of the times. As you can see, He counsels them to "be not troubled" (the first part of verse 35). Instead, they should use the fulfillment of these prophecies to strengthen their testimonies.
>
> Perhaps you have attended classes or been involved in discussions concerning the signs of the times in which the prevailing sentiment and feeling was that of fear and even an element of panic. If we follow the Savior's counsel (seen also in Joseph Smith—Matthew 1:23), we will avoid approaching these prophecies with fear and trepidation and instead look at them as faith and testimony builders as instructed by Jesus in the last part of verse 35, next.

35 And I said unto them: **Be not troubled**, for, **when all these things shall come to pass, ye may know that the promises which have been made unto you shall be fulfilled**. [*In other words, you can know that the gospel is true because of the obvious fulfillment of so many prophecies.*]

36 And when the light [*including the restoration of the gospel, the fulfillment of these prophecies, and so forth*] shall begin to break forth, it shall be with them [*the people who live in the last days*] like unto a parable which I will show you—

> Next, the Savior likens the signs of the times to the leaves sprouting on a tree, showing that summer is not far off. When we see the signs of the times being fulfilled, we know that the Second Coming is not far off.

37 **Ye look and behold** [*see*] **the fig-trees**, and **ye see them with your eyes** [*in other words, the evidence is obvious; there is no question as to what is happening*], and **ye say** when they begin to shoot forth [*when leaves begin to grow in spring*], and their leaves are yet tender, that **summer is now nigh at hand** [*summer is nearly here*];

38 **Even so it shall be in that day** [*in the last days*] **when they shall see all these things** [*the signs of the times being fulfilled; obvious evidence*], **then shall they know that the hour** [*for the Second Coming*] **is nigh** [*near*].

The word "fear," as used in verse 39, next, means living righteously, striving to stay on the covenant path, having respect and reverence for the Lord and for sacred things, including the scriptures. The message is that those who respect and study the scriptures and live the gospel will be familiar with the signs of the times. As they see them being obviously fulfilled, they will be looking forward to His coming.

39 And it shall come to pass that **he that feareth me shall be looking forth for the great day of the Lord to come**, even **for the signs of the coming of the Son of Man**.

Perhaps you've wondered why Jesus is often referred to in scripture as "the Son of Man" (verse 39, above) since you know that He is the Son of God and not the son of a mortal man. Did you notice that the word "Man" is capitalized? "Man" is short for "Man of Holiness," meaning Heavenly Father. Thus, Jesus is the "Son of Man of Holiness," or the Son of Heavenly Father. You can read this explanation in Moses 6:57. Sometimes, as in Matthew 20:28 and John 3:13, the phrase is "Son of man" (with "man" not capitalized), but it still means the same thing.

Next, in verses 40–43, the Savior tells us of yet more signs of the times, explaining that the righteous (spoken of in verse 39) will recognize them for what they are.

40 And **they** [*the righteous*] **shall see signs and wonders**, for they shall be shown forth **in the heavens above, and in the earth beneath** [*the signs of the times will be all around us*].

41 **And they shall behold** [*see*] **blood**, and **fire**, and **vapors of smoke**.

42 And **before the day of the Lord** [*Second Coming*] **shall come, the sun shall be darkened**, and the **moon** be **turned into blood**, and the **stars fall from heaven**.

In reference to verse 42, above, it is interesting to note that Joel 2:31 also speaks of the darkening of the sun and the moon being turned to blood as a prominent sign of the times. In the October 2001 general conference, in the Saturday morning session, President Gordon B. Hinckley taught that this has been fulfilled. He said (**bold** added for emphasis):

"The era in which we live is the fulness of times spoken of in the scriptures, when God has brought together all of the elements of previous dispensations. From the day that He and His Beloved Son manifested themselves to the boy Joseph, there has been a tremendous cascade of enlightenment poured out upon the world. The hearts of men have turned to their fathers in fulfillment of the words of Malachi. **The vision of Joel has been fulfilled wherein he declared**:

Joel 2:28–32

28 And it shall come to pass afterward, that I will pour out my spirit upon all flesh; and your sons and your daughters shall prophesy, your old men shall dream dreams, your young men shall see visions:

29 And also upon the servants and upon the handmaids in those days will I pour out my spirit.

30 And I will shew wonders in the heavens and in the earth, blood, and fire, and pillars of smoke.

31 The sun shall be turned into darkness, and the moon into blood, before the great and the terrible day of the LORD come.

32 And it shall come to pass, that **whosoever shall call on the name of the LORD shall be delivered**: for in mount Zion and in Jerusalem shall be deliverance, as the LORD hath said, and in the remnant whom the LORD shall call."

As soon as our living prophet said that these words of Joel had been fulfilled, I accepted it on faith. We are now left to wait for additional inspired details as to how this prophecy has been fulfilled.

Next, beginning with verse 43, we are given specific details about the events leading up to and surrounding the actual Second Coming.

43 And **the remnant** [*of the Jews*] **shall be gathered unto this place** [*Jerusalem*];

44 And then **they shall look for me, and, behold, I will come**; and **they shall see me in the clouds of heaven, clothed with power and great glory** [*when the resurrected Christ comes this time, it will be with full power and glory, as opposed to the humble circumstances of His first coming and mortal ministry*]; **with all the holy angels** [*the hosts of heaven will accompany Him; this will be a very large group*]; and **he that watches not for me shall be cut off** [*another way of saying that the wicked will be destroyed at His coming*].

It is important as we study these verses to be aware that they are not all in exact chronological sequence. Jesus is reviewing and giving additional details. For instance, as we get to verses 48–53, we will be taught about the Savior appearing to the Jews on the Mount of Olives. This is not the Second Coming; rather, it is an appearance of the Lord prior to it, similar to the appearance of the Savior at Adam-ondi-Ahman (Daniel 7:9–14; D&C 116) and to the city of New Jerusalem, spoken of in verses 66–67 in this section.

As He continues to teach us and give us marvelous doctrinal details, Jesus speaks of the resurrection of the righteous, often called "the morning of the first resurrection," and likewise frequently referred to as "the resurrection of the just." From this we learn that the righteous dead will be resurrected before the wicked are destroyed at the time of His coming (see also D&C 86:7).

45 But **before the arm of the Lord shall fall** [*before the wicked are destroyed*], an angel shall sound his trump, and **the saints that have slept** [*the righteous, celestial quality who are already dead; see D&C 88:97–98*] **shall come forth to meet me** in the cloud [*the "cloud" spoken of in (D&C 34:7)*].

46 Wherefore, **if ye have slept in peace** [*if you died righteous or have become righteous and worthy through the postmortal spirit world work for the dead and are now faithful and worthy of celestial glory*] **blessed** [*happy*] **are you**; for as you now behold me and know that I am, **even so shall ye come unto me and your souls shall live** [*your body and spirit will be reunited; (D&C 88:15)*], and **your redemption shall be perfected**; and the saints shall come forth from the four quarters of the earth [*the righteous dead will be resurrected from all over the earth*].

47 **Then shall the arm of the Lord fall upon the nations** [*then the wicked will be destroyed*].

It is encouraging to note that the righteous Saints who are still alive at the time of the Second Coming will also be caught up to meet the coming Lord (see D&C 88:96).

As mentioned previously, now the Savior goes back just a bit chronologically (in verse 48, next) and gives details about His appearance to the Jews on the Mount of Olives just outside of Jerusalem. This appearance to the Jews will occur before the actual Second Coming. President Ezra Taft Benson spoke of this as follows (**bold** added for emphasis):

"His **first appearance** will be to the righteous Saints who have gathered to the New Jerusalem. In this place of refuge they will be safe from the wrath of the Lord, which will be poured out without measure on all nations. . . .

"The **second appearance** of the Lord **will be to the Jews**. To these beleaguered sons of Judah, surrounded by hostile Gentile armies who again threaten to overrun

SECTION 45   33

Jerusalem, the Savior—their Messiah—will appear and set His feet on the Mount of Olives, 'and it shall cleave in twain, and the earth shall tremble, and reel to and fro, and the heavens also shall shake' (D&C 45:48).

"The Lord Himself will then rout the Gentile armies, decimating their forces (see Ezek. 38, 39). Judah will be spared, no longer to be persecuted and scattered. . . .

"The **third appearance** of Christ will be **to the rest of the world.**

"All nations will see Him 'in the clouds of heaven, clothed with power and great glory; with all the holy angels . . .

"'And the Lord shall utter his voice, and all the ends of the earth shall hear it; and the nations of the earth shall mourn, and they that have laughed shall see their folly.

"'And calamity shall cover the mocker, and the scorner shall be consumed; and they that have watched for iniquity shall be hewn down and cast into the fire.' (D&C 45:44, 49–50.)

"Yes, come He will!" (Ezra Taft Benson, "Five Marks of the Divinity of Jesus Christ," *Ensign*, December 2001).

48 And **then shall the Lord set his foot upon this mount** [*the Mount of Olives*], and **it shall cleave in twain** [*it will split in two (see Zechariah 14:4–7)*], and **the earth shall tremble, and reel to and fro** [*everyone on earth will feel this earthquake; the righteous will recognize it as a sign of the times*], and **the heavens also shall shake.**

In verses 49–50, next, He describes the awful awareness that will come upon the wicked as they realize that they have been caught up with.

49 And **the Lord shall utter his voice**, and **all** the ends of the earth **shall hear it**; and the nations of the earth **shall mourn**, and they that have laughed [*at the righteous and at morality and righteousness in general*] **shall see their folly** [*foolishness; lack of wisdom and foresight*].

50 And **calamity shall cover the mocker** [*who mocked sacred things*], and **the scorner** [*of righteousness*] **shall be consumed** [*will be burned*]; and **they that have watched for iniquity** [*in the righteous, in the leaders of the Church, in men and women of integrity; this can also mean those who constantly watch for new opportunities to commit sin*] **shall be hewn down and cast into the fire.**

In verses 51–53, next, the Savior returns to describing His appearance to the Jews on the Mount of Olives (before His actual Second

Coming to the entire world) and to their reaction upon seeing Him.

51 And **then shall the Jews look upon me and say: What are these wounds in thine hands and in thy feet?**

52 **Then shall they know that I am the Lord**; for **I will say unto them: These wounds are the wounds with which I was wounded in the house of my friends** [*in other words, these are the wounds that He received when those who should have been His friends crucified Him*]. **I am he who was lifted up** [*crucified*]. **I am Jesus** that was crucified. **I am the Son of God.**

53 And **then shall they weep** because of their iniquities [*they will be truly sorry for their wickedness*]; **then shall they lament** [*mourn*] **because they persecuted their king**.

Perhaps you can imagine and feel the tenderness of the scene described above as the Jews acknowledge and accept Jesus as the Christ, their Savior, and mourn for their sins. Elder Parley P. Pratt described this appearance of the Savior as follows (**bold** added for emphasis):

"Zechariah, chapter 14, has told us much concerning the great battle and overthrow of the nations who fight against Jerusalem, and he has said, in plain words, that the Lord shall come at the very time of the overthrow of that army; yes, in fact, even while they are in the act of taking Jerusalem, and have already succeeded in taking one-half the city, spoiling their houses, and ravishing their women. Then, behold, **their long-expected Messiah, suddenly appearing, shall stand upon the Mount of Olives**, a little east of Jerusalem, to fight against those nations and deliver the Jews. Zechariah says **the Mount of Olives shall cleave in twain**, from east to west, and one-half of the mountain shall remove to the north while the other half falls off to the south, suddenly forming **a very great valley into which the Jews shall flee for protection from their enemies** as they fled from the earthquake in the days of Uzziah, king of Judah; while the Lord cometh and all the Saints with Him. **Then will the Jews behold that long, long-expected Messiah, coming in power to their deliverance, as they always looked for him**. He will destroy their enemies and deliver them from trouble at the very time they are in the utmost consternation, and about to be swallowed up by their enemies. But what will be their astonishment when they are about to fall at the feet of their Deliverer and acknowledge him their Messiah! **They discover the wounds which were once made in his hands, feet, and side**; and on inquiry, at once recognize

Jesus of Nazareth, the King of the Jews, the man so long rejected. Well did the prophet say that **they shall mourn and weep**, every family apart, and their wives apart. But, thank heaven, **there will be an end to their mourning; for he will forgive their iniquities and cleanse them from uncleanness**" (Parley P. Pratt, *Voice of Warning*, 32–33; quoted in the *Doctrine and Covenants Student Manual*, 1981, 96–97).

Next, in verse 54, we are taught that those who have died and are worthy of terrestrial glory will have part in the first resurrection. The major resurrection at the beginning of the Millennium will take place in two parts—first, the celestial, and next, the terrestrial. The righteous dead, who are worthy of celestial glory, will be resurrected first (D&C 88:97–98). This is sometimes referred to as "the morning of the first resurrection." Then a major terrestrial resurrection will take place (D&C 88:99). This is sometimes referred to as the "afternoon of the first resurrection." Remember, this all takes place at or near the beginning of the Millennium.

54 And then shall the **heathen nations** [*a general term for those who will be in terrestrial glory; see notes included with D&C 76:71–73 in this study guide for more information*] be redeemed, **and they that knew no law shall have part in the first resurrection;** and it shall be tolerable for them [*perhaps implying that they will have a better experience on Judgment Day than the wicked; compare with D&C 75:22*].

Next, in verse 55, the Savior teaches us that Satan will be bound during the Millennium.

Doctrine
Vs. 55. Satan will be bound during the Millennium.

55 And **Satan shall be bound**, that he shall have no place in the hearts of the children of men.

Some Church members wonder whether Satan will be bound so that he cannot even try to tempt us or if the statement in verse 55, above, means that he will try but nobody will listen. Joseph Fielding Smith provided an answer as follows (**bold** added for emphasis):

"There are many among us who teach that the binding of Satan will be merely the binding which those dwelling on the earth will place upon him by their refusal to hear his enticings. This is not so. **He will not have the privilege during that period of time to tempt any man**. (D. & C. 101:28.)" (*Church History and Modern Revelation*, 1:192).

Next, the Lord refers back to the parable of the ten virgins, which

He gave as recorded in Matthew 25:1–13. This is one of those places in modern scripture that bless us with greater understanding of the Bible. For instance, in verse 57, below, the Savior explains what He meant by the "wise virgins."

56 And **at that day, when I shall come in my glory** [*the Second Coming*], **shall the parable be fulfilled which I spake concerning the ten virgins.**

57 For **they that are wise** and **have received the truth**, and **have taken the Holy Spirit for their guide**, and **have not been deceived**—verily I say unto you, they shall not be hewn down and cast into the fire, but shall abide the day [*they will not be destroyed at the Second Coming*].

Next, in verses 58–59, we are taught a few more details about how life will be during the Millennium.

Doctrine

Vs. 58. Children will grow up without sin during the Millennium.

58 And **the earth shall be given unto them** [*the "wise," as defined in verse 57, above*] **for an inheritance;** and **they shall multiply and wax strong** [*the population of righteous people will increase rapidly during the Millennium*], and **their children shall grow up without sin unto salvation.**

The phrase "without sin," in verse 58, above, could have at least two meanings. It could mean that children will grow up without "sinning" during the thousand years of peace. It could also mean that children born during the Millennium will grow up in an environment that is essentially without sin—without the wickedness and the sins of telestial lifestyles surrounding them, such as those with which we are plagued in these last days. The point at the end of verse 58, above, is wonderful, namely that, in that millennial environment, children will grow up "unto salvation."

Doctrine

Vs. 59. Christ will be the King over the entire world during the Millennium.

59 For **the Lord** [*Christ*] **shall be in their midst,** and **his glory shall be upon them,** and **he will be their king** and **their lawgiver.**

The type of government described in the last phrase of verse 59, above, is a "theocracy," which means "government by God."

This is the end of the Savior's quoting what He taught his disciples on the Mount of Olives concerning

His Second Coming as recorded in Matthew 24. As mentioned previously, the quote consists of section 45, verses 16–33 and 35–59, and contains more than three hundred additional words not found in Matthew 24 in the Bible.

Next, in verse 60, Jesus tells Joseph Smith in particular, and the Church in general, that he will receive no further explanation of Matthew 24 until additional work is done on the Joseph Smith Translation of the Bible (JST).

60 And now, behold, I say unto you, **it shall not be given unto you to know any further concerning this chapter** [*Matthew 24*], **until the New Testament** [*part of the Joseph Smith Translation of the Bible*] **be translated**, and in it all these things shall be made known [*in other words, as you continue to work on the translation of the New Testament, you will learn much more about this*];

61 Wherefore I give unto you that ye may now translate it [*go ahead now and work on correcting the New Testament as it now stands in the King James Bible*], that ye may be prepared for the things to come.

It is interesting to note that the very next day after this revelation was given, Joseph Smith resumed work on what is sometimes referred to as the inspired translation of the Bible, with Sidney Rigdon serving as his scribe. Up to this time, the Prophet had been working on the Old Testament and had done work up to and including Genesis 19:35. As a result of this revelation (D&C 45:60–62), Joseph and Sidney immediately began to work on the New Testament (while finishing a bit more of the Old Testament). In fact, they began working on it on March 8, 1831, beginning with Matthew, and by April 7, 1831, they had finished to Matthew 9:2. (See the table on page 96 in Robert J. Matthews's *A Plainer Translation: Joseph Smith's Translation of the Bible.*)

We will pause for a moment and provide a bit of background for the Joseph Smith Translation of the Bible, or the "JST" as it is commonly referred to today. We will quote from the institute of religion student manual, *Church History in the Fullness of Times*, 2003, 117–18.

"Joseph Smith's inspired translation of the Bible was one of the pivotal developments of his work as a prophet, and it has had a profound influence on the Church. Joseph's knowledge about the principles of the gospel and God's work with his ancient prophets and people increased immensely through this project. He considered it an important 'branch' of his calling and labored diligently at it. When he and

Sidney Rigdon were at home in Ohio, this was their major preoccupation. The frequency with which the "translation" is referred to in the revelations and historical documents of the period underscores the importance of this project. The Prophet first began this work in New York in 1830. When he arrived in Ohio in February 1831, he continued his work in the Old Testament with the help of his scribe, Elder Rigdon. But early in March, Joseph was commanded to work on the translation of the New Testament (see D&C 45:60–61). During the next two years Joseph and Sidney continued their work on both the New and the Old Testaments. They optimistically pronounced their work finished on 2 July 1833. See *History of the Church,* 1:368."

"In addition to the great legacy left to the Church in the Joseph Smith Translation (JST) itself, numerous revelations now recorded in the Doctrine and Covenants came to the Prophet while he worked on the inspired translation. The study of the Bible stimulated him to inquire of the Lord about significant doctrinal and organizational matters. Doctrine and Covenants sections 76, 77, and 91 have direct links with the translation effort, 'and probably much of the information in sections 74, 84, 86, 88, 93, 102, 104, 107, 113, and 132.' It is probable that many others are indirectly connected. (Robert J. Matthews, *A Plainer Translation:* *Joseph Smith's Translation of the Bible—A History and Commentary* (Provo: Brigham Young University Press, 1985), page 256; see also pages 264–65.)"

62 For verily I say unto you, that **great things await you** [*apparently referring to the additional revelations, spoken of above, triggered by questions arising from the work on the JST*];

As the Savior continues, He warns these early Saints about troubles in their own land, explaining that this is the reason He commanded them to move from their "eastern lands" to Ohio. (See D&C 37:3.) He also warns of future wars in the United States, no doubt including the Civil War as well as future troubles.

63 **Ye hear of wars in foreign lands; but**, behold, I say unto you, **they are nigh, even at your doors**, and **not many years hence ye shall hear of wars in your own lands**.

64 **Wherefore** [*this is why*] **I, the Lord, have said, gather ye out from the eastern lands**, assemble ye yourselves together ye elders of my church; go ye forth into the western countries [*the areas west of Kirtland, Ohio*], call upon the inhabitants to repent, and inasmuch as they do repent, build up churches [*units

and congregations of the Church] unto me.

> Next, the importance of unity and harmony (verse 65) is emphasized for those who desire to be the people of the Lord. These qualities are essential for those who ultimately wish to become celestial—in other words, worthy to live in a Zion society, of which the New Jerusalem (verse 66) is an example.

65 And **with one heart** and with **one mind**, gather up your riches that ye may purchase an inheritance which shall hereafter be appointed unto you.

Doctrine

Verses 66–71. The city of New Jerusalem will be built before the Second Coming of Christ.

66 And **it shall be called the New Jerusalem**, a land of **peace**, a city of **refuge**, a place of **safety** for the saints of the Most High God;

> We will take just a moment to learn a bit more about New Jerusalem, which is also referred to as "Zion" in this context.
>
> A city named New Jerusalem will be built in Independence, Jackson County, Missouri (D&C 57:2–3). It is spoken of in a number of places in the scriptures, including verse 66, next, and in Moses 7:61–62 in the Pearl of Great Price. At this point (section 45), the Saints have not yet been told where this city of Zion, or New Jerusalem, is to be built. They will be told in a little more than four months, on July 20, 1831, as the Prophet Joseph Smith receives the revelation now known as D&C 57.
>
> In the meantime, they are commanded to pool their resources in preparation for buying property for this city (verse 65, above). Perhaps one of the more important lessons we learn from this is that the Lord expects us to be obedient and to do our part to prepare for desired blessings that can come our way in the future.
>
> Here is just a bit more about New Jerusalem. It will become one of two headquarters or capitals during the Millennium (Old Jerusalem will become the other one). Joseph Fielding Smith explained this as follows (**bold** added for emphasis):
>
> "When Joseph Smith translated the Book of Mormon, he learned that America is the land of Zion which was given to Joseph and his children and that on this land the City Zion, or **New Jerusalem**, is to be built. He also learned that **Jerusalem in Palestine** is to be rebuilt and become a holy city. **These two cities**, one in the land of Zion and one in Palestine, are to **become capitals for the kingdom of God during the millennium**" (*Doctrines of Salvation*, 3:71).

We will learn more about New Jerusalem in verses 67–71.

67 And **the glory of the Lord shall be there**, and **the terror of the Lord also shall be there, insomuch tha**t [*such that*] **the wicked will not come unto it**, and **it shall be called Zion.**

68 And it shall come to pass among the wicked, that **every man that will not take his sword against his neighbor must needs flee unto Zion** [*including the stakes of Zion (see D&C 115:6)*] **for safety**.

69 And **there shall be gathered unto it out of every nation** under heaven; and it shall be **the only people that shall not be at war one with another.**

70 And **it shall be said among the wicked: Let us not go up to battle against Zion**, for the inhabitants of Zion are terrible; wherefore we cannot stand.

71 And it shall come to pass that **the righteous shall be gathered out from among all nations, and shall come to Zion, singing with songs of everlasting joy.**

It is important for us to realize that although New Jerusalem will be a literal city and that verses 65–71 apply to it, there is a much broader context for these verses. For instance, in D&C 115:6, we learn that in our day the stakes of Zion are to serve as "a defense and for a refuge" from the troubles and devastations that will be poured out upon the earth before the Second Coming. Thus, the advantages and protections provided by "Zion" and described in these verses can easily apply to Saints all over the world as they gather to the stakes of Zion in their own lands in the last days. The Prophet Joseph Smith spoke of this. He spoke of more than one gathering place for the Saints as follows (**bold** added for emphasis):

"Without Zion, and a place of deliverance, we must fall; because the time is near when the sun will be darkened, and the moon turn to blood, and the stars fall from heaven, and the earth reel to and fro. Then, if this is the case, and if we are not sanctified and **gathered to the places God has appointed**, with all our former professions and our great love for the Bible, we must fall; we cannot stand; we cannot be saved; for **God will gather out his Saints from the Gentiles**, and **then comes desolation and destruction**, and **none can escape except the pure in heart who are gathered**." (*Teachings of the Prophet Joseph Smith*, 71.)

Next, in verse 72, the Lord counsels the Saints not to talk to nonmembers about New Jerusalem, about Jackson County, Missouri, as a gathering place until

He tells them to. As you can well imagine, such talk could alarm and alienate people, including the locals in Missouri, and cause many misunderstandings and problems.

72 And now I say unto you, **keep these things from going abroad unto the world** until it is expedient in me [*until it is wise in the Lord's sight*], that ye may accomplish this work in the eyes of the people, and in the eyes of your enemies, **that they may not know your works until ye have accomplished the thing which I have commanded you;**

73 **That when they shall know it** [*when the enemies of the Church (verse 72, above) become aware of it*], that **they may consider these things** [*perhaps meaning the power and protection of the Lord, which will be upon the Saints in the last days as they gather together and strive to live the laws and commandments of a Zion people*].

74 For **when the Lord shall appear he shall be terrible unto them, that fear may seize upon them, and they shall stand afar off and tremble.**

75 And **all nations** [*meaning the wicked in all nations*] **shall be afraid** because of the terror of the Lord, and the power of his might. Even so. Amen.

SECTION 46

Background

This revelation was given through the Prophet Joseph Smith in Kirtland, Ohio, on March 8, 1831, just one day after the revelation recorded in section 45 was given. It deals with some important issues that require correction and additional instruction as the Church continues to grow. Remember, the Church is not quite one year old, and the converts come from several different religious backgrounds and persuasions that strongly affect their thinking as new members of the true Church. We see the Lord's patience and kindness as He gently teaches them.

Among other things at this period in the early history of the Church, particularly in the Kirtland, Ohio, region, some of the recent converts were exhibiting rather strange, even bizarre behaviors that they attributed to the manifestation of the Holy Ghost upon them. John Whitmer, David Whitmer's older brother, wrote "Some would fancy to themselves that they had the sword of Laban [see 1 Nephi 4:8–9], and would wield it as expert as a [soldier], . . . some would slide or scoot . . . [on] the floor, with the rapidity of a serpent, which the[y] termed sailing in the boat to the Lamanites, preaching the gospel. And many other vain and foolish manoeuvers (spelling in context) that are unseeming, and unprofitable to mention. Thus the devil blinded the eyes of some good and honest disciples" (in *The Joseph Smith Papers, Histories, Volume 2: Assigned Histories, 1831–1847*, 38).

In addition to these strange and false so-called spiritual manifestations among some members, the Saints in Kirtland had developed a practice of not allowing nonmembers of the Church to attend their worship services. Verses 3–6 will address this issue by instructing members not to exclude nonmembers from their public meetings.

Section 46 is probably best known for its listing of several gifts of the Spirit. As we study these spiritual gifts, you may wish to pay particular attention to which ones you may already have and which ones you feel you would like to strive to obtain according to the invitation of the Lord in verse 8.

President Dallin H. Oaks, while serving in the Quorum of the Twelve Apostles, taught us who can receive these gifts of the Spirit (**bold** added):

"**The Spirit of Christ is given to all men and women** that they may know good from evil, and manifestations of the Holy Ghost are given to lead earnest seekers to repentance and baptism. These are preparatory gifts. What we term spiritual gifts come next.

"**Spiritual gifts come to those who have received the gift of the Holy Ghost**. As the Prophet Joseph Smith taught, the gifts of the Spirit 'are obtained through that medium' [the Holy Ghost] and 'cannot be enjoyed without the gift of the Holy Ghost.' . . . (*Teachings of the Prophet Joseph Smith*, 243, 245)" ("Spiritual Gifts," *Ensign*, Sept. 1986, 68).

As we begin our verse-by-verse study, let's look first at verse 2. It is very important to anyone who has the stewardship to conduct meetings in the Church. While we know that there are guidelines and policies that are provided by the Church for the conducting of meetings, it is vital that those in charge listen to and follow the promptings of the Spirit as they preside and conduct.

1 HEARKEN, O ye people of my church; for verily I say unto you that these things were spoken unto you for your profit and learning.

2 But **notwithstanding those things which are written** [*in the handbooks, policy manuals, and such*], it always has been given to the elders of my church from the beginning, and ever shall be, to **conduct all meetings as** they are **directed and guided by the Holy Spirit**.

As you can no doubt see, the instructions given in verse 2, above, when followed, allow for meetings to better meet the needs of individuals in the congregation, class, quorum, or group. When the promptings of the Spirit are followed, it makes all the difference.

As mentioned in the background for this section, a practice of not admitting the public (unless they were serious investigators) to church meetings had become commonplace. The Lord addresses this issue directly in verses 3–6, next. We will point it out with **bold**.

3 Nevertheless **ye are commanded never to cast any one out from** [*prevent them from attending*] **your public meetings** [*there are obviously private meetings, such as temple, ward council, class presidency, and so forth, to which the public would not be invited*], **which are held before the world.**

4 **Ye are also commanded not to cast any one who belongeth to the church out of your sacrament meetings**; nevertheless, if any have trespassed, let him not partake [*of the sacrament*] until he makes reconciliation [*until he or she repents*].

5 And again I say unto you, **ye shall not cast any out of your sacrament meetings who are earnestly seeking the kingdom**—I speak this concerning those who are not of the church [*in other words, nonmembers*].

6 And again I say unto you, **concerning your confirmation meetings** [*meetings held to confirm recently baptized individuals; we usually do this in sacrament meetings now; see D&C 46:6, footnote a*], that **if there be any that are not of the church, that are earnestly seeking after the kingdom, ye shall not cast them out.**

President Russell M. Nelson also emphasized that nonmembers are invited to our public meetings and added counsel as to whether or not they should be allowed to take the sacrament. He said (**bold** added):

"Because we invite all to come unto Christ, friends and neighbors are always welcome **but not expected to take the sacrament. However, it is not forbidden. They choose for themselves**. We hope that newcomers among us will always be made to feel wanted and comfortable. Little children, as sinless beneficiaries of the Lord's Atonement, may partake of the sacrament as they prepare for covenants that they will make later in life" ("Worshiping at Sacrament Meeting," *Ensign*, Aug. 2004, 28).

Verse 7, next, is a transition between verses 3–6, above, which deal with the conducting of meetings according to the promptings of the Spirit, and the topic of spiritual gifts, which begins with verse 8. Among other things, this whole section points out the significant role of the Holy Ghost in the true Church of Jesus Christ. The beginning of verse 7 points out that not only does the Holy Ghost prompt for the proper conducting of meetings in the Church, but also that it should be listened to "in all things." The whole verse is a formula for avoiding deception.

7 But ye are commanded **in all things to ask of God**, who giveth liberally [*generously*]; and **that which the Spirit testifies unto you** even so I would **that ye should do** in all holiness of heart [*with pure motives*], walking uprightly before me [*living righteously*], considering the end [*goal*] of your salvation, doing all things with prayer and thanksgiving [*gratitude*], **that ye may not be seduced** [*overcome, fooled, deceived*] **by evil spirits**, or **doctrines of devils**, or the **commandments of men**; for some are of men, and others of devils.

Did you notice, near the end of verse 7, above, that not all dangers come directly from the devil? In addition to the dangers of being "seduced by evil spirits" and "doctrines of devils," there are dangers of being "seduced" by the philosophies, dangerous thinking, lack of wisdom, and foolish notions of other people.

As we move on to verse 8, next, we are taught that the gifts of the Spirit (given by the Holy Ghost; see verse 13) are key to avoiding any kind of deception.

8 Wherefore, **beware lest ye are deceived**; and **that ye may not be deceived seek ye earnestly the best gifts**, always remembering for what they are given [*including the purposes pointed out in verse 7, above*];

Did you notice in verse 8, above, that the Lord invites us to seek these spiritual gifts? While each member of the Church has been given at least one gift (verse 11), we are invited to seek additional gifts, choosing those that would be "best" for us. This can be a very important part of our personal spiritual growth and progression. We should obviously avoid seeking for those that could be damaging to us—for instance, seeking for the gift of tongues so that we can show off in testimony meeting or whatever. The last portion of verse 9 warns us against seeking these gifts for selfish or unwise purposes.

Also, verse 9, next, points out who will benefit from such gifts of the Spirit.

9 For verily I say unto you, **they**

are given for the benefit of those who love me and keep all my commandments, and him that seeketh so to do [*a comfort to those who are honestly striving to keep all the commandments but still fall short*]; that all may be benefited that seek or that ask of me, that ask and not for a sign that they may consume it upon their lusts [*to try to use these gifts to intentionally build one's self up in the eyes of others; to use to accomplish wicked or selfish goals*].

10 And again, verily I say unto you, I would that ye should **always remember**, and **always retain in your** minds what those gifts are, that are given unto the church.

> Did you notice that the Lord gives many cautions in the above verses with respect to motives and the use of spiritual gifts? Perhaps you are aware that these gifts are often counterfeited by the devil. It is one of his ways of deceiving people. His list of counterfeits includes healings, prophecy, tongues, interpretation of tongues, false spirits, visions, dreams, gathering, and so forth. The Prophet Joseph Smith gave the following counsel on this matter (**bold** added):
>
> "A man must have the discerning of spirits before he can drag into daylight this hellish influence and unfold it unto the world in all its soul-destroying, diabolical, and horrid colors; for **nothing is a greater injury to the children of men than to be under the influence of a false spirit when they think they have the Spirit of God**. Thousands have felt the influence of its terrible power and baneful effects. Long pilgrimages have been undertaken, penances endured, and pain, misery and ruin have followed in their train; nations have been convulsed, kingdoms overthrown, provinces laid waste, and blood, carnage and desolation are habiliaments [*usually spelled "habiliments," meaning attire, dress*] in which it has been clothed" (*History of the Church*, 4:573).
>
> Next, in verses 11 and 12, we see an element of teamwork built into the Lord's giving of some gifts to one member, other gifts to another, and different gifts to yet another, and so forth. In other words, one person has one gift, another a different one, and others additional ones, and when they work together in harmony, all are benefited.

11 For **all have not every gift** given unto them; for **there are many gifts**, and to **every man is given a gift** by the Spirit of God.

12 **To some is given one**, and **to some is given another, that all may be profited thereby.**

> Before we move ahead with our

study of the specific gifts of the Spirit referred to in section 46, beginning with verse 13, we will pause to note that there are other places in the scriptures where most of these same gifts are mentioned. In fact, if you are one who makes brief notes in the front or back of your scriptures for quick reference, or you have a "notes" section on your digital device, you may wish to turn there now and write the following note:

Gifts of the Spirit

D&C 46:8–29

1 Corinthians 12:3–11

Moroni 10:9–18

Romans 12:6–13 (including less commonly mentioned gifts)

Just one more observation, and then we will move on to verse 13. D&C 46, 1 Corinthians 12, and Moroni 10 basically review the same gifts of the Spirit. However, Moroni 10:14 mentions one not mentioned by the other two sources. It is the gift of seeing angels and ministering spirits.

Now, on to the gifts that are given by the Holy Ghost, mentioned in verses 13–25.

The gift of knowing that Jesus is the Christ

13 To some it is given by the Holy Ghost to know that Jesus **Christ is the Son of God**, and that he was crucified for the sins of the world.

The gift of believing the testimony of those who do know

14 To others it is given **to believe on their words**, that they also might have eternal life [*exaltation*] if they continue faithful. [*In other words, while they do not have their own sure testimony, if they keep the commandments because they believe others who do know for themselves, they will also gain exaltation in the highest degree in celestial glory.*]

The gift of leadership, including understanding and skillfully using the various organizations within the Church to save souls

15 And again, to some it is given by the Holy Ghost to know the **differences of administration**, as it will be pleasing unto the same Lord, according as the Lord will, suiting his mercies according to the conditions of the children of men. [*This gift is especially noticeable in the Prophet, General Authorities, General Auxiliary leaders, stake presidents, bishops, and local quorum and auxiliary leaders.*]

The gift of being able to distinguish between true philosophies and false philosophies, good ideas and bad ideas, wise counsel and foolish counsel, whether something is from God or from some other source

16 And again, it is given by the Holy Ghost to some **to know the diversities of operations**, whether they be of God, that the manifestations of the Spirit may be given to every man to profit withal. [*Sometimes a person with this gift will sense something wrong with a philosophy or idea being taught in a class at school or wherever, even if a complete understanding of what is wrong is not yet in place. This gift, along with other gifts of the Spirit, can be most valuable in distinguishing between the things of God and counterfeits.*]

> Elder Marion G. Romney (who later served in the First Presidency) explained "the diversities of operations" as follows (**bold** added for emphasis):
>
> "By the statement in the revelation on spiritual gifts, '... it is given by the Holy Ghost to some to **know the diversities of operations**, whether they be of God, ... and to others the discerning of spirits,' it appears that there are some apparently supernatural manifestations which are not worked by the power of the Holy Ghost. The truth is there are many which are not. **The world today is full of counterfeits**. It has always been so. Away back in the days of Moses, when Aaron's rod became a serpent, then Pharaoh's wise men, sorcerers and magicians '... cast down every man his rod, and they became serpents. ...' (Ex. 7:11–12.) Isaiah warned against seeking '... unto them that have familiar spirits, and unto wizards that peep, and that mutter: ...' (Isa. 8:19.)
>
> "The Saints were cautioned by the Lord to walk uprightly before him, doing all things with prayer and thanksgiving, that they might '... not be seduced by evil spirits, or doctrines of devils, or the commandments of men; ...' (D&C 47:7.)
>
> "These citations not only sustain the proposition that there are counterfeits to the gifts of the Spirit, but they also suggest the origin of the counterfeits. However, we are not required to rely alone upon their implications, plain as they are, for the Lord states specifically that **some of the counterfeits '... are of men, and others of devils.'** [D&C 46:7.]
>
> "**Some of these counterfeits are crude and easily detected, but others closely simulate true manifestations of the spirit**. Consequently, people are confused and deceived by them.

Without a key [*such as the gift of knowing "the diversities of operations"*]**, one cannot distinguish between the genuine and the counterfeit**" (In Conference Report, April 1956, 70–71).

The gift of wisdom

17 And again, verily I say unto you, to some is given, by the Spirit of God, the word of wisdom.

> It is important to note that the "word of wisdom" spoken of in verse 17, above, is not the "Word of Wisdom" known as section 89 of the Doctrine and Covenants in which the Lord counsels the Saints to avoid tobacco, alcohol, and hot drinks (tea and coffee) and to make wise use of fruits and grains and the like. Rather, it is the gift of having wisdom, seeing through the facade, and getting to the root cause. It includes the gift of seeing ahead to the ultimate consequences of a particular course of action.

The gift of knowledge and the gift of teaching

18 To another is given the word of knowledge, that all may be taught to be wise and to have knowledge.

> As indicated above, verse 18 can be viewed as having two gifts of the Spirit in it. Perhaps you have had the experience of having an instructor who had the gift of knowledge (able to learn and retain knowledge) but who did not have the gift of teaching. Still, one who has the gift of knowledge can be a valuable resource in classes, scientific research, and business.

The gift of having faith to be healed

19 And again, to some it is given to have faith to be healed;

This is a marvelous gift for those who possess it. There are many healings because of this gift of the Spirit. Yet, many do not have it. Under such circumstances, it might be easy for one not possessing it to feel less important than one who has it. The Lord addressed this situation in section 42 of the Doctrine and Covenants as follows (**bold** added for teaching purposes):

D&C 42:43–44, 48–52

43 And whosoever among you are sick, and have not faith to be healed, but believe, shall be nourished with all tenderness, with herbs and mild food [*perhaps this could include wise use of medicines and medical care today*], and that not by the hand of an enemy.

44 And the elders of the church, two or more, **shall** be called, and shall pray for and lay their hands upon them in my name [*administering to the sick*]; and if they die they shall die unto me, and if they live they shall live unto me.

48 And again, it shall come to pass that he that hath faith in me to be healed, and is not appointed unto death, shall be healed.

49 He who hath faith to see shall see.

50 He who hath faith to hear shall hear.

51 The lame who hath faith to leap shall leap.

52 And **they who have not faith to do these things, but believe in me, have power to become my sons** [*in other words, those who do not have the gift of having faith to be healed can still attain exaltation*]; and inasmuch as they break not my laws thou shalt bear their infirmities.

The gift of healing

20 And to others it is given to have **faith to heal**.

This gift applies both to healing physically as well as healing spiritually. Being healed spiritually, gaining a testimony, being converted to the Church, being healed of bitterness and anger, and so forth, are no doubt even more important than being healed physically in the eternal perspective.

A bit of a caution should perhaps go along with discussion of this gift. Those who have this gift are sometimes called upon to the point that they become the unofficial "designated blessers and healers" in a given ward or locality. As a result, those who would normally be called upon to administer to the sick, such as fathers, brothers, ministering brothers and sisters, and so forth, are excluded from consideration. There is, of course, no absolute rule that a "designated healer" should not be called, but wisdom should prevail.

By the way, the gift of healing is not limited to priesthood holders. Faithful women, including mothers, are often blessed with this gift and use it through their prayers of faith in behalf of the sick. The Prophet Joseph Smith spoke of faithful sisters healing the sick. He said "if the sisters should have faith to heal the sick, let all hold their tongues, and let everything roll on" (*Teachings of the Prophet Joseph Smith*, 224).

The gift of working miracles

21 And again, to some is given the working of miracles;

Here, as with the gift of healing, we may tend to think more in terms of the spectacular such as stopping rain or calming water, rather than the less conspicuous daily healings and miracles associated with these gifts. While there certainly are marvelous and obvious miracles—a definite blessing accompanying the gospel of Jesus Christ—if we don't pay attention, we may miss the "working of miracles" that abounds on a less-obvious level. For example, the gift of working miracles could be seen in the lessening of contention, the impression to call someone who has an urgent need to talk, the sudden inspiration to solve a problem on an assembly line, the avoidance of a traffic accident, the calming of a child in discomfort, and so on.

The gift of prophecy

22 And to others it is given to prophesy;

In John 16:13 we are taught that the Holy Ghost "shall shew you things to come." Therefore, we understand that, among other things, this gift (which all members can have and which must be kept within proper stewardship and realm of influence) can include the gift of knowing the future. Certainly, the First Presidency and the members of the Quorum of the Twelve have this gift for their stewardship over the entire world. We sustain them as "prophets, seers, and revelators." Other leaders within the Church can have this gift for those within their stewardships. Parents can have it for their families.

As a personal example, I was working late on a Saturday evening, studying and making notes for a talk I was to give on the following day. However, my mind kept focusing on the fact that one of our daughters was not yet home and it was getting late. Suddenly, I was given to know that she would be driving in within the next few minutes, and I was able to concentrate on preparing the talk. Sure enough, within ten minutes, I heard the unmistakable sound of our big Ford pickup driving into the driveway. She was home.

A faithful member could have the gift of prophecy by way of a good feeling or an uncomfortable feeling dealing with whether to marry the person he or she is currently dating. The gift of prophecy could be helpful in choosing a career path in college, choosing between employment options, deciding whether to relocate, and so forth.

The gift of discerning of spirits

23 And to others the discerning of spirits.

Elder Stephen L Richards explained that in addition to sensing hidden evil or good, this gift also enables one who possesses it to see the good in others. This is perhaps one of the most important manifestations of this gift. Elder Richards said that this gift consists largely "of an acute sensitivity to impressions—spiritual impressions, if you will—to read under the surface as it were, to detect hidden evil, and more importantly to find the good that may be concealed. **The highest type of discernment is that which perceives in others and uncovers for them their better natures, the good inherent within them** [bold added for emphasis]. It's the gift every missionary needs when he takes the gospel to the people of the world. He must make an appraisal of every personality whom he meets. He must be able to discern the hidden spark that may be lighted for truth. The gift of discernment will save him from mistakes and embarrassment, and it will never fail to inspire confidence in the one who is rightly appraised" (In Conference Report, April 1950, 162).

The gift of tongues

24 And again, it is given to some to speak with tongues;

This gift was manifest on the day of Pentecost, when Peter and the Apostles spoke to the multitudes in their own language, and those in the crowds (from many different countries) heard the preaching in their own languages. (See Acts 2:4–13.)

One of the most common manifestation of this gift is found in how fast and effectively our missionaries learn to speak foreign languages as part of their missionary work. This happens much to the amazement of people outside the Church. Representatives of large corporations and government entities have more than once approached the Church to ask if we could train them in our techniques for teaching foreign languages so effectively. Obviously, it is a bit difficult to explain to them that they and their people would have to join the Church so that they could get the gift of the Holy Ghost in order to receive this gift. And even then, it would have to be in harmony with the will of the Lord for them to receive and use the gift.

On occasions this gift is manifest in the sudden ability of people to understand or speak and understand a foreign language that they do not know. I experienced this as a young missionary in Austria. A member of the First Presidency was touring our mission and spoke to a large gathering of Saints in Vienna. Having been on my mission sufficiently long to understand German quite well, my companion missionaries and I, were amazed and deeply touched when we realized that many of the members in the congregation who did not understand English were understanding the sermon without needing interpretation into German. The gift of tongues had come upon them, and testimonies were greatly strengthened.

On the other hand, speaking in tongues is perhaps one of the most misunderstood gifts of the Holy Ghost and is often used by Satan and his evil spirits to deceive, divert, and detour people from the true gospel of Jesus Christ.

Because the gift of tongues is often used by the devil to counterfeit spirituality and to deceive, the Prophet Joseph Smith taught, "Be not so curious about tongues, do not speak in tongues except there be an interpreter present; the ultimate design of tongues is to speak to foreigners, and if persons are very anxious to display their intelligence, let them speak to such in their own tongues. The gifts of God are all useful in their place, but when they are applied to that which God does not intend, they prove an injury, a snare and a curse instead of a blessing" (*History of the Church*, 5:31–32).

The gift of the interpretation of tongues

25 And to another is given the interpretation of tongues.

This gift usually appears in conjunction with the gift of tongues. Elder Bruce R. McConkie taught, "Tongues and their interpretation are classed among the signs and miracles which always attend the faithful and which stand as evidences of the divinity of the Lord's work. (Mormon 9:24; Mark 16:17; Acts 10:46; 19:6.) In their more dramatic manifestations they consist in speaking or interpreting, by the power of the Spirit, a tongue which is completely unknown to the speaker or interpreter. Sometimes it is the pure Adamic language which is involved" (*Doctrinal New Testament Commentary*, 2:383).

This gift, as is the case with the gift of tongues, is most often found in the work of spreading the gospel throughout the earth. Certainly, those who work with translating the scriptures and Church curriculum materials into foreign languages for use as the Church spreads forth into all nations would experience this gift.

Next, in verse 26, we are reminded that all of these gifts of the Spirit are given for the benefit of God's children.

26 And all these gifts come from God, for the benefit of the children of God.

As you know, one of the responsibilities of the bishop of a ward is to keep the doctrine pure and to see that all things in the ward are done in accordance with established practices and policies of the Church. In order to do this, he doesn't necessarily have to have all the gifts of the Spirit himself, but he is given the ability to discern or distinguish between correct and proper use of gifts of the Spirit and counterfeit ones. This allows him to help his members avoid deception in any of many forms. This we are taught in verse 27, next.

27 And **unto the bishop** of the church, and unto such as God shall appoint and ordain to watch over the church and to be elders unto the church [*this would include General Authorities, stake presidents, and branch presidents*], are to have it **given** unto them **to discern all those gifts** lest there shall be any among you professing and yet be not of God. [*In other words, in case there are deceivers among them.*]

> Next, in verse 28, we are reminded that these spiritual gifts are to be received and used under the direction of the Holy Ghost. As you can see, this is a vital control over this aspect of God's work with His children.

28 And it shall come to pass **that he that asketh in Spirit shall receive in Spirit;**

> We understand from verse 29, next, that some have all these gifts. We suppose that this could refer to the prophet and other leaders, but we do not have a clear explanation from an authorized source. Therefore, we will apply Alma 37:11, which says, "Now these mysteries are not yet fully made known unto me; therefore I shall forbear." In other words, "I don't know; therefore, I won't say."

29 That **unto some it may be given to have all those gifts**, that there may be a head, in order that every member may be profited thereby.

> Earlier we mentioned that there are a number of less-commonly mentioned gifts of the Spirit. We will pause here and consider some of these gifts. In D&C 46:11, above, the Lord tells us "there are many gifts." We will quote Romans 12:6–13 here and use **bold** to point out some of these gifts that are not often referred to in discussions of gifts of the Spirit.

Romans 12:6–13

6 Having then **gifts differing** according to the grace that is given to us, whether **prophecy**, *let us prophesy* according to the proportion of faith;

7 Or **ministry** [*the gift of ministering to the needs of others*], let us wait on our ministering: or he that teacheth, on **teaching** [*the gift of being an effective teacher*];

8 Or he that exhorteth, on **exhortation** [*the gift of effectively explaining the urgency of living the gospel*]: he that **giveth** [*the gift of generosity*], let him do it with simplicity; he that **ruleth** [*the gift of leadership*], with diligence; he that sheweth **mercy**

[*the gift of being merciful*], with cheerfulness.

9 Let **love** [*the gift of showing sincere love*] be without dissimulation. **Abhor that which is evil** [*the gift of having a natural aversion to evil*]; **cleave to that which is good** [*the gift of wanting to be around goodness*].

10 **Be kindly affectioned** [*the gift of being sincerely kind*] one to another with brotherly love; in honour **preferring one another** [*the gift of putting the needs of others ahead of one's own needs*];

11 **Not slothful in business** [*the gift of being skilled in business dealings*]; **fervent in spirit** [*the gift of being truly spiritual*]; **serving the Lord** [*the gift of loving to serve the Lord*];

12 Rejoicing in **hope** [*the gift of hope, which in turn brings happiness and optimism*]; **patient** [*the gift of patience*] in tribulation; continuing **instant in prayer** [*the gift of praying always, continuously in tune with heaven*];

13 **Distributing to the necessity of saints** [*the gift of skillfully caring for the needy*]; given to **hospitality** [*the gift of hospitality, of being a gracious host*].

Elder Marvin J. Ashton spoke of these "less conspicuous gifts" as follows:

"Let us review some of these less-conspicuous gifts: the gift of **asking**; the gift of **listening**; the gift of **hearing** and **using a still, small voice**; the gift of **being able to weep**; the gift of **avoiding contention**; the gift of **being agreeable**; the gift of **avoiding vain repetition**; the gift of **seeking that which is righteous**; the gift of **not passing judgment**; the gift of **looking to God for guidance**; the gift of **being a disciple**; the gift of **caring for others**; the gift of **being able to ponder**; the gift of **offering prayer**; the gift of **bearing a mighty testimony**; and the gift of **receiving the Holy Ghost**" ("'There Are Many Gifts,'" *Ensign*, November 1987, 20).

Next, in verse 30, we are given a clue about how to get our specific prayers answered. It is rather simple and quite important. In effect, it says that when we are inspired by the Holy Ghost as to what to ask for, it is the will of God; therefore, it will happen. You may wish to write a cross-reference next to verse 30 in your own scriptures to D&C 50:29–30.

30 He that asketh in the Spirit asketh according to the will of God; wherefore it is done even as he asketh.

Next, in verse 31, the Savior reminds us that all our prayers as

SECTION 47

well as official ordinances and so forth in the Church must be done in the name of Jesus Christ.

31 And again, I say unto you, **all things must be done in the name of Christ**, whatsoever you do in the Spirit;

> The importance of expressing gratitude while still under the influence of the Spirit is emphasized next in verse 32. In D&C 59:21, we will again come across this emphasis on expressing gratitude to God for blessings received.

32 And **ye must give thanks unto God in the Spirit for whatsoever blessing ye are blessed with**.

> The Savior closes this revelation by stressing the fact that we must be consistent in living the gospel in our daily lives. We must not be on again, off again followers of Christ.

33 And **ye must practise virtue and holiness before me continually**. Even so. Amen.

SECTION 47

Background

> This revelation was given to John Whitmer, who was David Whitmer's older brother and one of the Eight Witnesses of the Book of Mormon. It was given through the Prophet Joseph Smith in Kirtland, Ohio, on March 8, 1831.

The heading to this section is an example of the minor changes that have been made to seventy-eight Doctrine and Covenants section headings in the 2013 edition compared to the headings in prior editions. We will show you both headings:

<u>2013 Edition</u>

Revelation given through Joseph Smith the Prophet, at Kirtland, Ohio, March 8, 1831. John Whitmer, who had already served as a clerk to the Prophet, initially hesitated when he was asked to serve as the Church historian and recorder, replacing Oliver Cowdery. He wrote, "I would rather not do it but observed that the will of the Lord be done, and if he desires it, I desire that he would manifest it through Joseph the Seer." After Joseph Smith received this revelation, John Whitmer accepted and served in his appointed office.

<u>1989 Printing</u>

Revelation given through Joseph Smith the Prophet, at Kirtland, Ohio, March 8, 1831. HC 1:166. Prior to this time Oliver Cowdery had acted as Church historian and recorder. John Whitmer had not sought an appointment as historian, but, being asked to serve in this capacity, he had said that he would obey the will of the Lord in the matter. He had already served as a secretary to the Prophet in recording many of the revelations received in the Fayette, New York, area.

Thus, in this revelation, John Whitmer was called to serve officially as Church historian and recorder. With Oliver Cowdery now on a mission to the Lamanites on the western frontier (see sections 30 and 32), Brother Whitmer's calling, as mentioned above, was to take over from Oliver as Church historian and recorder. His history, according to the latest research from the Joseph Smith Papers Project, consisted of ninety-six pages and spanned from 1831 to 1838. He gave much good and faithful service to the Church during most of these years, but toward the end of 1838, he became angry with Joseph Smith and refused to give the Church the history he had kept. For this and other reasons, he was excommunicated on March 10, 1838. He never returned to the Church but never denied his testimony of the Book of Mormon. In 1893 the Church finally obtained a copy of his history of the Church.

This revelation is a reminder to us that we are to be a record-keeping people and that the history of the Church is a vital part of the work of the Lord in these last days. Such has been the case in every dispensation of the gospel, beginning with Adam and Eve (see Moses 6:5).

We will now proceed with section 47, using **bold as usual** to point things out. You may wish to mark some of the bolded items in your own scriptures.

1 BEHOLD, it is expedient in me [*the Lord considers it necessary*] that my servant **John** [*Whitmer*] **should write and keep a regular history, and assist you, my servant Joseph, in transcribing all things which shall be given you**, until he is called to further duties.

2 Again, verily I say unto you that **he can also lift up his voice** [*speak*] **in meetings, whenever it shall be expedient** [*necessary, needed*].

3 And again, I say unto you that **it shall be appointed unto him to keep the church record and history continually**; for Oliver Cowdery I have appointed to another office [*including a mission to the Lamanites with Parley P. Pratt, Peter Whitmer Jr., and Ziba Peterson*].

4 Wherefore, **it shall be given him, inasmuch as he is faithful, by the Comforter, to write these things** [*in other words, this history is to be written under the direction of the Holy Ghost*]. Even so. Amen.

SECTION 48

Background

Early in 1831, the Saints began moving from the eastern United States, primarily New York, to settle in the Kirtland, Ohio, area as previously commanded by the Lord (see D&C 37:1–3). As they began arriving in Ohio, they had many questions, including whether or not Ohio was to be the place where New Jerusalem would be built. They had read about New Jerusalem in the Book of Mormon (for example, in Ether 13:6) and had recently been told more about it in D&C 42:9 and 62.

They were also wondering whether to buy land in the Kirtland area for the Saints to settle and build on as they arrived from the east. Should they plan on settling permanently in Ohio, or was it to be a temporary situation? In answer to these and other questions, the Lord gave the revelation contained in section 48 to Joseph Smith in Kirtland sometime in March 1831.

One of the lessons we can learn from this revelation is the importance of having faith and following the Lord's instructions, even if He only answers part of our question about a particular concern. For instance, as stated above, these Saints wanted to know if they were to settle permanently in Ohio. In verses 1 and 3, below, the Lord tells them three times that they will be there "for the present time." He could no doubt have told them that they would be in Kirtland for five years, as he did about six months later (see D&C 64:21), but He chose not to. Thus, we are reminded that one of the most important lessons we are to learn during mortality is to walk by faith and not demand complete answers before we start walking.

1 IT is necessary that ye should remain **for the present time** in your places of abode, as it shall be suitable to your circumstances.

2 And inasmuch as ye have lands, ye shall impart to the eastern brethren [*perhaps meaning that if they already have land in Ohio, they should share their land with incoming Saints so they too have land to settle on*];

3 And inasmuch as ye have not lands, let them buy **for the present time** in those regions round about, as seemeth them good, for it must needs be necessary that they have places to live **for the present time**.

Next, in verses 4–6, the Lord refers to "the city," meaning the city of New Jerusalem. Again, these Saints are expected to walk by faith and be obedient to the instructions of the Lord, without having all of their questions answered, including their wanting to know the location where New Jerusalem is to be built. By the way, they will be given a hint in about three months that Missouri will be "the land, which I will consecrate unto my people" (D&C 52:2–3), and then, in D&C 57:1–3, which was given in July 1831, they will finally be told that Independence, Missouri, is "the place for the city of Zion," meaning the New Jerusalem.

Thus, in this revelation, these early members of the Church are counseled to acquire land needed "for the present time" in Ohio, but also to save up as much money as they can appropriately come up with in order to be in a position eventually to buy land for the New Jerusalem. This is obviously a "curriculum" designed by our loving Savior for their growth and development, much the same as He does for each of us for our best good and development.

4 It must needs be necessary that ye **save all the money that ye can**, and that ye obtain all that ye can in righteousness, that in time ye may be enabled to purchase land for an inheritance, even the city [*New Jerusalem*].

5 **The place** [*the location for New Jerusalem*] **is not yet to be revealed; but** after your brethren come from the east **there are to be certain men appointed, and to them it shall be given to know the place**, or to them it shall be revealed.

In verse 5, above, and 6, next, notice how the Lord in His mercy and kindness gives these faithful Saints a bit more information about the eventual gathering to Zion, which, in this context, is another name for the New Jerusalem. This provides hope and encouragement as they walk in faith to fulfill what the Lord has instructed.

6 And **they shall be appointed to purchase the lands**, and to make a commencement to **lay the foundation of the city** [*the city of Zion—in other words, New Jerusalem*]; and **then shall ye begin to be gathered** with your families, every man according to his family, according to his circumstances, and **as is appointed to him by the presidency and the bishop** of the church, **according to the laws and commandments which ye have received, and which ye shall hereafter receive** [*more instructions are coming*]. Even so. Amen.

SECTION 49

Background

This is a fascinating revelation in which the Lord refuted a number of ideas and doctrines taught by a congregation of the Shaking Quakers, who lived not far from Cleveland, Ohio, about fifteen miles southwest of Kirtland. This revelation was given in Kirtland, Ohio, through the Prophet Joseph Smith on May 7, 1831, and was addressed to Sidney Rigdon, Parley P. Pratt, and Leman Copley. Brother Copley had been a member of the Shaking Quaker congregation before his conversion to the Church. Although Brother Copley had been baptized into the restored Church, he still felt that many of the teachings of the Shakers were true.

The Shaking Quakers (United Society of Believers in Christ's Second Appearing) were respectable and industrious citizens. Among other things, they had excellent schools, built fine furniture, invented the clothespin and flat broom as we know them today, washed hands often (unusual in that day), thus avoiding many of the epidemics of the times, and lived together in a type of united order. Many people not of their beliefs sent their own children to the Shaker schools because of the excellent education provided.

The Shaking Quakers originated in England, probably in the late 1700s, and immigrated to America in 1774 because of persecution. They were led by a woman named Ann Lee, who had been converted in England at age twenty-two to the "Shakers" (so called by many because they worshipped through dancing, shaking, clapping, whirling, chanting, and twisting, which they believed caused their sins to drop from their souls, thus leaving them clean before God).

Ann Lee married at age twenty-six and quickly had four children, three of whom died in infancy, and one of whom, Elizabeth, died at the age of six. Grief-stricken, she came to the conclusion that total denial of physical passion and desire was the only path to peace for her devastated soul. She decided that sexual relations and the institution of marriage were the basic cause of all evil. She claimed to have had a vision in which she saw Adam and Eve defy God's commands and engage in sexual relations, which purportedly led to their expulsion from the Garden of Eden. She thus concluded that sex was evil and the primal cause of the separation of mankind from God. Her husband eventually ended their marriage after thirteen years.

She proclaimed herself to be Christ, who had come the second time, this time coming in the form of a woman. Ann Lee served as the leader of the Shaking Quakers from about 1754 up to the time of her death near Albany, New York, on September 8, 1784, at the age of forty-eight. Shortly before her death, she told her followers that the Shakers would move to Ohio. Subsequently, a substantial number of them moved to Ohio and established a community of Shakers near Cleveland.

The teachings of the Shakers, as

established in America by Ann Lee, included the doctrine that Christ's Second Coming had already taken place and that He had come this time in the form of a woman (Ann Lee), the forbidding of the touching of members of the opposite sex (including the shaking of hands), the teaching that men and women are equals, that baptism was not necessary, that pork should not be eaten (many Shakers refused to eat any meat at all), and that celibacy (intentional avoidance of marriage as a matter of religion) was the highest form of worshipping God.

As we go through section forty-nine now, we will use **bold** to point things out, including the Lord's direct responses to the teachings of the Shaking Quakers.

1 **HEARKEN unto my word**, my servants **Sidney** [*Rigdon*], and **Parley** [*Pratt*], and **Leman** [*Copley*]; for behold, verily I say unto you, that I give unto you a commandment that you shall **go and preach my gospel which ye have received, even as ye have received it** [*in other words, don't water it down or change it*], **unto the Shakers.**

The three brethren mentioned in verse 1, above, did go as instructed, attending a Shaker service and receiving permission to read this revelation to the Shakers at the end of that meeting. Their message was rejected.

2 Behold, I say unto you, that **they desire to know the truth in part, but not all**, for they are not right before me and must needs repent.

It is interesting to note, in verses 3 and 4, next, that as the Lord instructs these three, He cautions Leman Copley not to cave in to the teaching and persuasion of his former associates in the Shaker community. Sadly, he wavered over the next few years, leaving and then coming back to the Church at least twice. He eventually joined with apostates who had left the Church. He died estranged from the Church in Ohio at about age eighty-one.

3 Wherefore, I send you, my servants Sidney and Parley, to preach the gospel unto them.

4 And **my servant Leman shall be ordained unto this work, that he may reason with them, not according to that which he has received of them** [*not reverting back to his old Shaker beliefs*], **but according to that which shall be taught him by you my servants**; and by so doing I will bless him, otherwise he shall not prosper.

Next, the Savior quotes His Father and identifies Himself as He begins addressing specific incorrect beliefs of the Shakers.

He first assures them that He has not yet come to earth for the Second Coming.

5 Thus saith the Lord; **for I am God, and have sent** [*note that this is past tense, in other words, it has already been done*] **mine Only Begotten Son** into the world for the redemption of the world, and have decreed that **he that receiveth him shall be saved**, and **he that receiveth him not shall be damned** [*stopped in progression*]—

6 And they have done unto **the Son of Man** [*Christ*] even as they listed [*just as they desired*]; and he **has taken his power on the right hand of his** [*the Father's*] **glory**, and **now reigneth in the heavens**, and **will reign till he descends on the earth** to put all enemies under his feet, **which time is nigh at hand** [*the Second Coming is getting close*]—

7 I, the Lord God, have spoken it; **but the hour and the day no man knoweth, neither the angels in heaven, nor shall they know until he comes.**

Remember that one of the beliefs of the Shakers was that they did not need baptism. In other words, their faithful members did not have sins.

8 Wherefore, I will that all men shall repent, for **all are under sin**, except those which I have reserved unto myself, holy men that ye know not of.

Joseph Fielding Smith explained the phrase "holy men that ye know not of" in verse 8, above. He said that they "are translated persons such as John the Revelator and the Three Nephites, who do not belong to this generation and yet are in the flesh in the earth performing a special ministry until the coming of Jesus Christ" (*Church History and Modern Revelation*, 1:209).

9 Wherefore, I say unto you that **I have sent unto you mine everlasting covenant** [*the restored gospel of Jesus Christ*], even that which was from the beginning.

10 And that which I have promised I have so fulfilled, and the nations of the earth shall bow to it; and, if not of themselves, they shall come down, for that which is now exalted of itself shall be laid low of power.

11 Wherefore, **I give unto you** [*Sidney, Parley, and Leman*] **a commandment that ye go among this people** [*the Shakers*], **and say unto them**, like unto mine Apostle of old, whose name was Peter:

12 **Believe on the name of the Lord Jesus, who** was on the

earth, and **is to come,** the beginning and the end;

13 **Repent and be baptized in the name of Jesus Christ,** according to the holy commandment, **for the remission of sins;**

14 And whoso doeth this shall **receive the gift of the Holy Ghost, by the laying on of the hands of the elders of the church.**

15 And again, verily I say unto you, that **whoso forbiddeth to marry is not ordained** [*authorized*] **of God,** for **marriage is ordained of God unto man** [*in other words, celibacy is a false doctrine*].

16 Wherefore, **it is lawful that he should have one wife, and they twain shall be one flesh** [*they should have children*], and **all this that the earth might answer the end** [*purpose*] **of its creation** [*in other words, if people don't have children, the spirit children of our Heavenly Parents cannot come to earth to obtain bodies and continue to progress*];

17 And **that it might be filled with the measure of man** [*that the earth might be populated*], according to his creation before the world was made [*as intended for the spirits who were created in premortality*].

Next, the Lord addresses the issue of whether or not to eat meat. This is an important verse for members of the Church who may wonder if we should avoid meat except in times of cold or famine (especially with respect to the proper interpretation of D&C 89:12–13).

18 And **whoso forbiddeth to abstain from meats, that man should not eat the same, is not ordained** [*authorized, approved*] **of God;**

As mentioned above, verse 18 provides a vital clarification regarding the eating of meat. It is okay to eat meat if we want to. And in case readers do not understand the wording in verse 18, above, our modern prophets have provided D&C 49, footnote 18a, making sure members of the Church realize that the Lord does not endorse abstinence from meat as a teaching of the true Church. We will reread verse 18, here, substituting the wording in footnote 18a for the wording as it stands. When we do so, it reads,

"And whoso **biddeth** [*requires*] to abstain from meats, that man should not eat the same, is not ordained of God."

Verse 19, next, confirms the interpretation of verse 18 given by the Brethren. You may also wish to make a cross-reference here to D&C 59:16–20 in your own scriptures since in them the Lord again teaches this principle.

19 For, behold, the **beasts** of the field and the **fowls** of the air, **and that which cometh of the earth, is ordained** [*authorized by the Lord*] **for the use of man for food** and for **raiment** [*clothing*], and that he might have in abundance.

20 **But it is not given that one man should possess that which is above another**, wherefore the world lieth in sin [*selfishness is an underlying reason for much of the sin and wickedness in the world*].

21 And **wo be unto man that sheddeth blood or that wasteth flesh and hath no need.**

Next, the Master addresses the false teaching of Ann Lee that Jesus will come in the form of a woman and also explains that the Second Coming will not be low key by way of a traveling man who announces himself as the Savior. In other words, the Second Coming will be just as spectacular and all-encompassing as foretold in prophecy.

22 And again, verily I say unto you, that **the Son of Man** [*Christ*] **cometh not in the form of a woman, neither of a man traveling on the earth.**

23 Wherefore, **be not deceived**, but continue in steadfastness, looking forth for the **heavens to be shaken**, and the **earth to tremble** and to **reel to and fro** as a drunken man, and for the **valleys to be exalted**, and for the **mountains to be made low**, and for the **rough places to become smooth**—and all this when the angel shall sound his trumpet [*in other words, all this will happen when the Savior comes; thus, it will be spectacular, and none will miss it or have any doubt about it*].

Having addressed specific false doctrines, the Savior now gives these three representatives of the Church (and the Shaking Quakers and all of us) some prophecies that will be fulfilled preceding His coming, and He tenderly invites them to repent and ask Him for help in understanding the true gospel. He assures them that He will "open the door" for them and support them in their mission.

24 But before the great day of the Lord shall come [*before the Second Coming of Christ*], **Jacob** [*Israel*] **shall flourish** in the wilderness [*the apostate world*], and **the Lamanites shall blossom as the rose** [*a wonderful prophecy that is being fulfilled dramatically in our day*].

25 **Zion shall flourish** upon the hills and rejoice upon the mountains, and shall be assembled together unto the place which I have appointed. [*Among other things,*

this verse can mean that the Church will grow dramatically and spread throughout the world before the Second Coming.]

26 Behold, I say unto you, **go forth as I have commanded you**; repent of all your sins; ask and ye shall receive; knock and it shall be opened unto you.

27 Behold, **I will go before you and be your rearward** [*your protection*]; and **I will be in your midst, and you shall not be confounded** [*stopped, confused*].

28 Behold, **I am Jesus Christ**, and I come quickly. Even so. Amen.

> The word quickly, as used in verse 28, above, does not necessarily mean "right away." It might better be understood as meaning that when the Savior comes, it will happen suddenly or "quickly," and there will be no time left for repenting.

SECTION 50

Background

This revelation was given through the Prophet Joseph Smith in Kirtland, Ohio, on May 9, 1831. During this period of time in the early days of the Church, there were many so-called "spiritual manifestations" among the Saints. The problem was that many of these "manifestations" were strange and even bizarre. And so, the Saints were not sure whether they came from God or the devil. One of Satan's well-used tools is the counterfeiting of revelation and spiritual manifestations.

For instance, after Parley P. Pratt had returned from the mission to the American Indians west of Missouri (see D&C 32) in late March 1831, he visited several branches of the Church around Kirtland and was dismayed to see what he considered to be disgusting spiritual manifestations among the members. He wrote, "As I went forth among the different branches, some very strange spiritual operations were manifested, which were disgusting, rather than edifying. Some persons would seem to swoon away, and make unseemly gestures, and be drawn or disfigured in their countenances. Others would fall into ecstacies, and be drawn into contortions, cramp, fits, etc. Others would seem to have visions and revelations, which were not edifying, and which were not congenial to the doctrine and spirit of the gospel. In short, a false and lying spirit seemed to be creeping into the Church.

"All these things were new and strange to me, and had originated in the Church during our absence, and previous to the arrival of President Joseph Smith from New York.

SECTION 50

"Feeling our weakness and inexperience, and lest we should err in judgment concerning these spiritual phenomena, myself, John Murdock, and several other Elders, went to Joseph Smith, and asked him to inquire of the Lord concerning these spirits or manifestations.

"After we had joined in prayer in his translating room, he dictated in our presence the following revelation [section 50]:—(Each sentence was uttered slowly and very distinctly, and with a pause between each, sufficiently long for it to be recorded, by an ordinary writer, in long hand.

"This was the manner in which all his written revelations were dictated and written. There was never any hesitation, reviewing, or reading back, in order to keep the run of the subject; neither did any of these communications undergo revisions, interlinings, or corrections. As he dictated them so they stood, so far as I have witnessed; and I was present to witness the dictation of several communications of several pages each. . . .)" (*Autobiography of Parley P. Pratt*, 61–62).

The Prophet Joseph Smith spoke of these strange manifestations in Kirtland. He said, "Soon after the Gospel was established in Kirtland, and during the absence of the authorities of the Church, many false spirits were introduced, many strange visions were seen, and wild, enthusiastic notions were entertained; men ran out of doors under the influence of this spirit, and some of them got upon the stumps of trees and shouted, and all kinds of extravagances were entered into by them; one man pursued a ball that he said he saw flying in the air, until he came to a precipice, when he jumped into the top of a tree, which saved his life; and many ridiculous things were entered into, calculated to bring disgrace upon the Church of God, to cause the Spirit of God to be withdrawn, and to uproot and destroy those glorious principles which had been developed for the salvation of the human family." (*History of the Church*, 4:580. See also *Manuscript History of the Church*, vol. C-1, page 1311, josephsmithpapers.org.)

What we learn from section 50 will be valuable in helping us avoid deception ourselves. First, in verses 1 and 2, we will be taught that there are indeed many evil and false spirits who attempt to deceive. In other words, such things are not merely the product of wild imaginations.

1 HEARKEN [*listen carefully*], O ye elders of my church, and **give ear to the voice of the living God**; and attend to the words of wisdom which shall be given unto you, according as ye have asked and are agreed **as touching the church, and the spirits which**

have gone abroad in the earth.

2 Behold, verily I say unto you, that **there are many spirits which are false spirits, which have gone forth in the earth, deceiving the world.**

> Revelation 16:14 reminds us that evil spirits have power to work miracles.

Revelation 16

14 For **they are the spirits of devils, working miracles,** which go forth unto the kings of the earth and of the whole world, to gather them to the battle of that great day of God Almighty.

President Boyd K. Packer of the Quorum of the Twelve warned us on several occasions that Satan and his evil spirits strive constantly to deceive us by counterfeiting true revelation. He said, "Be ever on guard lest you be deceived by inspiration from an unworthy source. You can be given false spiritual messages. There are counterfeit spirits just as there are counterfeit angels. (See Moro. 7:17.) . . .

"The spiritual part of us and the emotional part of us are so closely linked that [it] is possible to mistake an emotional impulse for something spiritual. We occasionally find people who receive what they assume to be spiritual promptings from God, when those promptings are either centered in the emotions or are from the adversary" ("The Candle of the Lord," *Ensign*, Jan. 1983, 55–56).

In another talk, President Packer spoke of the importance of distinguishing between a temptation from the devil and a true revelation from the Lord:

"There can be counterfeit revelations, promptings from the devil, temptations! As long as you live, in one way or another the adversary will try to lead you astray. . . .

"The Prophet Joseph Smith said that 'nothing is a greater injury to the children of men than to be under the influence of a false spirit when they think they have the Spirit of God' [*Teachings of the Prophet Joseph Smith*, 205]. . . .

"If ever you receive a prompting to do something that makes you feel uneasy, something you know in your mind to be wrong and contrary to the principles of righteousness, do not respond to it!" ("Personal Revelation: The Gift, the Test, and the Promise," *Ensign*, Nov. 1994, 61).

Continuing now with section 50, the Savior tells us what Satan is trying to do to us.

3 And also **Satan hath sought to deceive you,** that he might overthrow you.

Next, Jesus reminds these Saints

that He is aware of them and the evil things taking place among them. He assures the faithful of exaltation and warns the guilty of coming judgments.

4 Behold**, I, the Lord**, have looked upon you, and **have seen abominations in the church** [*among the members*] that profess my name [*who claim to be faithful members*].

5 But **blessed are they who are faithful** and endure, whether in life or in death, for **they shall inherit eternal life** [*exaltation*].

6 But **wo unto them that are deceivers and hypocrites** [*people who want to look good but don't want to be good*], for, thus saith the Lord, I will bring them to judgment.

> Next, in verse 7, we will find an important and reassuring lesson. Perhaps you have worried about a friend or loved one who was raised in a home or under circumstances where they did not get a fair chance to understand the gospel or see it in action. Perhaps there was much hypocrisy, including devastating abuse. Perhaps an acquaintance has been severely offended by hypocrisy on the part of an active member of the Church. Verse 7 reminds us that God is completely fair, and that victims of bad example and hypocrisy will "be reclaimed." In other words, they will be given a completely fair opportunity to understand and accept or reject the gospel, either in this life or the next. And, according to the Lord, they will be "reclaimed." This is most comforting!

Doctrine

Verses 7. God is completely fair. Those who do not get a completely fair set of opportunities to hear, understand, and accept or reject the gospel either later in this life or in the next life, will get them before the final judgment day.

7 Behold, verily I say unto you, there are **hypocrites among you**, who **have deceived some**, which has given the adversary power; but behold **such shall be reclaimed**;

> As you know from experience, all the wicked do not get punished during their mortal lives. In fact, some seem to prosper despite sinning and breaking God's commandments. Verse 8, next, reminds us that all such will eventually have their day of reckoning.

8 But **the hypocrites shall be detected and shall be cut off** [*from the full blessings of the gospel*], **either in life or in death**, even as I will; and wo unto them who are

cut off from my church, for the same are overcome of the world [*in other words, they have given in to sin and the ways of the world*].

9 Wherefore, **let every man beware lest he do that which is not in truth and righteousness before me.**

> Beginning with verse 10, next, the Savior deals directly with the question that led to the giving of this revelation; namely, how to tell if spiritual manifestations come from God or from the devil. Jesus tells these men that He will reason with them the same way they would reason with each other, and that He will use simple logic to help them understand Him.

10 And now **come**, saith the Lord, by the Spirit, unto the elders of his church, and **let us reason together**, that ye may understand;

11 **Let us reason even as a man reasoneth one with another face to face.**

12 Now, **when a man reasoneth he is understood of man**, because he reasoneth as a man; **even so will I, the Lord, reason with you that you may understand.**

> Next, the Lord uses a question-answer format to teach these early members and leaders how to tell whether or not the manifestations they are witnessing are from the Holy Ghost or the devil and his evil spirits.

Question

13 **Wherefore, I the Lord ask you this question—unto what were ye ordained** [*what were you called to do*]?

Answer

14 To **preach my gospel by the Spirit**, even the Comforter [*the Holy Ghost, which brings peace and harmony—unlike the strange manifestations they've seen*] which was sent forth to teach the truth [*in clear, easily recognizable terms*].

Question

15 **And then received ye spirits which ye could not understand, and received them to be of God** [*and you accepted strange and weird manifestations to be from God*]; and **in this are ye justified?**

Answer

16 Behold **ye shall answer this question yourselves** [*in other words, the answer is obvious—no, you were not justified in believing that such strange things had come from God*]; nevertheless, **I will be merciful unto you**; he that is weak among you hereafter shall be made strong [*if they keep learning these lessons—a kind reminder that these*

elders are still learning and that the Lord is merciful and patient].

Question

17 Verily I say unto you, he that is ordained of me and sent forth to preach the word of truth by the Comforter, in the Spirit of truth, doth he preach it by the Spirit of truth or some other way?

Perhaps you've noticed that when the Holy Ghost is present, testifying of the truthfulness of the gospel, helping you understand gospel principles, and so forth, there is a sweet feeling of peace, calm, and assurance that attends it. This is opposite the unsettling, jangling, and boisterous spirit that attends the types of "spiritual" manifestations these brethren were concerned about.

Answer

18 And if it be by some other way it is not of God. [*In other words, when you stop and think about it, it is easy to tell the difference.*]

Question

19 And again, he that receiveth the word of truth, doth he receive it by the Spirit of truth [*the peace and calm that attend the testifying of the Holy Ghost*] **or some other way?**

Answer

20 If it be some other way it is not of God.

Remember, the Lord told them He would reason with them "as a man reasoneth one with another face to face" (verse 11). We are seeing this and will see it again in verse 21, next.

Question

21 Therefore, why is it that ye cannot understand and know, that he that receiveth the word by the Spirit of truth receiveth it as it is preached by the Spirit of truth? [*In other words, the Holy Ghost does not do wild and weird things like jumping on stumps and shouting, twisting grotesquely, rolling and uttering strange sounds, and so forth, that are opposite the peace that accompanies the Spirit.*]

Next, in verses 22–25, the Savior summarizes this lesson on distinguishing between the truth from God and attempted deceptions from the devil and his evil spirits. We will summarize each point at the beginning of the relevant verse.

Point 1

When the Holy Ghost is involved, gospel understanding is the result (as opposed to not understanding the meaning and messages of strange and weird manifestations).

Point 2

When the Holy Ghost is involved, both the preacher and the hearer are edified (built up, strengthened in personal righteousness and understanding of the gospel).

Point 3

When the Holy Ghost is involved, there is rejoicing and harmony.

22 **Wherefore, he that preacheth and he that receiveth, understand one another, and both are edified and rejoice together.**

Point 4

Darkness is felt when the Holy Ghost is not involved.

23 And **that which doth not edify is not of God, and is darkness.**

Point 5

Things from God produce spiritual light and understanding. There is a progression from one level of understanding and light to the next. This progress continues for the faithful until they have all light and perfect understanding (see D&C 88:49, which tells the faithful that the day will come when they will actually comprehend God).

24 **That which is of God is light** [*that which comes from God produces light and understanding in our minds and hearts*]; and **he that receiveth light, and continueth in God, receiveth more light; and that light groweth brighter and brighter until the perfect day** [*until the person knows all things and becomes a god*].

Point 6

Spiritual light and truth from God enable us to chase deception and spiritual darkness out of our lives.

25 And again, verily I say unto you, and I say it that you may **know the truth, that you may chase darkness from among you**;

> Next, in verse 26, the Savior explains that in order to be greatest in His kingdom, one must be the humble servant of everyone. This seems to be the exact opposite of the arrogance and self-serving attitude seen commonly among worldly, powerful leaders.

26 **He that is ordained of God and sent forth, the same is appointed to be the greatest**, notwithstanding [*even though*] he is **the least and the servant of all.**

> One of the reasons such people (verse 26, above) are the

"greatest" is that the humble work of spreading the gospel enables sincere converts to eventually become gods, the greatest reward in the universe! We see this in verse 27, next.

27 Wherefore, **he is possessor of all things**; for **all things are subject unto him, both in heaven and on the earth** [*terms used to describe gods; see D&C 132:20*], **the life and the light, the Spirit and the power, sent forth by the will of the Father through Jesus Christ, his Son** [*all blessings and rewards of the gospel come through Jesus Christ's mission and Atonement*].

Next, we are reminded of the necessity of personal purity in order to progress in the gospel. Such purity is available through the Atonement of Jesus Christ.

28 **But no man is possessor of all things except he be purified and cleansed from all sin.**

Personal purity leads to power in prayer, as explained in verses 29–30, next.

29 And **if ye are purified** and cleansed from all sin, **ye shall ask whatsoever you will in the name of Jesus and it shall be done.**

30 **But know this, it shall be given you what you shall ask** [*in other words, if you are close to the Spirit, the Holy Ghost will inspire you as to what you may properly ask for*]; and as ye are appointed to the head, the spirits shall be subject unto you.

You may wish to cross-reference verse 30, above, with D&C 46:30, which carries a similar message regarding knowing if something is proper to pray for.

Next, the Savior teaches more about distinguishing between that which comes from God and that which comes from evil sources and gives instruction as to how to handle the situation when you become aware that something may be false or evil. Such falsehood or evil could come from other people as well as from evil spirits or the devil.

31 Wherefore, it shall come to pass, that **if you behold** [*see, sense*] **a spirit manifested that you cannot understand,** and you receive not that spirit, **ye shall ask of the Father in the name of Jesus; and if he give not unto you that spirit** [*if the situation or person does not bring light, understanding, rejoicing, edification, and so forth as explained in verses 22–25*], **then you may know that it is not of God.**

32 And **it shall be given unto you, power over that spirit**

[*including teachings, philosophies, persons, evil spirits*]; **and you shall proclaim against that spirit with a loud** [*firm, definite*] **voice that it is not of God—**

> Note the caution given here, next, to basically avoid arrogance and ego building, which are not in harmony with the ways of God.

33 **Not with railing accusation,** that ye be not overcome, **neither with boasting nor rejoicing,** lest you be seized [*overpowered*] therewith.

> Next, we are reminded of the importance of giving credit to God and avoiding the mistake of thinking we have power by ourselves to accomplish such things.

34 He that receiveth of God, **let him account it of God**; and let him rejoice [*humbly*] that he is accounted of God worthy to receive [*such help in discriminating between good and evil and dealing effectively with it*].

> In the final verses of this section, the Savior gives tender and somewhat personal counsel to several of the elders who asked Joseph Smith to inquire of the Lord concerning these matters. He also bears witness to them that Joseph Smith is His prophet, and He forgives them of their sins, thus giving them a fresh start and encouragement to continue learning and growing.

35 And **by giving heed and doing these things which ye have received, and which ye shall hereafter receive** [*more help and instructions come to those who obey initial counsel*]—**and the kingdom is given you of the Father, and power to overcome all things which are not ordained of him** [*which do not come from God*]—

36 And behold, verily I say unto you, **blessed are you who are now hearing these words of mine from the mouth of my servant** [*Joseph Smith*], for **your sins are forgiven you.**

37 Let my servant Joseph Wakefield, in whom I am well pleased, and my servant Parley P. Pratt go forth among the churches and strengthen them by the word of exhortation [*counseling and teaching, urging obedience to God's commandments*];

38 And also my servant John Corrill, or as many of my servants as are ordained unto this office, and let them labor in the vineyard [*the mission field, the earth, the Church*]; and let no man hinder them doing that which I have appointed unto them—

> In verse 39, next, the Lord expresses dissatisfaction with Edward Partridge, who was ordained

SECTION 50

as the first bishop of the Church (see D&C 41:9). He also gently reminds Bishop Partridge that he can be forgiven.

While we do not know for sure what the problem was, we do know that it was the bishop's responsibility to help the Saints moving into the area to get settled. It may be that he was not following counsel in fulfilling his responsibilities in this regard. In D&C 51:1–2, Edward Partridge is told that he must do things the way the Lord instructs, implying that perhaps he was ignoring some counsel and trying to do things his own way. We will see when we get to D&C 85:8 that Bishop Partridge was severely chastised for refusing to follow instructions. He did repent and was faithful to the end.

39 Wherefore, in this thing my servant **Edward Partridge is not justified** [*his behavior is not pleasing to God*]; nevertheless **let him repent and he shall be forgiven.**

One important message for us in verse 40, next, is that we must first learn to walk in faith and obedience before gaining more knowledge. Otherwise, we would be overwhelmed.

40 Behold, **ye are little children and ye cannot bear all things now; ye must grow in grace and in the knowledge of the truth.**

Next, the Master tenderly encourages all of us who feel our weaknesses and inadequacies by reminding us that we can achieve exaltation because of His Atonement.

41 **Fear not, little children, for you are mine**, and **I have overcome the world** [*Christ's Atonement has overcome all things for the righteous*], and **you are of them that my Father hath given me;**

42 **And none of them that my Father hath given me shall be lost.** [*This includes the fact that no power in earth or hell can tear the righteous away from the Savior, who will bring them safely to the Father.*]

Next, Jesus explains that He and His Father are united in purpose and work, and that those of us who accept and follow Him are, in effect, united with Him in purpose and work. In other words, if we unite with Christ, we are uniting with the Father.

43 And **the Father and I are one**. I am in the Father and the Father in me; and **inasmuch as** [*if*] **ye have received me, ye are in me and I in you.**

It is comforting and significant to know, as taught in verse 44, next, that the Savior is often in our midst. He is not an absentee God nor an uninterested deity who has finished His work and gives no more revelation and scripture as is taught by many religions.

44 Wherefore, **I am in your midst**, and **I am the good shepherd** [*the One we can safely follow back into the fold*], and **the stone of Israel** [*the promised Messiah, the sure foundation*]. **He that buildeth upon this rock shall never fall.**

> According to verses 45–46, we can plan on seeing the Savior, whether in this life or the next. It will happen. In the context of this section, this is beautiful assurance and encouragement to continue walking in faith until that day comes.

45 And **the day cometh that you shall hear my voice and see me, and know that I am.**

46 **Watch, therefore, that ye may be ready.** Even so. Amen.

SECTION 51

Background

> This is another example of an exact date, May 20, 1831, now being available because of research on the Joseph Smith Papers Project, whereas, editions of the Doctrine and Covenants prior to the 2013 edition simply said "May 1831" in the heading.

> In this section, we will learn more about the law of consecration. This revelation was given through the Prophet Joseph Smith at Thompson, Ohio, not far from Kirtland. It was given at the request of Bishop Edward Partridge, who had the main responsibility for dividing up community property and funds among the Saints as they continued to move into the Kirtland, Ohio, area from the eastern states, especially those Saints from Colesville, New York. In section 42, given about three months before, the basics of the law of consecration had been given by the Lord. Now, more details were needed about how to actually live the law of consecration.

> Perhaps you have attended a class or heard a discussion in which the "united order" or "law of consecration" was said to be basically similar to communism. Nothing could be farther from the truth. As we study this revelation, we will see foundational principles upon which the law of consecration is based. Among other things, we will see that the individual is top priority (opposite of communism), allowances are made to accommodate and foster individual talents and personalities (opposite of communism), and that private ownership of property is an integral part of living the law of consecration (opposite of communism).

> First, the Lord addresses thirty-seven-year-old Bishop Edward Partridge, the first bishop of the Church, and provides basic principles and guidelines throughout the revelation for implementing the law of consecration. This action in

Ohio is, in effect, a preparatory education that will be valuable for the Saints as they later relocate to Missouri and begin building a Zion society. We will note these principles as we come to them.

1 HEARKEN unto me, saith the Lord your God, and **I will speak unto my servant Edward Partridge, and give unto him directions**; for it must needs be that he receive directions how to organize this people.

2 **For it must needs be** [*it is necessary*] **that they be organized according to my laws** [*the law of consecration, basically, the laws of the celestial kingdom*]; if otherwise, they will be cut off.

Principle
There is not flat equality in the living of the law of consecration. Individual differences and wishes are respected and encouraged. (Obviously, all are expected to live the same basics of the gospel of Jesus Christ.)

3 Wherefore, let my servant Edward Partridge, and those whom he has chosen, in whom I am well pleased, appoint unto this people their portions [*assign the lands, means, and resources*], every man equal **according to** his family, according to his **circumstances** and his **wants** and **needs**.

Principle
Private ownership of property is a vital part of the law of consecration.

4 And let my servant Edward Partridge, when he shall appoint a man his portion, **give unto him a writing** [*a deed to his property*] **that shall secure unto him his portion, that he shall hold it**, even this right and this inheritance in the church, until he transgresses and is not accounted worthy by the voice of the church, according to the laws and covenants of the church, to belong to the church.

5 And **if he shall transgress and is not accounted worthy to belong to the church, he shall not have power to claim that portion which he has consecrated unto the bishop for the poor and needy of my church**; therefore, he shall not retain the gift, **but shall only have claim on that portion that is deeded unto him.**

6 And thus **all things shall be made sure, according to the laws of the land** [*the deeds are to be handled in accordance with the laws of the land*].

President J. Reuben Clark Jr. explained the principle of private ownership of property as applied in the United Order. He said, "One of the places in which some of the brethren are going astray is this: There is continuous reference in the revelations to equality among the brethren, but I think you will find only one place where that equality is really described, though it is referred to in other revelations. That revelation (D&C 51:3) affirms that every man is to be 'equal according to his family, according to his circumstances and his wants and needs.' (See also D&C 82:17; 78:5–6.) Obviously, this is not a case of 'dead level' equality. It is 'equality' that will vary as much as the man's circumstances, his family, his wants and needs, may vary" (In Conference Report, October 1942, 55).

President Clark went on to say, "The fundamental principle of this system was the private ownership of property. Each man owned his portion, or inheritance, or stewardship, with an absolute title, which he could alienate, or hypothecate, or otherwise treat as his own. The Church did not own all of the property, and the life under the United Order was not a communal life, as the Prophet Joseph himself said (*History of the Church*, 3:28). The United Order is an individualistic system, not a communal system" (In Conference Report, October 1942, 57).

7 And **let that which belongs to this people be appointed unto this people** [*probably an instruction to Bishop Partridge to stop holding back on giving deeds and to go ahead and do it. When we get to section 85, we will see that he had deep concerns and was holding back as to whether or not it was wise to have private ownership of property with legal deeds*].

8 And the money which is left unto this people—let there be an agent appointed unto this people, to take the money to provide food and raiment [*clothing*], **according to the wants** of this people.

In verse 8, above, we are again reminded that "wants" are important too in implementing the law of consecration. Many people have the mistaken notion that living the United Order would be a very basic lifestyle, almost a survival-only type of living. This would not be the case in a successful United Order.

Principle
Living the law of consecration requires honest people who are unselfish and united in harmony with each other—in other words, it requires celestial-quality individuals.

9 And let every man deal **honestly,** and **be alike** among this

SECTION 51

people, and **receive alike, that ye may be one** [*united*], **even as I have commanded you.**

> An explanation of the terms "be alike" and "receive alike," in verse 9, above, is given in the *Doctrine and Covenants Student Manual*, 1981, page 111, as follows (**bold** added for emphasis): "Under the united order everyone was alike in that they were independent and had full opportunity to use their gifts and talents in building the kingdom of God. They were also alike in that all had equal opportunity to benefit from whatever talents and abilities existed in the community. The idea that everyone was alike in goods possessed or income received is an erroneous one. The order was united in love, purpose, and commitment, but **unity does not mean sameness**. A man with seven children has needs different from those of couples just beginning married life."

10 **And let that which belongeth to this people** [*the Colesville Branch*] **not be taken and given unto that of another church** [*branch of the Church*].

> An explanation of the word "church" as used in verse 10, above, is given in the *Doctrine and Covenants Student Manual*, 1981, page 111, as follows: "The word 'church' in this paragraph stands for 'Branch,' as in Sec. 20:81, 45:64, and elsewhere. The meaning conveyed is that the property owned by the Colesville Branch could not be claimed by any other Branch. (Smith and Sjodahl, *Commentary*, 299.)"

As you can see, the Lord is giving Bishop Partridge rules and instructions that will very carefully control the living of the law of consecration among these Saints. Otherwise, there would be much misunderstanding, contention, and disharmony as a result.

11 Wherefore, **if another church** [*branch*] **would receive money of this church** [*as a loan*], **let them pay unto this church again** [*pay it back*] according as they shall agree;

12 And **this shall be done through the bishop or the agent**, which shall be appointed **by the voice of the church** [*the principle of common consent; see section 26*].

Principle

There is to be a bishop's storehouse where supplies are to be housed for distribution to the poor and needy.

13 And again, **let the bishop appoint a storehouse unto this church** [*similar to our bishop's storehouses today*]; **and let all things both in money and in**

meat [*food*], **which are more than is needful** for the wants of this people, **be kept in the hands of the bishop.**

Principle
Those whose callings require full-time service in the Church can have their needs and the needs of their families taken care of out of the funds and resources of the Church. (This can include some missionaries and some General Authorities today.)

14 And let him also reserve unto himself for his own wants, and for the wants of his family, as he shall be employed in doing this business.

15 And **thus I grant unto this people a privilege of organizing themselves according to my laws** [*according to the basic principles of the law of consecration*].

16 And **I consecrate unto them this land for a little season** [*the Saints will be in the Kirtland area for about five years; see D&C 64:21*], until I, the Lord, shall provide for them otherwise, and command them to go hence [*they will eventually be commanded to move to Missouri*];

There is great wisdom in what the Lord tells these members in verse 17, next. It can apply to many other situations also. The Lord tells them to settle down and live as if they were going to be in Ohio for many years, even though they know from revelation that they will only be there for "a little season" (verse 16, above, and in section 48).

17 And the hour and the day is not given unto them [*they don't yet know when they will be commanded to move again*], **wherefore** [*therefore*] **let them act upon this land** [*Ohio*] **as for years, and this shall turn unto them for their good.**

Next, in verse 18, the Lord says that the same principles given to Bishop Partridge will likewise apply in other settings. Then He explains that those who can successfully live the law of consecration will be qualified and worthy of exaltation.

18 Behold, **this shall be an example** unto my servant Edward Partridge, **in other places, in all churches** [*branches of the Church*].

19 And **whoso is found a faithful, a just, and a wise steward** shall enter into the joy of his Lord, and **shall inherit eternal life** [*exaltation, which is the highest degree of glory in the celestial kingdom*].

20 Verily, I say unto you, I am Jesus Christ, who **cometh quickly,**

in an hour you think not. Even so. Amen.

Just a thought in closing: it is interesting that, even though we have the signs of the times and other scriptures that alert us to the closeness of the Second Coming of Christ, He will still come at a time when we don't quite expect Him (see verse 20, above). One message we learn from this is that we need to be doing our best to live the gospel continuously and not risk periods of being intentionally less valiant in the gospel.

SECTION 52

Background

This revelation was given on June 6, 1831 (see heading in 2013 edition of the Doctrine and Covenants), in Kirtland, Ohio, through the Prophet Joseph Smith. The Church had just finished holding a four-day conference in Kirtland, which began on June 3 and finished on June 6. This revelation was given on the last day of this conference. During the conference, several of the brethren were ordained to the office of high priest, the first time this specific office was conferred upon men in this dispensation.

It was also during this conference that Joseph Smith revealed that John the Revelator (the Apostle who had served with Peter and James in the First Presidency and who was translated and is still on earth) was, at that time (1831) working with the lost ten tribes, preparing them for their return. John Whitmer, who served for a time as church historian, wrote, "The Spirit of the Lord fell upon Joseph in an unusual manner. And [Joseph] prophesied that John the Revelator was then among the ten tribes of Israel . . . to prepare them for their return from their long dispersion" (in *The Joseph Smith Papers, Histories, Volume 2: Assigned Histories, 1831–1847*, ed. Karen Lynn Davidson and others [2012], 39. See also *History of the Church*, 1:176.)

In this revelation, the Saints were told by the Lord that the next conference of the Church was to be held in Missouri. This was a brief but exciting hint that Missouri was to be significant in the future of the Church. Also, twenty-eight missionaries were specifically named and called to go forth and preach the gospel.

An important part of this section for us is verses 14–19, in which the Lord provides a pattern for avoiding deception. We will note eight specific points in this pattern when we get to them.

First, in verse 2, the Lord tells these elders what they should be doing between now and the next conference, which is to be held in Missouri. As usual, we will use **bold** for emphasis as well as a suggestion for things you might wish to mark in your own scriptures.

1 BEHOLD, thus saith the Lord unto the elders whom he hath called and chosen in these last days, by the voice of his Spirit—

2 Saying: **I, the Lord, will make known unto you what I will that ye shall do from this time until the next conference, which shall be held in Missouri**, upon the land which I will consecrate unto my people, which are a **remnant of Jacob** [*Israel*], and those who are heirs according to the covenant.

> You may wish to make a brief note in your own scriptures to the side of verse 2 explaining that "Jacob" is another name for "Israel." He was Abraham's grandson and the father of the twelve tribes of Israel. Israel is the covenant people through whom the gospel and priesthood covenants are to be taken to all the world. (See Abraham 2:9–11.) These faithful Saints in Kirtland are among the first of "scattered Israel" who are being gathered in the last days according to the covenant and promise of the Lord to do so. Thus, they are at the very forefront of the promised latter-day gathering of Israel.
>
> Next, Joseph and Sidney are told to leave for Missouri as soon as possible.

3 Wherefore, verily I say unto you, **let my servants Joseph Smith, Jun., and Sidney Rigdon** take their journey as soon as preparations can be made to leave their homes, and **journey to the land of Missouri.**

4 And inasmuch as they are faithful unto me, it shall be made known unto them what they shall do;

5 **And it shall also,** inasmuch as they are faithful, **be made known unto them the land of your inheritance** [*Missouri; see verse 42—in other words, if Joseph and Sidney are faithful, they will be guided by the Lord and will be told where the Saints will eventually settle in Missouri*].

> It may sound a bit strange to hear the Lord say, in effect, "if the Prophet and Church leaders are faithful . . ." (verses 4 and 5, above), but it is an important reminder that they too have agency. As noted in D&C 43:3–5, the Lord will never allow them to lead us astray. Verse 6, next, reemphasizes this fact.

6 And **inasmuch as they are not faithful, they shall be cut off**, even as I will, as seemeth me good.

> Next, several brethren are also instructed to leave on missions to

Missouri. In verse 9, they will be cautioned to preach and teach only that which is in the scriptures and what the Prophet Joseph Smith has taught as prompted by the Holy Ghost. In other words, they should avoid preaching personal opinions as doctrine—good advice for us today!

7 And again, verily I say unto you, let my servant **Lyman Wight** and my servant **John Corrill** take their journey speedily;

8 And also my servant **John Murdock**, and my servant **Hyrum Smith**, take their journey unto the same place [*Missouri*] by the way of Detroit.

9 And let them journey from thence [*from there*] preaching the word by the way, **saying none other things than that which the prophets and Apostles have written** [*in other words, the scriptures*], and that which is taught them by the Comforter [*the Holy Ghost*] through the prayer of faith.

10 **Let them go two by two** [*a precedent for modern missionary work*], and thus **let them preach** by the way in every congregation, **baptizing by water, and the laying on of the hands** [*confirming*] by the water's side.

In verse 11, next, we learn that the Lord will cut His work short with His righteous power—in other words, the Second Coming will come a little sooner than we think. Otherwise, according to Matthew 24:22, no one would still be alive at the Second Coming. Matthew wrote, "And except those days should be shortened, there should no flesh be saved; but for the elect's sake, those days shall be shortened." In D&C 84:97, the Lord again states that His work "shall be cut short in righteousness."

11 For thus saith the Lord, **I will cut my work short in righteousness,** for the days come that I will send forth judgment unto victory [*the day is coming when plagues and pestilences will be sent forth upon the earth, which, along with the Second Coming, will ultimately lead to the destruction of the wicked and the triumph of righteousness at the beginning of the Millennium*].

Next, in verses 12 and 13, Lyman Wight is given a warning and reminded that if he remains faithful, he will have major leadership responsibilities here on earth and be a "ruler over many things," which can imply that he can be a god in the next life.

12 **And let my servant Lyman Wight beware, for Satan desireth to sift him as chaff.**

Chaff (verse 12) is the husk that is

rubbed away from kernels of grain in the threshing process. Grain can be separated from the chaff through rubbing the grain between the hands and then tossing it into the wind. The wind blows the chaff away, and the grain kernels fall to the floor. The imagery in verse 12 is that Satan wants to blow Lyman every which way, like chaff in the wind, and separate him or "sift" him away from the Church.

13 And behold, **he that is faithful shall be made ruler over many things.**

It is sad to note that, although Lyman Wight did much good in the Church for a few more years (including being ordained an Apostle in 1841), his strong will and fiery temper began to cause trouble. He eventually left the Church and led about 150 members astray who followed him from Wisconsin to Texas. He died in Texas in 1858, having tried unsuccessfully to get the Church to join him there.

Satan desires to "sift" all of us "as chaff" (verse 12). In other words, he desires to deceive us and lead us away from the Church and God. Next, in verses 14–19, The Lord gives us a pattern for avoiding deception. First, we will call your attention to eight points in this pattern. Then we will do a bit more with it.

14 And again, **I will give unto you a pattern in all things, that ye may not be deceived**; for Satan is abroad in the land, and he goeth forth deceiving the nations—

15 Wherefore he that **[1] prayeth**, whose spirit **[2] is contrite** [*desires correction as needed from God through the scriptures, the Holy Ghost, or others, including Church leaders*], the same is accepted of me if he **[3] obey mine ordinances.**

16 He that speaketh, whose spirit is contrite, whose **[4] language is meek** and **[5] edifieth** [*builds others up and strengthens them*], the same is of God if he **[6] obey mine ordinances.**

17 And again, he that **[7] trembleth under my power** [*is humble and shows respect for God*] shall be made strong, and shall bring forth fruits of praise and wisdom, **[8] according to the revelations and truths which I have given you** [*lives in strict harmony with God's revealed word*].

18 And again, **he that** is overcome and **bringeth not forth fruits, even according to this pattern, is not of me.**

19 Wherefore, **by this pattern ye shall know the spirits in all cases under the whole heavens**

[*this pattern applies to all forms of deception, including people, philosophies, politics, groups, media, and so forth*].

Now, we will list these eight points again, along with brief commentary on each. In effect, if a person who is trying to persuade you toward a certain conclusion, course of action, belief, or whatever conforms to all eight points in this pattern, then you can rest assured that you will not be deceived by him or her.

(1) The person prays to God faithfully.

(2) The person humbly desires correction as needed.

(3) The person is living in harmony with the covenants he or she has made with God, including faithful church attendance, tithe paying, temple attendance, and so forth.

(4) The person's language is gentle and pleasant, not caustic and bitter.

(5) What you are hearing edifies you—in other words, brings you peace, light, and understanding (see D&C 50:22–24).

(6) The person keeps covenants made with God via ordinances such as baptism, sacrament, and in the temple.

(7) The person is humble and respects and carefully follows the leaders of the Church through whom the Lord extends His power and authority to all the world.

(8) The person's teachings and life are in strict harmony with the scriptures and the words of the modern prophets and Apostles.

20 **And the days have come** [*perhaps meaning that there will be extra persuasive deception in the last days preceding the Second Coming*]; **according to men's faith it shall be done unto them.**

In reference to the last phrase of verse 20, above, it is helpful to remember that "faith" usually implies action on our part. Thus, if we exercise "faith"—in other words, the "action" of studying and applying the principles of avoiding deception given by the Lord in this revelation—we will receive the extra help needed from the Holy Ghost to avoid being deceived.

Next, the Lord calls several more elders to serve missions to Missouri. You will probably recognize several of the names in this list of missionaries.

21 Behold, this commandment is given unto all the elders whom I have chosen.

22 And again, verily I say unto you, let my servant **Thomas B. Marsh** and my servant **Ezra Thayre** take their journey also,

preaching the word by the way unto this same land.

23 And again, let my servant **Isaac Morley** and my servant **Ezra Booth** take their journey, also preaching the word by the way unto this same land.

24 And again, let my servants **Edward Partridge** and **Martin Harris** take their journey with my servants **Sidney Rigdon** and **Joseph Smith, Jun**.

25 Let my servants **David Whitmer** and **Harvey Whitlock** also take their journey, and preach by the way unto this same land.

26 And let my servants **Parley P. Pratt** and **Orson Pratt** [*these are brothers*] take their journey, and preach by the way, even unto this same land.

27 And let my servants **Solomon Hancock** and **Simeon Carter** also take their journey unto this same land, and preach by the way.

28 Let my servants **Edson Fuller** and **Jacob Scott** also take their journey.

29 Let my servants **Levi W. Hancock** and **Zebedee Coltrin** also take their journey.

30 Let my servants **Reynolds Cahoon** and **Samuel H. Smith** also take their journey.

Just a quick note about Reynolds Cahoon (verse 30, above). In 1834, he and his wife had their seventh child, a boy. They asked the Prophet Joseph Smith to give him a name and blessing. As the Prophet prepared to do their bidding, he asked them what name they wanted him to give the infant. They declined to give one, instead asking Joseph to choose one. During the blessing, the Prophet named the baby "Mahonri Moriancumer Cahoon." You can perhaps imagine the surprise of the parents at now having a son named Mahonri Moriancumer Cahoon! At the end of the blessing, Joseph explained to them that the Lord had just revealed to him during the blessing that the name of the brother of Jared in the Book of Mormon was Mahonri Moriancumer. This event was recorded in an early Church publication, *The Juvenile Instructor*, as follows:

"While residing in Kirtland Elder Reynolds Cahoon had a son born to him. One day when President Joseph Smith was passing his door he called the Prophet in and asked him to bless and name the baby. Joseph did so and gave the boy the name of Mahonri Moriancumer. When he had finished the blessing he laid the child on the bed, and turning to Elder Cahoon he said, the name I have given your son is the name of the brother of Jared; the Lord has just shown [or revealed] it to me. Elder William F. Cahoon, who was standing near heard the Prophet make this statement to his father; and this was the first time the name of the brother of Jared was known in the Church in this dispensation" ("The Jaredites," *Juvenile Instructor,* 1 May 1892, 282; see also *Book of Mormon Student Manual,* 1979, 478).

31 Let my servants **Wheeler Baldwin** and **William Carter** also take their journey.

32 And let my servants **Newel Knight** and **Selah J. Griffin** both be ordained, and also take their journey.

> In verse 33, next, the Lord gives interesting counsel; namely, that these missionaries should take different routes as they preach the gospel en route to Missouri. When you stop to think about it, if they all followed the same path to Missouri, the first would do most of the preaching, and as others came along, there would be little opportunity left for effective preaching.

33 Yea, verily I say, let all these take their journey unto one place [*Missouri*], in their **several courses**, and **one man shall not build upon another's foundation, neither journey in another's track** [*in other words, go separate ways, but all end up in Missouri*].

34 **He that is faithful, the same shall be kept and blessed with much fruit** [*much success*].

35 And again, I say unto you, let my servants **Joseph Wakefield** and **Solomon Humphrey** take their journey into the **eastern lands**;

> It is interesting to note, in verse 35, above, that Elder Wakefield and Elder Humphrey were not sent to Missouri with the others but rather to the "eastern lands." This meant New York. In verse 36, next, they are told to stick to the scriptures as they preach about the restoration. The "families" mentioned apparently refer to relatives in Stockholm, New York.
>
> They went and had considerable success, including baptizing John Smith, a future patriarch to the Church, and George A. Smith, who would become an Apostle. Both of these converts were relatives of Solomon Humphrey.

36 Let them labor with their families [*relatives*], **declaring none other things than the prophets and Apostles**, that which they have seen and heard and most assuredly believe, that the prophecies may be fulfilled.

37 **In consequence of transgression**, let that which was bestowed upon **Heman Basset** be taken from him, and placed upon the head of **Simonds Ryder**.

Heman Basset (verse 37, above) left the Church shortly after this revelation was given. He was seventeen years old at this time and had already shown signs of being easily deceived. He had been living a type of "united order" with about one hundred others on Isaac Morley's farm in Kirtland before his baptism into the Church. He claimed to have had a revelation handed to him by an angel. Levi Hancock, who heard Heman tell the story of his vision, said, "Basset would behave like a baboon. He said he had a revelation he had received in Kirtland from the hand of an angel, he would read it and show pictures of a course of angels declared to be Gods, then would testify of the truth of the work and I believed it all, like a fool" (Levi Ward Hancock, autobiography, 18). During the conference of the Church immediately preceding this revelation (section 52), the Prophet Joseph Smith had sternly warned Heman. He said, "Heamon Basset you sit still the Devil wants to sift you" (Levi Ward Hancock, autobiography, quoted above).

Just a brief note about Simonds Ryder (verse 37, above). He was a member for just three months. Among his stated reasons for leaving the Church was that the Prophet misspelled his name on his call to go to Missouri to preach. His name was spelled "Rider" rather than "Ryder."

38 And again, verily I say unto you, let **Jared Carter** be ordained a priest, and also **George James** be ordained a priest.

Next, the Lord instructs the men who had not been called on missions to Missouri to take good care of the members in Ohio, to preach the gospel in the surrounding area, and to work for their own living rather than depending on contributions from the Church for their support.

39 **Let the residue of the elders** [*the remaining men*] **watch over the churches** [*the branches of the Church*], and **declare the word** [*preach the gospel*] in the regions round about them; and **let them labor with their own hands that there be no idolatry nor wickedness practiced** [*this word was spelled "practised" in editions of the Doctrine and Covenants prior to the 2013 edition. Just another example of the many relatively insignificant changes and corrections made in the 2013 edition by the Church. For more information on these changes, go online to Gospel Library/Scriptures/About the Scriptures/Adjustments to the Scriptures*].

An explanation of the word "idolatry" (verse 39, above,) is found in the *Doctrine and Covenants Student Manual*, 1981, page 113, as follows:

SECTION 52

"This instruction was given to those elders not assigned to go as missionaries to Missouri. These men were assigned to stay home and be the priesthood leaders for the Saints in Kirtland. By laboring with their own hands for their support rather than being paid for their priesthood service, these brethren would help prevent idolatry and priestcraft from springing up in the Church (see 2 Nephi 26:29). Modern readers may wonder at the use of the word idolatry, since idolatry is often thought of as a practice that went out of existence centuries ago. But in the preface to the Doctrine and Covenants, the Lord warned that one of the characteristics of the last days would be that 'every man walketh in his own way, and after the image of his God . . . whose substance is that of an idol' (D&C 1:16), and Paul defined covetousness as idolatry (see Ephesians 5:5; Colossians 3:5). In other words, when a man sets his heart on natural things, or prestige, or power to the point that God is no longer supreme, then that becomes as god to him. He worships, or gives his allegiance to, those things. This verse suggests that if the elders who remained in Ohio did not labor with their own hands, they might be guilty of this kind of covetousness, or idolatry."

40 And **remember in all things the poor and the needy, the sick and the afflicted**, for **he that doeth not these things, the same is not my disciple** [*is not a true follower of Christ*].

41 And again, let my servants Joseph Smith, Jun., and Sidney Rigdon and Edward Partridge **take with them a recommend from the church** [*similar to a temple recommend today, certifying that you are a member of the Church in good standing; see D&C 52:41, footnote a*]. And let there be one obtained for my servant Oliver Cowdery also.

42 And thus, even as I have said, if ye are faithful ye shall **assemble yourselves together to rejoice upon the land of Missouri**, which is **the land of your inheritance** [*a hint that they will be gathering there sometime in the future*], which is now the land of your enemies.

43 But, behold, **I, the Lord, will hasten the city** [*the city of New Jerusalem or Zion; see D&C 42:35*] **in its time** [*when the time is right*] and will crown the faithful with joy and with rejoicing.

44 Behold, **I am Jesus Christ, the Son of God**, and **I will lift them up** [*reward them with exaltation*] at **the last day** [*on the final judgment day*]. Even so. Amen.

SECTION 53

Background

This revelation was given through the Prophet Joseph Smith to a merchant named Algernon Sidney Gilbert in Kirtland, Ohio, on June 8, 1831. Brother Gilbert was baptized in 1830 and was about forty-one years old at the time of this revelation. He had a desire to know what the Lord wanted him to do in the Church and asked the Prophet to inquire for him. Joseph did and this revelation was the result.

A. Sidney Gilbert will live another three years and then die of cholera in Missouri after having hosted in his home several members of Zion's Camp (the little army of Saints that marched from Kirtland to Missouri in 1834 to assist members there who had been driven out by mobs) who were afflicted with the disease. He was known as a generous and good man as well as a skilled businessman. In fact, he was a business partner to Newel K. Whitney and co-owner of the Newel K. Whitney Store in Kirtland.

As you will see in this revelation, the Lord will request that Brother Gilbert move to Missouri and use his business skills to serve as an agent to the Church there. He will assist Bishop Edward Partridge (the first bishop in the Church) in handling the temporal affairs and needs of the Church.

Even though this revelation is given to a specific individual, you will see a number of lessons that can apply to all of us. For example, in verse 1, we are again reminded that God does hear our individual prayers and that He does know our thoughts and the desires of our hearts. In both verses 1 and 2, the Savior personally introduces Himself to Brother Gilbert, a sweet reminder that the Savior is humble and personable as described by Moroni in Ether 12:39.

1 BEHOLD, I say unto you, my servant Sidney Gilbert, that **I have heard your prayers**; and **you have called upon me that it should be made known unto you, of the Lord your God, concerning your calling and election** [*what the Savior wants Sidney to do now*] **in the church**, which I, the Lord, have raised up in these last days [*Jesus bears personal testimony to Brother Gilbert that this is His church*].

2 Behold**, I, the Lord**, who was crucified for the sins of the world, **give unto you a commandment that you shall forsake the world** [*avoid low worldly standards and behaviors and, instead, keep the commandments of God and the covenants you have made with Him*].

Next, in verse 3, the Master instructs Sidney Gilbert to be ordained an elder and to preach the

SECTION 53

first principles of the gospel, namely, faith, repentance, baptism, and the gift of the Holy Ghost.

3 Take upon you mine ordination, even that of an elder, to **preach faith** and **repentance** and **remission of sins,** according to my word, and **the reception of the Holy Spirit by the laying on of hands**;

> The instruction in verse 3, above, for Sidney to teach that the gift of the Holy Ghost is given by the "laying on of hands" is particularly important, because so many people in his day (and ours) believed that the receiving of the Spirit was a matter of "happening" rather than a gospel ordinance.
>
> Next, Brother Gilbert is called to be an agent to assist the bishop in handling the business and material needs of the members. In response to this, over the next three years until he dies, he will set up stores from which the Saints can purchase goods and supplies.

4 And also to be an agent unto this church in the place which shall be appointed by the bishop, according to commandments which shall be given hereafter.

> In verse 5, below, Sidney Gilbert is instructed to travel with the Prophet and Sidney Rigdon to Missouri. He will build a store in Independence, Missouri, which will eventually be broken into by mobs, and they will toss the merchandise out into the streets. He will build another store in Liberty, Missouri, and will again care for the needs of the Saints.

5 And again, verily I say unto you, you shall **take your journey with my servants Joseph Smith, Jun., and Sidney Rigdon.**

> Brother Gilbert's generosity as a merchant is described by Parley P. Pratt as he prepared to depart from Liberty, Missouri, on another mission. He said:
>
> "I next called on Sidney A. Gilbert, a merchant, then sojourning in the village of Liberty—his store in Jackson County having been broken up, and his goods plundered and destroyed by the mob. 'Well,' says he, 'brother Parley, you certainly look too shabby to start a journey; you must have a new suit; I have got some remnants left that will make you a coat,' etc. A neighboring tailoress and two or three other sisters happened to be present on a visit, and hearing the conversation, exclaimed, 'Yes, brother Gilbert, you find the stuff and we'll make it up for him.' This arranged, I now lacked only a cloak; this was also furnished by brother Gilbert" (*Autobiography of Parley P. Pratt,* 108).
>
> As we continue, verse 6, next, reminds us once again of the role of faith in moving ahead in obedience to the Lord's commands,

even when we do not know for sure what is going to happen next.

6 Behold, **these are the first ordinances which you shall receive; and the residue shall be made known in a time to come** [*the Lord will tell him more and give additional help and instructions when the time is right*], according to your labor in my vineyard.

Finally, as this revelation closes, we are reminded that remaining true and faithful to the end is a vital part of the gospel.

7 And again, I would that ye should learn that **he only is saved who endureth unto the end**. Even so. Amen.

SECTION 54

Background

Given through the Prophet Joseph Smith to Newel Knight, this revelation was received in Kirtland, Ohio, on June 10, 1831. Brother Knight was five years older than the Prophet and was the son of Joseph and Polly Knight, who had been generous to Joseph and Emma Smith on many occasions. Joseph had become acquainted with the Joseph Knight family while boarding with Isaac Hale's family in Harmony, Pennsylvania, prior to bringing the gold plates home. The Knights had been converted to the Church, along with several others in Colesville, New York.

In December 1830, the Lord had commanded the Saints to move to Ohio (see D&C 37:2). By this time, in June 1831, Newel Knight and a number of other members from New York had moved to Ohio and were living in Thompson not far from Kirtland. Newel was serving as president of the Thompson Branch of the Church, a group of about 60.

Problems had arisen in Thompson, which led Brother Knight to ask Joseph Smith to request counsel from the Lord. This resulted in the receiving of what is now known as section 54. Briefly put, the problem was that the rest of the Colesville Branch had now arrived in Thompson, and Leman Copley (perhaps you remember him from the background given along with section 49) had agreed to live the law of consecration by donating his large farm for the Colesville Saints to settle and build on. He had done this by covenant, as is required by the law of consecration. However, shortly after they arrived, he backed out of the agreement with encouragement from Ezra Thayre. This, of course, left the Colesville Saints in a difficult predicament, so they asked Newel Knight to go to the Prophet and find out what they should do. As you will see, after giving instructions on the seriousness of covenant breaking, the Lord instructs these faithful

SECTION 54

members to go on to Missouri. In verse 1, next, the Savior identifies Himself and introduces Himself.

1 BEHOLD, **thus saith the Lord**, even Alpha and Omega [*the "A" and the "Z" of the Greek alphabet, another scriptural term for the Savior*], **the beginning and the end**, even **he who was crucified for the sins of the world**—

> Next, in verse 2, Brother Knight is instructed to continue in his calling as branch president of the Colesville Saints. According to the *Doctrine and Covenants Student Manual*, 1981, page 115, Brother Knight is one of those leaders spoken of in D&C 38:34–36 who were to be sustained to take care of "the poor and the needy."

2 Behold, verily, verily, **I say unto you**, my servant **Newel Knight, you shall stand fast** [*continue to serve diligently*] **in the office** whereunto I have appointed you.

3 And if your brethren [*the members of the Thompson Branch*] desire to escape their enemies, let them **repent** of all their sins, and **become truly humble** before me and **contrite** [*be open and receptive to correction as needed*].

> Next, the Lord explains to Brother Knight that the covenant his people made with Him and Leman Copley for land on which to settle as a part of the law of consecration has been broken (by Leman Copley), and thus is no longer in effect. In other words, they are no longer bound by it.

4 And **as the covenant which they made unto me has been broken, even so it has become void and of none effect.**

> Verses 5 and 6, next, serve as a brief but important lesson concerning the two parties involved in a covenant that is broken. The guilty party is in serious trouble with the Lord, whereas the party that did its best to keep the covenant will obtain mercy (in other words, will ultimately receive great blessings from the Lord one way or another. Their exaltation is not in jeopardy because the other person or people involved in the covenant chose to break it).

5 And **wo to him by whom this offense cometh**, for **it had been better for him that he had been drowned in the depth of the sea.**

6 But **blessed are they who have kept the covenant and observed the commandment** [*kept their part of the agreement*]**, for they shall obtain mercy.**

> In verses 7–10, next, the Savior tells Brother Knight to take his branch to Missouri, to handle leadership and expenses according to their best judgment, and,

for the time being, to stop trying to live the law of consecration (United Order). In its place, they are to live "like unto men" (verse 9) until the time comes (in Missouri) to live the law of consecration again.

7 Wherefore, **go to now and flee the land**, lest your enemies come upon you; and **take your journey**, and appoint whom you will to be your leader, and to pay moneys for you.

8 And thus you shall **take your journey into the regions westward, unto the land of Missouri**, unto the borders of the Lamanites.

The "borders of the Lamanites" (verse 8, above) was a common term in that day for the western frontier. Many Indian tribes lived west of the Missouri River. Thus, Jackson County, Missouri, was on the extreme western edge of civilization at that time.

9 And **after you have done journeying** [*upon arriving in Missouri*], behold, I say unto you, **seek ye a living like unto men** [*don't keep striving to live the law of consecration, for now*], until I prepare a place for you.

10 And again, **be patient in tribulation** until I come; and, behold, I come quickly, and **my reward is with me** [*among other things, this phrase can mean that living the gospel of Jesus Christ carries with it its own rewards, independent of other benefits and blessings*], and **they who have sought me early shall find rest to their souls**. Even so. Amen.

This group of more than sixty faithful Colesville Saints followed instructions and traveled the almost nine hundred miles to Missouri, arriving in Independence, Missouri, near the end of July 1831.

SECTION 55

Background

This revelation was given to W. W. Phelps, age thirty-nine, through the Prophet Joseph Smith, on June 14, 1831, at Kirtland, Ohio. William Wines Phelps had not been baptized at the time of this revelation to him. A newspaper editor and printer by trade, he had read an announcement in a newspaper on March 26, 1830, that the Book of Mormon was about to come off the press and would be for sale. He later met Parley P. Pratt, from whom he purchased a copy on April 9, 1830. After reading the book, he desired to meet Joseph Smith and consequently left for Kirtland, Ohio, to do so.

Having just recently arrived in Kirtland with his family, he met the Prophet and, through him, asked what the Lord desired him to do now. Section 55 contains the Lord's answer. After the

SECTION 55

Savior introduces Himself to him, he is instructed to be baptized, confirmed, and ordained an elder. Shortly after this revelation, he will be baptized and ordained an elder.

1 BEHOLD, **thus saith the Lord** unto you, my servant William, yea, **even the Lord of the whole earth,** thou art called and chosen; and **after thou hast been baptized** by water, which if you do with an eye single to my glory [*meaning with pure motives*], **you shall have a remission of your sins and a reception of the Holy Spirit by the laying on of hands;**

2 And **then thou shalt be ordained by the hand of my servant Joseph Smith, Jun., to be an elder** unto this church, to preach repentance and remission of sins by way of baptism in the name of Jesus Christ, the Son of the living God.

Next, William is told that after he has been properly baptized and confirmed and has received the Melchizedek Priesthood through ordination to the office of elder in the Church, he will have the power to confer the gift of the Holy Ghost by the laying on of hands.

3 And on whomsoever you shall lay your hands, if they are contrite before me, **you shall have power to give the Holy Spirit.**

As you can see in verse 4, next, the Lord will put Brother Phelps right to work, using his talents and skills for printing and writing to bless the lives of children in the Church, as well as adults.

4 And again, you shall be ordained to **assist my servant Oliver Cowdery to do the work of printing,** and of **selecting and writing books for schools in this church, that little children also may receive instruction** before me as is pleasing unto me.

Brother Phelps commented on his role in making the gospel available to children. He said:

"As a people we are fast approaching a desired end, which may literally be called a beginning. Thus far, we cannot be reproached with being backward in instruction. By revelation, in 1831, I was appointed to 'do the work of printing, and of selecting and writing books for schools in this church, that little children might receive instruction;' and since then I have received a further sanction. We are preparing to go out from among the people, where we can serve God in righteousness; and the first thing is, to teach our children; for they are as the Israel of old. It is our children who will take the kingdom and bear it off to all the world. The first commandment with promise to Israel was, 'Honor thy father and thy mother, that thy days may be long in the land, which the Lord thy God giveth thee.' We will instruct our children in the paths of righteousness; and we want that instruction compiled in a book" (*Times and Seasons*, November 1, 1845, 1015).

In Missouri, Brother Phelps printed the Book of Commandments (the precursor to the Doctrine and Covenants) and the first Church newspaper, *The Evening and the Morning Star*. Later, back in Kirtland, he helped prepare and print the 1835 edition of the Doctrine and Covenants. He helped Emma Smith prepare the first hymn book for the Church. He wrote several of our Church hymns, including

- "The Spirit of God"
- "Now Let Us Rejoice"
- "Redeemer of Israel"
- "Now We'll Sing with One Accord"
- "Praise to the Man"
- "Adam-ondi-Ahman"
- "Gently Raise the Sacred Strain"
- "O God, the Eternal Father"
- "If You Could Hie to Kolob"

Continuing with section 55, next, in verse 5, William W. Phelps will be instructed to go to Missouri with Joseph Smith and Sidney Rigdon.

5 And again, verily I say unto you, for this cause [*to serve as a printer for the Church, as well as to carry out his other assignments*] you shall **take your journey with my servants Joseph Smith, Jun., and Sidney Rigdon**, that you may be planted [*a word which symbolizes being "planted in the Lord's vineyard to do His work*] in the land of your inheritance [*Missouri*] to do this work.

6 And again, let my servant **Joseph Coe** also **take his journey with them**. The residue shall be made known hereafter [*the Lord will tell them more when they get there*], even as I will. Amen.

Forty-eight-year-old Joseph Coe, born on November 12, 1784, was an early convert from New York. He joined the Saints in the Kirtland area in early 1831 and traveled to Missouri with the Prophet, Sidney Rigdon and others as instructed in verse 6, above. He was one of the eight elders present when Sidney Rigdon dedicated Missouri for the gathering of the Saints. Over time, he had disagreements with Joseph Smith that eventually led him to join with others in an attempt to overthrow Joseph as the Prophet. He was finally excommunicated in December 1838.

SECTION 56

Background

This revelation was given to the Prophet Joseph Smith at Kirtland,

SECTION 56

Ohio, on June 15, 1831. Perhaps you've noticed that there were several revelations given in June 1831. In fact, sections 52 through 56 were all given during that time.

We mentioned in the background to section 52 that many pairs of missionaries were called to go on missions to Missouri and preach along the way as they traveled. One of these sets of missionaries was Thomas B. Marsh and Ezra Thayre (D&C 52:22). In the background to section 54, we mentioned that Ezra Thayre was part of the problem that had arisen in Thompson, Ohio, near Kirtland over the consecration of a large farm for the settling of the Saints arriving from Colesville, New York.

The problem leading up to this revelation is that rebellious Ezra Thayre is embroiled in controversy in Thompson and doesn't particularly want to go to Missouri on a mission, even though the Lord has called him to go. As a result, he is dragging his feet on preparations to leave on the mission, which in turn has caused Thomas Marsh great concern because he does want to go. Consequently, Brother Marsh has gone to the Prophet Joseph, who has gone to the Lord for counsel on the matter. In verses 1–4, you will see the seriousness of making and then breaking covenants.

1 HEARKEN, O ye people who profess my name [*who claim to be members of the Lord's Church*], **saith the Lord your God;** for behold, **mine anger is kindled against the rebellious,** and **they shall know mine arm** [*symbolic of power in scriptural symbolism*] **and mine indignation** [*anger*], in the day of visitation [*punishment*] and of wrath upon the nations.

Some people wonder how God, who is perfect and righteous, can have "indignation" (verse 1, above). This type of anger is sometimes called "righteous indignation" and is often seen in the Lord's "parenting" situations when His children have not responded to a gentle approach. Therefore, He speaks and counsels in ways that are more likely to get their attention and appropriate response leading to repentance. When they still refuse to change their ways, the law of justice is eventually put into action, and wayward children often see that as anger. It is important to keep in mind that His "anger" or "indignation" is not out-of-control anger as is often the case with mortal parents. Rather, it is perfectly controlled and is mercifully designed to provide additional chances for the rebellious and wicked to come to their senses and repent.

Next, in verse 2, Jesus teaches a simple, basic doctrine.

2 And **he that will not take up his cross and follow me, and**

keep my commandments, the same shall not be saved [*will not be given exaltation, which is the highest of all blessings available on Judgment Day*].

The phrase "take up his cross," as used in verse 2, above, means to do whatever is necessary in order to follow Christ and keep His commandments and our covenants with Him. "Cross," of course, symbolizes trials and hardships encountered.

Next, in verse 3, we see the phrase "in mine own due time," which reminds us that the Lord is patient and that His punishments of His "children" come according to His timetable, not ours. Perhaps this is one of the reasons that some members who are striving to keep the commandments find themselves wondering why the wicked are not punished. They will be if they don't eventually repent. But in the meantime, as you have no doubt noticed, some of them do wake up spiritually and repent, bringing much joy in heaven as well as on earth. (Compare with D&C 18:13, 15.)

3 Behold, I, the Lord, command; and he that will not obey shall be cut off **in mine own due time**, after I have commanded and the commandment is broken.

Next, we find a brief lesson on the fact that some commandments and instructions can be revoked if people refuse to obey. This sometimes comes as a surprise to people who have the notion that once God says something, it cannot be revoked. We must carefully differentiate between "eternal laws," which cannot be revoked (such as the necessity of repenting, the necessity for an atonement, the law of justice, the law of mercy, and so forth) and commandments that can be revoked if people use their agency to disobey (such as the case here with Ezra Thayre, who is rebelling against going on a mission, thus leaving Thomas Marsh without a companion). Ezra Thayre would seem to have increased accountability since he was ordained a high priest at the fourth general conference of the Church held in June in Kirtland.

You may wish to make a cross-reference in your own scriptures next to verse 4, below, that sends you to D&C 58:30–33, which likewise deals with God's "revoking" instructions and blessings when people chose not to obey.

4 Wherefore **I, the Lord, command and revoke, as it seemeth me good**; and all this to be answered upon the heads of the rebellious [*the law of accountability*], saith the Lord.

5 **Wherefore** [*this is why*], **I revoke the commandment** which was given unto my servants Thomas B. Marsh and

SECTION 56

Ezra Thayre [*D&C 52:22*], **and give a new commandment** unto my servant Thomas, that he shall take up his journey speedily [*don't keep waiting for Ezra Thayre*] to the land of Missouri, and **my servant Selah J. Griffin shall also go with him**.

> The *Doctrine and Covenants Student Manual*, 1981, page 117, helps us understand what is happening in verses 6–8, next.
>
> "In these verses the Lord changed the assignments given in Doctrine and Covenants, section 52, verses 22 and 32. Selah J. Griffin, formerly assigned to Newel Knight, was assigned to Thomas B. Marsh. Newel Knight was called to go with the Colesville Saints to Missouri, and Ezra Thayre was released from his missionary calling."

6 For behold, **I revoke the commandment which was given unto my servants Selah J. Griffin and Newel Knight** [*D&C 52:32*], in consequence of the stiffneckedness of my people which are in Thompson, and their rebellions.

7 Wherefore, **let my servant Newel Knight remain with them** [*as their leader, rather than going on a preaching mission to Missouri with Selah Griffin*]; and as many [*of the Thompson Branch*] as will go [*to Missouri*] may go, that are contrite before me, and be led by him to the land which I have appointed.

8 And again, verily I say unto you, that my servant **Ezra Thayre must repent** of his **pride**, and of his **selfishness**, and **obey the former commandment** which I have given him concerning the place upon which he lives [*the farm in Thompson, Ohio*].

9 And **if he will do this**, as there shall be no divisions made upon the land, **he shall be appointed still to go to the land of Missouri**;

10 **Otherwise he shall receive the money which he has paid, and shall leave the place**, and shall be cut off out of my church [*excommunicated*], saith the Lord God of hosts;

> One possible explanation of verse 10, above, is that Ezra Thayre, in addition to supporting Leman Copley (who went back on his covenant to consecrate his large farm in Thompson for the settling of the Colesville Branch) appears to have given a sum of money to the Church. If he decides to leave the Church and the Thompson area, the money would be paid back.
>
> Next, in verse 11, the Lord assures that His words given above will be fulfilled.

11 **And though the heaven and the earth pass away, these words shall not pass away, but shall be fulfilled.**

12 And if my servant Joseph Smith, Jun., must needs pay the money [*pay back Ezra Thayre; see verse 10, above*], behold, I, the Lord, will pay it unto him again in the land of Missouri, that those of whom he shall receive may be rewarded again according to that which they do;

> It appears that Brother Thayre repented and remained faithful for a time, because he was again called to serve a mission with Thomas B. Marsh, this time on January 25, 1832 (D&C 75:31). He served this mission faithfully. He continued faithful in the Church until the Martyrdom of the Prophet Joseph Smith in 1844, at which time he refused to follow the leadership of the Quorum of the Twelve under Brigham Young. The last we hear of Ezra Thayre is that he was serving as a high priest in the Reorganized Church of Jesus Christ of Latter Day Saints in Michigan in 1860.

13 For according to that which they do they shall receive, even in lands [*in Missouri*] for their inheritance.

> Next, we are reminded of the danger of making our own rules and enjoying wickedness rather than following the Lord's counsel.

14 Behold, thus saith the Lord unto my people—**you have many things to do and to repent of**; for behold, your sins have come up unto me, and are not pardoned, **because you seek to counsel in your own ways** [*you are making your own rules*].

15 And **your hearts are not satisfied**. And **ye obey not the truth, but have pleasure in unrighteousness**.

> Sometimes it seems that the rich are the most likely to become prideful and selfish and to leave God. However, in verses 16 and 17, next, we are taught that the poor can also succumb to the temptation of being arrogant and prideful and of justifying their own unrighteousness.

16 **Wo unto you rich men**, that will not give your substance to the poor, for your riches will canker your souls [*will make spiritual "sores" upon your souls*]; and this shall be your lamentation [*this is what you will say, with great regret*] in the day of visitation [*when you are punished for your sins*], and of judgment [*on Judgment Day*], and of indignation [*when you feel the righteous anger of God*]: The harvest is past, the summer is ended [*my opportunities to repent are over*], and my soul is not saved!

17 **Wo unto you poor men**, whose hearts are not broken [*who are not humble*], whose spirits are not contrite [*who do not desire correction as needed from the Lord*], and whose bellies are not satisfied, and whose hands are not stayed [*stopped*] from laying hold upon [*stealing*] other men's goods, whose eyes are full of greediness, and who will not labor with your own hands!

18 But **blessed are the poor who are pure in heart**, whose hearts are broken, and whose spirits are contrite, **for they shall see the kingdom of God coming in power and great glory unto their deliverance**; for the fatness [*wealth; the best*] of the earth shall be theirs.

19 **For behold, the Lord shall come**, and **his recompense** [*reward*] **shall be with him**, and he shall reward every man, and the poor [*the righteous poor*] shall rejoice;

20 **And their generations** [*posterity*] **shall inherit the earth** [*compare with Matthew 5:5 and D&C 45:56–58*] from generation to generation, forever and ever. And now I make an end of speaking unto you. Even so. Amen.

SECTION 57

Background

Finally, the long-awaited day has arrived! The Prophet is in Missouri with other Church leaders and missionaries who have likewise traveled the approximately nine hundred miles from Kirtland. In this revelation, given to the Prophet Joseph Smith in "Zion" (Jackson County, Missouri) on July 20, 1831, the Lord reveals the location where Zion, the New Jerusalem, is to be built. The "center place" for the city of Zion is Independence, Missouri (see verse 3). Imagine the excitement and feelings of humility in the hearts of these brethren as they find themselves standing on this holy ground!

Leading up to this marvelous day, the Lord had given several revelations in which He gave hints and clues about this city of Zion, the city of New Jerusalem. For example, in the Book of Mormon, members of the Church had read about a New Jerusalem that would be located in America (see 3 Nephi 20:22; 21:23–24; Ether 13:2–10). In September 1830, the Lord had told the Saints that no one at that time knew where the city of Zion would be built (Hiram Page had claimed to know), but that it would be built "on the borders by the Lamanites" (D&C 28:9). And in D&C 42:62, the Lord told faithful members that He would tell them, when the time was right, "where the New Jerusalem shall be built."

Having departed from Kirtland on June 19, 1831, and arrived in Independence, Missouri, on July 14, 1831, with his traveling companions, the Prophet Joseph now spent time contemplating and wondering "When will the wilderness blossom as the rose; when will Zion be built up in her glory, and where will thy Temple stand unto which all nations shall come in the last days?" (in *Manuscript History of the Church*, vol. A-1, page 127, josephsmithpapers.org).

Now, with great rejoicing in their hearts, these elders receive the message through their Prophet that they are standing on the land of Zion, the place for the gathering of the Saints, and that the temple is to be built on a spot not far from the courthouse.

1 HEARKEN, O ye elders of my church, saith the Lord your God, who have assembled yourselves together, according to my commandments, in this land, which is **the land of Missouri**, which **is the land which I have appointed and consecrated for the gathering of the saints.**

2 Wherefore, this is the land of promise, and **the place for the city of Zion.**

3 And thus saith the Lord your God, if you will receive wisdom here is wisdom. Behold, the place which is now called **Independence is the center place**; and **a spot for the temple is lying westward, upon a lot which is not far from the courthouse.**

Apostle Bruce R. McConkie informed us that this temple will be built before the Second Coming of Christ. He Said, "As to the temple unto which all nations shall come in the last days, **it shall be built in the New Jerusalem before the Second Coming**, all as a part of the preparatory processes that will make ready a people for their Lord's return" (*A New Witness for the Articles of Faith*, 595).

We will include a quote from the 2018 *Doctrine and Covenants Student Manual*, chapter 21, which informs us that the temple in New Jerusalem will consist of a complex of 24 temples. "About two years after he received the revelation recorded in Doctrine and Covenants 57, the Prophet Joseph Smith received additional revelation concerning the spot where the temple would be constructed. In 1833, the Prophet had a plat map drawn for the city of Zion that depicted **a temple complex of 24 buildings** to be constructed next to each other in Independence (see *History of the Church*, 1:357–59). The gathering to and the building up of the city of Zion, or New Jerusalem, as declared by the Lord, will begin at 'the place of the temple' (D&C 84:4)."

Continuing our study of section 57, we move on to verse 4. In D&C 48:4, the Lord had told the members in Kirtland to begin saving money to purchase land for the New Jerusalem, or Zion. Now, in verses 4–6, the Church is instructed to begin actually buying land in this part of Missouri.

4 Wherefore, it is wisdom that **the land should be purchased by the saints**, and also **every tract lying westward**, even unto the line [*the border*] running directly between Jew [*the Indians, or Lamanites*] and Gentile [*the Missourians*];

> The use of the word "Jew" in verse 4, above, can be a bit confusing unless we stop to recall the origins of the Lamanites. As you know, Lehi and his group came from Jerusalem in 600 B.C. Regardless of specific genealogy, they were "Jews," politically and geographically. Since the Lamanites are descendants of Lehi and Sariah, they too can be referred to as "Jews."

5 And also **every tract bordering by the prairies, inasmuch as my disciples are enabled to buy lands**. Behold, this is wisdom, that they may obtain it for an everlasting inheritance.

It is interesting to note that land was available for purchase in this part of Missouri for $1.25 per acre. We will include a quote from the institute of religion *Church History Student Manual,* which describes this.

"The price of land and its ready availability also attracted the Saints. In 1831 whole sections of this undeveloped country could be purchased for $1.25 per acre. The Lord directed the brethren to purchase as much land as they were able (see D&C 57:3–5; 58:37, 49–52; 63:27), and Sidney Rigdon was appointed to 'write a description of the land of Zion' (D&C 58:50) to be circulated among eastern Saints in a quest for funds. Sidney Gilbert was appointed 'an agent unto the Church' to receive money from contributors and buy lands (D&C 57:6). Edward Partridge, already serving as a bishop, was commanded to divide the purchased land among the gathering Saints as 'their inheritance' (D&C 57:7). The Lord also cautioned regarding Zion, 'Let all these things be done in order. . . . And let the work of the gathering be not in haste, nor by flight' (D&C 58:55–56)." (*Church History in the Fulness of Times,* 1989, 107.)

6 And **let my servant Sidney Gilbert** [*the merchant spoken of in section 53; see background to section 53 in this study guide for more information about him*] **stand in the**

office to which I have appointed him [*D&C 53:4*], **to receive moneys, to be an agent unto the church, to buy land in all the regions round about**, inasmuch as can be done in righteousness, and as wisdom shall direct.

7 **And let my servant Edward Partridge** stand in the office to which I have appointed him [*the first bishop in the Church; see D&C 41:9*], and **divide unto the saints their inheritance** [*portion out the land purchased in Missouri to the arriving Saints*], even as I have commanded; and also those whom he has appointed to assist him.

As previously mentioned, Sidney Gilbert was a skilled businessman and merchant. In verse 8, next, the Lord gives him specific instructions concerning his responsibilities in Missouri.

8 And again, verily I say unto you, **let** my servant **Sidney Gilbert** plant himself in this place, and **establish a store, that he may sell goods without fraud** [*the Saints were subject to being cheated by local merchants who saw a chance to raise prices exorbitantly as members of the Church arrived in Missouri*], that he may **obtain money to buy lands** for the good of the saints, and that he may **obtain whatsoever things the disciples** [*members of the Church*] **may need** to plant them [*establish themselves*] in their inheritance [*in Missouri*].

Next, we see an important reminder that we are to conduct the business of the Church in accordance with the laws of the land in which it is being established. We suspect that the "license" was a business license required by local or state law at the time.

9 And also **let my servant Sidney Gilbert obtain a license**—behold here is wisdom, and whoso readeth let him understand—that he may send goods also unto the people, even by whom he will as clerks employed in his service;

10 And **thus provide for my saints**, that my gospel may be preached unto those who sit in darkness [*spiritual darkness; without the gospel*] and in the region and shadow of death.

You may recall from the background given for section 55, in this study guide as well as in the notes for that section, that William W. Phelps was, among other things, a printer by trade. In response to the instructions given by the Lord next, in verses 11–13, he established the first printing press for the Church in Missouri and published the first newspaper, the *Evening and the Morning Star*. He will also help select and prepare the revelations for the Book of Commandments (in effect, the first edition of the Doctrine and Covenants).

11 And again, verily I say unto you, **let my servant William W. Phelps** be planted in this place [*make this his home*], and **be established as a printer unto the church**.

12 And lo, if the world receive his writings—behold here is wisdom—**let him obtain whatsoever he can obtain in righteousness, for the good of the saints**.

13 And **let my servant Oliver Cowdery assist him**, even as I have commanded, in whatsoever place I shall appoint unto him, **to copy**, and to **correct**, and **select**, that all things may be right before me, as it shall be proved by the Spirit through him.

14 And thus **let those of whom I have spoken be planted** [*make their homes here*] **in the land of Zion, as speedily as can be, with their families**, to do those things even as I have spoken.

15 And **now concerning the gathering**—Let the bishop [*Edward Partridge (verse 7)*] and the agent [*Sidney Gilbert (verse 6)*] make preparations for those families which have been commanded to come to this land [*particularly the members of the Colesville Branch, who, at this time, are en route to Missouri, being led by Newel Knight; see D&C 56:7*], as soon as possible, and plant them in their inheritance.

16 **And unto the residue** [*those not specifically addressed in this revelation*] of both elders and members **further directions shall be given hereafter**. Even so. Amen.

Just a quick note about Kirtland before we move on: Perhaps you recall that the Lord had already told the Church that Kirtland, Ohio, was to be the gathering place "for the present time" (D&C 48:1, 3), thus indicating that it was a temporary gathering place. They were to position themselves financially to "purchase land for an inheritance, even the city," meaning the city of New Jerusalem (D&C 48:4), whose location was yet to be revealed (D&C 48:5). Now that the location of the city of Zion has been revealed (D&C 57:1–3), the money being collected will make its way to Bishop Partridge and will be used as instructed.

We know from D&C 64:21 that Kirtland was to serve as a "stronghold" for five years. Thus, over the next approximately five years, we will have, in effect, two headquarters for the Church—Kirtland and Jackson County, Missouri. If you keep this in mind, it will help avoid confusion regarding background and setting of several of the next revelations in the Doctrine and Covenants.

One other note. The Prophet Joseph Smith also revealed that Jackson County, Missouri, was the location of the Garden of Eden. According to Wilford Woodruff, President Brigham Young once said, "Joseph, the Prophet, told me that the Garden of Eden was in Jackson County, Missouri. When Adam was driven out he went to the place we now call Adam-ondi-Ahman, Daviess County, Missouri. There he built an altar and offered sacrifices" (Cowley, *Wilford Woodruff: History of His Life and Labors,* 481; see also 545–46).

SECTION 58

Background

This revelation was given through the Prophet Joseph Smith in Zion, Jackson County Missouri, on Monday, August 1, 1831, about eleven days after the revelation (section 57) designating Independence, Missouri, as the "center place" of Zion. Likewise, in section 57, many of these elders, including Edward Partridge, the first bishop of the Church, were commanded to "plant" themselves in Missouri now. This commandment to stay in Missouri now came as a shock to many of these men who had planned on returning shortly to their families, whom they had left back in Ohio just a month previously.

A quote from *Revelations in Context* helps us understand how difficult these commandments to remain in Missouri actually were for these early Saints. Bishop Partridge wrote to his wife, Lydia, and "broke the news that he wouldn't be returning to Ohio that summer and instead asked that she and their five daughters join him on the Missouri frontier. Additionally, instead of being able to return to Ohio to help them move that fall, he wrote, 'Brother Gilbert or I must be here to attend the sales in Dec. [and] not knowing that he can get back by that time I have thought it advisable to stay here for the present contrary to [my] expectations.' He also warned that once she joined him in Missouri, 'We have to suffer [and] shall for some time many privations here which you [and] I have not been much used to for year[s]' [Letter, Aug. 5, 1831, in Edward Partridge letters, 1831–1835, Church History Library].

"Lydia willingly obeyed the revelation to move, packing her home and gathering her five daughters to travel west to a place she had never seen before" (Sherilyn Farnes, "A Bishop unto the Church," in *Revelations in Context,* 79–80. See history.lds.org).

Most of these members had already recently moved from New York to Kirtland in the dead of winter, only to be told shortly after their arrival in Ohio that they were now to move to Missouri. We will be taught many lessons as we study section 58, beginning with the topic of tribulation and blessings and continuing with the topic of perspective in verses 1–4. You may wish to mark these verses in your own scriptures and place a brief note something to the effect of "tribulation and blessings" out to the side. Remember, the Savior is our teacher.

1 HEARKEN, O ye elders of my church, and give ear to my word, and **learn of me** [*Jesus*] what I will concerning you, and also concerning this land unto which I have sent you.

2 For verily I say unto you, **blessed is he that keepeth my commandments, whether in life or in death**; and **he that is faithful in tribulation, the reward of the same is greater in the kingdom of heaven.**

3 **Ye cannot behold with your natural eyes, for the present time, the design** [*plan*] **of your God concerning those things which shall come hereafter** [*right now you can't see what I see for the future of this land of Zion*], **and the glory which shall follow after much tribulation.**

4 For **after much tribulation come the blessings**. Wherefore **the day cometh that ye** [*the faithful*] **shall be crowned with much glory**; the hour is not yet, but is nigh at hand.

It is clear from the above verses that tribulation, properly endured, can lead to substantial personal growth and the highest blessings from God. A common but mistaken notion among some belief systems is that trials and tribulation are a result of personal transgression. In a very real way, the Lord is telling these faithful though imperfect Saints that the tribulations they have endured and will yet endure for the gospel's sake are a "curriculum" for their learning and growth. While we can't always see noble purposes in tribulation, the Lord can. And, in verse 3, He reminds us that we are not yet capable of seeing as He does during many of our trials and tribulations. So, we have to simply go forward with faith.

In verses 5–6, next, He tells us that one of the purposes of tribulation is that of teaching us obedience in the face of opposition.

5 **Remember this, which I tell you before, that you may lay it to heart** [*in scriptural symbolism, "heart" is the center of feelings and tends to be the basis for most behavior*], **and receive that which is to follow.**

In verses 6–9, the Savior gives several specific reasons for sending these Saints to Missouri at this time. We will number these reasons as we point them out. We can apply these to ourselves as we accept callings and responsibilities that severely tax our energies and resources.

6 Behold, verily I say unto you, **for this cause I have sent you** [*on this difficult journey to Jackson County, Missouri, among other things*]— **[1] that you might be obedient, and [2] that your hearts might be prepared to bear testimony of the things which are to come;**

7 And also **[3] that you might be honored in laying the foundation** [*for the growth of the Church*], **and in [4] bearing record of the land upon which the Zion of God shall stand** [*in other words, bearing record that the long-promised Zion will be established*];

8 And also **[5] that a feast of fat things** [*meaning the "very best"—in other words, the restored gospel of Jesus Christ*] **might be prepared for the poor**; yea, a feast of fat things, of wine on the lees well refined [*the very best*], **[6] that the earth may know that the mouths of the prophets shall not fail** [*so that the inhabitants of the earth may know that the words of prophets will be fulfilled*];

9 Yea, **a supper of the house of the Lord** [*a feast of the true gospel, prepared by God through His servants*], well prepared, **[7] unto which all nations shall be invited** [*the gospel will be preached to all people*].

Next, in verses 10–11, we are told that the gospel will go forth in two distinctive waves (after the early Saints have laid the foundation; see verse 7). In other words, the Lord says that there is an order as far as to whom the gospel will be preached in the last days. The first group is the "rich and the learned, the wise and the noble" (verse 10). After that, it will go to the economically severely disadvantaged and to those who are severely spiritually "blind and deaf" (verse 11).

While these are relative terms, it appears that there have been many converts since the beginning of the restoration who are among the "noble and great" spoken of by Abraham (Abraham 3:22). As such people have joined the Church and provided strength and resources, the Church has been positioned to take the gospel to all people. This is a rather interesting and exciting prophecy to see being fulfilled in our day.

10 **First, the rich and the learned, the wise and the noble;**

11 And **after that** cometh the day of my power; **then shall the poor**, the **lame**, and the **blind**, and

the **deaf**, come in unto the marriage of the Lamb [*the full gospel and its benefits, a reference to the parable given in Matthew 22:1–14*], and **partake of the supper of the Lord,** prepared for the great day to come.

12 Behold, I, the Lord, have spoken it.

In verse 13 and the first phrase of verse 14, the Lord reiterates that the reason He sent them to Missouri is so that the testimony of the restored gospel can go from Zion into all the world.

13 And **that the testimony might go forth from Zion,** yea, from the mouth of the city of the heritage of God—

14 Yea, **for this cause I have sent you hither** [*here to Missouri*], and have selected my servant Edward Partridge, and have appointed unto him his mission in this land.

Verses 14–16 contain strong words for Edward Partridge, whose responsibilities as bishop include dividing out tracts of land upon which the incoming Saints can settle and build. He is called to repentance and warned that he won't get another chance if he chooses not to be obedient to instructions. While we don't know for sure what the problem was, verse 17 leads us to suspect that the chastisement had to do with the allocating of Church-owned property to incoming members and that perhaps he was refusing to give written deeds to them (as instructed in D&C 51:4). We will deal more with this issue when we get to section 85, verse 8. Perhaps it was an entirely different problem, such as not properly using his counselors or listening to them (verse 18). Someday, we will know.

15 But **if he repent not of his sins,** which are **unbelief** and **blindness of heart,** let him take heed lest he fall.

16 Behold **his mission is given unto him, and it shall not be given again.**

17 And **whoso standeth in this mission** [*the calling of bishop*] **is appointed to be a judge in Israel,** like as it was in ancient days, **to divide the lands of the heritage of God unto his children;**

18 And to judge his people by the testimony of the just, and **by the assistance of his counselors,** according to the **laws of the kingdom** [*including private ownership of property in the United Order*] which are given by the prophets of God.

19 For verily I say unto you, **my law shall be kept on this land** [*the land of Zion*].

In the next several verses, we will be taught a number of mini lessons. We will point several of these out as we go. Many of these will probably be familiar to you. If not, once you hear them, you will notice them often in the sermons of Church leaders and in class discussions, as well as in sacrament meetings and so forth.

Lesson
Those in leadership positions must be humble enough to let God guide and direct them.

20 Let no man think he is ruler; but let God rule him that judgeth, according to the counsel of his own will, or—in other words, him that counseleth or sitteth upon the judgment seat.

Lesson
Being a loyal member of the Church is not an excuse for breaking the laws of the land.

21 Let no man break the laws of the land, for **he that keepeth the laws of God hath no need to break the laws of the land.**

Lesson
Respect and uphold the government in the land in which you live. (Some government, no matter how imperfect, is almost always better than no government.)

22 Wherefore, be subject to the powers that be [*man-made governments*], **until he** [*Christ*] **reigns whose right it is to reign, and subdues all enemies under his feet** [*this includes the millennial reign of Christ*].

Lesson
Keep a wise perspective between the laws of God and the laws of governments.

23 Behold, **the laws which ye have received from my hand are the laws of the church**, and in this light [*being subject to governments and so forth*] ye shall hold them forth. Behold, here is wisdom [*there is wisdom in doing this*].

24 And now, as I spake concerning my servant **Edward Partridge, this land** [*Zion, in Missouri*] **is the land of his residence**, and those whom he has appointed for his counselors; and also the land of the residence of him whom I have appointed to keep my storehouse [*the bishop's storehouse; see D&C 51:13*];

Lesson
There are many matters that are best left up to individuals and the Lord.

25 Wherefore, let them bring their families to this land, as they shall counsel between themselves and me.

Lesson
It is not necessary for us to be commanded in everything we do. We have a mind, and the Lord expects us to use it.

26 For behold, **it is not meet** [*necessary, wise*] **that I should command in all things**; for **he that is compelled in all things**, the same **is a slothful and not a wise servant**; wherefore he receiveth no reward.

27 Verily I say, **men should** be anxiously [*energetically, with sincere dedication*] engaged in a good cause, and **do many things of their own free will**, and bring to pass much righteousness;

28 **For the power is in them** [*they are capable of this*], wherein **they are agents unto themselves** [*they have moral agency*]. And inasmuch as men do good they shall in nowise lose their reward.

29 But **he that doeth not anything until he is commanded, and receiveth a commandment with doubtful heart, and keepeth it with slothfulness, the same is damned** [*does not progress*].

Lesson
Personal accountability is a basic principle of the gospel of Christ.

30 **Who am I** that made man, saith the Lord, **that will hold him guiltless that obeys not my commandments?** [*In other words, what kind of a god would our God be if He did not hold people accountable for how they use their agency?*]

Lesson
Do not blame the Lord when you, yourself, are responsible for not receiving promised blessings. He can command and revoke, depending on our response to His commandments.

31 **Who am I, saith the Lord, that have promised and have not fulfilled?**

32 **I command and men obey not; I revoke and they receive not the blessing.**

33 **Then they say in their hearts: This is not the work of the Lord, for his promises are not fulfilled** [*in other words, they blame God*]. But **wo unto such**, for their reward lurketh beneath, and not from above.

> As we continue, the Lord gives instructions for consecrating material means to the Church as the

Saints gather in Missouri. Martin Harris is given instructions to do so as an example to others.

34 And now I give unto you **further directions concerning this land** [*Zion, Jackson County, Missouri*].

35 It is wisdom in me that my servant **Martin Harris should be an example unto the church, in laying his moneys before the bishop of the church** [*the law of consecration in action*].

36 And also, **this is a law unto every man that cometh unto this land** [*Zion, Jackson County, Missouri*] **to receive an inheritance; and he shall do with his moneys according as the law** [*the law of consecration*] **directs**.

37 And it is wisdom also that **there should be lands purchased in Independence**, for the place of the storehouse [*the bishop's storehouse*], and also for the house of the printing.

Lesson

The Lord expects us to listen to the Holy Ghost and to exercise our agency in many things concerning our personal lives. Many decisions are left up to us.

38 And **other directions concerning my servant Martin Harris shall be given him of the Spirit, that he may receive his inheritance as seemeth him good** [*whatever he decides is fine*];

> Next, in verse 39, Martin Harris is given a warning to the effect that he is still afflicted with pride. In D&C 5:24 and 32, he was warned that he needed to be humble. It appears that he is still struggling with this problem at this time.

39 And let him repent of his sins, for **he seeketh the praise of the world**.

40 And also **let my servant William W. Phelps stand in the office to which I have appointed him** [*"as a printer unto the church" (D&C 57:11)*], and receive his inheritance in the land;

41 And **also he hath need to repent**, for I, the Lord, am not well pleased with him, for he **seeketh to excel** [*perhaps meaning that he wants to get ahead at the expense of others, an attitude that does not fit in with the law of consecration*], **and he is not sufficiently meek before me.**

> Having counseled the above brethren to repent, the Savior now gently reminds them (and all of us) that once we have truly repented,

our sins will not be brought up again. This includes on Judgment Day.

You may be interested to know that even in the case of members who are excommunicated, when they return to membership through baptism and confirmation, their original baptism and confirmation dates are put on their new membership records, thus preserving their privacy regarding their past problems and adhering to the Lord's promise in verse 42, next, wherein He says, "I, the Lord, remember them no more."

For those who have thus repented and been cleansed by the Atonement of Christ, the day of final judgment will be a pleasant experience, as taught in the last half of 2 Nephi 9:14 (**bold** added for emphasis).

2 Nephi 9:14

Wherefore, we shall have a perfect knowledge of all our guilt, and our uncleanness, and our nakedness; **and the righteous shall have a perfect knowledge of their enjoyment, and their righteousness, being clothed with purity, yea, even with the robe of righteousness.**

Verses 42 and 43 go together. You may wish to mark them in some way that indicates that they go together.

Lesson

When we truly repent, we are forgiven, and our sins will not be brought up again, not even on final Judgment Day.

42 Behold, he who has repented of his sins, the same **is forgiven, and I, the Lord, remember them no more.**

43 **By this ye may know if a man repenteth of his sins**—behold, **he will confess them** and **forsake them** [*stop doing them*].

Occasionally, over the years in classes, a student has asked me if verse 42 really means that God forgets our sins or simply that He will never bring them up to us again if we have truly repented. While the important thing is that He "remembers them no more," the technical answer may reside in D&C 82:7, in which we are told that if we commit the same sins we once repented of, "the former sins return."

Another question quite often brought up in classes has to do with what sins require that a member confess them to the bishop. Obviously, confession to the Lord and forsaking are required (see verse 43, above), and a member can confess anything of concern to his or her bishop or stake president. But a general guideline is that any sin that violates the commitments and issues involved in a temple recommend interview would need to be confessed to a person's bishop. Breaking the law of chastity, violating the Word of Wisdom, failure to pay tithing, criminal activity, preaching false doctrine, failure to sustain general or local officers in the Church, child abuse, and spouse abuse are among the sins that should be confessed to the bishop or stake president. Once such sins have been properly confessed to one's bishop or stake president, they do not need to be confessed again in additional temple recommend interviews over the years.

Yet another issue that has come up in class discussions over my years of teaching is whether it is permissible to confess to another bishop if a member is not comfortable confessing to his or her own bishop. The answer is simple. Our own bishop is the only one who has the keys of stewardship over us. While another bishop may be kind and a member may feel more comfortable going to him, he has no authority for that person, and thus, the requirement for confession is not met by visiting with him. One alternative is to go to one's stake president, who also has keys and authority to hear confessions from the members of his stake. In the case of a student, for instance, who may be away to college, he or she could confess to the home ward bishop or the college ward bishop.

In the remainder of this section, the Lord deals with a number of issues, including the matter of collecting money with which to purchase land in Missouri. First, He points out that the main gathering to Missouri will not take place for many years and that He will carefully control it when the time comes.

44 And now, verily, **I say concerning the residue of the elders** [*the ones not called to settle at this time in Missouri*] **of my church, the time has not yet come, for many years, for them to receive their inheritance in this land** [*Missouri*], except they desire it through the prayer of faith, only as it shall be appointed unto them of the Lord.

45 For, behold, **they shall push the people together from the ends of the earth.** [*In other words, there is much missionary work to be done before Zion is established in Missouri.*]

The **bolded** phrase in verse 45, above, is a quote from Deuteronomy 33:17, which speaks of Joseph's (who was sold into Egypt) posterity, pointing out the missionary duties of Ephraim and Manasseh. We will quote this Bible verse here. You will see that one word is different. The Doctrine and Covenants uses "from" rather than "to." In this verse in

Deuteronomy, Joseph is told in his father's blessing that his posterity will play a major role in the gathering of Israel in the last days.

Deuteronomy 33:17

His [*Joseph who was sold into Egypt*] glory is like the firstling of his bullock, and his horns are like the horns of unicorns [*"wild ox" in the Hebrew Old Testament*]: with them he shall push the people together **to** the ends of the earth: and they are the ten thousands of Ephraim, and they are the thousands of Manasseh.

Next, in verses 46–48, the Lord instructs the missionaries who are not called to settle in Missouri that they are to do much missionary work in the area, as well as along the way when they finally return to their homes in the Kirtland area.

46 Wherefore, assemble yourselves together; and **they who are not appointed to stay in this land** [*Missouri*]**, let them preach the gospel in the regions round about**; and **after that let them return to their homes.**

47 **Let them preach by the way** [*as they travel home*], and bear testimony of the truth in all places, and call upon the rich, the high and the low, and the poor to repent.

48 And **let them build up churches** [*branches of the Church*], inasmuch as the inhabitants of the earth will repent.

It is clear that the Church could not afford to purchase much land in Missouri at this time and that many more converts would be needed to finance the building up of Zion there. It is also a basic principle of the gospel that the sacrifices of the members, including financial sacrifices, bring strength and personal testimony into the lives and hearts of the members. This principle applies in the lives of members today as they pay tithes and offerings and reap the blessings of heaven.

Next, the members in Ohio are instructed to continue sacrificing and donating money for the purchase of land in Missouri.

49 And **let there be an agent appointed** by the voice of the church [*sustained by the members*], unto the church **in Ohio, to receive moneys to purchase lands in Zion** [*Jackson County, Missouri*].

Next, Sidney Rigdon is instructed to make a written description of the land on which Zion will be built and to write an official letter to all the branches of the Church at the time, requesting help in collecting money for purchasing land in Missouri.

50 And I give unto my servant **Sidney Rigdon** a commandment,

that he **shall write a description of the land of Zion, and a statement of the will of God**, as it shall be made known by the Spirit unto him;

> Brother Rigdon did write a description of the land, but his first attempt was not accepted by the Lord, as indicated a few weeks later in D&C 63:56. His second attempt was accepted. In volume one of *History of the Church,* we have a description of the land of Zion that was given by Joseph Smith in early August 1831. Whether this is a copy of Sidney Rigdon's description, we don't know, but we will include it here for your information.
>
> **Description of the Land of Zion.**
>
> "As we had received a commandment for Elder Rigdon to write a description of the land of Zion, we sought for all the information necessary to accomplish so desirable an object. The country is unlike the timbered states of the East. As far as the eye can reach the beautiful rolling prairies lie spread out like a sea of meadows; and are decorated with a growth of flowers so gorgeous and grand as to exceed description; and nothing is more fruitful, or a richer stockholder in the blooming prairie than the honey bee. Only on the water courses is timber to be found. There in strips from one to three miles in width, and following faithfully the meanderings of the streams, it grows in luxuriant forests. The forests are a mixture of oak, hickory, black walnut, elm, ash, cherry, honey locust, mulberry, coffee bean, hackberry, boxelder, and bass wood; with the addition of cottonwood, butterwood, pecan, and soft and hard maple upon the bottoms. The shrubbery is beautiful, and consists in part of plums, grapes, crab apple, and persimmons.
>
> **Agricultural Products; Animals, Domestic and Wild.**
>
> "The soil is rich and fertile; from three to ten feet deep, and generally composed of a rich black mold, intermingled with clay and sand. It yields in abundance, wheat, corn, sweet potatoes, cotton and many other common agricultural products. Horses, cattle and hogs, though of an inferior breed, are tolerably plentiful and seem nearly to raise themselves by grazing in the vast prairie range in summer, and feeding upon the bottoms in winter. The wild game is less plentiful of course where man has commenced the cultivation of the soil, than in the wild prairies. Buffalo, elk, deer, bear, wolves, beaver and many smaller animals here roam at pleasure. Turkeys, geese, swans, ducks, yea a variety of the feathered tribe, are among the rich abundance that grace the delightful regions of this goodly land—the heritage of the children of God.

SECTION 58

The Climate.

"The season is mild and delightful nearly three quarters of the year, and as the land of Zion, situated at about equal distances from the Atlantic and Pacific oceans, as well as from the Alleghany and Rocky mountains, in the thirty-ninth degree of north latitude, and between the sixteenth and seventeenth degrees of west longitude [from Washington], it bids fair—when the curse is taken from the land—to become one of the most blessed places on the globe. The winters are milder than the Atlantic states of the same parallel of latitude, and the weather is more agreeable; so that were the virtues of the inhabitants only equal to the blessings of the Lord which He permits to crown the industry of those inhabitants, there would be a measure of the good things of life for the benefit of the Saints, full, pressed down, and running over, even an hundred-fold. The disadvantages here, as in all new countries, are self-evident—lack of mills and schools; together with the natural privations and inconveniences which the hand of industry, the refinement of society, and the polish of science, overcome" (*History of the Church*, 1:197–98).

Next, in verse 51 (as mentioned above), Sidney Rigdon is instructed to write a letter from the Church to all branches, which includes a request for money from the members to assist in buying land in Missouri.

51 **And an epistle** [*an official letter*] **and subscription** [*request for funds*], **to be presented unto all the churches to obtain moneys**, to be put into the hands of the bishop, of himself or the agent, as seemeth him good or as he shall direct, **to purchase lands for an inheritance for the children of God** [*the righteous members of the Church*].

52 For, behold, verily I say unto you, **the Lord willeth that the disciples** [*members of the Church*] **and the children of men** [*nonmembers*] **should open their hearts**, even **to purchase this whole region of country**, as soon as time will permit.

In verse 53, next, we see a warning that if the members of the Church fail to purchase the land needed in Missouri, it will only be obtained through the shedding of blood. Over time, there was considerable reluctance on the part of a number of members in other areas to donate money to buy land in Missouri. As you know, there was much violence against the Saints in Missouri. In our day, there is considerable acquiring of land in Missouri, including in Adam-ondi-Ahman, due to the generous donations and tithing of the members of the Church, as well as through income to the Church from business ventures that bring in money from sources outside the Church.

53 Behold, here is wisdom. **Let them do this lest they receive none inheritance, save it be by the shedding of blood.**

54 And again, **inasmuch as there is land obtained, let there be workmen sent forth** of all kinds [*with all kinds of skills*] unto this land, to labor for the saints of God.

> In verses 55–56, next, the Master reminds these early members of the Church that the instructions given above must be carried out with wisdom and order. Part of doing these things "in order" would include purchasing land such that the Church would have clear legal title to it. Also, it was vital that the Saints themselves be as well prepared as possible to settle and build when they arrived in Missouri rather than "fleeing" helter-skelter to Zion.

55 **Let all these things be done in order;** and let the privileges of the lands [*probably meaning the advantages and blessings of settling on such fertile and sacred land*] be made known from time to time, by the bishop or the agent of the church.

56 And **let the work of the gathering be not in haste, nor by flight**; but let it be done as it shall be counseled by the elders of the church at the conferences, according to the knowledge which they receive from time to time.

> Next, in verse 57, Brother Rigdon is instructed to dedicate the land of Zion, which includes the "spot for the temple." Joseph Smith himself will dedicate the temple site.

57 And **let my servant Sidney Rigdon consecrate and dedicate this land, and the spot for the temple, unto the Lord.**

> The Prophet Joseph Smith recorded the dedication of the land by Sidney and the dedication of the temple site by him. He wrote,
>
> "On the second day of August, I assisted the Colesville branch of the Church to lay the first log, for a house, as a foundation of Zion in Kaw township, twelve miles west of Independence. The log was carried and placed by twelve men, in honor of the twelve tribes of Israel. At the same time, through prayer, the land of Zion was consecrated and dedicated by Elder Sidney Rigdon for the gathering of the Saints. It was a season of joy to those present, and afforded a glimpse of the future, which time will yet unfold to the satisfaction of the faithful" (*History of the Church*, 1:196).

"On the third day of August, I proceeded to dedicate the spot for the Temple, a little west of Independence, and there were also present Sidney Rigdon, Edward Partridge, W. W. Phelps, Oliver Cowdery, Martin Harris and Joseph Coe." (*History of the Church*, 1:199. See also *Manuscript History of the Church*, vol. A-1, page 139, josephsmithpapers.org.)

As the Lord finishes this revelation, He instructs Joseph Smith and others to finish up and then journey back to Kirtland. Remember, as mentioned in the notes at the end of section 57 in this book, that there will, in effect, be two headquarters or gathering places for the Saints over the next five years—Kirtland, Ohio, and Missouri.

58 And let a conference meeting be called; and **after that let my servants Sidney Rigdon and Joseph Smith, Jun., return** [*to Ohio*], **and also Oliver Cowdery with them**, to accomplish the residue [*the rest*] of the work which I have appointed unto them in their own land [*Ohio*], and **the residue** [*in Missouri, see verse 61*] as **shall be ruled by the conferences**.

59 And **let no man return** [*to Ohio*] **from this land** [*Missouri*] **except he bear record by the way**, of that which he knows and most assuredly believes [*all who return to Ohio should do missionary work as they travel back*].

60 **Let that which has been bestowed upon Ziba Peterson** [*possibly his license to preach the gospel*] **be taken from him**; and let him stand as a member in the church, and labor with his own hands, with the brethren, **until he is sufficiently chastened for all his sins; for he confesseth them not, and he thinketh to hide them.**

Just a quick note about Ziba Peterson (verse 60, above). In October 1830 he was called to go on a mission to the Lamanites along with Parley P. Pratt, Oliver Cowdery, and Peter Whitmer Jr. (See D&C 32:1–3.) He left from Fayette, New York, on October 17, 1830, and he and his companions traveled some 1,500 miles, preaching along the way and arriving in Independence, Missouri, in December 1830. They preached the gospel there and to the Indians across the Missouri River as late as April 1831.

Sadly, even though he responded to the chastisement in verse 60, above, and three days later confessed his sins, he withdrew from the Church in May 1833 and was excommunicated on June 25, 1833 (see *History of the Church*, 1:367). He never came back. He eventually moved his family to California, where he died in 1849 in Placerville.

61 **Let the residue** [*remainder*] **of the elders** of this church, **who are coming to this land** [*Missouri*], some of whom are exceedingly blessed even above measure, also hold a conference upon this land [*see verse 58, above*].

62 And **let my servant Edward Partridge** [*the bishop*] **direct the conference** which shall be held by them.

63 And **let them also return, preaching the gospel by the way**, bearing record of the things which are revealed unto them.

64 For, verily, **the sound** [*of gospel preaching*] **must go forth from this place into all the world**, and unto **the uttermost parts of the earth**—the **gospel must be preached unto every creature**, with signs [*blessings and miracles*] following them that believe.

> President Spencer W. Kimball explained the preaching of the gospel to "the uttermost parts of the earth." He said:
>
> "It seems to me that the Lord chose his words when he said 'every nation,' 'every land,' 'uttermost bounds of the earth,' 'every tongue,' 'every people,' 'every soul,' 'all the world,' 'many lands.'
>
> "Surely there is significance in these words!

> "Certainly his sheep were not limited to the thousands about him and with whom he rubbed shoulders each day. A universal family! A universal command! . . .
>
> "I feel that when we have done all in our power that the Lord will find a way to open doors. That is my faith. . . .
>
> "With the Lord providing these miracles of communication [radio, television, cassette tape players, satellites and receiving stations, and so on], and with the increased efforts and devotion of our missionaries and all of us, and all others who are 'sent,' surely the divine injunction will come to pass . . . (D&C 58:64.) And we must find a way. . . .
>
> "Using all the latest inventions and equipment and paraphernalia already developed and that which will follow, can you see that perhaps the day may come when the world will be converted and covered?
>
> "If we do all we can . . . I am sure the Lord will bring more discoveries to our use. He will bring a change of heart into kings and magistrates and emperors, or he will divert rivers or open seas or find ways to touch hearts. He will open the gates and make possible the proselyting" ("When the World Will Be Converted," *Ensign*, October 1974, 5, 10–11, 13).

65 And **behold the Son of Man**

[*the "Son of Man of Holiness"—in other words, the Son of God; see Moses 6:57*] **cometh**. Amen.

SECTION 59

Background

This revelation was given in Zion, Jackson County, Missouri, on Sunday, August 7, 1831, which was the day Polly Knight was buried.

This was a particularly tender occasion. Polly Knight was the wife of Joseph Knight Sr. and the mother of Newel Knight. Newel had just led the Thompson Branch (which included his parents) from the Kirtland area to Missouri (as instructed by the Lord in D&C 54:7–8). The Thompson Branch consisted primarily of members who had been converted in Colesville, New York, had gathered to Kirtland, and had then been instructed by the Lord to move on to Missouri.

The Prophet Joseph Smith knew the Knights well. In 1826, he had become well acquainted with them. They lived in Colesville, New York, at the time, and Joseph met them while boarding with the Isaac Hale family in Harmony, Pennsylvania (about fifteen miles from Colesville). During this time, Joseph occasionally lodged with the Knights, who listened attentively as he recounted his visions to them. It was Joseph Knight Sr. who loaned Joseph Smith a horse and buggy with which to bring the gold plates home from the Hill Cumorah in September 1827. The Knights believed his testimony and joined the Church shortly after it was organized on April 6, 1830. They were humble stalwarts in the faith.

Polly Knight's health had not been good for some time prior to beginning the nearly nine hundred-mile journey from Ohio to Missouri, but she insisted on going because she wanted to plant her feet on the sacred soil of Zion before she passed away. We will quote the Institute of Religion's *Church History in the Fulness of Times* manual for more detail on this:

"The journey to Missouri was not an easy one. This was particularly true for the Colesville Saints who left Thompson, Ohio, carrying their belongings and provisions in twenty-four wagons. At Wellsville, Ohio, they left the wagons and traveled by steamboat down the Ohio River to the junction of the Mississippi River. They then traveled up the Mississippi River to St. Louis. At St. Louis, Newel Knight and his company and some of the Prophet's companions elected to journey by steamboat on the Missouri River. This necessitated a wait of several days before passage could be secured.

"The case of Polly Knight illustrates the strong feelings of many members of the Church. Sister

Knight, mother of Newel and a member of the Colesville branch, risked her life making the trip to Zion. Polly's health was failing, but her anxiety to see the promised land was so great that she refused to be left behind in Ohio. Nor would she remain with friends along the route for rest and recuperation. Her son wrote, 'Her only, or her greatest desire, was to set her feet upon the land of Zion, and to have her body interred in that land.' Fearing that she might die at any time on the journey, Newel left the boat on one occasion and went ashore to purchase lumber for a coffin. He later reported that 'the Lord gave her the desire of her heart, and she lived to stand upon that land.' Polly died within two weeks of her arrival in the land of Zion and was the first Latter-day Saint to be buried in Missouri. The Lord gave these consoling words: 'Those that live shall inherit the earth, and those that die shall rest from all their labors, and their works shall follow them; and they shall receive a crown in the mansions of my Father, which I have prepared for them' (D&C 59:2)." (*Church History in the Fulness of Times*, 2003, 104–5.)

Section 59 is perhaps best known for its verses dealing with the Sabbath and the blessings of Sabbath Day observance (verses 9–17). We will move ahead now with our verse-by-verse study. As mentioned above, Polly Knight had died, having walked upon the soil of the land of Zion. It is Sunday, August 7, 1831, the day they buried her, and verses 1–2 have direct reference to her and her faithfulness in coming to Zion.

1 BEHOLD, **blessed**, saith the Lord, **are they who have come up unto this land** [*Missouri*] **with an eye single to my glory** [*with proper motives*], according to my commandments.

2 For those that live shall inherit the earth, and **those that die shall rest from all their labors, and their works shall follow them; and they shall receive a crown in the mansions of my Father, which I have prepared for them**.

Verses 3–8 give counsel and encouragement. They also emphasize that the Ten Commandments are still in force.

3 Yea, **blessed are they whose feet stand upon the land of Zion, who have obeyed my gospel**; for they shall receive for their reward the good things of the earth, and it shall bring forth in its strength.

Perhaps you've heard someone complain that there are too many commandments and that there doesn't seem to be much freedom in living the gospel. People who think this do not understand freedom. They fail to realize that it is the breaking of God's commandments that limits freedom and reduces options. Verse 4, next, is a clear lesson on the fact that commandments are great blessings. In effect, they are the "instruction manual" for true human freedom and happiness. They bring us from spiritual darkness and confusion into the light of the gospel and eternal perspective and understanding. They enable us to exercise our moral agency in ways that lead to the highest blessings and most satisfying lifestyle in the universe, namely, godhood. The truly wise seek the commandments of God. The foolish reject them until they are bound by consequences.

4 And **they shall** also **be crowned with blessings** from above, yea, and **with commandments not a few**, and with revelations in their time—they that are faithful and diligent before me.

Next, in verse 5 and the first part of verse 6, we see similar wording to that in Matthew 22:37–39.

5 Wherefore, I give unto them a commandment, saying thus: **Thou shalt love the Lord thy God with all thy heart, with all thy might, mind, and strength**; and in the name of Jesus Christ thou shalt serve him.

6 **Thou shalt love thy neighbor as thyself.** Thou shalt not steal; neither commit adultery, nor kill, nor do anything like unto it.

Did you notice an important doctrine that the Savior added here in the Doctrine and Covenants? We will quote Matthew 22:37–39 here so you can pick it out.

Matthew 22:37–39

37 Jesus said unto him, Thou shalt love the Lord thy God with all thy heart, and with all thy soul, and with all thy mind.

38 This is the first and great commandment.

39 And the second is like unto it, Thou shalt love thy neighbour as thyself.

The answer to our question is that He added, "and in the name of Jesus Christ thou shalt serve him."

Continuing with our study, you have probably observed that many people today claim that the Ten Commandments are outdated, that they do not apply in modern society. In the last part of verse 6, the Savior clearly indicates that they are still in force. We will repeat verse 6 here and use **bold** to emphasize this point.

Doctrine

The Ten Commandments are still in force today.

6 Thou shalt love thy neighbor as thyself. **Thou shalt not steal;**

neither **commit adultery, nor kill**, nor do anything like unto it.

A most important principle is taught in the last phrase of verse 6, above. It is that we must avoid "anything like unto it." This is the answer when someone says, in effect, that the scriptures do not mention a specific sin, and therefore it is not forbidden. For example, a student once said to me in class that there is no specific mention in the scriptures of certain types of sexual physical intimacy other than adultery or fornication; therefore, any sexual activity, other than actual adultery or fornication must be permissible. The simple answer to him and the entire class was to quote D&C 59:6: "nor do anything like unto it." He was somewhat startled and disappointed and exclaimed, "Oh, so there is something in there about it!"

Next, in verse 7, we find that we are commanded to have gratitude. This may sound a bit strong, that is, to refer to it as a commandment. But the wording is "Thou shalt," the same as in the Ten Commandments. Remember, "commandments" are given for our good (verse 4, above), and gratitude is one of the most healing and beneficial of all human attributes. No wonder we are commanded to express it. We will see more about gratitude in verse 21.

7 Thou shalt thank the Lord thy God in all things.

One of the most important and beneficial of all personal sacrifices we can give is mentioned next, in verse 8.

8 Thou shalt offer a sacrifice unto the Lord thy God in righteousness, even that **of a broken heart and a contrite spirit.**

The words "broken heart" and "contrite spirit" in verse 8, above, obviously mean humility. However, if we take a closer look, we can find additional fine-tuned meanings in these expressions.

One of my students, while pondering the phrase "broken heart," asked if it meant that truly righteous people should be crying most of the time—an interesting observation with a definite "no" for an answer. As we chatted, we used the comparison of a "well-broken" or "well-trained" horse, strong and powerful with much spirit and energy but very quickly yielding to the slightest touch of the reins or directions of the "master." Thus, one way of looking at "broken heart" is that of having our hearts willingly and easily controlled by the "Master" through His gospel and our eagerness to keep His commandments.

The word "contrite" can be defined as being "humble" or "meek," but it has the additional fine-tuned scriptural meaning of seeking correction as needed. Thus, having a "contrite spirit" includes the desire to receive correction from the Lord as needed in order to grow and progress.

Next, in verses 9–17, the Savior teaches these Saints and all of us about the purposes of the Sabbath. As expressed in verse 9, a major benefit of keeping the Sabbath holy is that of keeping ourselves more nearly "unspotted" or untarnished by the world.

Doctrine

Where possible, we should go to church on the Sabbath day.

9 And **that thou mayest more fully keep thyself unspotted from the world, thou shalt** [a *commandment*] **go to the house of prayer** [*the church*] and offer up thy sacraments **upon my holy day;**

> Perhaps you are acquainted with someone who claims that he or she can get closer to God by going to the mountains, or wherever, on Sunday than by going to church. While it may be true that we can have spiritual thoughts and experiences among God's creations in nature and feel close to Him, there is a major flaw in such thinking. The problem is that such a person is making his or her own rules and is completely ignoring the "thou shalt" of verse 9. It is not an optional matter for those who desire salvation.

10 For verily this is a day appointed unto you to **rest from your labors,** and to **pay thy devotions unto the Most High;**

11 **Nevertheless thy vows shall be offered up in righteousness on all days and at all times** [*we must live the gospel all week, not just on Sunday*];

12 But remember that **on this, the Lord's day, thou shalt offer thine oblations and thy sacraments** unto the Most High, **confessing thy sins unto thy brethren** [*in this context, this likely includes making peace with people you have offended*], **and before the Lord.**

> The word "oblations," as used in verse 12, above, means "offerings, whether of time, talents, or means, in service of God and fellowman," as stated in D&C 59:12, footnote b.

> From verses 13–15, next, we see that it is up to us to make the Sabbath a special day of dedication to the Lord and personal growth toward Him. The focus should be on what to do on the Sabbath in order to accomplish this goal rather than focusing on what we can't or shouldn't do. It is to be a pleasant day of "rejoicing . . . with cheerful hearts and countenances." In fact, if we fill the Sabbath with appropriate things, there will probably not

be time to do things that violate the purpose of the Sabbath.

As an Apostle, President Russell M. Nelson taught us how to more readily keep the Sabbath Day holy. He said:

"How do we hallow the Sabbath day? In my much younger years, I studied the work of others who had compiled lists of things to do and things not to do on the Sabbath. It wasn't until later that I learned from the scriptures that my conduct and my attitude on the Sabbath constituted a sign between me and my Heavenly Father. With that understanding, I no longer needed lists of dos and don'ts. When I had to make a decision whether or not an activity was appropriate for the Sabbath, I simply asked myself, 'What sign do I want to give to God?' That question made my choices about the Sabbath day crystal clear. . . .

"How can you ensure that your behavior on the Sabbath will lead to joy and rejoicing? In addition to your going to church, partaking of the sacrament, and being diligent in your specific call to serve, what other activities would help to make the Sabbath a delight for you? What sign will you give to the Lord to show your love for Him?" ("The Sabbath Is a Delight," *Ensign* or *Liahona*, May 2015, 130).

13 And **on this day thou shalt do none other thing**, only let thy food be prepared with singleness of heart that thy fasting may be perfect, or, in other words, **that thy joy may be full**.

14 Verily, **this is fasting and prayer, or in other words, rejoicing and prayer**.

15 And inasmuch as ye **do these things with thanksgiving, with cheerful hearts and countenances**, not with much laughter, for this is sin, but with a glad heart and a cheerful countenance—

There are some words and phrases in verses 13–15, above, that can help us keep the Sabbath day holy. We will take time to take a closer look at some of them here.

Singleness of heart (verse 13)

This phrase is considered by some to mean "simplicity." Yet others define it as meaning "with specific purpose." Thus, in a family or as an individual where it means "simplicity," meal preparation might be simple and easy, with minimal effort to prepare and clean up.

On the other hand, for those to whom it means "specific purpose," the focus might intentionally include a more elaborate meal, with the desired result of attracting the family to join together and spend more time in food and conversation, during which family ties are strengthened and the family counsels together one with another.

In either case or in any of several other scenarios, if the focus in the heart is on keeping the Sabbath, the meal preparation will most likely be appropriate. This is one of those matters where we are taught correct principles and expected to govern ourselves. John Taylor explained that the Prophet Joseph Smith said, "I teach the people correct principles, and they govern themselves" (In *Journal of Discourses*, 10:57–58).

Fasting (verse 13)

President Joseph F. Smith taught the following about fasting:

"Now, while the law requires the Saints in all the world to fast from 'even to even' and to abstain both from food and drink, it can easily be seen from the Scriptures, and especially from the words of Jesus, that it is more important to obtain the true spirit of love for God and man, 'purity of heart and simplicity of intention,' than it is to carry out the cold letter of the law. The Lord has instituted the fast on a reasonable and intelligent basis, and none of his works are vain or unwise. His law is perfect in this as in other things. Hence, those who can are required to comply thereto; it is a duty from which they cannot escape; but let it be remembered that the observance of the fast day by abstaining twenty-four hours from food and drink is not an absolute rule, it is no iron-clad law to us, but it is left with the people as a matter of conscience, to exercise wisdom and discretion. Many are subject to weakness, others are delicate in health, and others have nursing babies; of such it should not be required to fast. Neither should parents compel their little children to fast. I have known children to cry for something to eat on fast day. In such cases, going without food will do them no good. Instead, they dread the day to come, and in place of hailing it, dislike it; while the compulsion engenders a spirit of rebellion in them, rather than a love for the Lord and their fellows. Better teach them the principle, and let them observe it when they are old enough to choose intelligently, than to so compel them.

"But those should fast who can, and all classes among us should be taught to save the meals which they would eat, or their equivalent, for the poor. None are exempt from this; it is required of the Saints, old and young, in every part of the Church. It is no excuse that in some places there are no poor. In such cases the fast donation should be forwarded to the proper authorities for transmission to such stakes of Zion as may stand in need" (*Gospel Doctrine*, 243–44).

There is perhaps another aspect of "fasting" that may be seen in the context of verse 13. It is the added dimension that "fasting" can also mean "fasting" from the things of the world—the daily work and toil, entertainments and so forth—that use up much of our time and attention during the week.

Not with much laughter (verse 15)

There is a tendency on the part of some people to never take sacred things seriously. For them, "laughter" is a means of brushing serious matters aside. D&C 88:69 speaks of "excess of laughter," and D&C 88:121 associates "laughter" with "light-mindedness," which is another term for not taking sacred things seriously. Thus, we understand that "laughter," in the context of the Sabbath, can mean showing irreverence and disrespect for the sacred purposes of the Lord's "holy day."

As we continue with section 59, the Savior teaches us the benefits of keeping the Sabbath holy.

16 Verily I say, that **inasmuch as ye do this** [*keep the Sabbath day holy*]**, the fulness of** [*everything in*] **the earth is yours, the beasts of the field** and the **fowls of the air,** and **that which climbeth upon the trees and walketh upon the earth**;

17 Yea, and **the herb,** and **the good things which come of the earth,** whether **for food** or for **raiment** [*clothing*]**,** or for **houses,** or for **barns,** or for **orchards,** or for **gardens,** or for **vineyards**;

In verses 18–19, next, the Savior tells us one of the major purposes of His creations for us. We will use **bold** to point it out.

18 Yea, all things which come of the earth, in the season thereof, are made for the benefit and the use of man, both **to please the eye and to gladden the heart**;

19 Yea, for food and for raiment, for taste and for smell, to strengthen the body **and to enliven the soul**.

20 And **it pleaseth God** [*it makes God happy*] **that he hath given all these things unto man**; for unto this end [*purpose; "to please the eye and to gladden the heart . . . and to enliven the soul"*] were they made to be used, with judgment [*wisdom and common sense*], not to excess, neither by extortion [*to take by force, overcharge, greediness*].

In the note accompanying verse 7, we mentioned that we would return to the topic of gratitude when we got to verse 21. It is significant to note that the importance of gratitude is pointed out rather dramatically in verse 21. If you look carefully, you will see that the Lord groups all other commandments into one but places gratitude into a category of its own. Thus, gratitude is mentioned exclusively, in effect being compared in importance to all the other commandments combined. While we need to be careful not to go overboard in our analogy here, it is obvious that the Lord considers gratitude to be one of the most important and saving attributes. Failing to have and express gratitude is apparently one of the most serious and damaging of all human traits.

21 And **in nothing doth man offend God, or against none is his wrath kindled, save** [*except*] **those who confess not his hand in all things** [*who do not express gratitude*]**, and obey not his commandments.**

The phrase "the law and the prophets," as used in verse 22, next, means the Bible, specifically the Old Testament. The "law" consists of the first five books of the Old Testament (Genesis, Exodus, Leviticus, Numbers, and Deuteronomy). The "prophets" is a reference, basically, to the rest of the Old Testament and includes the words of the prophets such as Isaiah, Jeremiah, Ezekiel, and so forth.

22 Behold, **this is according to the law and the prophets** [*in other words, what the Lord has explained in the above verses is also taught in the Bible*]**; wherefore, trouble me no more concerning this matter.**

In closing, the Master reminds us of the rewards that come to the righteous. As you can see, we do not have to wait until the next life to receive one of the greatest rewards of all.

23 But learn that he who doeth the works of righteousness shall receive his reward, even **peace in this world and eternal life** [*exaltation*] **in the world to come.**

24 I, the Lord, have spoken it, and the Spirit beareth record. Amen.

Before we leave section 59, we will include one more quote regarding keeping the Sabbath day holy. President Spencer W. Kimball taught,

"The Sabbath is a holy day in which to do worthy and holy things. Abstinence from work and recreation is important, but insufficient. The Sabbath calls for constructive thoughts and acts, and if one merely lounges about doing nothing on the Sabbath, he is breaking it. To observe it, one will be on his knees in prayer, preparing lessons, studying the gospel, meditating, visiting the ill and distressed, writing letters to missionaries, taking a nap, reading wholesome material, and attending all the meetings of that day at which he is expected" ("The Sabbath—A Delight," *Ensign*, January 1978, 4).

SECTION 60

Background

This revelation was given through the Prophet Joseph Smith in Jackson County, Missouri, on August 8, 1831. A number of Saints, including the Prophet and other Church leaders, had come to Missouri, as commanded by the Lord. They had dedicated the land of Zion for the eventual gathering of the Lord's people (D&C 58:57), had dedicated a temple site, and had accomplished other things as instructed. Having completed these assigned tasks, many of them had been instructed by the Lord to return east (D&C 58:46, 58, 63) to their homes and responsibilities in the Kirtland, Ohio, area for a season.

As you no doubt have observed, one of the main focuses of the Restoration at this point in time is that of missionary work. It is vital for the continued establishment of the Church that there be a large influx of new converts. The Lord has sent many of His "noble and great" (Abraham 3:22) spirits to earth and placed them in strategic locations where they can be found by these early missionaries. When these faithful ones from our premortal life hear the gospel, they will recognize it as the truth and will join the Church. But first, these early missionaries must find them.

Thus, in this revelation, the Lord gives specific instructions to those brethren who are now to return from Jackson County, Missouri, to their homes in the East. They are told to go out of their way to make every reasonable effort to preach the gospel as they travel rather than simply focusing on getting home.

By the way, if you look at a map, you will see that much of the journey between Missouri and Ohio could be made by river (particularly the Missouri, Mississippi, and Ohio Rivers). This helps understand the use of the "craft" (boat) mentioned in verse 5. Waterways were indeed the preferred mode of travel for many in that day.

As we begin our specific study of the verses in this section, you will see that the Lord emphasizes the importance of preaching and spreading the gospel as they travel. This focus certainly applies to us also in our day.

1 BEHOLD, thus saith the Lord unto the elders of his church, who are to return speedily to the land from whence they came [*back east to the Kirtland area*]: Behold, **it pleaseth me, that you have come up hither** [*to Missouri*];

2 But **with some I am not well pleased,** for **they will not open their mouths** [*to preach the gospel*], but **they hide the talent** [*the gospel; the ability to teach the gospel*] which I have given unto them,

SECTION 60

because of the fear of man. Wo unto such, for mine anger is kindled against them.

> As you can see from verse 2, above, it is a serious matter not to share the gospel when the opportunity is available. From verse 3, next, it appears that some of the twenty-eight elders called by the Lord to come to Missouri (see section 52) and preach the gospel en route did not do an adequate job of it in the eyes of the Lord. Now, as they return to Ohio, they are being given a chance to do better.

3 And it shall come to pass, **if they are not more faithful** unto me, **it shall be taken away, even that which they have** [*perhaps meaning their calling to serve missions or the small "talent" they have, which can be developed more if they will be obedient*].

4 For **I, the Lord, rule in the heavens above, and among the armies of the earth** [*in other words, the Lord has the power to help them succeed with their missions*]; and in the day when I shall make up my jewels [*a scriptural phrase meaning exaltation; jewels are symbolic of the best; the imagery is that they will become jewels in the Lord's crown of glory on the final Judgment Day*], all men shall know what it is that bespeaketh [*foretells; indicates by obvious signs; represents*] the power of God.

5 But, verily, **I will speak unto you concerning your journey unto the land** [*Ohio*] **from whence you came. Let there be a craft made, or bought, as seemeth you good, it mattereth not unto me,** and take your journey speedily for the place which is called St. Louis [*go straight to St. Louis before you stop to preach the gospel*].

> There is perhaps an important message for us couched in verse 5, above. The phrase "it mattereth not unto me" may be a bit of a surprise to some who believe that there is always a right and wrong for every situation we face. Similar verses are found in D&C 61:22, 62:5, 63:44, and 80:3. In this case, the Lord is saying that it makes no difference to Him whether these brethren buy a boat or build one themselves.

> In applying this principle to our lives, there may be situations and decisions we face in which we seek an answer from the Lord but can't seem to get one. For example, suppose you had two job offers, one for a position with a company in Rochester, New York, and one in San Diego, California. You pray and receive a peaceful feeling about the job in Rochester. Therefore, you assume that you should get a negative feeling when praying about the opportunity in San

Diego. You pray and get a peaceful feeling. Confused, you try again, with the same result. You must make a decision soon, and in an attempt to draw closer to the Spirit, you turn to the scriptures, opening your Doctrine and Covenants to a random page. It is section 60. As you read, "it mattereth not unto me" jumps out at you, and you now realize that either job would be fine with the Lord. He will use you in the Church no matter which location you settle in. With great relief, you offer a prayer of gratitude and proceed with making your choice.

Next, in verses 6 and 7, the Savior instructs the Prophet, Sidney, and Oliver to travel straight to Cincinnati before they begin preaching, whereas others are told to get off the river at St. Louis and begin preaching (verse 8).

Notice also that they are to preach "without wrath" (verse 7). As you have perhaps noticed, some preachers in some religions seem to believe that preaching should be fiery, with much loud condemnation of the wicked. This is not to be the mode of preaching for these true servants of God.

6 And from thence let my servants, Sidney Rigdon, Joseph Smith, Jun., and Oliver Cowdery, take their journey for Cincinnati;

7 And in this place let them lift up their voice and declare my word with loud voices [*speaking up so people can hear*], **without wrath** or doubting, lifting up holy hands upon them. For **I am able to make you holy** [*clean, pure, without sin, worthy of blessings*], **and your sins are forgiven you.**

> We find another beautiful and simple "gem" couched in verse 7, above. It is a marvelous understatement by our humble Savior as He says, "I am able to make you holy."

8 And let the residue [*the others*] **take their journey** from St. Louis, **two by two**, and preach the word, **not in haste** [*don't hurry along home*], among the congregations of the wicked, until they return to the churches [*the branches of the Church*] from whence they came.

> We have to be a bit careful with the phrase "congregations of the wicked" as used in verse 8, above. It is clear that many wicked, riotous, and rebellious people had come west and settled on the fringes of society where they could live their chosen lifestyle in relative freedom. However, there were many good people also, with Christian standards and virtues, who had settled in these western lands. The term "wicked" is sometimes used to mean those who do not have the gospel. We find this use of the word in the Doctrine and Covenants. We will take time to point this out.

D&C 88:52–53

52 And whoso receiveth not my voice is not acquainted with my voice, and is not of me.

53 And by this you may know the righteous from **the wicked**, and that the whole world groaneth under sin and darkness even now.

A quote from the 2018 *Doctrine and Covenants Student Manual*, chapter 22, further helps us in understanding the use of "wicked" here:

"The phrase 'congregations of the wicked' as used in Doctrine and Covenants 60:8 and other revelations (see also D&C 61:33; 62:5) does not necessarily mean that all people in these places were guilty of gross wickedness. Rather, the phrase likely refers to people who did not have a knowledge or understanding of the restored gospel of Jesus Christ."

As we continue, it is helpful to recall that these missionaries baptized a number of people and established branches of the Church along the way as they traveled from Ohio to Missouri. Now, as they return to Ohio, it is likely that they will visit many of these converts again and thus strengthen the little branches as they go, as indicated in verse 9, next.

9 And **all this for the good of the churches** [*branches of the Church*]; for this intent have I sent them.

> We see a principle of the law of consecration in action in verses 10–11, next. Bishop Edward Partridge is handling the consecrated funds of the "united order" in Missouri and is instructed by the Lord to supply money to these missionaries to help with their needs as they return to Ohio. Those who are able to pay the money back after they get home are requested to do so. Those who can't are not required to. No one will tell them who can and who can't. It is up to them to decide. This illustrates the fact that a very high level of personal honesty and integrity is required to successfully live the law of consecration. It is a celestial law, and we must be able to live it in order to qualify for the celestial kingdom.
>
> Similarly, no one tells us exactly how much fast offering to pay. It is up to us. We decide.

10 **And let my servant Edward Partridge impart of the money** which I have given him, **a portion unto mine elders who are commanded to return**;

11 And **he that is able, let him return it** by the way of the agent [*men assigned to assist the bishop in handling the funds of the Church*]; and **he that is not, of him it is not required.**

12 And **now I speak of the residue** [*others*] **who are to come unto this land** [*Missouri; see verse 14*].

> As you can see, verses 13–14, next, contain good counsel for today's missionaries as well as for these early elders in 1831.

13 Behold, **they have been sent to preach my gospel among the congregations of the wicked**; wherefore, **I give unto them a commandment**, thus: **Thou shalt not idle away thy time, neither shalt thou bury thy talent that it may not be known.**

14 And after thou hast come up unto the land of Zion, and hast proclaimed my word, thou shalt speedily return, **proclaiming my word** among the congregations of the wicked, **not in haste, neither in wrath nor with strife.**

> The Lord explains that shaking "off the dust of thy feet," in verse 15, next, is a "testimony against" those who reject the missionaries. In this context, it appears to be a witness that they had a valid chance to hear and accept the gospel but rejected it. In a way it can be considered a curse in the sense that people who reject the gospel are "cursed" by their own choice to continue living in spiritual darkness and ignorance of the plan of salvation.

15 And **shake off the dust of thy feet against those who receive thee not**, not in their presence, lest thou provoke them, but in secret; and **wash thy feet, as a testimony against them** in the day of judgment.

> As a follow-up to verse 15, above, we will include two quotes from the 1981 *Doctrine and Covenants Student Manual* here.
>
> "The ordinance of washing the dust from one's feet was practiced in New Testament times and was reinstituted in this dispensation (see D&C 88:139–40; John 11:2; 12:3; 13:5–14). The action of shaking or cleansing the dust from one's feet is a testimony against those who refuse to accept the gospel (see D&C 24:15; 84:92; 99:4). Because of the serious nature of this act, Church leaders have directed that it be done only at the command of the Spirit. President Joseph Fielding Smith explained the significance of the action as follows: 'The cleansing of their feet, either by washing or wiping off the dust, would be recorded in heaven as a testimony against the wicked. This act, however, was not to be performed in the presence of the offenders, "lest thou provoke them, but in secret, and wash thy feet, as a testimony against them in the day of judgment." The missionaries of the Church who faithfully perform their duty are under the obligation of leaving their testimony with all with whom they come in contact in their work. This

testimony will stand as a witness against those who reject the message, at the judgment.' (*Church History and Modern Revelation,* 1:223.)" *Doctrine and Covenants Student Manual,* 1981, 130–31).

"Cursings as well as blessings may be administered by the power and authority of the priesthood (see D&C 124:93) and include the sealing up of the unbelieving and rebellious to punishment (see D&C 1:8–9). The act of cleansing the feet as a testimony against those who reject the servants of the Lord is an ordinance of cursing and is not just a demonstration that a witness of the truth has been given and has been rejected. Through this cleansing ordinance, those who rejected the truth are on their own, and those who preached the gospel to them are no longer responsible for them before the Lord (see D&C 88:81–82). It is apparent in this and other scriptures given later in the Doctrine and Covenants that this ordinance is to be performed only when the Lord expressly commands it (see also D&C 75:20–22)" (*Doctrine and Covenants Student Manual,* 1981, 50).

16 Behold, **this is sufficient for you, and the will of him** [*Christ*] **who hath sent you.**

17 And by the mouth of my servant Joseph Smith, Jun., it shall be made known concerning Sidney Rigdon and Oliver Cowdery [*Sidney and Oliver will be told more about their specific responsibilities by the Prophet*]. The residue [*the others*] hereafter. Even so. Amen.

SECTION 61

Background

This revelation was given through the Prophet Joseph Smith at McIlwaine's Bend, on the bank of the Missouri River, Friday, August 12, 1831.

Section 61 stirs much interest in the minds of members today on the subject of "curses on the waters." It also is subject to misinterpretation and misapplication because it is not kept in its proper context.

We will first give some historical background and then strive to differentiate between verses that apply to Joseph Smith's day and to those that have application in our day. Since many verses apply specifically to the 1830s, it becomes a problem when they are applied to our day.

In early August 1831, several leaders and elders were instructed to return to Ohio (D&C 58:46, 58, 63). In D&C 60:5, they were told to buy or build watercraft, whichever they preferred, in which to travel by river as they pursued their journey home. Their first destination was St. Louis. On August 9, Joseph Smith, along with ten others began their journey in canoes down the Missouri River. We will quote again from the 2018 institute manual for Doctrine and Covenants:

On August 9, 1831, the Prophet Joseph Smith and 10 elders departed Independence, Missouri, in canoes heading down the Missouri River for St. Louis. The river was difficult to navigate due to the many fallen trees submerged in the river. During the first few days of traveling, there was some conflict that arose in the group, and feelings of discord were present for a time. On the third day of the journey, a submerged tree nearly capsized the canoe that Joseph Smith and Sidney Rigdon were in. At the Prophet's urging, the group camped on the banks of the Missouri River at a place called McIlwaine's Bend. After leaving the river to make camp, William W. Phelps saw in broad daylight 'the Destroyer, in his most horrible power, ride upon the face of the waters' (*Manuscript History of the Church*, vol. A-1, page 142, josephsmithpapers.org). That evening the group discussed their difficulties, resolved their contentious feelings, and forgave one another. The next morning the Prophet received the revelation recorded in Doctrine and Covenants 61."

With these things in mind, we will now proceed with our study of this revelation. First, the Savior reminds these brethren of His power and stewardship, which gives Him power to forgive sins (which He does in verse 2).

1 BEHOLD, and **hearken unto the voice of him** [*Jesus Christ*] **who has all power, who is from everlasting to everlasting, even Alpha and Omega, the beginning and the end** [*involved in all things relating to our salvation, from premortality to the final judgment*].

2 Behold, verily [*listen carefully*] **thus saith the Lord** unto you, O ye elders of my church, who are assembled upon this spot [*on the bank of the Missouri River, by McIlwaine's Bend; see heading to section 61 in your Doctrine and Covenants*], **whose sins are now forgiven you,** for **I, the Lord, forgive sins, and am merciful unto those who confess their sins with humble hearts;**

Verse 2, above, must have been very comforting and humbling to those in the group who had been short-tempered and disagreeable with each other. Apparently, they had made peace with each other by now (see verse 20).

Next, in verse 3, they are instructed to be more missionary-minded.

3 But verily I say unto you, that **it is not needful for this whole company of mine elders to be**

moving swiftly upon the waters, whilst the inhabitants on either side are perishing in unbelief.**

4 Nevertheless, **I suffered** [*allowed*] **it** [*probably a reference to W. W. Phelps's vision of Satan riding upon the waters—see heading to this section*] **that ye might bear record**; behold, **there are many dangers upon the waters, and more especially hereafter** [*this can include things such as pollution, acid rain, warfare, tidal waves, oil spills, and so forth in the last days*];

5 For I, the Lord, have decreed in mine anger **many destructions upon the waters**; yea, and **especially upon these waters** [*the Missouri and Mississippi Rivers; the destruction can include cholera and disastrous flooding*].

> Verse 6, next, applies to the elders to whom the Lord was speaking in this revelation and can easily apply to missionaries today in the islands and elsewhere who are required to travel by water as they do their work.

6 Nevertheless, **all flesh is in mine hand** [*the Lord has all power to help and bless us*], and **he that is faithful among you shall not perish by the waters.**

7 Wherefore, it is expedient [*necessary*] that my servant Sidney Gilbert and my servant William W. Phelps be in haste upon their errand and mission [*to purchase a printing press and bring it back to Missouri*].

> According to what the Lord says next, we understand that the perils and problems that these men had experienced during the previous day were allowed in order to humble them and help them learn to work together in harmony. In context, the last phrase of verse 8 indicates that disharmony and bickering can be a serious form of wickedness.

8 Nevertheless, **I would not suffer** [*allow*] **that ye should part** [*go your separate ways to fulfill your assignments*] **until you were chastened** [*scolded*] **for all your sins, that you might be one** [*be united in harmony with each other*], **that you might not perish in wickedness;**

9 But now, verily I say, it behooveth me [*it is the Lord's will*] that ye should part. Wherefore let my servants Sidney Gilbert and William W. Phelps take their former company, and let them take their journey in haste that they may fill their mission [*to buy a printing press and take it back to Missouri*], and **through faith they shall overcome;**

The word "faith" in the last phrase of verse 9, above, is a reminder that faith is a major tool for us to use in obtaining the Lord's help.

10 And **inasmuch as they are faithful they shall be preserved, and I, the Lord, will be with them.**

11 And let the residue [*the others*] take that which is needful for clothing.

12 Let my servant Sidney Gilbert take that which is not needful [*the leftover clothing and equipment*] with him, as you shall agree [*you decide*].

> Having addressed immediate needs and given instructions, the Lord now invites these men, in effect, to come to "class" and let Him teach them about the land and the water and the cursings and blessings pronounced upon them. He will reason with them and teach them as He did His people in ancient times—see for example Isaiah 1:18, where He reasons together with them. First, in verse 13, He reminds them that commandments are given for their benefit.

13 And now, behold, **for your good I gave unto you a commandment concerning these things;** and **I, the Lord, will reason with you as with men in days of old.**

14 Behold, **I, the Lord, in the beginning blessed the waters** [*Genesis 1:20–22*]; **but in the last days,** by the mouth of my servant John [*the Apostle, who recorded the Book of Revelation*], **I cursed the waters** [*Revelation 8:8–11; 16:3–4*].

15 Wherefore, **the days will come that no flesh shall be safe upon the waters** [*this can apply to Joseph Smith's day, indicating that there will be times during flooding that no travelers will be safe on these rivers; it could also refer to the last days, when, because of warfare, tidal waves, severe pollution, terrorists, and so on, no one will be safe traveling to a particular destination on the water; see also Moses 7:66*].

Joseph Fielding Smith taught about these verses as follows:

"In the beginning the Lord blessed the waters and cursed the land, but in these last days this was reversed, the land was to be blessed and the waters to be cursed. A little reflection will bear witness to the truth of this declaration. In the early millenniums of this earth's history, men did not understand the composition of the soils, and how they needed building up when crops were taken from them. The facilities at the command of the people were primitive and limited, acreage under cultivation was limited, famines were prevalent and the luxuries which we have today were not obtainable. Someone may rise up and say that the soil in those days was just as productive as now, and this may be the case. It is not a matter of dispute, but the manner of cultivation did not lend itself to the abundant production which we are receiving today. It matters not what the causes were, in those early days of world history there could not be the production, nor the varieties of fruits coming from the earth, and the Lord can very properly speak of this as a curse, or the lack of blessing, upon the land. In those early periods we have every reason to believe that the torrents, floods, and the dangers upon the waters were not as great as they are today, and by no means as great as what the Lord has promised us. The early mariners among the ancients traversed the seas as they knew them in that day in comparative safety. . . . Today this manner of travel in such boats would be of the most dangerous and risky nature. Moreover, we have seen the dangers upon the waters increase until the hearts of men failed them and only the brave, and those who were compelled to travel the seas, ventured out upon them. In regard to the Missouri-Mississippi waters, we have seen year by year great destruction upon them, and coming from them. Millions upon millions of dollars, almost annually are lost by this great stream overflowing its banks. Many have lost their lives in these floods as they sweep over the land, and even upon this apparently tranquil or sluggish stream there can arise storms that bring destruction. Verily the word of the Lord has been, and is being, fulfilled in relation to those waters. While the Lord has spoken of the sea heaving itself beyond its bounds, and the waves roaring, yet we must include the great destruction upon the waters by means of war, and especially by submarine warfare as we have learned of it in recent years" (*Church History and Modern Revelation*, 1:224; see also Genesis 3:17–19; Ether 7:23–25; 9:16, 28; Revelation 16:1–6; Alma 45:16; D&C 59:3; 16–19).

Verse 16, next, seems to apply to Joseph Smith's day.

16 And it shall be said in days to come that **none is able to go up to the land of Zion** [*Missouri*] **upon the waters, but he that is upright in heart** [*righteous*].

Next, in verse 17, the Lord continues explaining the "blessings and curses" referred to above.

17 And, as **I, the Lord, in the beginning cursed the land** [*Genesis 3:17*], even so **in the last days have I blessed it,** in its time, for the use of my saints, that they may partake the fatness thereof.

The Lord states that He "has blessed" the land "in the last days." Verse 17, above, is a clear reference to this fact. Perhaps you've noticed that agricultural science has now made it possible to grow abundant crops in much smaller gardens and upon much smaller farms. Surely, this is a clear sign that the Lord has blessed the land in the last days.

Verses 18–29, next, seem to primarily refer to the travels of the Saints in Joseph Smith's day upon the Missouri, Mississippi, and Ohio Rivers.

18 And **now I give unto you a commandment** that what I say unto one I say unto all, that **you shall forewarn your brethren concerning these waters** [*the rivers upon which the Saints often traveled*], that they come not in journeying upon them, lest their faith fail and they are caught in snares;

19 I, the Lord, have decreed, and **the destroyer** [*Satan*] **rideth upon the face thereof**, and I revoke not the decree.

20 **I, the Lord, was angry with you yesterday** [*because of their disharmony and ill feelings toward each other; see notes in Background*], **but today mine anger is turned away.**

21 Wherefore, let those concerning whom I have spoken, that should take their journey in haste—again I say unto you, let them take their journey in haste.

Verse 22, next, is important in understanding this section. As previously stated, it is prophesied that there will be special dangers upon the waters in the last days, and there are. But verse 22 clearly shows that all water is not dangerous, and from it we understand that most water use and travel is just fine, as long as common sense is used.

22 And **it mattereth not unto me**, after a little, if it so be that they fill their mission, **whether they go by water or by land; let this be** as it is made known unto them **according to their judgments** [*common sense and wisdom*] hereafter.

23 And now, **concerning my servants, Sidney Rigdon, Joseph Smith, Jun., and Oliver Cowdery, let them come not again upon the waters, save it be upon the canal**, while journeying unto their homes [*they journeyed as instructed, arriving in Kirtland in late August*]; or in other words they shall not come upon the waters to journey, save upon the canal.

24 Behold, **I, the Lord, have appointed a way for the journeying of my saints**; and behold, this is the way—that **after they leave the canal they shall journey by land**, inasmuch as they are commanded to journey and

go up unto the land of Zion [*Missouri*];

25 And they shall do like unto the children of Israel, pitching their tents by the way.

26 And, behold, this commandment you shall give unto all your brethren.

> Verses 27–28, next, are a reminder that, when prompted by the Holy Ghost, a faithful priesthood holder could be allowed to command and the water will obey. (See D&C 61:27, footnote a.) It is also possible that these verses could apply specifically to the Prophet Joseph Smith.

27 Nevertheless, **unto whom is given power to command the waters**, unto him **it is given by the Spirit** to know all his ways;

28 Wherefore, **let him do as the Spirit of the living God commandeth him**, whether upon the land or upon the waters, as it remaineth with me to do hereafter.

29 And unto you is given the course for the saints, or the way for the saints of the camp of the Lord, to journey [*as stated in verse 24*].

> In verses 30–31, Joseph Smith and his two traveling companions are told to go straight to Cincinnati before they start to preach. Cincinnati was just a village at this time, with many dwelling there who had fled civilization to the east after having broken the law.

30 And again, verily I say unto you, my servants, **Sidney Rigdon, Joseph Smith, Jun., and Oliver Cowdery, shall not open their mouths** [*preach the gospel*] in the congregations of the wicked **until they arrive at Cincinnati**;

31 **And in that place they shall lift up their voices unto God against that people**, yea, unto him whose anger is kindled against their wickedness, **a people who are well–nigh ripened for destruction** [*just about ready to be destroyed*].

32 **And from thence** [*from Cincinnati*] **let them** [*Joseph, Sidney, and Oliver*] **journey for the congregations of their brethren** [*they may travel on home to Kirtland*], **for their labors even now are wanted more abundantly among them than among the congregations of the wicked** [*they are wanted urgently back home*].

33 And now, **concerning the residue** [*the other elders in this group of eleven to whom this revelation was given*], **let them journey and declare the word** among the congregations of the wicked,

inasmuch as it is given [*they should take time to preach along the way from here, as inspired by the Spirit*];

34 And **inasmuch as** [*if*] **they do this they shall rid their garments** [*be relieved of the responsibility for the sins of these people*], and **they shall be spotless before me** [*they will be forgiven of their own sins*].

> The phrase "they shall rid their garments" in verse 34, above, is seen in other forms elsewhere in scripture. For example, in 2 Nephi 9:44, Jacob says, "I take off my garments, and I shake them before you," symbolizing that he is "shaking their sins off his clothing" that they have now heard the gospel, and that their souls are in their own hands. He has fulfilled his duty by preaching it to them. Therefore, their sins are no longer his responsibility. In Jacob 2:2, he teaches his people in order "that I might rid my garments of your sins." Likewise, King Benjamin assembled his people in order to teach them, in order "that I might rid my garments of your blood."
>
> Next, in verse 35, the remaining elders are told that they can stay together as a group en route home to Ohio, or they can split up and go two by two. However, Reynolds Cahoon and Samuel H. Smith (the Prophet's younger brother) are to stay together regardless of what the other four decide to do.

35 And **let them journey together, or two by two**, as seemeth them good, only let my servant **Reynolds Cahoon, and my servant Samuel H. Smith**, with whom I am well pleased, **be not separated until they return to their homes**, and this for a wise purpose in me [*the Lord doesn't tell them why; they are to take it on faith*].

36 And now, verily I say unto you, and what I say unto one I say unto all, **be of good cheer, little children; for I am in your midst, and I have not forsaken you**;

> Verse 36, above, is a pleasant reminder that the Savior is often among us, as He said to these men. ("I am in your midst.")

37 And **inasmuch as you have humbled yourselves before me, the blessings of the kingdom** [*ultimately exaltation*] **are yours.**

38 Gird up your loins [*prepare for the journey*] and be watchful and be sober [*be serious about their responsibilities*], looking forth for the coming of **the Son of Man** [*Jesus, the Son of Man of Holiness (Son of the Father); see Moses 6:57*], for he **cometh in an hour you think not.**

> The end of verse 38, above, is another reminder that no one knows the exact timing of the Savior's

Second Coming. It can be cross-referenced to Matthew 24:36 and Mark 13:32.

The Prophet Joseph Smith likewise taught that no one knows the timing. He said, "Jesus Christ never did reveal to any man the precise time that He would come. Go and read the Scriptures, and you cannot find anything that specifies the exact hour He would come; and all that say so are false teachers" (*History of the Church*, 6:254).

39 Pray always that you enter not into temptation, that you may abide [*be able to survive*] the day of his coming, **whether in life or in death**. Even so. Amen.

SECTION 62

Background

Given August 13, 1831, at Chariton, Missouri, on the bank of the Missouri River, this revelation through the Prophet Joseph Smith was given to his group, who were returning to the Kirtland area from Missouri, and a group of elders who were on their way to Missouri. The Prophet gave background for this revelation as follows:

"On the 13th [August] I met several of the Elders on their way to the land of Zion, and after the joyful salutations with which brethren meet each other, who are actually 'contending for the faith once delivered to the Saints,' I received the following: [section 62]" (*History of the Church* 1:205).

The *Doctrine and Covenants Student Manual*, 1981, page 132, has a quote in which these elders coming from Kirtland to Missouri are identified. It reads,

"Reynolds Cahoon named them as follows: Hyrum Smith, John Murdock, Harvey Whitlock, and David Whitmer (see *Journal History*, 13 August 1831)."

This is a short section that contains sweet insights into the Savior's personal attention and care for His humble followers here on earth.

1 BEHOLD, and hearken, O ye elders of my church, saith the Lord your God, even **Jesus Christ, your advocate, who knoweth the weakness of man and how to succor them who are tempted**.

We will mention two things from verse 1, above. First, the term "advocate" in this context means "one who wants us to succeed and does everything in his power to help us."

Second, the word "succor" means "to hurry to help someone in distress or need."

2 And verily **mine eyes are upon those who have not as yet gone up unto the land of Zion**; wherefore **your mission is not yet full**

[*these elders have not yet completed their mission*].

Next, the Master tells them (John Murdock, David Whitmer, Harvey Whitlock, and Hyrum Smith—the Prophet's older brother) that their testimonies are recorded in heaven.

3 Nevertheless, ye are blessed, for **the testimony which ye have borne is recorded in heaven for the angels to look upon**; and they rejoice over you, and your sins are forgiven you.

We find ourselves hoping that verse 3, above, applies likewise to us. If it does, we may be able to hope that our loved ones who have already died might be able to read our testimonies when we bear them, provided that they too are recorded in heaven.

Next, the Savior instructs these men to continue on to Missouri and to hold a sacrament meeting when they get there.

4 And now **continue your journey. Assemble** yourselves **upon the land of Zion**; and **hold a meeting** and **rejoice together**, and **offer a sacrament unto the Most High**.

Did you notice in verse 4, above, that one of the major purposes of church meetings is so that we have an opportunity to get together and enjoy one another's company?

5 And then you may return [*to Kirtland*] to bear record, yea, even altogether, or two by two, as seemeth you good, **it mattereth not unto me** [*see note for D&C 60:5 for more on this*]; only **be faithful, and declare glad tidings unto the inhabitants of the earth, or among the congregations of the wicked.**

Remember, as pointed out previously, that the term "wicked," as used in this context (verse 5, above), doesn't always mean evil, truly wicked people. Rather, it can simply mean people who don't have the gospel. This is a much different meaning than we use today.

6 Behold, I, the Lord, have brought you together that the promise might be fulfilled, that the faithful among you should be preserved and rejoice together in the land of Missouri. **I, the Lord**, promise the faithful and **cannot lie**.

It helps, as we continue to verse 7, to understand that John Murdock was so sick and weak at this time that he was unable to continue the journey to Jackson County. After the Lord's counsel to them in verse 7, these four men pooled their money and bought a horse for Brother Murdock to ride the rest of the way to Zion.

7 I, the Lord, am willing, **if any among you desire to ride upon horses, or upon mules, or in chariots, he shall receive this blessing**, if he receive it from the hand of the Lord, **with a thankful heart in all things** [*another reminder of the importance of gratitude*].

8 These things remain with you to do according to judgment and the directions of the Spirit.

> The phrase "the kingdom is yours," in verse 9, next, is most reassuring. It is another way of saying that if we keep sincerely progressing, we can make it to celestial exaltation despite present weaknesses and imperfections.

9 Behold, **the kingdom is yours**. And behold, and lo, I am with the faithful always. Even so. Amen.

SECTION 63

Background

> In editions previous to the 2013 edition of the Doctrine and Covenants, the date of this revelation was given as "late in August 1831." However, based on research for the Joseph Smith Papers Project, the date is now known to be August 30, 1831. It was given through Joseph Smith in Kirtland, Ohio. The Prophet had now arrived back in Kirtland, having traveled the nine hundred miles from Jackson County, Missouri, in nineteen days.
>
> Although many members of the Church in the Kirtland area were faithful and deeply committed to the Lord and His newly restored Church, some were not. They claimed to be members and wanted the blessings of the gospel but were not keeping the commandments. In fact, while the Prophet was gone to Missouri, many in Kirtland had grumbled, and some had apostatized. Some apparently wanted more obvious evidence from God that this was His church. Lustful thinking and sexual immorality also seem to have become a problem among some of the members in Kirtland. These conditions among the members in Ohio seem to make up the background and setting for verses 1–21. The wicked and rebellious in the Kirtland area receive a severe chastisement from the Savior Himself in these verses.
>
> Continuing on, beginning with verse 22, the Lord gives these members specific instructions concerning Kirtland as well as Zion (in Jackson County, Missouri), giving much prophecy and pointing their minds forward to the time of His Second Coming and the Millennium. He gives encouragement to the righteous (example: verses 47–49) and warns all of the members not to be among the "foolish virgins" (verse 54).

The revelation concludes with specific instructions to Sidney Rigdon about his written description of Zion (verses 55–56) and a clear reminder of the importance of missionary work, the seriousness of covenants, the necessity of respect for the name of God, and the need for patience with themselves as the Saints strive to overcome sins and shortcomings.

It's a good idea at times as you are studying the scriptures to "step back," so to speak, and look for major messages and patterns. By so doing, you give the Spirit additional opportunities to teach you. Section 63 lends itself nicely to this approach in studying. If you "step back" and look at this section from an overall perspective, you will see an interesting pattern in how the Savior is dealing with the problems among the Saints in Kirtland. It is similar to how He sometimes deals with us as we have need to repent. In a very real sense, this is a pattern for parenting.

Pattern for Parenting

<u>First</u>—He explains the problems (verses 1–21).

<u>Second</u>—He gives them specific things to do and gives counsel that will help them repent and overcome the problems (verses 22–46, 55–66).

<u>Third</u>—He gives them something to look forward to by pointing their minds ahead to the blessings and rewards of obedience and living the gospel (verses 47–54).

With this in mind, we will use **bold** to point out the problems He addresses in the text of verses 1–21. We will go through these verses first without commentary, other than using **bold** for emphasis, so that you can see at a glance what the Lord's concerns are. Then we will repeat the verses and add commentary. You may wish to read just the **bolded** words and phrases the first time through.

1 **HEARKEN**, O ye people, and open your hearts and give ear from afar; and listen, **you that call yourselves the people of the Lord,** and hear the word of the Lord and his will concerning you.

2 Yea, verily, I say, **hear the word of him whose anger is kindled against the wicked and rebellious**;

3 Who willeth to take even them whom he will take, and preserveth in life them whom he will preserve;

4 Who buildeth up at his own will and pleasure; and destroyeth when he pleases, **and is able to cast the soul down to hell.**

5 Behold, **I, the Lord, utter my voice, and it shall be obeyed.**

6 Wherefore, verily I say, **let the wicked take heed,** and **let the rebellious fear and tremble;** and **let the unbelieving hold their lips, for the day of wrath shall come** upon them as a whirlwind, and all flesh shall know that I am God.

7 And **he that seeketh signs shall see signs, but not unto salvation.**

8 Verily, I say unto you, **there are those among you who seek signs,** and there have been such even from the beginning;

9 But, behold, **faith cometh not by signs, but signs follow those that believe.**

10 Yea, **signs come by faith, not by the will of men, nor as they please, but by the will of God.**

11 Yea, signs come by faith, unto mighty works, for **without faith no man pleaseth God;** and **with whom God is angry he is not well pleased;** wherefore, **unto such he showeth no signs, only in wrath unto their condemnation.**

12 Wherefore, **I, the Lord, am not pleased with those among you who have sought after signs and wonders for faith, and not for the good of men unto my glory.**

13 Nevertheless, I give commandments, and **many have turned away from my commandments and have not kept them.**

14 **There were among you adulterers and adulteresses; some of whom have turned away from you, and others remain with you** that hereafter shall be revealed.

15 **Let such beware and repent speedily, lest judgment shall come upon them as a snare, and their folly shall be made manifest, and their works shall follow them in the eyes of the people.**

16 And verily I say unto you, as I have said before, **he that looketh on a woman to lust after her, or if any shall commit adultery in their hearts, they shall not have the Spirit, but shall deny the faith and shall fear.**

17 Wherefore, I, the Lord, have said that **the fearful, and the unbelieving, and all liars, and whosoever loveth and maketh a lie, and the whoremonger, and the sorcerer, shall have their part in that lake which burneth with fire and brimstone, which is the second death.**

18 Verily I say, that **they shall not have part in the first resurrection.**

19 And now behold, I, the Lord,

say unto you that **ye are not justified, because these things are among you.**

20 **Nevertheless, he that endureth in faith and doeth my will, the same shall overcome, and shall receive an inheritance upon the earth when the day of transfiguration shall come;**

21 **When the earth shall be transfigured**, even according to the pattern which was shown unto mine Apostles upon the mount; of which account the fulness ye have not yet received.

> As you can see, there are many problems among the Saints in Ohio at this point in Church history, not unlike those among members today. As mentioned previously, we will now repeat verses 1–21, adding commentary. First, the Lord addresses the members who call themselves faithful members but who are actually not.

1 **HEARKEN**, O ye people, and open your hearts and give ear from afar; and listen, **you that call yourselves the people of the Lord** [*implying that they "call" themselves Saints but are not*], and hear the word of the Lord and his will concerning you.

> Next, in verses 2–6, the Lord gives a concise, to-the-point warning and lesson about the reality of His role in disciplining the rebellious. Such strong wording from a loving God is often needed to get the attention of people who think they are doing rather well but in reality are blinded to the dangers of the direction their life is taking. In D&C 95:1, the Savior reminds us that "whom I love I also chasten that their sins may be forgiven, for with the chastisement I prepare a way for their deliverance in all things out of temptation."

2 Yea, verily, I say, **hear the word of him** [*Christ*] **whose anger is kindled against the wicked and rebellious;**

3 **Who willeth to take even them whom he will take** [*remove from the earth*], **and preserveth in life them whom he will preserve;**

4 **Who buildeth up** at his own will and pleasure; **and destroyeth** when he pleases, **and is able to cast the soul down to hell** [*Jesus is our final judge; see John 5:22*].

5 Behold, **I, the Lord, utter my voice, and it shall be obeyed.**

6 **Wherefore** [*therefore*], verily I say, **let the wicked take heed, and let the rebellious fear and tremble;** and **let the unbelieving hold their lips** [*including that they should stop murmuring and complaining*], for the day of wrath [*punishments*] shall come upon

them as a whirlwind, and **all flesh shall know that I am God.**

> Next, in verses 7–12, the topic of seeking signs is addressed. This is a context-sensitive issue. Faith-obedience brings "signs" or blessings, which are appropriate and strengthen testimony and build character. Signs that are demanded as proof of God's existence or as obvious evidence of His involvement are inappropriate and a sign of rebellion and arrogance on the part of those who demand them.
>
> Thus, the "signs" spoken of here, which are out of order, are those that people demand from God before they will be obedient. In effect, they are saying, "Show me the blessings, and then I will obey the commandments. Bless me first and then I will pay tithing. Bless me first and then I will donate money to buy land in Zion." Demanding evidence from God first, before obedience, hardens and damages the soul. On the other hand, faith softens the soul and makes it moldable and pliable in the hands of the Master. When people move ahead with faith, before the blessings or results are known, they grow in character and strength toward God.

7 And **he that seeketh signs shall see signs, but not unto salvation** [*in other words, those who arrogantly demand proof of potential blessings before they will obey God will ultimately see plenty of evidence that God exists when He punishes them; see last part of verse 11*].

8 Verily, I say unto you, **there are those among you who seek signs**, and there have been such even from the beginning;

> Next, we are reminded that faith in the hearts and actions of the righteous does produce signs, and that God carefully controls these miracles and blessings so that they are truly a benefit to His Saints.

9 But, behold, **faith cometh not by signs, but signs follow those that believe.**

10 Yea, **signs come by faith, not by the will of men, nor as they please, but by the will of God.**

11 Yea, signs come by faith, unto mighty works, for **without faith no man pleaseth God** [*no accountable person can be saved without faith*]; and **with whom God is angry he is not well pleased; wherefore, unto such he showeth no signs, only in wrath unto their condemnation** [*in the form of punishments and being stopped in personal progression*].

> As this lesson on sign-seeking continues, we are reminded that it is usually the case that signs demanded by the wicked and

rebellious are generally not the kind of signs that would be for the good of others. This could include such signs as would not foster spiritual growth and goodness, rather, the building up of one's self in the eyes of others, selfish pleasure, pride, and so forth.

12 Wherefore, **I, the Lord, am not pleased with those among you who have sought after signs and wonders for faith**, and **not for the good of men** unto my glory.

13 Nevertheless, I give commandments, and **many have turned away from my commandments and have not kept them**.

Next, in verses 14–16, the Lord addresses the spiritually damaging effects of lustful thinking and sexual immorality, which had apparently become a serious problem among some of the Ohio Saints. He mercifully also reminds these members that such sins can be repented of and thus forgiven.

14 **There were among you adulterers and adulteresses; some** of whom **have turned away from you, and others remain with you** that hereafter shall be revealed.

15 **Let such beware and repent speedily**, lest judgment shall come upon them as a snare, and **their folly shall be made manifest, and their works shall follow them in the eyes of the people**.

One of my students once asked why sexual intimacy outside of marriage is such a serious sin since science and modern medicine make it so easy and convenient to prevent conception. This question, of course, got the immediate full attention of everyone in class. I was most grateful for verse 16, next, in which the Lord gives an answer to this question.

16 And verily I say unto you, as I have said before [*in D&C 42:23*], **he that looketh on a woman to lust after her, or if any shall commit adultery in their hearts, they shall not have the Spirit, but shall deny the faith and shall fear.**

As you can see, from the bolded portion of verse 16, above, one reason that immoral behavior is so serious is that it drives the Spirit away, leaving people insensitive to spiritual things and vulnerable to becoming inactive in the Church, as well as living in fear of the punishments of God.

Next, in verse 17, we see a list of several sins that when not repented of will lead the sinner to being turned over to Satan to pay for his or her own sins and ultimately end up in the telestial kingdom on the day of final judgment (see also D&C 76:103 and Revelation 22:15).

17 Wherefore [*this is why*], I, the Lord, have said that **the fearful** [*afraid to do right*], and the **unbelieving, and all liars, and whosoever loveth and maketh a lie, and the whoremonger** [*people whose lives are centered on sexual immorality*], **and the sorcerer** [*including witchcraft, devil worship, and the occult*], **shall have their part in that lake which burneth with fire and brimstone** [*will be punished for their own sins; see D&C 19:15–17; 76:84–85*], **which is the second death** [*being cut off from living in the direct presence of God*].

18 Verily I say, that **they shall not have part in the first resurrection** [*telestials are not resurrected with the righteous but must wait until the end of the Millennium for resurrection; see D&C 88:100–101*].

> Verse 19, next, uses the word "justified." In a general sense, as most often used in the scriptures (for example, see Moses 6:60), "justified" means those who are ratified at the final judgment as worthy to live forever in the presence of God and Christ in celestial glory.
>
> The word "justified" as used in verse 19, next, means to "be right before God." In other words, to be worthy for the full blessings of the Lord.

19 And now behold, I, the Lord, say unto you that **ye are not justified** [*worthy to enter celestial glory*]**, because these things** [*the sins and concerns mentioned in the above verses*] **are among you.**

> As you read verse 20, next, notice the encouragement given by the Savior to these members who are being chastised for their sins. It is not too late for them to "overcome" and be found worthy to "inherit the earth" (the earth will become the celestial kingdom for those of us who live worthy of obtaining celestial glory; see D&C 130:9–11).

20 Nevertheless, **he that endureth in faith and doeth my will, the same shall overcome** [*overcome sin and evil with the help of Christ and His Atonement*]**, and shall receive an inheritance upon the earth when the day of transfiguration shall come;**

21 **When the earth shall be transfigured**, even according to the pattern which was shown unto mine Apostles upon the mount [*the Mount of Transfiguration; see Matthew 17:1–3, 9*]; of which account the fulness ye have not yet received [*we have not yet been given a full account of what took place when Jesus was transfigured on the mountain about six months before His crucifixion and resurrection*].

> Looking back at verses 20–21, the earth will actually go through

two "transfigurations." One is when it is transfigured from a "telestial" globe to a "terrestrial" globe as it receives its "paradisiacal glory" at the beginning of the Millennium (Articles of Faith 1:10). The second is when it is changed into a celestial planet (D&C 130:9), moved back into the presence of the Father where it was first created (*Teachings of the Prophet Joseph Smith*, 181), and becomes the celestial kingdom for those from this earth who are worthy of celestial glory.

As we continue with verse 22, we see an insightful phrase reminding us of the Lord's kindness and patience with us. Notice that He says, "not by the way of commandment." Then, in verse 23, He says that there are special blessings for those who keep the commandments.

22 And now, verily I say unto you, that as I said that I would make known my will unto you, behold I will make it known unto you, **not by the way of commandment,** for **there are many who observe not to keep my commandments.**

23 **But unto him that keepeth my commandments I will give the mysteries of my kingdom** [*the doctrines, principles, and ordinances of the plan of salvation; not "mysterious and strange things"; see the Bible Dictionary under* "*Mystery*"]**, and the same** [*the gospel*] **shall be in him a well of living water, springing up unto everlasting life** [*bringing him to exaltation*].

Do you see the messages in verses 22–23, above? Certainly, one major message is that we can't be forced to heaven. Another is that those who have a good attitude toward studying the gospel and abiding by its teachings will want to live by every word from God, whether it comes by way of commandment or counsel. Attitude is critically important in becoming celestial.

Next, the Lord gives additional instructions concerning Zion in Jackson County, Missouri. Again, the Saints are reminded that the gathering to Missouri is to be done in order and with wisdom.

24 And now, behold, **this is the will of the Lord your God concerning his saints,** that **they should assemble** themselves together **unto the land of Zion, not in haste,** lest there should be confusion, which bringeth pestilence [*all kinds of trouble*].

A quote from the 2018 Doctrine and Covenants Student Manual helps us understand "not in haste" in verse 24, above.

"To manage the number of Saints gathering to Zion, Church leaders

SECTION 63

required those in Ohio desiring to go to Missouri to obtain a Church-issued certificate before they could migrate and participate in the law of consecration in Missouri. However, many enthusiastic members disregarded the instruction and went to Missouri in large numbers. A Church historian appointed by the Prophet Joseph Smith later wrote, 'The church immediately began to gather in Jackson County, and on this subject they became quite enthusiastic. They had been commanded not to go up in haste, nor by flight, but to have all things prepared before them. Money was to be sent up to the bishop, and as fast as lands were purchased, and preparations made, the bishop was to let it be known, that the church might be gathered in. But this regulation was not attended to, for the church got crazy to go up to Zion, as it was then called. The rich were afraid to send up their money to purchase lands, and the poor crowded up in numbers, without having any places provided, contrary to the advice of the bishop and others, until the old citizens began to be highly displeased' (John Corrill, *A Brief History of the Church of Christ of Latter Day Saints* [1839], 18–19, josephsmithpapers.org; see also *The Joseph Smith Papers, Histories, Volume 2: Assigned Histories, 1831–1847*, ed. Karen Lynn Davidson and others [2012], 146)."

25 **Behold, the land of Zion—I, the Lord, hold it in mine own hands** [*the Lord owns the whole earth, including Zion, and has power over it*];

26 Nevertheless, **I, the Lord, render unto Caesar the things which are Caesar's.** [*A reference to Luke 20:25. In effect, the Lord could clear the land of Zion and simply turn it over to the Saints; however, it is proper that the members purchase land in Zion from the legal owners. In other words, "Pay Caesar for the things Caesar owns." Respect man-made governments. Among other things, they prevent chaos and anarchy.*]

27 Wherefore, **I the Lord will that you should purchase the lands**, that you may have advantage of the world, that you may have claim on the world [*so that the civil government's legal system will be obligated to support their ownership of the land*], that they may not be stirred up unto anger.

28 **For Satan putteth it into their hearts to anger against you, and to the shedding of blood.**

Next, we see that there are basically just two options for obtaining the land on which to build Zion in Missouri.

29 Wherefore, the land of Zion shall not be obtained but [*except*]

by purchase or by blood [*bloodshed*], otherwise there is none inheritance for you.

30 And **if by purchase,** behold **you are blessed**;

31 And **if by blood**, as you are forbidden to shed blood, lo, your enemies are upon you, and **ye shall be scourged from city to city, and from synagogue to synagogue,** and but few shall stand to receive an inheritance.

> Next, in verse 32, we see that as people reject truth and righteousness, going against their consciences and the commandments of God, His Spirit withdraws, with the resulting wars and devastations described in verse 33. The world is experiencing this now.

32 I, the Lord, am angry with the wicked; **I am holding my Spirit from the inhabitants of the earth.**

33 **I have** sworn in my wrath, and **decreed wars** upon the face of the earth, **and the wicked shall slay the wicked**, and **fear shall come upon every man;**

> Left alone, verses 32–33, above, could be quite discouraging for the righteous. Verse 34, next, must be included with them for a complete picture. With it included, we see that the Saints will have difficulties because of the wickedness of the world but that the Lord will be with them.

34 **And the saints also shall hardly escape; nevertheless, I, the Lord, am with them**, and will come down in heaven from the presence of my Father and consume the wicked with unquenchable fire [*a reference to the Second Coming*].

It is important to understand the phrase, in verse 34, above, that says, "the Saints also shall hardly escape." The Prophet Joseph Smith addressed this subject. He said:

"It is a false idea that the Saints will escape all the judgments, whilst the wicked suffer; for all flesh is subject to suffer, and 'the righteous shall hardly escape;' still many of the Saints will escape, for the just shall live by faith; yet many of the righteous shall fall a prey to disease, to pestilence, etc., by reason of the weakness of the flesh, and yet be saved in the Kingdom of God. So that it is an unhallowed principle to say that such and such have transgressed because they have been preyed upon by disease or death, for all flesh is subject to death; and the Savior has said, 'Judge not, lest ye be judged'" (*History of the Church*, 4:11).

The messages and counsel of our current prophet and other Church leaders must also be included with

SECTION 63

verses 32–34, above, if we are to avoid gloom, despair, and pessimism in our own lives. One of the strongest messages from them is for us to avoid getting caught up in gloom and doom. Rather, we are reminded that this is a wonderful time to be alive. President Gordon B. Hinckley said during general conference in October 2001 (**bold** added for emphasis):

"I do not know what we did in the preexistence to merit the wonderful blessings we enjoy. We have come to earth in this great season in the long history of mankind. **It is a marvelous age, the best of all**" ("Living in the Fulness of Times," *Ensign,* November 2001, 4).

Verse 35, next, tells us that, even though the Second Coming is close, it is not yet here. This may sound obvious, but remember that there were some in Joseph Smith's day, such as the Shaking Quakers (see heading to section 49 in your Doctrine and Covenants) who taught that the Savior had already come. Likewise, there are some today who teach that He is already here, that His Second Coming has occurred but that the Millennium has not yet begun.

35 And behold, **this** [*the Second Coming*] **is not yet, but by and by**.

As you know, there are usually many different messages and lessons we can get from a given verse or set of verses. What the Holy Ghost teaches us is determined by our situation and needs at the time or for future use. Therefore, as we read our scriptures, we get one message one time and another the next time, and so forth. There are many different messages we could get from verses 36–37, next. We will choose to read them for helps in surviving the last days and will use **bold** to point them out.

36 Wherefore, seeing that I, the Lord, have decreed all these things [*the last day's calamities and destructions leading up to the Second Coming*] upon the face of the earth, **I will that my saints should be assembled** upon the land of Zion [*in terms of our surviving the last days, this verse can mean for us to gather with the faithful Saints, in our branches, wards, and stakes, no matter where we live*];

37 And that every man should **take righteousness** in his hands [*use personal righteousness as a weapon to defend yourself against wickedness*] **and faithfulness** upon his loins [*clothe yourself with faithfulness to God*], **and lift a warning voice** unto the inhabitants of the earth [*explain and teach the gospel to those around you*]; and **declare both by word and by flight that desolation shall come upon the wicked** [*teach the gospel with words and by example as you*

avoid and flee (when necessary) the wickedness that is enveloping the world].

38 Wherefore, **let my disciples** [*members of the Church*] **in Kirtland arrange their temporal concerns**, who dwell upon this farm [*the farm in Kirtland upon which Titus Billings and others were living*].

> Next, the Lord tells Titus Billings to sell the farm, mentioned in verse 38, above, and move to Jackson County, Missouri, in the spring, along with several other Saints currently living on that farm. (Some Saints were to remain in Kirtland until later). Brother Billings did so, leading a small company of Latter-day Saints to Zion in the spring and consecrating the proceeds from the sale of the farm to the Church in Zion. He died faithful to the Church, in Provo, Utah, on February 6, 1866, at age seventy-two. Obedience pays big dividends.

39 **Let my servant Titus Billings**, who has the care thereof, **dispose of** [*sell*] **the land**, that he may be prepared in the coming spring to take his journey up unto the land of Zion, with those that dwell upon the face thereof [*with others who live on the farm*], excepting those whom I shall reserve unto myself, that shall not go until I shall command them.

40 And let all the moneys which can be spared [*you decide how much you need for traveling and how much can be given for building Zion*], **it mattereth not unto me whether it be little or much**, be sent up unto the land of Zion, unto them whom I have appointed to receive.

> Did you notice the important message in verse 40, above? The Lord said that it does not matter to Him how much or how little money is given in such donations. This can apply to us in the sense that it is up to us to decide how much we pay for fast offering, humanitarian aid, missionary fund, and so forth (except tithing in which it does matter; it is 10 percent). Perhaps you've noticed that the Brethren steadfastly avoid giving you a dollar amount to pay with respect to these other voluntary contributions to the Church. They likewise counsel local leaders of the Church to avoid setting quotas for temple attendance. It is up to each member to decide since it is a part of the law of consecration. And the law of consecration operates on celestial standards—in other words, on the basic goodness, generosity, unselfishness, honesty, and integrity of participants. The same principles apply to the visiting of the sick, the number of children to have and when to have them, seniors serving missions, and so forth.

Next, in verse 41, the Savior tells these Saints that He will instruct the Prophet as to who is to go to Missouri and who is to stay in Ohio for a season.

41 Behold, **I, the Lord, will give unto my servant Joseph Smith, Jun., power** that he shall be enabled **to discern** by the Spirit those **who shall go up unto the land of Zion, and** those of my disciples **who shall tarry** [*stay put*].

42 **Let my servant Newel K. Whitney retain his store** [*the Newel K. Whitney Store in Kirtland*], or in other words, the store, **yet for a little season.**

43 Nevertheless, **let him impart** [*donate*] **all the money which he can impart, to be sent up unto the land of Zion.**

44 Behold, **these things are in his own hands, let him do according to wisdom** [*he is free to decide for himself; another illustration of the principles of agency and integrity inseparably associated with the law of consecration.*]

45 Verily I say, **let him be ordained** [*set apart*] **as an agent unto the disciples that shall tarry** [*the Church members who remain in Ohio*], and let him be ordained unto this power;

Next, in verse 46, Newel K. Whitney and Oliver Cowdery are instructed to spread the word quickly among the branches of the Church in Ohio, explaining the need for donations to buy land in Zion, and to collect donations as they go. The present value as well as the eternal value of obedience to God's instructions is emphasized in verses 47–48.

46 And now **speedily visit the churches**, expounding [*explaining and teaching*] these things unto them, **with my servant Oliver Cowdery.** Behold, this is my will, **obtaining moneys** even as I have directed.

47 **He that is faithful and endureth shall overcome the world** [*will overcome the sins and temptations of the world*].

48 He that sendeth up treasures unto the land of Zion shall receive an inheritance in this world, **and his works shall follow him, and also a reward in the world to come.**

In verses 49–54, the Lord points the minds and hearts of these Saints to the future, to the Second Coming and the Millennium, giving them perspective as to the blessings that will someday come to the righteous. Such perspective gives strength that helps with present burdens and difficulties encountered because of obedience to God's commandments and counsel.

49 Yea, and **blessed are the dead that die in the Lord** [*who die righteous*], from henceforth, **when the Lord shall come** [*the Second Coming*], and old things shall pass away, and all things become new [*D&C 29:24*], **they shall rise from the dead** and shall not die after, **and shall receive an inheritance before the Lord, in the holy city.**

Among other possibilities, the "holy city" mentioned at the end of verse 49, above, could be a reference to Zion, or the New Jerusalem in Missouri, which will be one of two cities that will serve as headquarters for the Savior and His Church during the Millennium (see Ether 13:1–11).

Also, in Revelation 21:2, a "holy city" is spoken of that symbolizes the celestialized earth (see heading to Revelation 21 in your Bible); or, in other words, the celestial kingdom for those from this earth.

Either way, to "receive an inheritance before the Lord, in the holy city," verse 49, above, can be interpreted to mean that the faithful Saints can look forward to being with the Savior in the future, no matter what happens to them in this mortal life.

Next, we are taught that faithful Saints who are still alive when the Savior comes will live during the Millennium to a specified age and then die. This answers the question sometimes asked as to whether mortals who live during the Millennium will actually die or simply be resurrected without dying. They will die but will be resurrected immediately, "in the twinkling of an eye" (see verse 51, and D&C 101:31).

50 And **he that liveth when the Lord shall come, and hath kept the faith** [*was faithful on earth*], blessed is he; nevertheless, **it is appointed to him to die at the age of man.**

How old is the "age of man" (verse 50, above)? Isaiah said that people will live to be one hundred years old during the Millennium (Isaiah 65:20). Joseph Fielding Smith also spoke of this. He said (**bold** added for emphasis):

"When Christ comes the saints who are on the earth will be quickened and caught up to meet him. This does not mean that those who are living in mortality at that time will be changed and pass through the resurrection, for mortals must remain on the earth until after the thousand years are ended. A change, nevertheless, will come over all who remain on the earth; they will be quickened so that they will not be subject unto death until they are old. Men shall die when they are **one hundred years of age**, and the change shall be made suddenly to the immortal state. Graves will not be made during this thousand years. . . . Death shall come as a peaceful transition from the mortal to the immortal state" (*Way to Perfection*, 298–99, 311).

51 Wherefore, **children shall grow up until they become old; old men shall die; but they shall not sleep in the dust** [*they will not be buried*], **but they shall be changed in the twinkling of an eye** [*resurrected immediately*].

52 Wherefore, **for this cause preached the Apostles unto the world the resurrection of the dead** [*perhaps meaning that the Savior's Apostles of old likewise preached about these things to strengthen faithful Saints back then in living the gospel despite difficulties and persecutions*].

53 **These things are the things that ye must look for** [*it helps us live the gospel when we understand and look forward to these things*]; and, **speaking after the manner of the Lord** [*speaking in terms of the Lord's time*], **they are now nigh at hand**, and in a time to come, even in **the day of the coming of the Son of Man.**

Next, the Lord uses imagery and symbolism from the parable of the ten virgins (Matthew 25:1–13) as He explains that some members of the Church will be wise and some foolish when it comes to being prepared to meet the Savior. The righteous will not be completely separated from the wicked until the Second Coming.

54 And **until that hour** [*up until the Second Coming*] **there will be foolish virgins among the wise**; and **at that hour cometh an entire separation of the righteous and the wicked**; and in that day will I send mine angels to pluck out the wicked and cast them into unquenchable fire [*the wicked will be destroyed at the Second Coming*].

The topic now changes to the description of Zion in Jackson County, Missouri, which the Lord asked Sidney Rigdon to write (see D&C 58:50–51). As you will see in verses 55–56, his first attempt was not acceptable to the Lord. He will make another attempt and it will be accepted.

55 And now behold, verily I say unto you, **I, the Lord, am not pleased with my servant Sidney Rigdon**; he exalted himself in his heart, and received not counsel, but grieved the Spirit;

56 Wherefore **his writing** [*written description of Zion*] **is not acceptable unto the Lord,** and **he shall make another**; and if the Lord receive it not, behold he standeth

no longer in the office to which I have appointed him.

> In a sense, the prospective missionaries spoken of in verse 57, next, could be like potential senior missionaries today. If they desire to serve, they are to make it known and they will be called on missions.

57 And again, verily I say unto you, **those who desire in their hearts**, in meekness, **to warn sinners to repentance, let them be ordained unto this power.**

58 For **this is a day of warning, and not a day of many words** [*missionaries need to preach the gospel simply and directly*]. For I, the Lord, am not to be mocked in the last days.

> Next, in verses 59–60, the Lord reminds us of His power and influence over all things. One message we gain from this is that the wicked cannot successfully escape from Him and the consequences of sin. A more pleasant message is that it is completely safe for us to follow Him.

59 Behold, **I am from above**, and **my power lieth beneath. I am over all**, and **in all**, and **through all**, and **search all things** [*He knows all that is going on*], and the day cometh [*likely a direct reference to the Second Coming and the Millennium*] that all things shall be subject unto me.

60 Behold, **I am Alpha and Omega, even Jesus Christ**.

> While verses 61–64 can easily be used to preach against swearing and profanity and using the name of God in vain, there is another aspect of these verses in the context of this section that also fits.
>
> As stated earlier, those addressed directly in this section are members of the Church. They have taken upon them the name of Christ, having made covenants with the Father in the Savior's name. They have, in effect, spoken His name with their lips as they have made covenants and taken His name upon them through baptism, and some of them have taken it "in vain" because they are now breaking their covenants and rebelling. They have offended the Spirit (verse 64) as they have mocked and ridiculed the sacred things that have come "from above," either by their complaining or their sinful acts.
>
> Thus, taking "the name of the Lord ... in vain" can mean making covenants and then breaking them, treating lightly "that which cometh from above" (the gospel of Jesus Christ, revelation, inspiration, the words of the prophets, and so forth).

61 Wherefore, **let all men beware how they take my name in their lips—**

SECTION 63

62 For behold, verily I say, that **many there be who are under this condemnation** [*have committed this sin*], **who use the name of the Lord, and use it in vain,** having not authority [*among other things, perhaps meaning that they are not the leaders of the Church and do not have the authority to correct the Prophet and criticize the leaders*].

63 Wherefore, **let the church repent of their sins, and I, the Lord, will own them** [*Jesus will accept them now and on Judgment Day*]; otherwise they shall be cut off.

> Elder James E. Talmage explained various aspects of taking the name of the Lord in vain. He said:
>
> "1. We may take the name of God in vain by profane speech.
>
> "2. We take it in vain when we swear falsely, not being true to our oaths and promises.
>
> "3. We take it in vain in a blasphemous sense when we presume to speak in that name without authority.
>
> "4. And we take his name in vain whenever we willfully do aught [anything] that is in defiance of his commandments, since we have taken his name upon ourselves" (In Conference Report, October 1931, 53).

Yet another important message, in verse 64, next, is that we must speak about sacred things with reverence and respect, avoiding inappropriate humor involving deity and Church leaders, not reducing sacred and holy things to the common and crude.

64 Remember that **that which cometh from above is sacred, and must be spoken with care, and by constraint of the Spirit**; and in this there is no condemnation, and **ye receive the Spirit through prayer**; wherefore, without this there remaineth condemnation.

> Joseph and Sidney followed the instructions given in verse 65, next, and accepted the invitation of John Johnson to live with him and his family on their farm in Hiram, Ohio, about thirty miles southeast of Kirtland. Joseph and Emma moved in with the Johnsons on September 12, 1831. The great revelation known as section 76, giving details about the three degrees of glory and perdition, will be given in the Johnson home in February 1832.
>
> The John Johnson home has now been restored by the Church and is one of the prime Church history attractions in the Kirtland area.

65 **Let my servants, Joseph Smith, Jun., and Sidney Rigdon,**

seek them a home [*in the Kirtland area*], as they are taught through prayer by the Spirit.

In verse 66, the Savior gives a final word of counsel and comfort.

66 **These things remain to overcome through patience** [*the concerns and instructions addressed in this section must still be overcome, and patience will be needed*], **that such may receive a more exceeding and eternal weight of glory** [*it is worth overcoming sins and shortcomings*], **otherwise, a greater condemnation. Amen.**

Before we leave this section, it is worth taking another look at the word "patience" in verse 66, above. We will mention three aspects of patience here:

1. Patience with others, in order to work together with them in harmony.

2. Patience with yourself, so that you don't cripple personal progress with self-criticism and condemnation.

3. Patience with the leaders of the Church so that you don't find yourself criticizing them.

You may wish to read Alma 32 again and look at the important role of "patience," especially as emphasized in verses 41, 42, and 43.

SECTION 64

Background

This revelation through the Prophet Joseph Smith was given in Kirtland, Ohio, on September 11, 1831, just one day before Joseph moved his family to the John Johnson home in Hiram, Ohio, about thirty miles southeast of Kirtland. Sidney Rigdon likewise moved to the Johnson farm. One of the main reasons for the move was to have the uninterrupted time necessary to resume the translation of the Bible, which work had been temporarily set aside during the Prophet's recent travels to Missouri.

Sidney Rigdon was serving as scribe for Joseph during the inspired revision of the Bible. This work today is known as the Joseph Smith Translation of the Bible, or JST. As you have perhaps noticed, there are many footnotes in our Church's edition of the Bible that give corrections and additions to the Bible text. There is also a short section at the back of our Bible titled the "Joseph Smith Translation," which contains longer corrections and additions.

Joseph Fielding Smith gave some background to this section. He said:

"Because of interference and because he needed a quiet place in which to work, the Prophet on

SECTION 64

September 12, 1831, moved to the home of John Johnson in the township of Hiram. This was in Portage County, Ohio, about thirty miles southeast of Kirtland. From the time he moved until early in October, the Prophet spent most of his spare time preparing for the continuation of the translation of the Bible. By translation is meant a revision of the Bible by inspiration or revelation as the Lord had commanded him, and which was commenced as early as June 1830. (D.H.C. 1:215.) Sidney Rigdon continued to write for the Prophet in the work of revision. The day before the Prophet moved from Kirtland he received an important revelation, section 64, as it now appears in the Doctrine and Covenants. This revelation contained a wealth of information, counsel and warning, for the guidance of the members of the Church. In it the Lord said: 'Behold, thus saith the Lord your God unto you, O ye elders of my church, hearken ye and hear, and receive my will concerning you. For verily I say unto you, I will that ye should overcome the world; wherefore I will have compassion upon you.' Then it is made known that the keys of the mysteries of the kingdom were to remain with Joseph Smith while he lived inasmuch as he should obey the Lord's ordinances. We learned in an earlier revelation that this same promise was made to him, with the warning that if he should fail he would still have power to appoint or ordain his successor, and the Church was instructed that no other was appointed or would be, to give revelations for the Church and this was to be a law unto the Church. This might have saved some ambitious individuals from the pitfalls laid by the adversary, and some who were foolish enough to follow them, if they had been properly impressed with this plain and logical doctrine. (Sec. 43:3–6.) The Lord declared that there were some who had sought occasion against the Prophet, but without cause. This has been true in the case of each of his successors in the Presidency of the Church. The Lord pointed out the fact that the Prophet had sinned, nothing very grievous, but he had shown repentance, and there are 'sins unto death.' (See 64:7; 1 John 5:16.) A sin unto death merits no forgiveness" (Joseph Fielding Smith, *Church History and Modern Revelation,* 2:7–8).

Additional background that is helpful in understanding this section has to do with Ezra Booth (verse 15). He was a Methodist minister and close friend of John Johnson. He was converted to the Church in about May 1831 when he saw the Prophet Joseph Smith command Brother Johnson's wife, Elsa, to be healed. Ezra witnessed the immediate healing of her lame arm (see *History of the Church*, 1:215–16). Ezra was ordained a high priest on June 3, 1831, and served a mission to Missouri as instructed by the Lord in D&C 52:23 (given

June 7, 1831). He became upset about having to walk the entire distance to Missouri, preaching as they went. It was apparently not the comfort and attention to which he had become accustomed as a popular minister prior to joining the Church. He began to find fault with Joseph Smith and other leaders of the Church.

One of the things that seemed to bother Booth about Joseph Smith was that the Prophet's naturally pleasant and jovial personality was not serious enough for a true prophet of God. He felt that Joseph had a "spirit of lightness and levity, a temper of mind easily irritated, and an habitual proneness to jesting and joking" (in *The Joseph Smith Papers, Documents, Volume 2: July 1831–January 1833*, ed. Matthew C. Godfrey and others [2013], 60, note 332).

By September 1831, Ezra Booth was back in Kirtland and was in a condition of apostasy, criticizing the Prophet and rejecting the Church. He was excommunicated on September 6, 1831 (see *Church History in the Fulness of Times*, 2003, 114), and he formally denounced the Church at a Methodist camp meeting on September 12, 1831. He went on to become the first apostate to write and publish anti-Mormon literature, publishing nine articles against the Church in the *Ohio Star* newspaper from October to December 1831. Ezra Booth participated in the tarring and feathering of the Prophet Joseph Smith on the night of March 24, 1832, at the John Johnson farm in Hiram, Ohio.

Section 64 is perhaps best-known because of its counsel on forgiving others. You may wish to glance ahead and see if you recognize verses 9–11. As you will see, it has many other important messages also.

As we begin our verse-by-verse study, we feel the tenderness and compassion of the Savior in verses 1–4 as He forgives sins and encourages efforts to improve and do better.

1 BEHOLD, **thus saith the Lord your God unto you**, O ye elders of my church, hearken ye and hear, and **receive my will concerning you.**

2 For verily I say unto you, **I will that ye should overcome the world** [*the Savior wants us to succeed*]; wherefore [*this is one of the reasons*] **I will have compassion upon you.**

3 **There are those among you who have sinned; but verily I say, for this once, for mine own glory** [*because the Savior also has joy, happiness, and success as we repent; see first phrase of Mosiah 14:11*], **and for the salvation of**

souls, I have forgiven you your sins.

4 I will be merciful unto you, for I have given unto you the kingdom.

> Next, in verse 5, we have another witness from the Savior Himself, that the living prophet, although not perfect, leads us under His direction. This verse, when coupled with D&C 43:3–4, serves as a reminder that the living prophet will never be allowed to lead us astray.

5 And **the keys of the mysteries of the kingdom shall not be taken from my servant Joseph Smith, Jun.**, through the means I have appointed [*in D&C 43:3–4*], **while he liveth, inasmuch as he obeyeth mine ordinances.**

> The last phrase of verse 5 is important because it says, in effect, that the living prophet still has agency, and if he were to choose to disobey God and refuse to lead the Church according to the Lord's will, he would be removed from office.
>
> Next, beginning with verse 6, the focus turns to forgiving others in order to receive forgiveness from the Lord.

6 **There are those who have sought occasion against him** [*Joseph Smith*] **without cause** [*they do not have a valid case against the Prophet*];

7 **Nevertheless, he has sinned** [*Joseph is not perfect*]; **but** verily I say unto you, **I, the Lord, forgive sins unto those who confess their sins before me and ask forgiveness**, who have not sinned unto death [*become sons of perdition; see D&C 76:31–35*]. [*In other words, Joseph confesses his sins and asks for forgiveness, and the Lord forgives him, just as is the case with you and me and all others who sincerely repent.*]

8 **My disciples, in days of old** [*followers of Christ in ancient times*], sought occasion [*had complaints*] against one another and **forgave not one another in their hearts**; and for this evil they were afflicted and sorely [*severely*] chastened [*disciplined*].

> As stated in the background notes for this section, verses 9–11, next, are probably some of the most often-quoted in the Doctrine and Covenants. The doctrine is clear. We must forgive others and turn their judgment over to the Savior in order to be forgiven ourselves.

9 Wherefore, I say unto you, that **ye ought to forgive one another**; for **he that forgiveth not** his brother his trespasses **standeth condemned** [*stopped in personal progress; in trouble on Judgment Day*] before the Lord; for **there**

remaineth in him the greater sin.

10 I, the Lord, will forgive whom I will forgive, but of you it is required to forgive all men [*including yourself*].

The last phrase of verse 9, above, bears further comment. At first glance, it sounds unfair, especially in the case of serious and damaging actions against us by others. For instance, in cases of robbery, rape, child abuse, spouse abuse, and other traumatizing "trespasses" against someone, how can the victim be guilty of a "greater sin" by not forgiving the perpetrator? There are several possible answers to this question. We will consider two.

First, another term for sin, trespass is "spiritual damage." Thus, anger, hatred, desires for revenge, and so forth, if allowed to remain "in" us, can do "greater" damage over time than the original "trespass" against us. They can cripple spiritual and emotional growth as well as preventing healing.

Second, if those who have trespassed against us do get to the point where they are repenting and asking our forgiveness, and we refuse their pleas for forgiveness, we can do even "greater" damage to them than they did to us.

There is another question we must address with these verses. Does forgiving mean allowing additional "trespasses"? Does the Lord require that we continue to be "walked on"? We find an answer by reading what Nephi was commanded by the Lord to do after repeated trespasses against him by Laman and Lemuel. He was commanded to "flee" his brethren (2 Nephi 5:5) and to go with those who would follow him to a place and situation in which they could have peace.

Yet another question must be considered. What if a person who has been severely traumatized by another's actions tries to forgive, prays for help, seeks counsel from others, reads the scriptures, and so forth, but still finds that he or she is emotionally incapable of forgiving? What then?

Mercifully, the answer is found in verse 11, next.

11 And ye ought to say in your hearts—let God judge between me and thee, and reward thee according to thy deeds.

In other words, they are invited to turn the burden of "judging" and punishing over to God and thus get on with their lives.

Over many years serving as a bishop and stake president, I found verse 11, above, to be most helpful in such situations. The major step for people who had not yet been able to muster the strength emotionally to forgive their "trespasser" was to turn things over to the Savior. I asked them if they felt that they could support the Savior's decision and actions with respect to their abuser. Usually, the immediate answer was "yes," which brought visible relief. In some cases, they had to pray for strength first over a period of time to simply turn the person or persons over to the Lord. Having taken this step, it was not long before they began seeing their "enemy" with pity and with a hope that he or she could someday change and avoid the misery that awaited them if they refused to repent.

Next, in verses 12–14, the Master explains the necessity of Church disciplinary action on occasions and that such action by Church leaders does not constitute lack of forgiving on their part (as commanded in verses 9–10, above); rather, it is sometimes necessary to meet the requirements of the Lord in preserving the strength and purity of the Church. We will learn more about this in section 102.

12 **And him that repenteth not of his sins, and confesseth them not, ye shall bring before the church**, and do with him as the scripture saith unto you, either by commandment or by revelation [*either according to the commandments and instructions already given, such as in D&C 42:24, 26, 75, 80–91, or as directed by the Spirit at the time*].

13 And this ye shall do that God may be glorified—**not because ye forgive not, having not compassion, but that ye may be justified in the eyes of the law, that ye may not offend him who is your lawgiver**—

14 Verily I say, **for this cause** [*in order not to disobey God*] **ye shall do these things**.

As mentioned in the background given in this study guide for this section, Ezra Booth apostatized after a few weeks in the Church. Both Ezra Booth and Isaac Morley are mentioned in verses 15–16, next. They served as companions (D&C 52:23) as they traveled on their missions to Missouri. They had both complained against Church leaders. Note that Isaac Morley is forgiven, but Ezra Booth is not. Ezra left the Church and fought against it, never coming back. In contrast, Isaac repented and remained faithful, serving as a patriarch, stake president, and high counselor through mobbings and persecutions in Missouri and Illinois and the trials and difficulties of moving west with the pioneers. He died true to the Church, in Fairview, Utah, on June 24, 1865, at age seventy-nine.

15 Behold, **I, the Lord, was angry with** him who was my

servant **Ezra Booth**, and **also** my servant **Isaac Morley**, for they kept not the law, neither the commandment;

16 They sought evil in their hearts, and I, the Lord, withheld my Spirit. They condemned for evil that thing in which there was no evil [*possibly a reference to the instruction from the Lord for Isaac Morley to sell his farm in Kirtland and consecrate the money from the sale to the Church as part of the law of consecration*]; nevertheless **I have forgiven my servant Isaac Morley** [*who repented and did sell his farm after all; see verse 20*].

17 And **also my servant Edward Partridge**, behold, he **hath sinned**, and **Satan seeketh to destroy his soul; but when these things are made known unto them, and they repent of the evil, they shall be forgiven.**

As is the case with so many verses in the Doctrine and Covenants, verse 17, above, has a simple but important message and reminder for all of us. It is that when we find out that we have been wrong, and if we humble ourselves and repent, we will be forgiven.

Next, the Lord requests that Sidney Gilbert (business partner to Newel K. Whitney and co-owner of the Newel K. Whitney store in Kirtland) return to Zion in Jackson County, Missouri, to continue setting up a store there (see note accompanying D&C 53:4 in this study guide) and to handle other business affairs of the Church as needed.

18 And now, verily I say that **it is expedient in me that** my servant **Sidney Gilbert**, after a few weeks, **shall return upon his business, and to his agency in the land of Zion;**

19 And that which he hath seen and heard may be made known unto my disciples [*members of the Church, faithful followers of Christ*], that they perish not. And for this cause have I spoken these things.

Along with the background already given in the note following verse 14, above, verse 20, next, gives us an important insight as to why the Lord asked Isaac Morley to sell his farm in Kirtland and consecrate the money gained from the sale to the Church. The insight is that this apparently was a critical moment in Isaac's life. He seems to have been sorely tempted to keep the farm and the personal wealth it provided for him and his family. At first, he refused to sell but quickly rethought the issue and determined to be obedient and sell, thus strengthening his testimony by obedience during a moment of temptation. With the spiritual momentum gained by this act of obedience, he gained strength to endure faithfully for the rest of his life.

Watch now, in verse 20, as the Lord explains why He had Isaac Morley sell his farm.

20 **And again, I say unto you, that my servant Isaac Morley may not be tempted above that which he is able to bear,** and counsel wrongfully to your hurt, **I gave commandment that his farm should be sold.**

> Frederick G. Williams also owned a farm in the area, but the Lord instructs him not to sell. It consisted of about 144 acres.

21 **I will not that my servant Frederick G. Williams should sell his farm, for I, the Lord, will to retain a strong hold in the land of Kirtland, for the space of five years,** in the which **I will not overthrow the wicked, that thereby I may save some.**

> If we use our imagination, we might hear some members gossiping and complaining because Isaac Morley was told by the Prophet to sell his farm (verse 20), whereas Frederick G. Williams (an extra close friend of the Prophet and physician to Joseph and Emma and their family) was told to keep his farm (verse 21). Such chatter is folly! From what you know, you can readily see that such criticism is foolish and shows lack of faith in the Lord's prophet. But how many situations do we run into where we do not have the understanding and insights that we have here? For example, one bishop may handle a seemingly similar situation completely differently than another bishop. This is just a reminder to have faith in the inspiration of the Lord to His leaders, and to avoid gossip and criticism.

Looking again at verse 21, above, we see two more messages. First, Kirtland is to remain a stronghold of the Church for another five years. During this time, a temple will be built. And when it is dedicated, on March 27, 1836 (D&C 109), marvelous manifestations will attend it. And just a week later, on April 3, 1836, the Savior, Moses, Elias, and Elijah will appear and bestow priesthood keys upon the Prophet and Oliver Cowdery (D&C 110). Obviously, these Saints didn't know all this when instructions were given to keep Kirtland as a headquarters of the Church for five years.

Thus, having some members remain in Kirtland while excitement for relocating to Missouri was running high was both a test of faith for those who were asked to remain, as well as a significant opportunity for the faithful to learn a lesson through blessings that came through obedience.

A second message is found at the

end of verse 21, above. It is that the Lord holds off on "smiting" the wicked and disobedient, because by being patient, He still might save some of them. It is well to keep this in mind when, at times, we are tempted to wish that the Lord would "smite" those who make life difficult and miserable for us.

In verse 22, next, the Lord tells these members that after five more years in Kirtland, all who wish to move to Missouri are welcome to do so, as long as they do it with humble and receptive hearts.

22 And **after that day** [*after five years; verse 21, above*], **I, the Lord, will not hold any guilty that shall go with an open heart up to the land of Zion**; for **I, the Lord, require the hearts of the children of men.**

We ought not to miss the important message at the end of verse 22, above. The Lord requires our "hearts," our center of feelings and emotions. The mind is the center of rational thought and intellectual understanding, but we tend to act and behave based on our feelings. Thus, when we give our hearts to the Lord, we are giving our deepest loyalty to Him. We find ourselves wanting to obey Him rather than needing to obey Him in order to get blessings we want. When we give our hearts to Him, we find ourselves being truly good rather than playing it safe.

Next, we see another verse that is quite well-known. It deals with paying tithing so we don't get burned at the Second Coming.

23 Behold, **now it is called today until the coming of the Son of Man** [*this is your opportunity to prepare to meet God; compare with D&C 45:6 and Alma 34:32–33*], and verily **it is a day of sacrifice, and a day for the tithing of my people**; for **he that is tithed shall not be burned at his coming.**

Obviously, a person who lives in sin and wickedness but pays tithing to avoid being burned with the wicked when the Savior comes would not avoid burning. Such people, if there be any, would be forgetting that the Lord requires the "heart," as explained in verse 22.

24 For **after today** [*the time between now and the Second Coming*] **cometh the burning**—this is speaking after the manner of the Lord [*according to the symbolic language used by God*]—for verily I say, **tomorrow** [*when the Second Coming arrives*] **all the proud and they that do wickedly shall be as stubble**; and **I will burn them up**, for I am the Lord of Hosts; and I will not spare any that remain in Babylon [*symbolic of personal as well as mass wickedness*].

People often wonder how the

SECTION 64

wicked will actually be burned. The scriptures have a simple answer. They will be burned by the glory of the coming Christ. We find this in D&C 5:19, as well as in 2 Nephi. We will quote 2 Nephi here (**bold** added for emphasis):

2 Nephi 12:10, 19, 21

10 O ye wicked ones, enter into the rock, and hide thee in the dust, for the fear of the Lord and the glory of his majesty shall smite thee.

19 And they shall go into the holes of the rocks, and into the caves of the earth, for the fear of the Lord shall come upon them and **the glory of his majesty shall smite them**, when he ariseth [*at the time of the Second Coming*] to shake terribly the earth.

21 To go into the clefts of the rocks, and into the tops of the ragged rocks, for the fear of the Lord shall come upon them and **the majesty of his glory shall smite them**, when he ariseth to shake terribly the earth.

25 Wherefore, **if ye believe me, ye will labor while it is called today** [*you will prepare to meet God now*].

Next, in verse 26, the Lord instructs Newel K. Whitney and Sidney Gilbert not to sell the Newel K. Whitney store in Kirtland (which they own together) until the five years (verse 21) are up. The Saints who remain in Kirtland will need its goods and services.

26 And **it is not meet** [*necessary*] **that** my servants, **Newel K. Whitney and Sidney Gilbert, should sell their store** and their possessions here; for this is not wisdom until the residue [*remaining members*] of the church, which remaineth in this place [*Kirtland*], shall go up unto the land of Zion [*Jackson County, Missouri*].

It appears that, in verses 27–33, next, the Lord is reminding Brothers Whitney and Gilbert that they will need to do business with nonmembers along with their business with and for the Church in Kirtland, and that the Lord will inspire them as they work to carry out their stewardships. The importance of their role in supplying goods and services for the Saints through their business skills and talents is emphasized in verse 30. That they will become tired and weary in carrying out their responsibilities is implied by verse 33.

27 Behold, it is said in my laws, or forbidden, to get in debt to thine enemies;

28 But behold, it is not said at any time that the Lord should not

take when he please, and pay as seemeth him good.

29 Wherefore, **as ye are agents, ye are on the Lord's errand; and whatever ye do according to the will of the Lord is the Lord's business.**

30 And **he hath set you to provide for his saints** in these last days, that they may obtain an inheritance in the land of Zion.

31 And behold, I, the Lord, declare unto you, and my words are sure and shall not fail, that they shall obtain it.

32 But all things must come to pass in their time.

33 Wherefore, **be not weary in well-doing**, for ye are laying the foundation of a great work. And **out of small things proceedeth that which is great**.

34 Behold, **the Lord requireth the heart and a willing mind;** and the willing and obedient shall eat the good of the land of Zion [*symbolic of obtaining the blessings of the Lord temporally and physically*] in these last days.

35 And **the rebellious shall be cut off out of the land of Zion, and shall be sent away, and shall not inherit the land** [*symbolic of the fact that the wicked will not "inherit" a place in the kingdom of God*].

36 For, verily I say that **the rebellious are not of the blood of Ephraim** [*symbolic of all those who come into the Church and make and keep covenants, regardless of which tribe of Israel they come from*], wherefore they shall be plucked out.

In verses 37–40, next, the Lord symbolically and literally presents the Church, the righteous Saints, and the pure gospel of Jesus Christ, as the standard against which all things are to be judged.

37 Behold, **I, the Lord, have made my church in these last days like unto a judge** sitting on a hill, or in a high place, to judge the nations.

38 For it shall come to pass that **the inhabitants of Zion shall judge all things pertaining to Zion.**

39 And **liars and hypocrites shall be proved by them, and they who are not Apostles and prophets shall be known.**

40 And **even the bishop, who is a judge, and his counselors, if they are not faithful in their stewardships shall be condemned,**

and others shall be planted in their stead [*all leaders of the Church are subject to obeying the principles and commandments of the gospel; there is no "privilege because of position" in the Church, as is the case in almost all man-made governments and organizations*].

> Finally, in verses 41–43, the Savior prophesies about the successful gathering of Israel in the last days. We are watching this even now as it happens before our very eyes!

41 For, behold, I say unto you that **Zion shall flourish**, and **the glory of the Lord shall be upon her**;

42 And **she shall be an ensign** [*a flag, a signal to gather; a rallying point*] unto the people, and **there shall come unto her out of every nation under heaven**.

43 And **the day shall come when the nations of the earth shall tremble because of her, and shall fear because of her terrible** [*mighty and strong*] **ones**. The Lord hath spoken it. Amen.

SECTION 65

Background

> This revelation was given in Hiram, Ohio, thirty miles southeast of Kirtland on October 30, 1831. The Prophet Joseph Smith said that he received it as a prayer "in the fore part of October" (*History of the Church*, 1:218).

A number of revelations were received by the Prophet while he and his family, along with Sidney Rigdon, were living on the John Johnson farm. Many of these revelations were given as a result of questions that came up in the minds of Joseph and Sidney as they continued the work of translating the Bible (known today as the JST, or the Joseph Smith Translation) in the Johnson home. Perhaps the most notable of these revelations is section 76 (the three degrees of glory and perdition), which was occasioned by working on John 5:29 as they were translating the New Testament.

One of the main messages in this section is that the kingdom of God is going forth as a result of the restoration of the gospel so that the kingdom of heaven can come.

We will see the term "kingdom of God" in verses 2, 5, and 6. The Prophet Joseph Smith explained his role in setting up the kingdom of God in the last days as follows:

"The ancient prophets declared that in the last days the God of heaven should set up a kingdom which should never be destroyed, nor left to other people [Daniel 2:44]; and the very time that was calculated on, this people were struggling to bring it out. . . .

"I calculate to be one of the instruments of setting up the kingdom of Daniel by the word of the Lord, and I intend to lay a foundation that will revolutionize the whole world. . . . It will not be by sword or gun that this kingdom will roll on: the power of truth is such that all nations will be under the necessity of obeying the Gospel" (*History of the Church*, 6:364–65).

Basically, the "kingdom of God" (verse 2) means the Church here on earth. The "kingdom of heaven" (verse 6) means Christ's millennial kingdom, which will be set up on earth when He comes again and which will be the ruling government for all nations and people during the thousand years.

Remember, the Prophet Joseph Smith said that this revelation came in the form of a prayer when it was given to him.

1 HEARKEN, and lo, a voice as of one sent down from on high, who is mighty and powerful, whose going forth is unto the ends of the earth, yea, whose voice is unto men—**Prepare ye the way of the Lord**, make his paths straight.

2 **The keys of the kingdom of God are committed unto man on the earth** [*by way of the restoration of the gospel, through Joseph Smith*], and from thence [*"thence," likely meaning the small beginnings in New York*] shall the gospel roll forth unto the ends of the earth, as the stone which is cut out of the mountain without hands [*Daniel 2:34–35*] shall roll forth, until it has filled the whole earth.

3 **Yea, a voice crying—Prepare ye the way of the Lord, prepare ye the supper of the Lamb** [*the restored gospel is the "supper of the Lamb" to be offered to all people; see the parable in Matthew 22:1–14*], **make ready for the Bridegroom** [*prepare for the coming of Christ who is the "Bridegroom"*].

Verse 4, next, in this prayer, contains a request for all of us to preach the gospel.

4 **Pray unto the Lord, call upon his holy name, make known his wonderful works among the people**.

In verse 5, next, we see, through this prayer, that the gospel is to be restored and offered to all people upon the earth in preparation for the coming of the Lord, at which time the Savior will come in full glory.

5 **Call upon the Lord, that his kingdom may go forth upon the earth, that the inhabitants thereof may receive it, and be prepared for the days to come, in the which the Son of Man**

[*Christ, "Son of Man of Holiness" (Heavenly Father); see Moses 6:57*] **shall come** down in heaven, **clothed in the brightness of his glory, to meet the kingdom of God** [*the Church*] **which is set up on the earth.**

6 Wherefore [*the prayer continues*], **may the kingdom of God** [*the Church*] **go forth, that the kingdom of heaven may come**, that thou, O God, mayest be glorified in heaven so on earth, that thine enemies may be subdued; for thine is the honor, power and glory, forever and ever. Amen.

In conclusion, we will include a quote from Elder James E. Talmage of the Quorum of the Twelve in which he explained the terms "kingdom of God" and "kingdom of heaven." He said:

"The expression 'Kingdom of God' is used synonymously with the term 'Church of Christ'; but the Lord had made plain that He sometimes used the term 'Kingdom of Heaven' in a distinctive sense. In 1832 He called attention to that in these words, addressing Himself to the elders of the Church [D&C 65:1–6]:

"As Christ gave power to bear off the kingdom in his day, so has he given the same power in this day.

"Such was the prayer, such is the prayer, prescribed for this people to pray, not to utter in words only, not to say only, but to pray—that the Kingdom of God may roll forth in the earth to prepare the earth for the coming of the Kingdom of Heaven. That provision in the Lord's prayer, 'Thy kingdom come, thy will be done on earth as it is in heaven' has not been abrogated [*annulled, done away with*]. We are praying for the Kingdom of Heaven to come, and are endeavoring to prepare the earth for its coming. The Kingdom of God, already set up upon the earth, does not aspire to temporal domination among the nations. It seeks not to overthrow any existing forms of government; it does not profess to exercise control in matters that pertain to the governments of the earth, except by teaching correct principles and trying to get men to live according to the principles of true government, before the Kingdom of Heaven shall come and be established upon the earth with a King at the head. But when He comes, He shall rule and reign, for it is His right" (In Conference Report, April 1916, 128–29).

SECTION 66

Background

The 2013 edition of the Doctrine and Covenants heading for this section is another example of the great value of the research being done for the Joseph Smith Papers Project. If you have a prior edition, the heading for this section is:

"Revelation given through Joseph Smith the Prophet, at Orange, Ohio, October 25, 1831. HC 1:219–221. This was the first day of an important conference. In prefacing this revelation, the Prophet wrote: 'At the request of William E. McLellin, I inquired of the Lord, and received the following.'"

The heading in the 2013 edition reflects additional research.

Revelation given through Joseph Smith the Prophet, at Hiram, Ohio, October 29, 1831. William E. McLellin had petitioned the Lord in secret to make known through the Prophet the answer to five questions, which were unknown to Joseph Smith. At McLellin's request, the Prophet inquired of the Lord and received this revelation.

Brother McLellin was slightly less than a month younger than Joseph Smith (having been born on January 18, 1806). He was a widower and had been a school teacher in Paris, Tennessee. He had heard the gospel preached by Harvey Whitlock and David Whitmer, had traveled to Independence, Missouri, to see Joseph Smith but missed him, and had subsequently joined the Church, being baptized in Jackson County, Missouri, by Hyrum Smith on August 20, 1831. He was ordained an elder on August 24, 1831, and then left the next day for Tennessee, traveling with Hyrum Smith on a missionary journey. William preached his first sermon as an elder in the Church on August 28. After spending some time in Tennessee, he left for Kirtland, Ohio, with Hyrum Smith and finally met the Prophet Joseph Smith in October 1831.

After becoming acquainted with the Prophet, William E. McLellin asked him to inquire of the Lord for him (which resulted in section 66). William had approached the Lord previously in secret prayer and specifically asked Him to answer five questions for him through Joseph Smith. He shared this information with no one, but after the revelation of the Lord through Joseph, Brother McLellin wrote, "I now testify in the fear of God, that every question which I had thus lodged in the ears of the Lord of Sabbath, were answered to my full and entire satisfaction" (William E. McLellin, in Susan Easton Black's *Who's Who in the Doctrine & Covenants*, 191).

As we proceed with our study of this brief section, we will see that William E. McLellin has many good attributes and much potential but also that he has some weaknesses about which the Lord warns him.

He will be called as a member of the Quorum of the Twelve Apostles in 1835, but, sadly, he

SECTION 66

will go into apostasy and will be excommunicated in 1838.

The Joseph Smith Papers Project gives us some additional information about William. We will quote from the 2018 *Doctrine and Covenants Student Manual*:

"William served the Lord faithfully for a time, and in 1835 he was called to serve as a member of the Quorum of the Twelve Apostles. Sadly, William did not heed the Lord's counsel to continue faithful to the end and later apostatized and turned against the Prophet Joseph Smith. When he was excommunicated from the Church in May 1838, he admitted that he had 'quit praying, and keeping the commandments, and indulged himself in his lustful desires' (Joseph Smith, in *Manuscript History of the Church*, vol. B-1, page 796, josephsmithpapers.org."

1 BEHOLD, thus saith the Lord unto my servant William E. McLellin—**Blessed are you, inasmuch as you have** [*because you have*] **turned away from your iniquities** [*sins*]**, and have received my truths**, saith the Lord your Redeemer, the Savior of the world, even of as many as believe on my name.

In verse 2, next, the Savior bears His personal testimony to Brother McLellin as to the truthfulness of the restored gospel.

2 Verily I say unto you, **blessed are you for receiving mine everlasting covenant** [*for being baptized and confirmed*], even **the fulness of my gospel, sent forth unto the children of men** [*inhabitants of the earth*], that they might have life [*eternal life, exaltation*] and be made partakers of the glories which are to be revealed in the last days, as it was written [*prophesied*] by the prophets and Apostles in days of old.

Next, the Master reminds William McLellin that he needs to improve. It is a much-needed blessing to have our faults pointed out, but, as you probably know, it takes a humble person to accept such correction. Brother McLellin will have difficulty accepting it.

3 Verily I say unto you, my servant William, that **you are clean, but not all**; **repent, therefore, of those things which are not pleasing in my sight**, saith the Lord, for **the Lord will show them unto you** [*so he can repent—a great kindness from God*].

4 And **now, verily, I, the Lord, will show unto you what I will concerning you**, or what is my will concerning you.

The Lord now asks William to do missionary work and gives specific instructions.

5 Behold, verily I say unto you, that **it is my will that you should proclaim my gospel from land to land, and from city to city**, yea, in those regions round about where it has not been proclaimed [*in areas where no one has yet formally preached the gospel*].

6 **Tarry not many days** [*don't stay long*] **in this place** [*the Kirtland area*]; **go not up unto the land of Zion** [*Missouri*] **as yet; but inasmuch as you can send** [*money*], **send; otherwise, think not of thy property.**

7 **Go unto the eastern lands**, bear testimony in every place, unto every people and in their synagogues, reasoning with the people.

8 **Let my servant Samuel H. Smith** [*Joseph Smith's younger brother*] **go with you**, and forsake him not, and give him thine instructions; and he that is faithful shall be made strong in every place; and **I, the Lord, will go with you**.

> William did go to "the eastern lands" (verse 7) and preached in Pennsylvania, but his mission was cut short because of disobedience and sickness.
>
> In verse 9, next, William is told by the Lord that he will be privileged to have the gift of healing (one of the gifts of the Spirit mentioned in D&C 46:20), and in verses 9–10, he is counseled in things that he particularly needs, including patience. He is specifically told to avoid adultery.

9 **Lay your hands upon the sick, and they shall recover**. Return not till I, the Lord, shall send you. **Be patient** in affliction. **Ask**, and ye shall receive; knock, and it shall be opened unto you.

10 **Seek not to be cumbered** [*possibly meaning to avoid distractions that would take him away from his missionary work*], **forsake all unrighteousness. Commit not adultery—a temptation with which thou hast been troubled.**

11 **Keep these sayings**, for they are true and faithful [*play close attention to what the Lord has said, and be obedient, because it deals with exact and specific issues for William*]; **and thou shalt magnify thine office, and push many people to Zion** [*a reference to Deuteronomy 33:13–17, in which Joseph's (Joseph, who was sold into Egypt) posterity is blessed to lead the gathering of Israel in the last days*] with songs of everlasting joy upon their heads.

12 **Continue in these things even unto the end, and you shall have**

a crown of eternal life [*symbolism meaning exaltation*] **at the right hand** [*the covenant hand, symbolic of receiving promised blessings from God through personal worthiness*] **of my Father,** who is full of grace and truth [*is full of help and truth*].

13 Verily, thus saith the Lord your God, your Redeemer, even Jesus Christ. Amen.

SECTION 67

Background

This revelation was given at Hiram, Ohio, in November 1831 through the Prophet Joseph Smith. The Prophet had called a special conference, held at the John Johnson home, during which the top priority business was preparing sixty-five revelations for publication in what was to be known as the "Book of Commandments." The plan was to print ten thousand copies (later reduced to 3,000) of this book of scripture in Missouri, on a printing press set up by William W. Phelps and Oliver Cowdery, as commanded by the Lord in D&C 57:11–14. The Book of Commandments was the predecessor to what we now know as the Doctrine and Covenants.

During the first day of this conference, on November 1, 1831, the Lord gave His own "preface" (see D&C 1:6) to the Book of Commandments. It is now section 1 of the Doctrine and Covenants.

During the conference, there was some criticism by William E. McLellin (and apparently others; see verse 5) of the wording in the revelations. As you will see, in section 67, verses 5–8, the Lord invited anyone who cared to challenge the wording of the revelations given through Joseph Smith to choose the least significant revelation from the Book of Commandments and try to come up with a better one. William E. McLellin volunteered to take up the challenge. Of him, Joseph Smith wrote (**bold** added for emphasis):

"After the foregoing was received [section 67], **William E. M'Lellin**, as the wisest man, in his own estimation, **having more learning than sense**, endeavored to write a commandment like unto one of the least of the Lord's, but failed; it was an awful responsibility to write in the name of the Lord. The Elders and all present that witnessed this vain attempt of a man to imitate the language of Jesus Christ, renewed their faith in the fulness of the Gospel, and in the truth of the commandments and revelations which the Lord had given to the Church through my instrumentality" (*History of the Church,* 1:226; see also in *Manuscript History of the Church,* vol. A-1, page 162, josephsmithpapers.org).

We will proceed now with section 67. First, in verses 1–2, the Savior assures these elders that their prayers have been heard, that He knows them personally, and that He has power to bless them.

1 BEHOLD and hearken, O ye elders of my church, who have assembled yourselves together [*for the conference that began on November 1, 1831*], **whose prayers I have heard**, and whose **hearts** I know, and whose **desires have come up before me.**

2 Behold and lo, **mine eyes are upon you**, and the heavens and the earth are in mine hands, and **the riches of eternity** [*including exaltation*] **are mine to give.**

We do not know what the blessing was that is referred to in verse 3, next. But there is a lesson for us in it; namely, that fear can stand in the way of receiving desired blessings.

3 Ye endeavored to believe that ye should receive the blessing which was offered unto you; but behold, verily I say unto you **there were fears in your hearts**, and verily **this is the reason that ye did not receive.**

Next, beginning with verse 4, the Lord offers a tangible testimony that the revelations given through Joseph Smith are from Him. The testimony is a simple one. No man can duplicate the revelations that come from God. Man-made attempts are hollow and empty. They may have words, but they do not have the Spirit.

4 And now **I, the Lord, give unto you a testimony of the truth of these commandments** [*the sixty-five revelations given through the Prophet Joseph Smith, which were to make up the Book of Commandments*] which are lying before you [*which the Prophet and others were preparing for publication*].

5 **Your eyes have been upon my servant Joseph Smith, Jun.**, and **his language you have known**, and **his imperfections you have known**; and you have sought in your hearts knowledge that you might express beyond his language [*you think you can do a better job of writing than he has done*]; this you also know.

Next, in verses 6–8, comes the challenge from the Lord to the Prophet's critics among this group of elders.

6 Now, **seek ye out of the Book of Commandments** [*the sixty-five revelations about to be published*], even **the least that is among them,** and **appoint him that is the most wise among you;**

SECTION 67

7 Or, **if there be any among you that shall make one like unto it, then ye are justified in saying that ye do not know that they are true;**

8 **But if ye cannot make one like unto it, ye are under condemnation if ye do not bear record that they are true.**

9 For **ye know that there is no unrighteousness in them**, and that which is righteous cometh down from above, from the Father of lights [*the Father; the source of light; the same expression is used in the Bible in James 1:17*].

10 And again, verily I say unto you that it is your privilege, and a promise I give unto you that have been ordained unto this ministry, that **inasmuch as you strip yourselves from jealousies and fears, and humble yourselves before me, for ye are not sufficiently humble**, the veil shall be rent and **you shall see me and know that I am—not with the carnal neither natural mind, but with the spiritual.**

> There is more than one scriptural meaning for the phrase to "see [God]." This is explained in the last part of verse 10, above, combined with verses 11–14, next.
>
> Of course, it is possible to literally see God, as was the case with Joseph Smith. Some have seen the Father and many have seen the Savior literally. In order to have this experience, a person must be "quickened" (verse 11) by the Holy Ghost. Otherwise, their mortal bodies would not survive the occasion (verse 12; compare with Moses 1:11).
>
> All can "see" the Savior in the sense spoken of in verse 10, above. Through the power of the Holy Ghost, we can know that Jesus is the Christ and "see" the reality of His existence. We can "see" His tenderness, mercy, kindness, and charity for us. We can feel His love and understand His gospel. All this and more is "seeing" the Savior with our "spiritual" mind (end of verse 10).
>
> We will **bold** what we have said in the above notes as taught in the next verses.

11 For **no man has seen God at any time in the flesh** [*literally*], **except quickened by the Spirit of God.**

12 **Neither can any natural man** [*unprepared mortal*] **abide** [*survive*] **the presence of God**, neither after the carnal mind [*the spiritually unprepared mind*].

> Next, the Savior tells the men to whom this revelation specifically applies that they are not yet prepared to literally see angels, let alone the Savior.

13 Ye [*some of the men in the room with Joseph Smith*] **are not able to abide the presence of God now, neither the ministering of angels**; wherefore, **continue in patience** until ye are perfected.

14 Let not your minds turn back [*don't give up hope*]; and **when ye are worthy, in mine own due time** [*when the timing is right according to the wisdom of the Lord*], **ye shall see and know** that which was conferred upon you by the hands of my servant Joseph Smith, Jun. Amen.

Two more notes before we leave section 67.

First, Elder Orson F. Whitney spoke of the Lord's challenge, given in section 67, to write a revelation. He said:

"Well, one of them, who thought himself the wisest, and who possessed some learning, took up the challenge and actually attempted to frame a revelation; but it was a flat failure. He could utter, of course, certain words, and roll out a mass of rhetoric; but the divine spirit was lacking, and he had to acknowledge himself beaten.

"It is not so easy to put the spirit of life into things. Man can make the body, but God alone can create the spirit" (In Conference Report, April 1917, 42).

Second, William E. McLellin (by the way, we find several different spellings of his name in historical documents) served a mission with Parley P. Pratt in the winter of 1832. He became a member of the high council in Clay County, Missouri, in 1834. On February 15, 1835, he was called to be a member of the Quorum of the Twelve Apostles.

In 1835 he wrote a letter criticizing the First Presidency, and he left the Church in August 1836. In 1838 he was excommunicated, after which he joined in mobbing and robbing the Saints in Missouri and in driving them from the state. Entries and notes found in the *History of the Church*, 3:215, tell of McLellin's activities while the Prophet and others were held in jails in Missouri. We will quote two of these here. One is an entry by the Prophet. The second is a footnote.

"During our trial William E. McLellin, accompanied by Burr Riggs and others, at times were busy in plundering and robbing the houses of Sidney Rigdon, George Morey, the widow Phebe Ann Patten, and others, under pretense or color of law, on an order from General Clark, as testified to by the members of the different families robbed" (*History of the Church,* 3:215).

"While the brethren were imprisoned at Richmond it is said that 'McLellin, who was a large and

SECTION 68

active man, went to the sheriff and asked for the privilege of flogging the Prophet. Permission was granted on condition that Joseph would fight. The sheriff made known to Joseph McLellin's earnest request, to which Joseph consented, if his irons were taken off. McLellin then refused to fight unless he could have a club, to which Joseph was perfectly willing; but the sheriff would not allow them to fight on such unequal terms. McLellin was a man of superficial education, though he had a good flow of language. He adopted the profession of medicine.'—Mill. Star, 36:808, 809" (*History of the Church*, 3:215, footnote).

William E. McLellin eventually moved to Illinois and then on to Kirtland, Ohio, where, in early 1847, he joined with Martin Harris, who was organizing a new church called the Church of Christ. William soon visited David Whitmer in Richmond, Missouri, encouraging him to be the prophet of this new church. The church apparently died out by the end of 1849.

On June 5, 1869, McLellin joined the Hedrickites, an apostate church set up by Granville Hedrick after the martyrdom of the Prophet Joseph Smith. He left that church by November 1869. His wife joined the Reorganized Church of Jesus Christ of Latter Day Saints (note that it is "Latter Day Saints" rather than "Latter-day Saints," as is the spelling for our church) and they moved to Independence, Missouri, in 1870. William E. McLellin died on April 24, 1883, at age seventy-seven. Despite his opposition to the First Presidency and his bitterness toward the Church, he bore witness to his dying day of the truthfulness of the Book of Mormon.

SECTION 68

Background

This revelation was given through the Prophet Joseph Smith in Hiram, Ohio, on November 1, 1831. It was given at the request of Orson Hyde, Luke S. Johnson, Lyman E. Johnson, and William E. McLellin. Perhaps you've noticed that several revelations were given in Hiram. If you turn to the front of your Doctrine and Covenants to the "Chronological Order of Contents" and count the revelations given in Hiram (at the John and Elsa Johnson home), you will count sixteen!

Among many doctrines in section 68, perhaps the most widely known and often-quoted are the instructions to teach children to understand repentance, faith, baptism, the gift of the Holy Ghost (verse 25), and the doctrine that children may be baptized at age eight (verse 25).

The Prophet Joseph Smith gave a brief background to this section. He said:

"As the following Elders—Orson Hyde, Luke Johnson, Lyman E. Johnson, and William E. M'Lellin—were desirous to know the mind of the Lord concerning themselves, I inquired, and received the following [section 68]: (*History of the* Church, 1:227).

First, in verse 1, next, Orson Hyde is told that he is to teach the gospel "from people to people, and from land to land." This was literally fulfilled, including his dedicating the Holy Land for the gathering of the Jews.

1 MY servant, **Orson Hyde, was called by his ordination to proclaim the everlasting gospel, by the Spirit of the living God, from people to people, and from land to land**, in the congregations of the wicked [*a phrase often used to mean people who don't have the gospel*], in their synagogues, reasoning with and expounding [*explaining*] all scriptures unto them.

A quote from the *Doctrine and Covenants Student Manual*, 1981, pages 143–44, gives additional detail about the travels of Orson Hyde, as prophesied in verse 1, above.

"The prophecy in this verse was literally fulfilled. Orson Hyde proclaimed the gospel 'from people to people, from land to land.' In 1832, he and Samuel H. Smith traveled in the States of New York, Massachusetts, Maine, and Rhode Island—two thousand miles—on foot. In 1835 he was ordained an Apostle, and in 1837 he went on a mission to England. In 1840 he was sent on a mission to Jerusalem. He crossed the Ocean, traveled through England and Germany, visited Constantinople, Cairo, and Alexandria, and, finally, reached the Holy City. On October 24th, 1841, he went up on the Mount of Olives and offered a prayer, dedicating Palestine for the gathering of the Jews. (Smith and Sjodahl, *Commentary*, 409.)"

Next, the Savior gives instructions to missionaries as they go forth.

2 And, behold, and lo, **this is an ensample** [*example*] **unto all those** who were ordained unto this priesthood, **whose mission is appointed unto them to go forth**—

3 And this is the ensample unto them, that **they shall speak as they are moved upon by the Holy Ghost** [*teach according to the promptings of the Spirit*].

Next, in verses 4–5, the Lord explains the significance of teaching by the Spirit.

4 And **whatsoever they shall speak when moved upon by the Holy Ghost shall be scripture**, shall be **the will of the Lord**, shall be **the mind of the Lord**, shall be

the word of the Lord, shall be the voice of the Lord, and the power of God unto salvation [*will lead those who listen and obey to salvation in celestial glory*].

Verse 4, above, is a good example of a verse of scripture that must be interpreted in context. The word "scripture" is defined concisely as that which is being taught by the missionary and which, when followed, will lead to salvation.

Often in our gospel conversations, the term "scripture" is used to mean the word of the Lord to the whole Church, in fact, to the entire world. If this definition is applied to the word "scripture" in verse 4, then the phrase "whatsoever they shall speak" must be limited to the living prophets, seers, and revelators, and more specifically, to **the** prophet (the President of the Church). Elder Harold B. Lee addressed this issue. He said:

"It is not to be thought that every word spoken by the General Authorities is inspired, or that they are moved upon by the Holy Ghost in everything they read and write. Now you keep that in mind. I don't care what his position is, if he writes something or speaks something that goes beyond anything that you can find in the standard church works [the scriptures], unless that one be the prophet, seer, and revelator—please note that one exception—you may immediately say, 'Well, that is his own idea.' And if he says something that contradicts what is found in the standard church works (I think that is why we call them 'standard'—it is the standard measure of all that men teach), you may know by that same token that it is false, regardless of the position of the man who says it" ("The Place of the Living Prophet, Seer, and Revelator" address delivered to seminary and institute of religion faculty, July 8 1964, 14; quoted in *Doctrine and Covenants Student Manual*, 1981, 144).

Joseph Fielding Smith also spoke on this matter. He said:

"When one of the brethren stands before a congregation of the people today, and the inspiration of the Lord is upon him, he speaks that which the Lord would have him speak. It is just as much scripture as anything you will find written in any of these records, and yet we call these the standard works of the Church. We depend, of course, upon the guidance of the brethren who are entitled to inspiration.

"There is only one man in the Church at a time who has the right to give revelation for the Church, and that is the President of the Church. But that does not bar any other member in this Church from speaking the word of the Lord, as indicated here in this revelation, section 68, but a revelation that is to be given as these revelations are given in this book, to the

Church, will come through the presiding officer of the Church; yet, the word of the Lord, as spoken by other servants at the general conferences and stake conferences, or wherever they may be when they speak that which the Lord has put into their mouths, is just as much the word of the Lord as the writings and the words of other prophets in other dispensations" (*Doctrines of Salvation*, 1:186).

5 Behold, **this is the promise of the Lord** unto you, O ye my servants.

Verses 6–12 can generally be read as advice and counsel to missionaries today.

6 Wherefore, **be of good cheer**, and **do not fear**, for **I the Lord am with you, and will stand by you**; and **ye shall bear record of me, even Jesus Christ, that I am the Son of the living God, that I was, that I am, and that I am to come.**

7 **This is the word of the Lord** unto you, my servant Orson Hyde, and also unto my servant Luke Johnson, and unto my servant Lyman Johnson, and unto my servant William E. McLellin, and **unto all the faithful elders of my church—**

8 **Go ye into all the world, preach the gospel to every creature, acting in the authority which I have given you, baptizing in the name of the Father, and of the Son, and of the Holy Ghost.**

9 And **he that believeth and is baptized shall be saved, and he that believeth not shall be damned** [*stopped in progression*].

10 And **he that believeth shall be blest with signs following, even as it is written** [*the scriptures contain many promises and blessings to those who are baptized and faithfully keep their covenants*].

11 And **unto you it shall be given to know the signs of the times, and the signs of the coming of the Son of Man** [*the Holy Ghost will teach missionaries many things, including how to understand and recognize the "signs of the times," which are prophecies that will be fulfilled in the last days, indicating that the Second Coming is getting close*];

12 And of as many as the Father shall bear record, to you shall be given power to seal them up unto eternal life [*those who accept baptism can then work faithfully toward the sealing ordinances available in temples*]. Amen.

The topic now changes, and verses 13–21 deal with the office of bishop, more particularly, with the calling of Presiding Bishop of the Church. It is helpful to know that at this time in the history of the Church, there was only one bishop and that was Bishop Edward Partridge, who had been called as bishop in February 1831 (see D&C 41:9).

First, in verse 14, the Lord explains that there will be other bishops called in the future, and He explains that they are to be worthy high priests, appointed by the First Presidency (verse 15). Perhaps you are aware in our day that before a bishop is called, the stake president receives a letter from the First Presidency, authorizing him to issue a call to a particular man, who has been approved by them to be called to serve as a bishop.

13 And now, concerning the items in addition to the covenants and commandments, they are these—

14 **There remain hereafter, in the due time of the Lord, other bishops to be set apart** unto the church, to minister even according to the first [*like Bishop Partridge did*];

15 Wherefore **they shall be high priests who are worthy**, and they shall be **appointed by the First Presidency** of the Melchizedek Priesthood, **except they be literal descendants of Aaron** [*Moses's older brother; see Exodus 7:7*].

16 And **if they be literal descendants of Aaron they have a legal right to the bishopric, if they are the firstborn among the sons of Aaron**;

17 For the firstborn holds the right of the presidency over this priesthood, and the keys or authority of the same.

18 No man has a legal right to this office [*Presiding Bishop of the Church*], to hold the keys of this priesthood, except he be a literal descendant and the firstborn of Aaron.

> Elder Joseph Fielding Smith explained the phrase "except they be literal descendants of Aaron" in verse 15, above. He pointed out that this applies only to the office of Presiding Bishop of the Church. Furthermore, such a literal descendant of Aaron would have to be worthy and be called by the First Presidency. He could not simply walk into Church headquarters and announce that he is here and ready to begin serving as Presiding Bishop. Elder Smith taught:
>
> "It has no reference whatever to bishops of wards. Further, such a one must be designated by the First Presidency of the Church and receive his anointing and ordination under their hands. The revelation comes from the Presidency, not from the patriarch, to

establish a claim to the right to preside in this office. In the absence of knowledge concerning such a descendant, any high priest, chosen by the Presidency, may hold the office of Presiding Bishop and serve with counselors" (*Doctrines of Salvation*, 3:92–93).

"The office of Presiding Bishop of the Church is the same as the office which was held by Aaron. . . . It was this office which came to John the Baptist, and it was by virtue of the fact that he held the keys of this power and ministry that he was sent to Joseph Smith and Oliver Cowdery to restore that Priesthood, May 15, 1829. The person who has the legal right to this presiding office has not been discovered; perhaps is not in the Church, but should it be shown by revelation that there is one who is the 'firstborn among the sons of Aaron,' and thus entitled by birthright to this presidency, he could 'claim' his 'anointing' and the right to that office in the Church" (*Church History and Modern Revelation*, 1:259).

19 But, **as a high priest of the Melchizedek Priesthood has authority to officiate in all the lesser offices he may officiate in the office of bishop when no literal descendant of Aaron can be found, provided he is called and set apart and ordained unto this power, under the hands of the First Presidency** of the Melchizedek Priesthood.

20 And a literal descendant of Aaron, also, **must be designated by this Presidency**, and **found worthy**, and anointed, and **ordained under the hands of this Presidency, otherwise they are not legally authorized to officiate in their priesthood.**

These instructions (verses 15–21) regarding a literal descendant of Aaron and the office of Presiding Bishop may well be a matter that will come into play sometime in the future, and if and when it does, we will probably exclaim, "Oh, that is what it meant!"

21 But, by virtue of the decree concerning their right of the priesthood descending from father to son, **they may claim their anointing if at any time they can prove their lineage, or do ascertain it by revelation from the Lord under the hands of the above named Presidency.**

Verses 22–24, next, explain that the Presiding Bishop of the Church, should occasion demand, could not be tried for his membership in the Church, except by the First Presidency.

22 And again, **no bishop** [*Presiding Bishop*] or high priest who shall be set apart for this ministry [*who is called to serve as Presiding Bishop*] **shall be tried or condemned for any crime**

SECTION 68

[*meaning worthiness issues, not civil law issues; see D&C 42:79, 84, 85, 86, 87*], **save it be before the First Presidency of the church;**

23 And inasmuch as he is found guilty before this Presidency, by testimony that cannot be impeached [*by evidence that cannot be refuted*], he shall be condemned;

24 And **if he repent he shall be forgiven**, according to the covenants and commandments of the church.

> In verses 25–28, the topic now turns to the responsibility that parents in the Church have to teach their children to understand the basic commandments, ordinances, and principles of the gospel by the time they are eight years old.
>
> As a bishop, one of my most pleasant duties was that of interviewing children for baptism. Time and time again, I was impressed (and sometimes almost startled) by the knowledge and depth of understanding of these young candidates for baptism. They were living proof that young children can indeed be taught by age eight as instructed by the Lord in these next verses.

25 And again, **inasmuch as parents have children in Zion**, or in any of her stakes which are organized, **that teach them not to understand the doctrine of repentance, faith in Christ the Son of the living God, and of baptism and the gift of the Holy Ghost by the laying on of the hands, when eight years old, the sin be upon the heads of the parents.**

> As you will see, additional instructions for parents to teach their children are included in verse 28.
>
> Before moving on, we will pause for a moment and consider the phrase "the sin be upon the heads of the parents" at the end of verse 25, above. Note that in this context the word "sin" is singular and not plural. Therefore, we understand it to be saying, in effect, "the sin of not teaching the gospel to their children." Otherwise, an unfortunate false doctrine arises that states that parents are responsible for all sins committed by their children if they did not teach them the gospel. President Spencer W. Kimball said:
>
> "I have sometimes seen children of good families rebel, resist, stray, sin, and even actually fight God. In this they bring sorrow to their parents, who have done their best to set in movement a current and to teach and live as examples. But I have repeatedly seen many of these same children, after years of wandering, mellow, realize what they have been missing, repent, and make great contribution to the spiritual life of their community. The reason I believe this can take

place is that, despite all the adverse winds to which these people have been subjected, they have been influenced still more, and much more than they realized, by the current of life in the homes in which they were reared. When, in later years, they feel a longing to recreate in their own families the same atmosphere they enjoyed as children, they are likely to turn to the faith that gave meaning to their parents' lives.

"There is no guarantee, of course, that righteous parents will succeed always in holding their children, and certainly they may lose them if they do not do all in their power. The children have their free agency.

"But if we as parents fail to influence our families and set them on the 'strait and narrow way,' then certainly the waves, the winds of temptation and evil will carry the posterity away from the path.

"'Train up a child in the way he should go; and when he is old, he will not depart from it.' (Prov. 22:6.) What we do know is that righteous parents who strive to develop wholesome influences for their children will be held blameless at the last day, and that they will succeed in saving most of their children, if not all" ("Ocean Currents and Family Influences," *Ensign*, November 1974, 111–12).

Brigham Young taught:

"If Brother Brigham shall take a wrong track, and be shut out of the Kingdom of heaven, no person will be to blame but Brother Brigham. I am the only being in heaven, earth, or hell, that can be blamed.

"This will equally apply to every Latter-day Saint. Salvation is an individual operation. I am the only person that can possibly save myself. When salvation is sent to me, I can reject or receive it. In receiving it, I yield implicit obedience and submission to its great Author throughout my life, and to those whom he shall appoint to instruct me; in rejecting it, I follow the dictates of my own will in preference to the will of my Creator" (*Discourses of Brigham Young*, 390).

26 For **this shall be a law unto the inhabitants of Zion, or in any of her stakes** which are organized.

In verse 27, next, the Lord specifically repeats what He said in verse 25, above, regarding the age for baptism and confirmation for young children.

27 And **their children shall be baptized for the remission of their sins when eight years old,** and receive the laying on of the hands [*be confirmed*].

In verse 28, the Savior adds additional items for parents to teach children.

28 And **they shall also teach their children to pray, and to walk uprightly before the Lord.**

> In verses 29–31, the emphasis seems to be, among other things, on the importance of parents teaching by example and avoiding being lazy.

29 And the inhabitants of Zion shall also **observe the Sabbath day to keep it holy.**

30 And the inhabitants of Zion also shall remember their labors, inasmuch as they are appointed to **labor, in all faithfulness; for the idler shall be had in remembrance** [*will be brought to judgment*] **before the Lord.**

31 Now, I, the Lord, am not well pleased with the inhabitants of Zion, for **there are idlers among them**; and **their children are also growing up in wickedness; they also seek not earnestly the riches of eternity, but their eyes are full of greediness.**

32 **These things ought not to be**, and must be done away from among them; wherefore, let my servant Oliver Cowdery carry these sayings [*the manuscript for the Book of Commandments; see D&C 69 section heading as well as 69:1*] unto the land of Zion [*Jackson County, Missouri*].

33 And a commandment I give unto them—that **he that observeth not his prayers** before the Lord in the season thereof, let him be had in remembrance before the judge of my people.

34 **These sayings are true and faithful; wherefore, transgress them not, neither take therefrom** [*don't minimize their importance nor water them down*].

35 Behold, I am Alpha and Omega, and I come quickly. Amen.

SECTION 69

Background

This revelation was given in Hiram, Ohio, on November 11, 1831, through the Prophet Joseph Smith.

As stated in the background to section 67 in this study guide, sixty-five revelations had been approved (at a special conference held November 1, 1831, at Hiram) to be published as the Book of Commandments (the predecessor to the Doctrine and Covenants). The manuscript containing copies of these revelations was to be carried to Zion, in Jackson County, Missouri, by Oliver Cowdery. In addition, money that had been collected in the Kirtland area was also to be carried by Oliver to Missouri for the building up of the Church in Zion.

Since much of the journey to Zion would take Oliver through dangerous frontier territory, the Lord called John Whitmer to accompany him. This we see in verses 1–2, next. The remainder of the section, verses 3–8, deals primarily with John Whitmer's duties as Church historian. You may wish to read the background notes in this study guide for section 47, where you will see more detail about John Whitmer as historian for the Church.

1 HEARKEN unto me, saith the Lord your God, for my servant Oliver Cowdery's sake. It is not wisdom in me that he should be entrusted with [*have full responsibility for the safety of*] the commandments [*the manuscript for the Book of Commandments*] and the moneys which he shall carry unto the land of Zion, except one go with him who will be true and faithful [*like Oliver*].

2 Wherefore, I, the Lord, will that my servant, **John Whitmer, should go with my servant Oliver Cowdery;**

John Whitmer did accompany Oliver Cowdery as instructed. They started for Missouri on November 20, 1831, and arrived in Independence on January 5, 1832, after a long and difficult journey in winter cold.

B. H. Roberts gave additional background for verses 1–2, above. He said:

"The fact was that much of the journey between Kirtland and Independence, or Zion, was through a sparsely settled country, the western portion of it through a frontier country where there is always a gathering, more or less, of lawless people; and it was at considerable risk that a person traveled through such a country, especially when alone and carrying money with him. It was wisdom then, for the sake of Oliver Cowdery, and to insure the safety of the money and the sacred things he was to carry with him, that one should go with him that would be a true and faithful companion, hence the appointment of John Whitmer" (*Comprehensive History*, 1:268n).

As mentioned above, in the background to this section, verses 3–8 contain instructions to John Whitmer, who was called by the Lord on March 8, 1831, to replace Oliver Cowdery as the Church Historian (D&C 47:1, 3–4). John Whitmer was one of the Eight Witnesses to the Book of Mormon and was an older brother to David Whitmer (one of the Three Witnesses).

3 And also that **he** [*John Whitmer*] **shall continue in writing and making a history** [*of the Church*] of all the important things which he shall observe and know concerning my church;

4 And **also that he receive counsel and assistance from my servant Oliver Cowdery and others.**

> As you can see, in verse 5, next, missionaries scattered abroad were to send accounts and histories to Zion, where John Whitmer could use them in preserving and recording the history of the growing restored Church.

5 And also, **my servants who are abroad in the earth should send forth the accounts of their stewardships to the land of Zion;**

6 For **the land of Zion shall be a seat** [*headquarters*] and a place **to receive and do all these things** [*for the keeping of this history*].

> Next, the Lord instructs John to do much traveling from place to place in the Church in order to gather and record details to be used in writing the history of the Church.

7 Nevertheless, **let my servant John Whitmer travel many times from place to place, and from church to church** [*from branch to branch*], that he may the more easily obtain knowledge [*for the history*]—

8 **Preaching** and **expounding** [*explaining*]**, writing, copying, selecting, and obtaining all things which shall be for the good of the church**, and **for the rising generations** [*the major purpose of keeping a history*] that shall grow up on the land of Zion, to possess it from generation to generation, forever and ever. Amen.

SECTION 70

Background

This revelation was given through the Prophet Joseph Smith at Kirtland, Ohio, on November 12, 1831.

Section 70 would be particularly difficult to understand without a knowledge of the background and setting. You will see this as we study it verse by verse.

As you know from the background notes to sections 67 and 69, the Book of Commandments (the first publication of revelations through Joseph Smith) was to be printed in Missouri. The printing press was set up in Independence by W. W. Phelps. Oliver Cowdery and John Whitmer were to take the manuscript for the Book of Commandments, along with money collected to help build Zion, to Independence. The plan was to print ten thousand copies. The number was later reduced to three thousand. The Book of Commandments contained sixty-five revelations, plus the Lord's "preface" (now section 1) and an appendix (now section 133).

As we study, you will see many attributes and character qualities required of those who desire to obtain celestial glory. These are the same qualities as are required of those who live the law of consecration.

First, though, in verses 1–4, the Lord names those men who are serving on what we could call "the scripture publication committee." He reminds them of their responsibility and stewardship.

1 BEHOLD, and **hearken** [*defined in the 1828 Noah Webster Dictionary (American Dictionary of the English Language) as "to give heed to what is uttered; to observe or obey"*], O ye inhabitants of Zion, and **all ye people of my church who are afar off, and hear the word of the Lord** [*in this context, the Book of Commandments*] which I give unto my servant **Joseph Smith, Jun.**, and also unto my servant **Martin Harris**, and also unto my servant **Oliver Cowdery**, and also unto my servant **John Whitmer**, and also unto my servant **Sidney Rigdon**, and also unto my servant **William W. Phelps**, by the way of commandment unto them.

2 For **I give unto them a commandment**; wherefore hearken and hear, for thus saith the Lord unto them—

3 **I, the Lord, have appointed them, and ordained them to be stewards over the revelations and commandments** which I have given unto them, and which I shall hereafter give unto them [*continuing revelation*];

4 And **an account of this stewardship will I require of them in the day of judgment**.

The main topic of verses 5–7, next, is what to do with the money that will come from sales of copies of the Book of Commandments.

5 Wherefore, I have appointed unto them, and **this is their business** in the church of God, **to manage them** and the concerns thereof, yea, **the benefits** [*proceeds from sales*] thereof.

6 Wherefore, a commandment I give unto them, that **they shall not give these things** [*the proceeds from sales of the Book of Commandments*] **unto the church, neither unto the world**;

Verse 16 tells them that they are to use this money in caring for themselves and their families.

Beginning with verse 7, next, we are given insights to the high character and unselfishness required of those who live the law of consecration. If you have wondered if you could live celestial law, you may wish to pay close attention to what we **bold** in the next verses as well as to the notes we add.

You will see that it is up to them to decide what is surplus.

7 Nevertheless, **inasmuch as** [*if*] **they receive more than is needful for their necessities** and their **wants**, it shall be given into my storehouse [*the bishop's storehouse, to assist the poor and the needy*];

8 And **the benefits shall be consecrated unto the inhabitants of Zion,** and unto their generations, inasmuch as they become heirs according to the laws of the kingdom.

9 Behold, **this** [*deciding what to keep for your own use and what to consecrate to the Church to bless the lives of others*] **is what the Lord requires of every man in his stewardship** [*based on what he or she personally owns and earns*], even as I, the Lord, have appointed or shall hereafter appoint unto any man.

10 And behold, **none are exempt from this law** [*of having a celestial attitude*] **who belong to the church of the living God** [*the true, real God, as opposed to dead idols—inanimate objects that are commonly worshipped in many religions*];

11 Yea, **neither the bishop, neither the agent who keepeth the Lord's storehouse, neither he who is appointed in a stewardship over temporal things** [*"none are exempt" (verse 10) from these rules—in other words, everyone who desires to attain celestial glory must develop celestial attitudes, feelings, and behaviors, regardless of where or how he or she serves*].

Next, in verse 12, the Lord explains that as the Saints live the law of consecration, there will be some who are occupied full time in managing temporal and spiritual aspects of the Church, and thus they and their families will need to be supported out of the funds and supplies of the Church.

12 **He who is appointed to administer spiritual things**, the same **is worthy of his hire** [*is worthy of being supported by the funds of the Church*], even as those who are appointed to a stewardship to **administer in temporal things**;

13 Yea, even more abundantly, which abundance is multiplied unto them **through the manifestations of the Spirit** [*the funds of the Church are to be allocated as directed by the Holy Ghost*].

The importance of having a Christlike, celestial attitude is again emphasized in verse 14, next.

14 Nevertheless, **in your temporal things** [*physical needs*] **you shall be equal**, and this **not grudgingly**, otherwise the abundance of the manifestations of the Spirit shall be withheld.

> Verses 15–18 seem to refer mainly to the men named in verse 1, who are involved full time in their responsibilities for the preparation and publication of the Book of Commandments, and, thus, cannot work to support and sustain their families. This revelation explains why they are to keep the proceeds from the sale of copies of the Book of Commandments.

15 Now, this commandment [*to keep the money from sales of the Book of Commandments*] I give unto my servants **for their benefit** while they remain [*while they are so heavily involved in this work*], **for a manifestation of my blessings** upon their heads, and **for a reward** of their diligence and **for their security**;

16 **For food** and for **raiment** [*clothing*]; for an **inheritance**; for **houses** and for **lands**, in whatsoever circumstances I, the Lord, shall place them [*in whatever full-time callings the Lord gives them*], and whithersoever I, the Lord, shall send them.

17 For **they have been faithful over many things**, and have done well inasmuch as they have not sinned.

18 Behold, **I, the Lord, am merciful and will bless them**, and they shall enter into the joy of these things [*they will have great satisfaction for jobs well done*]. Even so. Amen.

> Before we leave this section, we will take a moment, as we did in section 51, to remind you that living the law of consecration preserves individuality and personal identity. There is private ownership of property and respect for and encouragement of the development and use of individual talents and abilities. Unselfishness, generosity, concern for the welfare of others, and Christlike attitudes are essential. Otherwise, it won't work.
>
> President J. Reuben Clark Jr., of the First Presidency, explained that the "equality" in the law of consecration is not flat equality without consideration of individual wants, desires, and needs. He said:
>
> "There is continuous reference in the revelations to equality among the brethren, but I think you will find only one place where that equality is really described, though it is referred to in other revelations. That revelation (D. & C. 51:3) affirms that every man is to be 'equal according to his family,

according to his circumstances and his wants and needs.' (See also D. & C. 82:17; 78:5–6.) Obviously, this is not a case of 'dead level' equality. It is 'equality' that will vary as much as the man's circumstances, his family, his wants and needs, may vary" (In Conference Report, October 1942, 55).

SECTION 71

Background

This revelation was given to Joseph Smith and Sidney Rigdon, on December 1, 1831, while they were working on the translation of the Bible (the JST) at the John Johnson home in Hiram, Ohio.

In the background to section 64, we mentioned that a member of the Church by the name of Ezra Booth had apostatized from the Church and had written nine bitter and inflammatory anti-Mormon articles that had caused much sentiment against the Church in the Kirtland area. At the time of this revelation, Symonds Ryder, also an apostate and former member, had joined Ezra Booth in publicly attacking the Church.

As you know, we are generally counseled to ignore the efforts and writings of such people. Missionaries especially are so instructed. If we were to take our time and energy to rebut such attacks, it would take away from the time and energy we spend in serving others and fulfilling our responsibilities with our families, Church, employment, missionary work, and so forth. If we debated with every individual who desires to debate and confront us about the Church, there would be much more tension and animosity, and few would be able to hear the peaceful call of the Church to follow Christ.

Therefore, the instruction of the Lord to Joseph and Sidney in this revelation is unusual (verse 7). In fact, a friend of mine who was serving as a mission president at the time told me that a set of elders excitedly called him one day at his office and told them that they had just found a scripture that would allow them to debate the local minister in public. The minister had been causing much trouble for them as they attempted to do their missionary work in that area.

Curious and concerned, the president asked them to tell him what verse they were using. They pointed him to D&C 71:7. Luckily, my friend knew the background to this verse and counseled the elders that this was a special context-sensitive case, and it did not constitute a license for all missionaries to debate in public. Disappointed but understanding, the elders settled back and continued to follow the counsel in D&C 19:30 ("reviling not against revilers"), which does apply to the preaching of the gospel.

Going back to the background and setting for this section, because of the damage being done to the Church and individual members in Ohio, the Lord instructs Joseph and Sidney to go ahead and engage in public as well as private debate with these enemies of the gospel. They did, with much success, and in D&C 73:3, they will be told to go back to the work of translating the Bible.

1 BEHOLD, **thus saith the Lord unto you my servants Joseph Smith, Jun., and Sidney Rigdon, that the time has verily come** that it is necessary and expedient [*necessary*] in me **that you should open your mouths** in proclaiming my gospel, the things of the kingdom, expounding [*explaining*] the mysteries thereof out of the scriptures, according to that portion of Spirit and power which shall be given unto you, even as I will.

2 Verily I say unto you, **proclaim unto the world** [*to nonmembers*] **in the regions round about** [*in this part of Ohio*], and in the church [*among the members*] also, **for the space of a season** [*for a while*], even **until it shall be made known unto you** [*until the Lord asks them to stop*].

3 Verily **this is a mission for a season**, which I give unto you.

4 Wherefore, labor ye in my vineyard. **Call upon the inhabitants of the earth**, and bear record, and prepare the way for the commandments and revelations which are to come. [*In effect, the Lord is asking them to soften the attitudes and concerns held by nonmembers as a direct result of Ezra Booth's writings.*]

Verses 5–6, next, explain the importance of obedience.

5 Now, behold **this is wisdom**; whoso readeth, let him understand and receive also;

6 **For unto him that receiveth it shall be given more abundantly, even power.**

In verses 7–9, next, the Savior tells Joseph and Sidney that they will be blessed with success if they faithfully follow this counsel.

7 Wherefore, **confound your enemies; call upon them to meet you both in public and in private; and inasmuch as ye are faithful their shame shall be made manifest.**

8 Wherefore, **let them bring forth their strong reasons against the Lord.**

9 Verily, thus saith the Lord unto you—there is **no weapon that is formed against you shall prosper**;

SECTION 72

Background

The heading to section 72 in the 2013 printing of the Doctrine and Covenants states that this section "is a compilation of three revelations received on the same day." They were given through the Prophet Joseph Smith in Kirtland, Ohio, on December 4, 1831. Verses 1–8 are the first revelation. Immediately after they were received, Newel K. Whitney was ordained a bishop. Then verses 9–23 were received, outlining the duties of a bishop, and verses 24–26 were given providing instructions for the gathering to Zion.

You will see that several practices of the Church today have their precedents in this section, such as requiring that a priesthood holder have a temple recommend or have a written recommendation from his bishop in order to perform an ordinance outside his own ward.

As background to the receiving of this revelation, Joseph Smith recorded that "several of the Elders and members assembled together to learn their duty, and for edification, and after some time had been spent in conversing about our temporal and spiritual welfare, I received the following: [D&C 72]" (*History of the Church*, 1:239).

Joseph Fielding Smith tells us what happened as Joseph and Sidney carried out the Lord's instructions at this time. He said:

"Quite generally the Lord counsels his servants not to engage in debates and arguments, but to preach in power the fundamental principles of the Gospel. This was a condition that required some action of this kind, and the Spirit of the Lord directed these brethren to go forth and confound their enemies, which they proceeded immediately to do, as their enemies were unable to substantiate their falsehoods and were surprised by this sudden challenge so boldly given. Much of the prejudice was allayed and some friends made through this action" (*Church History and Modern Revelation*, 1:269).

Next, in verse 10, we see that anyone who fights against the Lord's work will eventually be stopped, but that it will happen according to the wisdom and timing of the Lord.

10 And if any man lift his voice against you **he shall be confounded** [*stopped*] **in mine own due time**.

11 Wherefore, **keep my commandments; they are true and faithful** [*the commandments are, in effect, loyal and faithful "traveling companions," right on target, for us during our mortal sojourn, and will bring us safely home to God*]. Even so. Amen.

The First Revelation Given This Day, Verses 1–8

1 HEARKEN, and **listen to the voice of the Lord**, O ye who have assembled yourselves together, who are the high priests of my church, to whom the kingdom and power have been given.

2 For verily thus saith the Lord, **it is expedient in me** [*it has become necessary*] **for a bishop to be appointed unto you**, or of you, unto the church in this part of the Lord's vineyard [*in the Kirtland, Ohio, area*].

3 And verily in this thing ye have done wisely, for **it is required of the Lord, at the hand of every steward, to render an account of his stewardship, both in time and in eternity.**

4 For **he who is faithful and wise in time is accounted worthy to inherit the mansions prepared for him of my Father.**

5 Verily I say unto you, **the elders of the church in this part of my vineyard** [*the Kirtland area*] **shall render an account of their stewardship unto the bishop, who shall be appointed of me** in this part of my vineyard.

At this point, some members of the Church in the Kirtland area were living the law of consecration, but the only bishop in the Church, Edward Partridge, was living in Zion in Missouri at that time. Thus, a bishop was needed in Kirtland. This sets the stage for Newell K. Whitney to be called as a bishop (verse 8).

6 **These things shall be had on record, to be handed over unto the bishop in Zion** [*Bishop Edward Partridge, the first bishop to be called in this dispensation (D&C 41:9), in effect, the Presiding Bishop of the Church*].

7 And the duty of the bishop shall be made known by the commandments which have been given, and the voice of the conference.

8 And now, verily I say unto you, my servant **Newel K. Whitney is the man who shall be appointed and ordained unto this power** [*to be bishop in Kirtland*]. This is the will of the Lord your God, your Redeemer. Even so. Amen.

As noted above, verses 9–23 were given after Newel K. Whitney was ordained a bishop. They give additional details about the duties of a bishop as well as more about the law of consecration, the need for "certificates" (equivalent to recommends today) to be carried by priesthood holders in order to function in their priesthood, and so forth.

SECTION 72

The Second Revelation Given This Day, Verses 9–23

9 The word of the Lord, in addition to the law [*perhaps referring to the revelation given earlier that day, in which instructions were given to ordain Newel K. Whitney a bishop*] which has been given, **making known the duty of the bishop who has been ordained unto the church in this part of the vineyard** [*Kirtland*], **which is verily this—**

Next, specific duties of a bishop are listed. They still apply today.

10 To **keep the Lord's storehouse** [*the bishop's storehouse*]; to **receive the funds of the church** [*such as tithing, fast offering, humanitarian aid, missionary fund, and so forth today*] in this part of the vineyard;

11 To **take an account of the elders** as before has been commanded; **and to administer to their wants** [*administer welfare funds to the needy*], who shall pay for that which they receive, inasmuch as they have wherewith to pay;

12 That **this also may be consecrated** to the good of the church, **to the poor and needy.**

One of the things that we see in action, next, in verse 13 (which likewise is done in the Church today), is this: when a local ward or branch does not have sufficient fast offering funds to meet the needs of the poor and the needy among them, funds can be given from the general Church funds to assist the local bishop in meeting local needs.

13 **And he who hath not wherewith to pay**, an account shall be taken and handed over to **the bishop of Zion** [*Edward Partridge, the Presiding Bishop*], who **shall pay the debt out of that which the Lord shall put into his hands** [*general Church funds, particularly fast offering funds today*].

14 And **the labors of the faithful** [*those who are called to full-time service in the Church, such as General Authorities and missionaries today*] **who labor in spiritual things**, in administering the gospel and the things of the kingdom unto the church, and unto the world, **shall answer the debt unto the bishop in Zion** [*in other words, those who serve full time in the Church are not required to reimburse the Church for their support and the support of their families*];

15 **Thus it** [*the needed funds*] **cometh out of the church**, for according to the law [*the law of consecration*] **every man that**

cometh up to Zion must lay all things before [*must consecrate all he has to*] the bishop in Zion.

16 And now, verily I say unto you, that as **every elder in this part of the vineyard** [*in Kirtland*] **must give an account of his stewardship unto the bishop in this part of the vineyard** [*Bishop Newel K. Whitney*]—

> In verses 17–18, next, we see also that a "recommend" from Bishop Whitney, in Kirtland, was required in order for members who moved from Ohio to Zion, in Jackson County, Missouri, to participate in the law of consecration there.

17 **A certificate** [*equivalent to a recommend today*] **from the judge or bishop** [*Bishop Whitney*] **in this part of the vineyard** [*in the Kirtland area*], **unto the bishop in Zion** [*Bishop Partridge*], **rendereth every man acceptable, and answereth all things, for an inheritance, and to be received as a wise steward and as a faithful laborer** [*in Missouri*];

18 **Otherwise he shall not be accepted of the bishop** [*Bishop Partridge*] **of Zion.**

> Next, the Lord instructs that every elder in the Ohio area who desires a "recommend" from Bishop Newel K. Whitney (and who doesn't live under his immediate supervision), should bring a recommend from his branch president, and then Bishop Whitney can give him a recommend to be used in Missouri.

19 And now, verily I say unto you, **let every elder** who shall give an account unto the bishop of the church in this part of the vineyard [*Bishop Whitney in Kirtland*] **be recommended by the church or churches** [*the branch or branches of the Church*], **in which he labors**, that he may render himself and his accounts approved in all things.

> Verses 20–22 refer specifically to the brethren in D&C 70:1–3 who had the direct responsibility to see that the Book of Commandments was published. They referred to themselves as the "Literary Firm" (*History of the Church*, 2:482–83). Because their responsibilities required their full time, they were to receive assistance from the funds of the Church to support themselves and their families.

20 And again, **let my servants who are appointed as stewards over the literary concerns of my church have claim for assistance upon the bishop or bishops in all things—**

21 **That the revelations** [*the Book of Commandments*] **may be published**, and go forth unto the ends of the earth; that they also may

obtain funds which shall benefit the church in all things;

22 That they also may render themselves approved in all things [*in order for them to be able to carry out their responsibilities*], and be accounted as wise stewards.

> According to verse 23, the pattern described in the above verses for "recommends" and so forth is to be applied throughout the Church as it grows and spreads throughout the earth.

23 And now, behold, **this shall be an ensample** [*example*] **for all the extensive** [*numerous*] **branches of my church, in whatsoever land they shall be established.** And now I make an end of my sayings. Amen.

> As the Church grows and as converts are baptized in areas where an organized branch of the Church does not exist, such converts won't have a branch president to give them a recommend for Bishop Whitney or Bishop Partridge. In verses 24–26, next, the Master explains how to handle this situation.

The Third Revelation Given This Day, Verses 24–26

24 A few words in addition to the laws of the kingdom, respecting the members of the church—**they that are appointed by the Holy Spirit to go up unto Zion**, and they who are privileged to go up unto Zion—

25 **Let them carry up unto the bishop a certificate from three elders** of the church, **or a certificate from the bishop**;

26 **Otherwise** he who shall go up unto the land of Zion **shall not be accounted as a wise steward** [*will not be allowed to participate in the Church and the law of consecration in Jackson County, Missouri*]. This is also an ensample [*example*]. Amen.

SECTION 73

Background

> This revelation was given to Joseph Smith and Sidney Rigdon, in Hiram, Ohio, on January 10, 1832. You may wish to read the background notes for section 71 in this study guide. In section 71, Joseph and Sidney had been told to put aside work on the translation of the Bible (the JST) for a season in order to face the wild rumors and falsehoods being circulated in the area as a result of nine anti-Mormon articles published by apostate Ezra Booth in a local newspaper. The articles ran from October to December and had done much damage to the Church.
>
> The Prophet wrote of the success

of their efforts in confronting the libel of Ezra Booth and others. He said: "From this time until the 8th or 10th of January, 1832, myself and Elder Rigdon continued to preach in Shalersville, Ravenna, and other places, setting forth the truth, vindicating the cause of our Redeemer; showing that the day of vengeance was coming upon this generation like a thief in the night; that prejudice, blindness and darkness filled the minds of many, and caused them to persecute the true Church, and reject the true light; by which means we did much towards allaying the excited feelings which were growing out of the scandalous letters then being published in the Ohio Star, at Ravenna, by the before-mentioned apostate, Ezra Booth. On the 10th of January, I received the following revelation [D&C 73] making known the will of the Lord concerning the Elders of the Church until the convening of the next conference" (*History of the Church*, 1:241).

Having successfully followed the instructions given in section 71, the Prophet and Sidney are now told to return to the work of translating the Bible (verse 3). Some verses in this section are directed to various elders serving missions in the Ohio area (see D&C 73, footnote 1a in your Doctrine and Covenants), whereas some instructions are specifically to Joseph and Sidney.

1 FOR verily, thus saith the Lord, it is expedient in me that **they** [*various missionaries in the Ohio area*] **should continue preaching the gospel, and in exhortation to the churches in the regions round about, until conference** [*to be held in Amherst, Ohio, January 25, 1832; see heading to section 74 in your Doctrine and Covenants*];

2 And **then**, behold, **it shall be made known** unto them, by the voice of the conference, **their several missions.**

Verses 3 and 4 are directed specifically to the Prophet and Sidney Rigdon.

3 Now, verily I say unto you my servants, Joseph Smith, Jun., and Sidney Rigdon, saith the Lord, **it is expedient to translate again**; [*they are to resume work on the translation of the Bible, which we know today as the Joseph Smith Translation of the Bible, or JST*]

4 And, inasmuch as it is practicable, to preach in the regions round about until conference; and **after that it is expedient to continue the work of translation until it be finished.**

Again, verse 5 appears to apply to several elders.

5 And **let this be a pattern unto**

the elders until further knowledge, even as it is written.

6 Now **I give no more unto you at this time.** Gird up your loins [*continue preparations for further assignments*] and be sober [*be serious about the work*]. Even so. Amen.

SECTION 74

Background

This section is yet another example of the great value coming to us from research for the Joseph Smith Papers Project. Editions of the Doctrine and Covenants prior to the 2013 edition give the date of this revelation as January 1832. It was actually sometime in 1830. A quote from the 2018 *Doctrine and Covenants Student Manual* shows that this is incorrect:

"When Church historian and recorder John Whitmer copied the revelation recorded in Doctrine and Covenants 74 into the official record book, he recorded the date as 1830 (see *The Joseph Smith Papers, Documents, Volume 1: July 1828–June 1831*, ed. Michael Hubbard MacKay and others [2013], 228). Years later, those editing the Prophet Joseph Smith's history mistakenly wrote that the Prophet received this revelation in January 1832 while he was making inspired revisions to the New Testament.

However, John Whitmer identified Wayne County, New York, as the place where Joseph Smith dictated the revelation and 1830 as the date when it was received. The Prophet's later history described this revelation as 'an Explanation of the epistle to the first Corinthians, 7th Chapter, 14th verse' (in *Manuscript History of the Church*, vol. A-1, page 178, josephsmithpapers.org). The passage in 1 Corinthians 7:14 had often been cited in Joseph Smith's day to justify infant baptism."

1 Corinthians 7:14 is the subject of this revelation. It is helpful, by way of background and setting for this revelation, to understand that the Jews had a traditional belief that little children were born unclean or unholy (see verse 6).

Verse 1, next, quotes 1 Corinthians 7:14 as it stands in the King James Bible.

1 FOR the unbelieving husband [*nonmember husband*] is sanctified [*helped toward being cleansed*] by the wife [*faithful member*], and the unbelieving wife [*nonmember*] is sanctified by the husband [*faithful member*]; else [*otherwise*] were your children unclean, but now are they holy.

Beginning with verse 2, next, the Lord explains the background to this verse. The law of circumcision was part of the law of Moses and was still being practiced by the Jews who had rejected Christ. Thus, if a woman joined the Church, set up by the Savior during His mortal ministry, her nonmember husband still wanted their children to be subject to the law of Moses, including the law of circumcision for males.

2 Now, **in the days of the Apostles the law of circumcision was had among all the Jews who believed not the gospel of Jesus Christ.**

3 And it came to pass that **there arose a great contention among the people** [*members of the Church*] **concerning the law of circumcision,** for **the unbelieving husband was desirous that his children should be circumcised and become subject to the law of Moses, which law was fulfilled** [*the law of Moses had now been fulfilled by Jesus Christ and the law of circumcision was no longer in force*].

4 And it came to pass that **the children, being brought up in subjection to the law of Moses, gave heed to the traditions of their fathers and believed not the gospel of Christ, wherein they became unholy.**

We see from verse 4, above, that the problem was that if children were brought up keeping the law of Moses, even though they may have belonged to the true Church and attended its meetings, they still ended up believing the law of Moses and the false traditions of the Jews. Thus, they grew up to become "unholy" or unworthy of salvation.

Next, in verse 5, we are told that Paul had given his opinion that a woman or a man should not marry outside the Church unless they had an agreement that the children who were born to them would not be raised according to the law of Moses.

5 Wherefore, **for this cause the Apostle** [*Paul*] **wrote unto the church** [*wrote to the Corinthian members of the Church*], giving unto them a commandment, not of the Lord, but of himself [*expressing his opinion*], **that a believer should not be united** [*married*] **to an unbeliever; except the law of Moses should be done away among them,**

6 **That their children might remain without circumcision; and that the tradition might be done away,** which saith **that little children are unholy; for it was had among the Jews;**

Next, in verse 7, we are taught one of the most beautiful of all doctrines regarding little children. It will be repeated again in D&C 137:10.

7 But **little children are holy, being sanctified** [*saved; made holy and fit to be in the presence of God*] **through the atonement of Jesus Christ**; and this is what the scriptures mean [*such as Mosiah 3:16; Moroni 8; D&C 29:47, 50; and D&C 137:10*].

SECTION 75

Background

This revelation was given through the Prophet Joseph Smith at a conference held at Amherst, Ohio, about fifty miles east of Kirtland on January 25, 1832. It consists of two revelations given on the same day (similar to section 73, which consists of three revelations given on the same day). The first revelation is verses 1–22. The second, verses 23–36.

One of the significant things to watch as we study the Doctrine and Covenants is the gradual development of the structure of Church leadership as we know it today. Rather than organizing it all at once, the Lord did it step by step as the growth and development of the Church warranted it. In a way, it was similar to what happens in outlying areas of the Church today. First, there may be a few members, then a dependent branch with a minimum of leadership, then a branch with a branch president, then with a full branch presidency, and finally, a ward with the full normal organization of officers and teachers.

For example, when the Church was organized on April 6, 1830, there were four priesthood offices to which men were ordained—deacon, teacher, priest, and elder (see D&C 20:38). And Joseph Smith was "called a seer, a translator, a prophet, an apostle of Jesus Christ, an elder of the church" (D&C 21:1).

In 1831, a new office was added, that of bishop. Edward Partridge was called to be the first bishop in February 1831 (D&C 41:9).

In 1832, at the time of this revelation (section 75), Joseph Smith was sustained and ordained as the President of the High Priesthood of the Church. Thus, he is now the "President of the Church." In early March 1832, he will get counselors for the first time, and on March 15, 1832, the Lord announced that the First Presidency held "the keys of the kingdom, which belong always unto the Presidency of the High Priesthood" (D&C 81:2).

In December 1833, the first patriarch was called (Joseph Smith's father, Joseph Smith Sr.).

In 1834, the first stake was organized at Kirtland on February 17.

In 1835, the Quorum of the Twelve Apostles was organized.

The above serves to remind us

that the Lord did things "line upon line" as He gradually established the organization of the Church as we know it today.

At the time of this revelation, some elders had approached the Prophet, concerned that they were having difficulty in getting people to understand the message of the Restoration as they preached and taught it. They asked Joseph to ask the Lord for counsel on this matter. As the Savior responds, He first identifies Himself to these elders in verse 1.

The First Revelation Given on This Day, Verses 1–22

(given to elders who had submitted their names to serve missions).

1 VERILY, verily, I say unto you, **I who speak** even **by the voice of my Spirit**, even **Alpha and Omega, your Lord and your God**—

"Alpha and Omega" (verse 1) are the first and last letters of the Greek alphabet—in other words, "A and Z." The symbolism is that all things are encompassed by the Savior. He knows all things and has all power to help us and bring us to exaltation if we are willing. He can help us in everything from A to Z in our lives.

Next, the Lord addresses these elders who have come to seek counsel from Him.

2 **Hearken, O ye who have given your names to go forth to proclaim my gospel**, and **to prune my vineyard** [*the imagery is that of cutting out the old dead wood of falsehood and apostasy, the false doctrines and philosophies of the world that stand in the way of new growth, as in pruning a fruit tree*].

3 Behold, I say unto you that **it is my will that you should go forth and not tarry** [*don't delay longer*], neither be idle but labor with your might—

4 **Lifting up your voices as with the sound of a trump** [*the imagery is that of a clear, easily discernible, simple, uncluttered message of the Restoration, like a trumpet or French horn in an orchestra is easy to pick out*], **proclaiming the truth according to the revelations and commandments which I have given you** [*as they preach, they should stick to the scriptures and revelations through the prophet*].

5 And thus, **if ye are faithful ye shall be laden with many sheaves** [*you will have a great harvest of souls*], and crowned with honor, and glory, and immortality, and eternal life [*exaltation in celestial glory*].

Verses 6–12 are directed to William E. McLellin and Luke Johnson.

SECTION 75

In D&C 66:7 (given about three months previous to this revelation), the Lord had told Elder McLellin to go to the "eastern lands" to preach. He did go to Pennsylvania and preached some, but returned soon because of disobedience and illness. (You may wish to read more about William McLellin in the background notes for sections 66 and 67 in this study guide.) Now, the Lord revokes that mission for William and asks him to go south to preach.

One lesson that we learn from this change in missions for Brother McLellin is that the Lord keeps trying with us, even when we make mistakes, and even when our attitude is poor. He loves us and gives us every opportunity to succeed.

6 Therefore, verily I say **unto** my servant **William E. McLellin, I revoke the commission** [*mission call*] **which I gave unto him to go unto the eastern countries** [*the eastern United States*];

7 And **I give unto him a new commission** and a new commandment, in the which I, the Lord, **chasten him for the murmurings of his heart**;

8 And **he sinned; nevertheless, I forgive him** and say unto him again, **Go ye into the south countries** [*the Savior is giving him another chance to succeed*].

9 And let my servant **Luke Johnson** [*son of John and Elsa Johnson*] go with him, and proclaim the things which I have commanded them—

10 **Calling on the name of the Lord for the Comforter** [*the Holy Ghost*], **which shall teach them all things that are expedient** [*necessary*] **for them**—

11 **Praying always that they faint not** [*so they don't get too discouraged and give up*]; and **inasmuch as they do this, I will be with them even unto the end.**

12 Behold, this is the will of the Lord your God concerning you. Even so. Amen.

Verses 13–22 give instructions to several pairs of missionaries to serve in various parts of the United States.

13 And again, verily thus saith the Lord, let my servant **Orson Hyde** and my servant **Samuel H. Smith** take their journey into the eastern countries, and proclaim the things which I have commanded them; and inasmuch as they are faithful, lo, I will be with them even unto the end.

14 And again, verily I say unto my servant **Lyman Johnson**, and unto my servant **Orson Pratt**, they shall also take their journey

into the eastern countries; and behold, and lo, I am with them also, even unto the end.

15 And again, I say unto my servant **Asa Dodds**, and unto my servant **Calves Wilson**, that they also shall take their journey unto the western countries, and proclaim my gospel, even as I have commanded them.

16 And **he who is faithful shall overcome all things** [with the help of the Atonement of Christ], **and shall be lifted up** [given exaltation] **at the last day** [on the final Judgment Day].

17 And again, I say unto my servant **Major N. Ashley**, and my servant **Burr Riggs**, let them take their journey also into the south country.

> Verses 18–22 contain a context for shaking "off the dust of your feet as a testimony against them" (verse 20). The word "testimony" means "witness"—in other words, "evidence" that they rejected the missionaries.
>
> In many conversations among members of the Church, the word "curse" enters into such discussions. In a sense, rejecting the gospel brings the "curse" of not having the gospel and its attendant blessings upon those who reject the missionaries. However, we must be very careful in what we do with such words. Remember, God is completely fair, and all people will ultimately have had a fair chance to hear and understand the gospel before the day of final judgment. You may wish to read section 138, especially verses 30–34, to reaffirm this doctrine.

18 Yea, **let all those take their journey**, as I have commanded them, going **from house to house, and from village to village, and from city to city**.

19 **And in whatsoever house ye enter, and they receive you, leave your blessing upon that house**.

20 And **in whatsoever house ye enter, and they receive you not**, ye shall **depart speedily** from that house, and **shake off the dust of your feet as a testimony against them**.

21 And you shall be filled with joy and gladness; and **know this, that in the day of judgment you shall be judges of that house, and condemn them** [unless they accept the gospel later; see D&C 138];

22 And **it shall be more tolerable for the heathen** [those who didn't get a chance to hear the gospel] **in the day of judgment, than

for that house; therefore, gird up your loins [*prepare to serve*] and be faithful, and ye shall overcome all things, and be lifted up [*receive exaltation*] at the last day. Even so. Amen.

Before we leave the subject of shaking dust off feet "as a testimony against them" (verse 20, above), we will include a quote from the *Doctrine and Covenants Student Manual*, 1981, pages 130–31 on this subject.

"The ordinance of washing the dust from one's feet was practiced in New Testament times and was reinstituted in this dispensation (see D&C 88:139–40; John 11:2; 12:3; 13:5–14). The action of shaking or cleansing the dust from one's feet is a testimony against those who refuse to accept the gospel (see D&C 24:15; 84:92; 99:4). Because of the serious nature of this act, Church leaders have directed that it be done only at the command of the Spirit. President Joseph Fielding Smith explained the significance of the action as follows: 'The cleansing of their feet, either by washing or wiping off the dust, would be recorded in heaven as a testimony against the wicked. This act, however, was not to be performed in the presence of the offenders, "lest thou provoke them, but in secret, and wash thy feet, as a testimony against them in the day of judgment." The missionaries of the Church who faithfully perform their duty are under the obligation of leaving their testimony with all with whom they come in contact in their work. This testimony will stand as a witness against those who reject the message, at the judgment.' (*Church History and Modern Revelation*, 1:223.)"

In verses 23–28, the Lord gives instructions concerning how the families of missionaries should be cared for in their absence.

The Second Revelation Given on This Day, Verses 23–36

(given to a group of elders who wanted to know the Lord's will for them).

23 And again, thus saith the Lord unto you, **O ye elders** of my church, **who have given your names** [*in other words, the elders who requested this revelation*] **that you might know his will concerning you**—

24 Behold, I say unto you, that **it is the duty of the church to assist in supporting the families of those** [*who have already been called on missions*], **and also to support the families of those who are called** [*those who will yet be called*] and must needs be sent unto the world to proclaim the gospel unto the world.

25 **Wherefore, I, the Lord, give unto you this commandment**, that ye **obtain places for your**

families, inasmuch as [*if*] your brethren are willing to open their hearts [*in other words, if others who are not called to go on missions are willing to help support your families while you are gone*].

26 And **let all such as can obtain places for their families, and support of the church for them, not fail to go** [*on the missions to which they have been called*] **into the world, whether to the east or to the west, or to the north, or to the south.**

27 **Let them ask and they shall receive, knock and it shall be opened unto them, and be made known from on high, even by the Comforter** [*the Holy Ghost*], **whither they shall go.**

> Next, because the Saints were generally poor in worldly means and goods at this time in Church history, it was difficult to find others who had the means themselves to support their own families plus others. Therefore, those who are unable to find support for their families, if they go on missions, are counseled to stay home and support them themselves. They will not lose blessings from the Lord by so doing.

28 And again, verily I say unto you, that **every man who is obliged to provide for his own family** [*who can't find others to support his family*], let him provide [*he should stay home and provide for them himself*], and **he shall in nowise lose his crown** [*he will not lose his salvation*]; **and let him labor in the church** [*he should serve faithfully in the Church at home*].

> In a significant sense, the principle explained by the Savior in verse 28, above, could apply to any faithful members who desire to serve a mission but can't because of difficulties beyond their control. They are to stay home and serve faithfully in the Church there. They will not lose eternal blessings as a result.
>
> Another general principle is taught in verse 29, next. Personal industry and diligence need to be developed by all who wish to become celestial.

29 **Let every man be diligent in all things.** And **the idler shall not have place in the church, except he repent and mend his ways.**

> In the final verses of this section, several other missionary pairs are identified.

30 Wherefore, let my servant **Simeon Carter** and my servant **Emer Harris** be united in the ministry;

31 And also my servant **Ezra**

Thayre and my servant **Thomas B. Marsh**;

32 Also my servant **Hyrum Smith** and my servant **Reynolds Cahoon**;

33 And also my servant **Daniel Stanton** and my servant **Seymour Brunson**;

34 And also my servant **Sylvester Smith** and my servant **Gideon Carter**;

35 And also my servant **Ruggles Eames** and my servant **Stephen Burnett**;

36 And also my servant **Micah B. Welton** and also my servant **Eden Smith**. Even so. Amen.

SECTION 76

Background

This revelation includes a vision (consisting of six visions) given to the Prophet Joseph Smith and Sidney Rigdon while living at the home of John and Alice (Elsa) Johnson in Hiram, Ohio. The vision was given on February 16, 1832, and provides doctrinal details about the three degrees of glory and perdition (meaning complete loss, complete destruction). Section 76 is thus one of the major doctrinal sections of the Doctrine and Covenants.

One of the main reasons Joseph and Emma Smith, along with Sidney Rigdon, had moved into the John Johnson home was so that Joseph and Sidney would have time to continue work on the translation of the Bible (the *Joseph Smith Translation of the Bible*, or JST) as commanded by the Lord in D&C 45:60–61.

Joseph had started work on the JST in June 1830 and continued for about three years. During the work of translating, correcting, and revising, many questions came up in the Prophet's mind. As was his way, he turned to the Lord for answers.

The question that led to the vision recorded in section 76 had to do with the Christian concept of heaven and hell, and, in particular, John 5:29, which is usually interpreted as meaning that there is just one heaven and one hell. We will quote it here, including verse 28 for context:

John 5:28–29

28 Marvel not at this: for the hour is coming, in the which all that are in the graves shall hear his voice,

29 And shall come forth; they that have done good, unto the resurrection of life; and they that have done evil, unto the resurrection of damnation.

The question that came up in the Prophet's mind had to do with the problem of believing in just one heaven in view of the fact that there are so many different lifestyles and degrees of righteousness or wickedness among people.

Joseph Smith gave the background to this vision. He wrote:

"Upon my return from Amherst [Ohio] conference, I resumed the translation of the Scriptures. From sundry [various] revelations which had been received, it was apparent that many important points touching the salvation of man, had been taken from the Bible, or lost before it was compiled. It appeared self-evident from what truths were left, that if God rewarded every one according to the deeds done in the body the term 'Heaven,' as intended for the Saints' eternal home must include more kingdoms than one. Accordingly, on the 16th of February, 1832, while translating St. John's Gospel, myself and Elder Rigdon saw the following vision [D&C 76]" (*History of the Church*, 1:245).

About 12 other men were in the room at the Johnson home when the vision was given. Brother Philo Dibble was one of them, and he recorded the experience as follows:

"The vision which is recorded in the Book of Doctrine and Covenants was given at the house of 'Father Johnson,' in Hiram, Ohio, and during the time that Joseph and Sidney were in the spirit and saw the heavens open, there were other men in the room, perhaps twelve, among whom I was one during a part of the time—probably two-thirds of the time,—I saw the glory and felt the power, but did not see the vision.

"The events and conversation, while they were seeing what is written (and many things were seen and related that are not written,) I will relate as minutely as is necessary.

"Joseph would, at intervals, say: 'What do I see?' as one might say while looking out the window and beholding what all in the room could not see. Then he would relate what he had seen or what he was looking at. Then Sidney replied, 'I see the same.' Presently Sidney would say 'what do I see?' and would repeat what he had seen or was seeing, and Joseph would reply, 'I see the same.'

"This manner of conversation was reported at short intervals to the end of the vision, and during the whole time not a word was spoken by any other person. Not a sound nor motion made by anyone but Joseph and Sidney, and it seemed to me that they never moved a joint or limb during the time I was there, which I think was over an hour, and to the end of the vision.

"Joseph sat firmly and calmly all the time in the midst of a magnificent glory, but Sidney sat limp and pale, apparently as limber as a rag, observing which, Joseph remarked, smilingly, 'Sidney is not used to it as I am'" (*Juvenile Instructor*, May 1892, 303–4).

We mentioned earlier that this vision consisted of a series of six separate visions within the overall vision. The overall vision is recorded in verses 19–113. For purposes of study, the six visions within the vision can generally be grouped as given in the following list (you may wish to include this list as notes in your own scriptures):

Overall Vision
Verses 19–113

Six Visions within the Vision
1. The Glory of the Son (verses 19–24)

2. The Fall of Lucifer (Satan) (verses 25–29)

3. The Sons of Perdition (verses 30–39, 43–49)

4. Celestial Glory (verses 50–70, 92–96)

5. Terrestrial Glory (verses 71–80, 87, 91, 97)

6. Telestial Glory (verses 81–89, 98–106, 109–12)

We will now begin our verse-by-verse study of this section. In verses 1–10, we are taught about the glory and power of God. We are also given many insights as to the desire of God to bless us and show respect and honor toward us. This is almost unique in a world in which many Christian religions, along with numerous non-Christian religions, demean and debase mankind in order to elevate God.

1 **HEAR**, O ye heavens, and give ear, O earth, **and rejoice** ye inhabitants thereof, for **the Lord is God, and beside him there is no Savior.**

2 **Great is his wisdom, marvelous are his ways, and the extent of his doings none can find out.**

3 **His purposes fail not, neither are there any who can stay his hand** [*none can stop the Lord*].

4 **From eternity to eternity he is the same** [*He uses the same plan of salvation to save*], **and his years never fail** [*He will never cease to exist*].

5 For thus saith the Lord—**I, the Lord, am merciful and gracious unto those who fear** [*respect*] **me, and delight to honor those who serve me in righteousness and in truth unto the end.**

6 **Great shall be their reward and eternal shall be their glory.**

Before reading verse 7, next, it is helpful to check the Bible Dictionary (in our Latter-day Saint edition of the Bible) for the definition of "mystery." Otherwise, we might think that it means mysterious and obscure facts and details. It does not. We will use **bold** for emphasis.

Mystery

"Denotes in the N.T. [*New Testament*] **a spiritual truth that was once hidden but now is revealed, and that, without special revelation, would have remained unknown**. It is generally used along with words denoting revelation or publication (e.g., Rom. 16:25–26; Eph. 1:9; 3:3–10; Col. 1:26; 4:3; 1 Tim. 3:16). **The modern meaning of something incomprehensible forms no part of the significance of the word as it occurs in the N.T.** *See also* Alma 12:9–11; 40:3; D&C 19:10; 42:61–65; 76:5–10. On the other hand, there is no spiritual gain in idle speculation about things the Lord has not revealed. See Deut. 29:29; Alma 37:11."

7 And **to them will I reveal all mysteries**, yea, all the hidden mysteries of my kingdom from days of old, and for ages to come, will I make known unto them the good pleasure of my will concerning all things pertaining to my kingdom.

8 Yea, **even the wonders of eternity shall they know**, and things to come will I show them, even the things of many generations.

9 And **their wisdom shall be great, and their understanding reach to heaven**; and **before them the wisdom of the wise shall perish, and the understanding of the prudent shall come to naught** [*nothing*].

Verse nine, above, reminds us of the "wise," including many philosophers, highly educated individuals, the teachings of most other religions, Christian and non-Christian, and others who present their confusing and conflicting views about God and religion, completely missing the simple doctrines and truths of the true gospel of Jesus Christ. Thus, these "plain and simple things" (1 Nephi 13:29) are "mysteries" to them. And their teachings and mysterious wonderings and musings will come to nothing when exposed to the full light and wonderful intelligence of the pure gospel of Jesus Christ.

10 For **by my Spirit will I enlighten them** [*the righteous who "fear" God—verse 5*]**, and by my power will I make known unto them the secrets of my will— yea, even those things which eye has not seen, nor ear heard, nor yet entered into the heart of man.**

> In verses 11–18, Joseph Smith and Sidney Rigdon tell us what led up to this vision.

11 **We, Joseph Smith, Jun., and Sidney Rigdon**, being in the Spirit [*working under the influence of the Holy Ghost*] on the sixteenth day of February, in the year of our Lord one thousand eight hundred and thirty–two—

12 **By the power of the Spirit our eyes were opened and our understandings were enlightened**, so as to see and understand the things of God—

13 Even those things which were from the beginning before the world was, which were **ordained of the Father** [*authorized and put into action*]**, through his Only Begotten Son**, who was in the bosom of the Father [*who worked in complete harmony with the Father*], even from the beginning;

> In verse 14, next, we are told that the Prophet and Sidney Rigdon saw the Savior and talked with Him during this vision.

14 **Of whom we bear record**; and the record which we bear is the fulness of the gospel of Jesus Christ, who is the Son, **whom we saw and with whom we conversed in the heavenly vision.**

15 For **while we were doing the work of translation** [*working on the translation of the Bible, which became the Joseph Smith Translation (the JST)*]**, which the Lord had appointed unto us, we came to the twenty–ninth verse of the fifth chapter of John**, which was given unto us as follows—

16 **Speaking of the resurrection of the dead**, concerning those who shall hear the voice of the Son of Man [*speaking of those who will have had a fair chance to hear and understand the gospel by the day of final judgment*]:

17 **And shall come forth; they who have done good in the resurrection of the just; and they who have done evil, in the resurrection of the unjust.**

18 Now **this caused us to marvel, for it was given unto us of the Spirit.**

> Did you notice the wonderful doctrine in verse 18? The Holy Ghost can cause us to wonder about things, to prepare us to be taught by the Spirit, and to receive answers from above to our prayers and wonderings.
>
> Perhaps you have had the experience of wondering about something and then going to church and the sacrament meeting speaker or a teacher in one of your classes

answered your question. It may have seemed to you that he or she was talking directly to you! And because you had been wondering about that very thing, the answer meant much more than it otherwise would have because you were prepared by the Spirit to hear it. In fact, you still remember it today. Such is the power of the Holy Ghost to prepare and teach us.

Next, the vision that Joseph Smith and Sidney Rigdon had of the Savior is described. Remember that the entire vision they had, consisting of six visions, goes from verse 19 to 113.

Vision #1
The Glory of the Son
(verses 19–24)

19 And while we meditated upon these things, the Lord touched the eyes of our understandings and they were opened, and the glory of the Lord shone round about.

20 And we beheld the glory of the Son, on the right hand of the Father, and received of his fulness;

From verse 21, next, we learn that they saw others, besides the Father and Son, in this vision.

21 And **saw the holy angels, and them who are sanctified** [*"sanctified" means those who have proven themselves worthy of living with God forever—compare with Moses 6:60*] before his throne, worshiping God, and the Lamb, who worship him forever and ever.

The idea in the scriptures of worshipping God "forever and ever" is often misunderstood. It has caused some to wonder if they even want to go to heaven. It conjures up visions of standing on clouds, playing harps forever, and becoming terribly bored.

However, when we realize that "worshipping God" includes doing things that bring Him honor and glory, such as serving others, even creating our own worlds and using the same plan of salvation for our spirit children that He used for us, the term "worship" becomes exciting and fascinating, the complete opposite of boredom.

You may wish to mark verses 22–24 in your own scriptures. They are often quoted and are very powerful.

22 **And now, after the many testimonies which have been given of him** [*Christ*]**, this is the testimony, last of all, which we give of him: That he lives!**

23 **For we saw him, even on the right hand** [*the covenant hand, symbolizing that the Savior kept the covenants He made with the Father to be the Redeemer*] **of God; and**

we heard the voice bearing record that he is the Only Begotten of the Father—

On occasions, students of the gospel become confused at the term "Only Begotten of the Father" (verse 23, above). The confusion comes when they consider the fact that all of us are spirit sons and daughters of God (as stated in the proclamation on the family), born to Him in the premortal life. How can Christ be the "Only Begotten" when we too are begotten spirit children of God?

The answer is simple and important. Jesus is the Only Begotten of the Father in the flesh. In other words, He is the only one whose father in mortality was God. President Heber J. Grant explained this. He said (**bold** added for emphasis):

"We believe absolutely that Jesus Christ is the Son of God, begotten of God, the first-born in the spirit and **the only begotten in the flesh**; that He is the Son of God just as much as you and I are the sons of our fathers" (Heber J. Grant, "Analysis of the Articles of Faith," *Millennial Star*, January 5, 1922, 2).

24 That by him [Christ], and through him, and of him, the worlds are and were created [*all the worlds He has created or will yet create*]**, and the inhabitants thereof are begotten sons and daughters unto God.**

Verse 24, above, answers an interesting question that often comes up in gospel classes and discussions. The question is whether Jesus is the savior of other worlds in addition to ours. Can you pick out the answer? It is found in the last phrase, which states that the inhabitants of all those worlds ("worlds without number" according to Moses 1:33) "are begotten sons and daughters **unto** God." The word "unto" is significant. It is not "of." (We are all begotten spirit sons and daughters "of" God.) It is "unto," implying the action of bringing them unto the Father through the gospel and the Atonement. In other words, through our Savior, the inhabitants of all of Father's worlds have the opportunity to be brought back to the Father and live with Him in celestial glory forever. Thus, "begotten sons and daughters unto God" is another term for exaltation.

Just in case someone challenges this interpretation of verse 24, it is helpful to read verses 22–24 in poetic form, as written by the Prophet Joseph Smith (who put the whole vision in poetic form):

And now after all of the proofs
  made of him,
By witnesses truly, by whom
  he was known,
This is mine, last of all, that he lives;
  yea, he lives!
And sits on the right hand of God
  on his throne.

*And I heard a great voice bearing
    record from heav'n,
He's the Saviour and Only
    Begotten of God,
By him, of him, and through him,
    the worlds were all made,
Even all that career [orbit] in
    the heavens so broad.*

*Whose inhabitants, too, from the
    first to the last,
Are sav'd by the very same
    Saviour of ours;
And of course, are begotten Gods
    daughters and sons
By the very same truths and the
    very same powers.*

—Millennial Star, 4:49–55

Vision #2
The Fall of Lucifer
(verses 25–29)

25 And this we saw also, and bear record, that an angel of God [*Lucifer, Satan*] **who was in authority** [*Lucifer held considerable authority in premortality before he rebelled*] **in the presence of God, who rebelled against the Only Begotten Son** [*Christ*] **whom the Father loved** [*was able to bless with His highest blessings*] **and who was in the bosom of the Father** [*who was in complete harmony and unity with the Father*]**, was thrust down from the presence of God and the Son,**

The word "loved" in the phrase "whom the Father loved" in verse 25, above, must be understood correctly. Otherwise, it sounds like the Father loves some of His children more than others.

In an article titled "Divine Love," written for the February 2003 *Ensign*, then Elder Russell M. Nelson described several different types of "love" as it pertains to God. Among other things, he wrote (**bold** added for emphasis):

"While **divine love** can be called perfect, infinite, enduring, and universal, it **cannot correctly be characterized as** *unconditional*. The word does not appear in the scriptures. On the other hand, many verses affirm that **the higher levels of love the Father and the Son feel for each of us—and certain divine blessings stemming from that love—are** *conditional*.

"The resplendent bouquet of God's love—including eternal life—includes **blessings for which we must qualify**, not entitlements to be expected unworthily."

With this instruction from Elder Nelson in mind, we can define the phrase "whom the Father loved" as meaning "whom the Father was enabled to bless because of Christ's obedience."

SECTION 76

We will now continue with the vision of the fall of Lucifer.

26 And was called Perdition [*which means complete loss, irreparably damaged*], for **the heavens wept over him**—he was **Lucifer, a son of the morning** [*all of us wept and were sorry to see him fall*].

By the way, the name "Lucifer" (verse 26) means "light bearer" or "light bringer" (common dictionary definitions). Continuing, we must be careful to read the last phrase of verse 26, above, exactly as it is. Some people inadvertently read it as "the son of the morning" rather than "a son of the morning." The difference is important. If it were "the son of the morning," it would imply that Lucifer was one of the highest in authority. Whereas "a son of the morning" implies that he was one of many who held authority and wielded influence in our premortal life. President George Q. Cannon of the First Presidency explained this. He said:

"Some have called him *the* son of the morning, but here it is *a* son of the morning—one among many, doubtless. This angel was a mighty personage, without doubt. The record that is given to us concerning him clearly shows that he occupied a very high position; that he was thought a great deal of, and that he was mighty in his sphere, so much so that when the matter was debated concerning the earth and the plan of salvation, he was of sufficient importance to have a plan, which he proposed as the plan by which this earth should be peopled and the inhabitants thereof redeemed. His plan, however, was not accepted; but it was so plausible and so attractive that out of the whole hosts of heaven one-third accepted his plan and were willing to cast their lot with him [Moses 4:1–4; D&C 29:36–37]. Now, the difference between Jesus and Lucifer was this: Jesus was willing to submit to the Father" (*Millennial Star,* September 5, 1895, 563–64; quoted in the *Doctrine and Covenants Student Manual,* 1981, 160).

27 And we [*Joseph Smith and Sidney Rigdon*] beheld, and lo, **he is fallen! is fallen, even a son of the morning!**

28 And while we were yet in the Spirit, the Lord commanded us that we should write the vision; for **we beheld Satan, that old serpent, even the devil, who rebelled against God, and sought to take the kingdom of our God and his Christ—**

29 Wherefore [*this is why*], **he maketh war with the saints of God,** and encompasseth them round about [*surrounds them with temptation to sin*].

The "war" referred to in verse 29, above, started with the War in Heaven (see Revelation 12:7–9), which started with the rebellion of Lucifer in premortality. It is still continuing here on earth. It will not be over until the final defeat of Satan and his evil followers in the battle of Gog and Magog, which will take place after the Millennium comes to an end. (See D&C 88:110–115.) The War in Heaven was a battle for our loyalty and, ultimately, for our souls. President Gordon B. Hinckley said (**bold added for emphasis**):

"The book of Revelation speaks briefly of what must have been **a terrible conflict for the minds and loyalties** of God's children" ("War and Peace," *Ensign*, May 2003, 78). He then went on to quote Revelation 12:7–9.

Next, we will study what the Prophet Joseph Smith and Sidney Rigdon saw regarding the sons of perdition.

Vision #3

The Sons of Perdition, sometimes referred to in gospel conversations as those who will end up in "outer darkness" (verses 30–39, 43–49)

This final place, reserved for the devil and those who follow him completely, is referred to variously as "hell," "perdition," and sometimes "outer darkness." You can find it referred to as "outer darkness" in "*Guide to the Scriptures,*" under "Hell," where it says, "The scriptures sometimes refer to hell as outer darkness."

Before we move on, it is important to understand that Satan makes war (verse 30) against all of us who have lived beyond the age of accountability (see D&C 29:46–47). A key phrase in verse 30, next, is "made war <u>and</u> overcame." Satan cannot completely overpower and forever claim anyone without that person's consent. Thus, sons of perdition are those who have intentionally made unwise agency choices and have thus gradually turned themselves completely over to Lucifer.

For teaching purposes, we will number the qualifications for becoming sons of perdition as we go along.

30 And **we saw a vision of the sufferings of those with whom he** [*Lucifer*] **made war and overcame** [*a gradual process*], for thus came the voice of the Lord unto us:

31 Thus saith the Lord concerning all those who **[1] know my power, and [2] have been made partakers thereof,** and **[3] suffered themselves through the power of the devil to be overcome,** and to **[4] deny the truth** and **[5] defy my power—**

We will add some notes for each of the five items numbered in verse 31, above.

(1) "know my power"

In order to "know" God and His power, one must have the witness of the Holy Ghost. Joseph Smith taught this as follows: "All sins shall be forgiven, except the sin against the Holy Ghost; for Jesus will save all except the sons of perdition. What must a man do to commit the unpardonable sin? He must receive the Holy Ghost, have the heavens opened unto him, and know God, and then sin against Him. After a man has sinned against the Holy Ghost, there is no repentance for him. He has got to say that the sun does not shine while he sees it; he has got to deny Jesus Christ when the heavens have been opened unto him, and to deny the plan of salvation with his eyes open to the truth of it; and from that time he begins to be an enemy. This is the case with many apostates of the Church of Jesus Christ of Latter-day Saints" (*Teachings of the Prophet Joseph Smith*, 358).

(2) "have been made partakers thereof"

They are members of the Church, have received all ordinances, endowments, and such that we have available here in this life to prepare for exaltation. President Joseph F. Smith explained this (**bold** added for emphasis):

"And he that believes, is baptized, and receives the light and testimony of Jesus Christ . . . **receiving the fulness of the blessings of the gospel in this world**, and **afterwards turns wholly unto sin**, violating his covenants . . . will taste the second death" (*Gospel Doctrine*, 476–77).

(3) "suffered themselves through the power of the devil to be overcome"

They must exercise their moral agency to intentionally go against knowledge and truth. In other words, they must intentionally allow themselves to be overcome by Satan.

(4) "deny the truth"

They become complete liars, completely lacking integrity. In other words, they become totally dishonest, like Satan, denying the truth when they fully know it.

(5) "defy my power"

They don't simply go inactive. Rather, they fight against God and the Church, against all that is good, with the same evil energy with which Satan and his evil hosts fight truth and right.

Next, in verse 32, the Lord defines such people as being sons of perdition.

32 **They are** they who are **the sons of perdition,** of whom I say

that it had been better for them never to have been born;

> From the last phrase of verse 32, above, we understand that sons of perdition do not come through the veil as such. Rather, they retrogress during this life and become sons of perdition.

33 For **they are vessels of wrath** [*have become full of anger, bitterness, and hatred of that which is good. In other words, they actually become like Satan. They think as he does, act as he does, and react against good as he does. This is the full opposite of becoming like Christ through following His commandments and striving to live His gospel*], **doomed to suffer the wrath of God, with the devil and his angels in eternity** [*they will ultimately be cast out completely with Satan and the evil spirits who followed him in the War in Heaven; see D&C 88:114*];

34 Concerning whom I have said **there is no forgiveness in this world nor in the world to come** [*in other words, this sin, often termed "the sin against the Holy Ghost," cannot be forgiven; the reason is simple: it is that, among other things, such individuals have become just like Satan and would not have any use for or interest in forgiveness if it were offered to them*]—

In verse 35, next, we see three more qualifications for becoming sons of perdition.

35 Having **[6] denied the Holy Spirit after having received it**, and having **[7] denied the Only Begotten Son of the Father**, having **[8] crucified him unto themselves and put him to an open shame**.

We will add notes for each of the three items listed in verse 35, above.

(6) "denied the Holy Spirit after having received it"

> In order to become a son of perdition, one must have received the gift of the Holy Ghost. The following quote helps us understand this.
>
> "To become a son of perdition one must sin against the Holy Ghost; but before that is possible, one must receive the gift of the Holy Ghost. Elder Melvin J. Ballard explained that 'unto the Holy Ghost has been given the right and the privilege of manifesting the truth unto men as no other power will. So that when he makes a man see and know a thing he knows it better than he shall ever know anything else; and to sin against that knowledge is to sin against the greatest light there is, and consequently commit the greatest sin there is.' (*Millennial Star*, 11 Aug. 1932, 499–500.)" (See also

SECTION 76

Doctrine and Covenants Student Manual, 1981, 161.)

(7) "denied the Only Begotten Son of the Father"

After receiving a sure testimony that Jesus is the Christ, they reject Him completely, just as Satan has.

(8) "crucified him unto themselves and put him to an open shame"

They become so bitter that they themselves would gladly crucify Christ again if they had the opportunity. In other words, as stated above, they have become like Satan. They think as he does, hate as he does, and have the same desires and goals as he does. Brigham Young summarized the topic of becoming sons of perdition. He said:

"How much does it take to prepare a man, or woman . . . to become angels to the devil, to suffer with him through all eternity? Just as much as it does to prepare a man to go into the Celestial Kingdom, into the presence of the Father and the Son, and to be made an heir to his kingdom and all his glory, and be crowned with crowns of glory, immortality, and eternal lives" (*Journal of Discourses*, 3:93).

Additional information about the fate and ultimate condition of sons of perdition is given in verses 36–48.

36 These are **they** who **shall go away into the lake of fire and brimstone** [*there is no literal "lake of fire and brimstone"; brimstone is molten sulfur; thus, this phrase is symbolic of the worst, unimaginable suffering*], **with the devil and his angels** [*the evil spirits who followed him in the War in Heaven*]—

37 And **the only ones on whom the second death** [*being completely cut off from God's presence*] **shall have any power** [*the only ones who will not have at least some degree of glory and be free from Satan forever*];

38 Yea, verily, **the only ones who shall not be redeemed in the due time of the Lord** [*redeemed to at least telestial glory or better*], **after the sufferings of his wrath** [*after being punished for their own sins; see D&C 19:15–17*].

Before we read verse 39, next, we must be aware that everyone who has ever been born on earth will be resurrected. This includes those who become sons of perdition. (See 1 Corinthians 15:22, D&C 88:32.) Lucifer and the evil spirits who followed him (Revelation 12:4) will, of course, not get resurrected because they do not receive mortal bodies.

If we do not understand the above doctrine, we will be apt to interpret verse 39, next, as saying that everyone except sons of perdition will be resurrected. This would be false doctrine.

39 For all the rest [*all except those mortals who become sons of perdition*] shall be brought forth by the resurrection of the dead, **through the triumph and the glory of the Lamb** [*all who attain telestial, terrestrial, or celestial glory, will, at least to some degree, partake of the "triumph and glory" of Christ; they will all be completely free from Satan in the eternities, and will live in kingdoms of glory*], **who was slain**, who was in the bosom of the Father before the worlds were made [*whose Atonement was planned in the premortal councils*].

Verses 40–44 break from describing sons of perdition long enough to rejoice in the Atonement of Christ.

40 And **this is the gospel, the glad tidings**, which the voice out of the heavens bore record unto us—

41 **That he came into the world**, even Jesus, **to be crucified for the world**, and **to bear the sins of the world**, and **to sanctify** [*to make holy, to cleanse and make fit to be in the presence of God*] **the world**, and **to cleanse it from all unrighteousness**;

42 That **through him** [*Christ*] **all might be saved whom the Father had put into his power** [*through the means of the gospel and the Atonement*] **and made** [*made worthy of salvation*] **by him**;

43 **Who glorifies the Father** [*Christ brings honor and glory to the Father*], **and saves all** the works of his hands [*saves everyone, to one degree of glory or another*], **except those sons of perdition** who deny [*completely reject*] the Son after the Father has revealed him [*after they know full well that Jesus is the Christ*].

44 Wherefore [*therefore*], **he saves all except them—they shall go away into everlasting punishment, which is endless punishment, which is eternal punishment, to reign with the devil and his angels** [*including the wicked spirits who followed him in premortality*] **in eternity**, where their worm dieth not [*where they cannot cease to exist*], and the fire [*perhaps meaning spiritual agony*] is not quenched, which is their torment—

45 And **the end** thereof, **neither the place** thereof, **nor their**

torment, no man knows [*no mortal can comprehend how miserable they will be*];

46 Neither was it revealed, neither is, neither will be revealed unto man, **except to them who are made partakers thereof**;

47 Nevertheless, **I, the Lord, show it by vision unto many** [*including Joseph Smith and Sidney Rigdon; see verse 30, above*], but straightway shut it up again;

48 Wherefore, **the end**, the **width**, the **height**, the **depth**, and the **misery** thereof, **they understand not, neither any man except those who are ordained** [*not "foreordained" or "predestined" or "preselected" by God to this condemnation, but rather "ordained" or "'qualified for" by the law of justice*] **unto this condemnation** [*being stopped in spiritual progression*].

> In a technical sense, there is another way to know what happens to them. Those who become gods will know all things. Therefore, they will know the final fate of sons of perdition. (This is by far the best way to find out!)

49 And **we heard the voice, saying: Write the vision**, for lo, **this is the end of the vision of the sufferings of the ungodly**.

Vision #4
Celestial Glory
(verses 50–70, 92–96)

> These are faithful, baptized members of the Church, who have the gift of the Holy Ghost and strive to keep the commandments, thus qualifying them to be "washed and cleansed from all their sins" (verse 52). Little children who die before the age of accountability will be in the highest degree of glory in the celestial kingdom—in other words, in exaltation. We will discuss more about this when we get to D&C 137:10.

50 And again we bear record—for **we saw and heard**, and this is the testimony of the gospel of Christ **concerning them who shall come forth in the resurrection of the just** [*"resurrection of the just" is another term for those who gain celestial glory*]—

51 **They are they who [1] received the testimony of Jesus**, and **[2] believed on his name** and **[3] were baptized** after the manner of his burial, being buried in the water in his name, and this according to the commandment which he has given—

52 That by **[4] keeping the commandments** they might be **[5] washed and cleansed from all their sins**, and **[6] receive the Holy Spirit by the laying on of the hands** of him who is ordained and sealed unto this power;

53 And who **[7] overcome by faith**, and **[8] are sealed by the Holy Spirit of promise** [*the Holy Ghost*], which the Father sheds forth upon all those who are just and true.

> We will add some notes to the numbered items in verses 51–53, above.

(1) "received the testimony of Jesus"

> "Received" is an active verb, one that calls for action on our part. The action required here is that of receiving the gospel into one's life and sincerely striving to live in conformity to its commandments and covenants.

(2) "believed on his name"

> "Belief" in this context is much more than mere acknowledging. It includes actively living the gospel and believing that it will lead to salvation because of the Atonement of Christ.

(3) "were baptized"

> These people were baptized by immersion by those who had the priesthood authority to do so.

(4) "keeping the commandments"

> Keeping the commandments leads to the cleansing expressed in number 5, next.

(5) "washed and cleansed from all their sins"

> Although none of us will be perfect in all ways at the time we leave this mortal life, by striving sincerely and honestly to keep the commandments, we qualify to be cleansed from all sins by the Atonement of Jesus Christ. We are thus made pure, clean, and worthy to enter into the presence of God. Not only that, but we are also enabled to be comfortable in His presence (compare with 2 Nephi 9:14, last half of verse).

(6) "receive the Holy Spirit by the laying on of the hands"

> The gift of the Holy Ghost is given at the time of confirmation. If we actively "receive" the Holy Ghost into our lives thereafter, He will guide us in all things throughout our lives. By following His promptings, we will be led to greater and greater understanding of the

gospel and will be enabled to have the Atonement of Christ active in our lives. This leads to number 7, next.

(7) "overcome by faith"

The foregoing steps lead to overcoming the sins and temptations of the world through faith in the Lord Jesus Christ, thus qualifying us to receive number 8, next.

(8) "are sealed by the Holy Spirit of promise"

The Holy Ghost is the "Holy Spirit of promise." The name comes from the fact that He is the Holy Spirit that is promised by Jesus Christ to His worthy followers after baptism.

One of the roles of the Holy Ghost is to seal or ratify ordinances performed here on earth so that they are binding in heaven also. Thus, when a worthy member is "sealed by the Holy Spirit of promise," it means that he or she has proven worthy of exaltation and is "sealed up" for that blessing.

When ordinances are not performed by proper authority, or they are performed by proper authority but the person does not live worthily, the Holy Ghost does not seal them, thus, the ordinances are not binding in heaven. We are taught this clearly in the Doctrine and Covenants as follows:

D&C 132:7

7 And verily I say unto you, that the conditions of this law are these: All covenants, contracts, bonds, obligations, oaths, vows, performances, connections, associations, or expectations, that are not made and entered into and sealed by the Holy Spirit of promise, of him who is anointed, both as well for time and for all eternity, and that too most holy, by revelation and commandment through the medium of mine anointed, whom I have appointed on the earth to hold this power (and I have appointed unto my servant Joseph to hold this power in the last days, and there is never but one on the earth at a time on whom this power and the keys of this priesthood are conferred), **are of no efficacy, virtue, or force in and after the resurrection from the dead; for all contracts that are not made unto this end have an end when men are dead.**

Elder David A. Bednar taught, "The Holy Spirit of Promise is the ratifying power of the Holy Ghost. When sealed by the Holy Spirit of Promise, an ordinance, vow, or covenant is binding on earth and in heaven. (See D&C 132:7.) Receiving this 'stamp of approval' from the Holy Ghost is the result of faithfulness, integrity, and steadfastness in honoring gospel covenants 'in [the] process of time' (Moses 7:21). However, this sealing can be forfeited through unrighteousness and transgression" ("Ye Must Be Born Again," *Ensign or Liahona*, May 2007, 22).

Before we move on, you may wish to glance back over verses 51–53 and take note of the fact that it is not complicated to qualify for celestial glory. Some people get the notion that being a faithful, active member of the Church is too complex and difficult to understand and do. In reality, being faithful to God is the simplest of all lifestyles. Even children can do it (see D&C 68:25–28). Complexity enters in when people sin and try to hide it or rationalize sin away.

As we continue, we see a number of different terms for "exaltation" in verses 54–58 and in verses 66–67. "Exaltation" means attaining the highest degree of glory in the celestial kingdom and becoming gods. It is also referred to as "eternal life." We know that the terms in these next verses refer to exaltation, not just to entering one of the other levels in celestial glory (see D&C 131:1–4), because verse 58 says "they are gods." We will **bold** these words and phrases to point them out. A number of these terms may be familiar to you. (On a sad note, some apostates who have broken off from our church have taken some of these terms as the names of the churches they have formed.)

54 **They are they who are the church of the Firstborn.**

55 **They are they into whose hands the Father has given all things** [*in other words, they have been given exaltation*]—

56 **They are they who are priests and kings, who have received of his fulness, and of his glory;**

Faithful women in the Church are also included in the context of verse 56, above. Elder Bruce R. McConkie said (**bold** added for emphasis):

"If righteous men have power through the gospel and its crowning ordinance of celestial marriage to become kings and priests to rule in exaltation forever, it follows that the women by their side (without whom they cannot attain exaltation) will be **queens and priestesses**. (Rev. 1:6; 5:10.) Exaltation grows out of the eternal union of a man and his wife. Of those whose marriage endures in eternity, the Lord says, "Then shall they be gods" (D. & C. 132:20); that is, **each of them, the man and the woman, will be a god. As such they will rule over their dominions forever** (*Mormon Doctrine*, 613).

57 And are priests of the Most High, after the order of Melchizedek, which was **after the order of Enoch**, which was **after the order of the Only Begotten Son** [*Jesus Christ*].

58 Wherefore, as it is written, they are gods, even the **sons of God** [*meaning that they have done all things necessary to become "heirs" of God—in other words, gods*]—

> Rewards and blessings of exaltation in celestial glory are detailed in verses 59–70. Again, we will use **bold** to point these out.

59 Wherefore, all things are theirs, whether life or death, or things present, or things to come, all are theirs and **they are Christ's, and Christ is God's**.

60 And they shall overcome all things.

> The word "shall," in verse 60, above, is important. In fact, it is very comforting. It lets us know that we will be allowed to continue progressing in the next life provided that we have qualified for that privilege during this life. None of us will be perfect when we die. There will be much progress and growth yet to be made after we pass away. However, once being judged worthy of exaltation on Judgment Day, those who receive this blessing will go on to "overcome all things." The Prophet Joseph Smith taught this. He said (**bold** added for emphasis):
>
> "When you climb up a ladder, you must begin at the bottom, and ascend step by step, until you arrive at the top; and so it is with the principles of the Gospel—you must begin with the first, and go on until you learn all the principles of exaltation. **But it will be a great while after you have passed through the veil before you will have learned them. It is not all to be comprehended in this world; it will be a great work to learn our salvation and exaltation even beyond the grave**" (*Teachings of the Prophet Joseph Smith*, 348).

61 Wherefore, let no man glory in man [*don't build your life upon the philosophies and false wisdom of man*], **but rather let him glory in God**, who shall subdue all enemies under his feet [*those who remain loyal to God are guaranteed to overcome all obstacles to exaltation*].

62 These shall dwell in the presence of God and his Christ forever and ever.

> Next, in verse 63, we find that those who qualify for celestial glory will be privileged to accompany Christ as He comes to earth at the time of the Second Coming.

63 These are they whom he shall bring with him, when he shall come in the clouds of heaven to reign on the earth [*during the Millennium*] over his people.

64 These are they who shall have part in the first resurrection.

65 These are they who shall come forth in the resurrection of the just.

> In the context of verses 64–65, above, the terms "first resurrection" and "resurrection of the just" both refer to those who will be in the celestial kingdom. Another term for this resurrection is "the morning of the first resurrection."
>
> However, be aware that in a broader sense, the "first resurrection" includes all who will inherit the celestial and terrestrial kingdoms, since these resurrections will take place near the beginning of the Millennium (see D&C 88:96–99). First, the celestials will be resurrected, then the terrestrials, all near the front end of the Millennium. We will quote from the 2018 *Doctrine and Covenants Student Manual* for this:
>
> "The Resurrection of the just is also known as the 'first resurrection' (D&C 76:64) and includes all those who will inherit the celestial and terrestrial kingdoms (see D&C 88:96–99). The First Resurrection began when the graves of the righteous were opened after the Resurrection of Jesus Christ (see Matthew 27:52–53; Mosiah 15:21–24; 3 Nephi 23:9–10). The Doctrine and Covenants refers to the First Resurrection as the time when the just will come forth from their graves at the Second Coming of Jesus Christ (see D&C 29:13; 45:54; 88:96–99). The Resurrection of the unjust, or the 'last resurrection' (D&C 76:85), will include those who will inherit the telestial kingdom and those who are sons of perdition, and it will occur at the end of the Millennium (see D&C 76:85; 88:32, 100–102)" (*Doctrine and Covenants Student Manual*, 2018, chapter 28, 76:50–119).
>
> One more important technical point. Obviously, there will be many righteous people during the Millennium itself, including children who are born and who "shall grow up without sin unto salvation" (D&C 45:58). These will also inherit celestial glory, but their resurrection will occur at the end of their mortal millennial lives of 100 years (Isaiah 65:20), regardless of when, during the Millennium, they live. When referring to their resurrection, we say something to the effect that they are part of the "first resurrection," or, in other words, they will join the first resurrection when their turn comes.

66 These are they who are come unto Mount Zion [*symbolizing celestial glory, and including those* *who will dwell with Christ in New Jerusalem; see D&C 84:2]*, **and unto the city of the living God** [*in this context, this means celestial kingdom; see Revelation 21, heading, and verse 2]*, **the heavenly place, the holiest of all** [*celestial glory*].

In addition to giving more names for exaltation, verse 67, next, contains an important doctrine. It is that "innumerable" people will attain exaltation.

67 These are they who have come to an **innumerable** company of angels, to **the general assembly** and **church of Enoch, and of the Firstborn**.

Revelation chapter seven also teaches that great numbers of people will enter exaltation. We will include it here and use **bold** to point this doctrine out.

Revelation 7:9

After this I beheld, and, lo, a great multitude, which no man could number, of all nations, and kindreds, and people, and tongues, stood before the throne, and before the Lamb, **clothed with white robes** [*symbolic of celestial glory*], **and palms in their hands** [*palm fronds are symbolic of triumph and victory; thus, these have "overcome" all things and will receive exaltation*];

Some may wonder how "innumerable" people can attain celestial glory when other scriptures say that only a few will make it. An example of this is found in Matthew 7:14, which says, "Strait is the gate, and narrow is the way, which leadeth unto life, and few there be that find it."

The answer is simple. Such scriptures as Matthew 7:14 are context sensitive. At various times in the history of the world, including our day, because of gross and widespread wickedness, "few" have been doing the things necessary to qualify for celestial glory.

However, "few there be that find it" would not have applied during the two hundred years of peace among the Nephites after the appearance and teaching of the resurrected Christ. Likewise, it will not apply during the Millennium when virtually all will join the Church and be faithful (see D&C 84:98).

Add to these numbers of righteous all the faithful from the Fall of Adam and Eve to the Second Coming, all the babies and children who have died before reaching the age of accountability (D&C 137:10), which is about 50–80 percent of the earth's total population, plus all those who accept the gospel in the spirit world (D&C 138:32, 58–59), and you have large numbers who will enter celestial glory and exaltation.

As we continue, we see more descriptive terms for those who attain exaltation.

68 These are they whose names are written in heaven [*in the "Book of Life"; see Revelation 3:5*], where God and Christ are the judge of all.

69 These are they who are just men made perfect [*a process*] **through Jesus the mediator of the new covenant, who wrought out this perfect atonement through the shedding of his own blood.**

> President Russell M. Nelson, when he was an Apostle, taught about the process by which we become perfect. He said, "Brothers and sisters, let us do the best we can and try to improve each day. When our imperfections appear, we can keep trying to correct them. We can be more forgiving of flaws in ourselves and among those we love. We can be comforted and forbearing. The Lord taught, 'Ye are not able to abide the presence of God now . . . ; wherefore, continue in patience until ye are perfected' [D&C 67:13].
>
> "We need not be dismayed if our earnest efforts toward perfection now seem so arduous and endless. Perfection is pending. It can come in full only after the Resurrection and only through the Lord. It awaits all who love him and keep his commandments. It includes thrones, kingdoms, principalities, powers, and dominions [see D&C 132:19]. It is the end for which we are to endure. It is the eternal perfection that God has in store for each of us" ("Perfection Pending," *Ensign*, Nov. 1995, 88).

70 These are they whose bodies are celestial [*they will have celestial resurrected bodies*], **whose glory is that of the sun, even the glory of God, the highest of all, whose glory the sun of the firmament is written of as being typical.**

We will be taught that there are differences between the resurrected bodies of those who gain celestial glory and the bodies of those who go to other places when we study verse 78 and D&C 88:28–32.

We will also see additional blessings and details about those who attain celestial exaltation when we get to verses 92–96.

Next, we will study the vision of those who enter terrestrial glory.

Vision #5
Terrestrial Glory
(verses 71–80, 87, 91, 97)

71 And again, we saw the terrestrial world, and behold and lo, **these are they** who are of the terrestrial, **whose glory differs from that of the church of the Firstborn** [*celestial glory, specifically, exaltation; see verses 54 and*

67] who have received the fulness of the Father [*who have received exaltation*], **even as that of the moon differs from the sun** in the firmament. [*In other words, the terrestrial kingdom is as different in glory from the celestial kingdom as the moon is different from the sun*].

We will use numbers and **bold** to point out qualifications for terrestrial glory.

72 Behold, these are **[1] they who died without law**;

Verses 73 and 74 go together.

73 And also they who are **[2] the spirits of men kept in prison** [*in spirit prison*], **whom the Son visited** [*see 1 Peter 3:18–2; 4:6, D&C 138*], and preached the gospel unto them, that they might be judged according to men in the flesh [*so that they can be judged by the same standards as people on earth who have the gospel*];

74 **Who received not the testimony of Jesus in the flesh, but afterwards received it.**

75 These are they who are **[3] honorable men of the earth, who were blinded by the craftiness of men.**

76 **These are they who receive of his glory** [*they get some glory*], **but not of his fulness** [*but not full glory like celestials*].

77 **These are they who receive of the presence of the Son** [*Jesus will visit them*], **but not of the fulness of the Father.**

78 Wherefore, **they are bodies terrestrial**, and not bodies celestial [*their resurrected bodies are terrestrial, not celestial*], and differ in glory as the moon differs from the sun.

In D&C 88:28–32, we are taught that there will be differences between celestial resurrected bodies and the resurrected bodies of those who are given terrestrial glory, telestial glory, and outer darkness (sons of perdition). Joseph Fielding Smith explained this. He said:

"In the resurrection there will be different kinds of bodies; they will not all be alike. The body a man receives will determine his place hereafter. There will be celestial bodies, terrestrial bodies, and telestial bodies, and these bodies will differ as distinctly as do bodies here. . . .

"Bodies will be quickened [*resurrected*] according to the kingdom which they are judged worthy to enter. . . .

"Some will gain celestial bodies with all the powers of exaltation and eternal increase. These bodies will shine like the sun as our Savior's does, as described by John. Those who enter the terrestrial kingdom will have terrestrial bodies, and they will not shine like the sun, but they will be more glorious than the bodies of those who receive the telestial glory.

"In both of these kingdoms there will be changes in the bodies and limitations. They will not have the power of increase, neither the power or nature to live as husbands and wives, for this will be denied them and they cannot increase.

"Those who receive the exaltation in the celestial kingdom will have the 'continuation of the seeds forever.' They will live in the family relationship. In the terrestrial and in the telestial kingdoms there will be no marriage. Those who enter there will remain 'separately and singly' forever.

"Some of the functions in the celestial body will not appear in the terrestrial body, neither in the telestial body, and the power of procreation will be removed" (*Doctrines of Salvation*, 2:286–88).

79 These are [4] they who are not valiant in the testimony of Jesus; wherefore, they obtain not the crown over the kingdom of our God [*"crown" is symbolic of exaltation, of ruling and reigning as gods*].

We will add some notes for the numbered items in verses 72 through 79.

(1) "they who died without law"

Elder Melvin J. Ballard explained this as follows:

"Now, I wish to say to you that those who died without law, meaning the pagan nations, for lack of faithfulness, for lack of devotion, in the former life, are obtaining all that they are entitled to. I don't mean to say that all of them will be barred from entrance into the highest glory. Any one of them who repents and complies with the conditions might also obtain celestial glory, but the great bulk of them will only obtain terrestrial glory" (Bryant S. Hinckley, *Sermons and Missionary Services of Melvin J. Ballard*, 251; quoted in the *Doctrine and Covenants Student Manual*, 1981, 164).

(2) "the spirits of men kept in prison, whom the Son visited ... Who received not the testimony of Jesus in the flesh, but afterwards received it"

In short, this appears to mean those who had a valid opportunity to "receive" the gospel (to incorporate the gospel into their lives) during mortality, but who intentionally chose not to, and then "afterwards received it" (in the spirit world).

Since God is completely fair, we have to consider that such people would have had a completely fair opportunity to hear and understand the gospel before rejecting it. Also, since we understand that many in the spirit world mission field will accept the gospel and (when their temple work is completed by mortals) go on to celestial exaltation (D&C 138), we are compelled to believe that those spoken of in verses 73 and 74, who "afterwards received it," must yet lack something that would allow them to attain celestial glory and be comfortable there. Perhaps they are not as deeply committed as those who ultimately qualify for the celestial reward. We don't know. Thus, we will have to wait for additional knowledge from authorized sources before being able to answer all the questions that come up regarding these verses.

(3) "honorable men of the earth, who were blinded by the craftiness of men"

These are good and honorable people, who are honest, keep the law of chastity, keep their word, help others, and live respectable, clean lives. Yet, among other things, it appears that they do not want to be tied down by church obligations, time-consuming meetings, and so forth. Joseph Fielding Smith spoke of this category of people. He said:

"Into the terrestrial kingdom will go all those who are honorable and who have lived clean virtuous lives, but who would not receive the Gospel, but in the spirit world repented and accepted it as far as it can be given unto them. Many of these have been blinded by tradition and the love of the world, and have not been able to see the beauties of the Gospel" (*Church History and Modern Revelation*, 1:287–88).

He also said:

"All who enter this kingdom [*terrestrial glory*] must be of that class who have been morally clean." (*Answers to Gospel Questions*, 2:208–10.)

(4) "they who are not valiant in the testimony of Jesus"

Those who have a testimony but intentionally do not live according to it fall into this category. They still fulfill the other qualifications for terrestrial glory, such as being honorable and keeping the law of chastity, but they are not valiant and faithful in living the gospel, keeping their covenants, fulfilling their church obligations, and so forth.

Be careful not to imply from this that those who attain celestial glory must be perfect here on earth. That, of course, is not the case. But there is a big difference in attitude and loyalty between members who know the gospel is true and strive to live it and those who know the gospel is true but live it when it is convenient or fits their current needs.

Bruce R. McConkie summarized the qualifications for terrestrial glory as follows:

"To the terrestrial kingdom will go: 1. Accountable persons who die without law (and who, of course, do not accept the gospel in the spirit world under those particular circumstances which would make them heirs of the celestial kingdom); 2. Those who reject the gospel in this life and who reverse their course and accept it in the spirit world; 3. Honorable men of the earth who are blinded by the craftiness of men and who therefore do not accept and live the gospel law; and 4. Members of The Church of Jesus Christ of Latter-day Saints who have testimonies of Christ and the divinity of the great latter-day work and who are not valiant, but who are instead lukewarm in their devotion to the Church and to righteousness. (D. & C. 76:71–80.)" (*Mormon Doctrine*, 784).

By the way, it is interesting to note that those who enter celestial glory will live on this earth (D&C 130:9–11) after it has been celestialized and glorified, whereas those who go to terrestrial and telestial glory will live on other planets prepared for them. Joseph Fielding Smith taught this. He said (**bold** added for emphasis):

"This earth will become a celestial kingdom when it is sanctified. Those who enter **the terrestrial** kingdom will **have to go to some other sphere** which will be prepared for them. Those who enter **the telestial** kingdom, **likewise will have to go to some earth which is prepared for them**, and there will be **another place which is hell where the devil and those who are punished to go with him will dwell**. Of course, those who enter the telestial kingdom, and those who enter the terrestrial kingdom will have the eternal punishment which will come to them in knowing that they might, if they had kept the commandments of the Lord, have returned to his presence as his sons and his daughters. This will be a torment to them, and in that sense it will be hell" (*Answers to Gospel Questions*, 2:210).

80 And now **this is the end of the vision which we saw of the terrestrial**, that **the Lord commanded us to write** while we were yet in the Spirit.

Before we continue, we will mention one other question that occasionally comes up in gospel discussions. It asks why the Lord, as a matter of kindness and mercy, couldn't place all people into heaven, whether they are worthy or not. Brigham Young addressed this question. He said:

"Some might suppose that it

SECTION 76

would be a great blessing to be taken and carried directly into heaven and there set down, but in reality that would be no blessing to such persons; they could not reap a full reward, could not enjoy the glory of the kingdom, and could not comprehend and abide the light thereof, but it would be to them a hell intolerable and I suppose would consume them much quicker than would hell fire. It would be no blessing to you to be carried into the celestial kingdom, and obliged to stay therein, unless you were prepared to dwell there (*Discourses of Brigham Young*, Deseret Book, 95).

We will now proceed to study the telestial glory.

Vision #6

Telestial Glory (verses 81–89, 98–106, 109–112)

81 And again, we saw the glory of the telestial, which glory is that of the lesser, even **as the glory of the stars differs from that of the glory of the moon** in the firmament [*there is much difference between the telestial glory and the terrestrial glory*].

We will use numbers and **bold** to point out qualifications of those who receive telestial glory.

82 These are [1] they who received not the gospel of Christ, neither the testimony of Jesus.

83 These are [2] they who deny not the Holy Spirit [*they did not deny the Holy Ghost, therefore, they are not sons of perdition*].

We will add some notes for the numbered items in verses 82–83.

(1) "they who received not the gospel of Christ"

These are people who willfully rejected Christ and His full gospel after being given fair opportunities to accept it.

(2) "they who deny not the Holy Spirit"

In other words, they are wicked, but they did not deny the Holy Ghost, therefore, they do not qualify to be sons of perdition.

We will add additional numbers when we get to verses 99–101 and 103.

As we continue, we see details as to what happens to those who qualify for telestial glory.

84 These are they who are thrust down to hell.

These people will be turned over to Satan to suffer for their own sins because they were not willing to repent and allow Christ's Atonement to pay for their sins. See verse 106 and D&C 19:15–19. Elder Joseph Fielding Smith explained this. He said (**bold** added for emphasis):

"Into this kingdom will go all of those who have been unclean in their lives. See verses 98 to 112, in section 76. These people who enter there will be the unclean; the liars, sorcerers, adulterers, and those who have broken their covenants. Of these the Lord says: 'These are they who are cast down to hell and suffer the wrath of Almighty God, until the fulness of times, when Christ shall have subdued all enemies under his feet, and shall have perfected his work (D&C 76:106).' Yet **these, after they have been punished for their sins and having been turned over to the torments of Satan, shall eventually come forth, after the millennium**, to receive the telestial kingdom" (*Answers to Gospel Questions*, 12:208).

85 These are **they who shall not be redeemed from the devil until the last resurrection**, until the Lord, even Christ the Lamb, shall have finished his work.

In D&C 88:100–101, we are taught that those who receive telestial glory must wait until the end of the Millennium (the thousand years of peace) to be resurrected. Combining this reference with verse 85, above, we learn that telestials will be turned over to Satan to suffer for their sins during the time that the Millennium is going on upon the earth. They will not be redeemed from the devil until they are resurrected into telestial bodies.

86 These are **they who receive not of his fulness in the eternal world** [*they will not gain the blessings of celestial glory and exaltation*], **but of the Holy Spirit through the ministration of the terrestrial** [*the Holy Ghost can have influence in the telestial kingdom; also, those in the terrestrial kingdom can visit those in the telestial kingdom*];

Elder James E. Talmage summarized telestial glory as follows:

"There is another grade [*telestial*], differing from the higher orders as the stars differ from the brighter orbs of the firmament; this is for those who received not the testimony of Christ, but who, nevertheless, did not deny the Holy Spirit; who have led lives exempting them from the heaviest punishment [*perdition*], yet whose redemption will be delayed until the last resurrection. In the telestial world there are innumerable degrees comparable to the varying light of the stars. Yet all who receive of any one of these orders of glory are at last saved, and upon them Satan will finally have no claim" (James E. Talmage, *The Articles of Faith*, 92).

As you saw in verse 86, above, those who live in the terrestrial kingdom can visit the telestial kingdom. Next, in verse 87, we are taught that inhabitants of the celestial kingdom can visit people who live in the terrestrial glory. As you can see, there is no doctrine here to the effect that celestials can visit telestials.

87 And **the terrestrial through the ministration of the celestial.**

88 **And also the telestial receive it** [*the limited blessings for them as mentioned in verse 86, above*] **of** [*through*] **the administering of angels who are appointed to minister for them**, or who are appointed to be ministering spirits for them; for **they** [*those who go to telestial glory*] **shall be heirs of salvation** [*will receive a degree of salvation, not celestial, not terrestrial, but telestial, which is still so wonderful we cannot imagine it; see verse 89, next*].

With very few exceptions, the term "salvation," as used in the scriptures, means exaltation. One of the exceptions appears in verse 88, above. In this case, it means "salvation in telestial glory." Indeed, being free from Satan forever and being in a kingdom of glory that "surpasses all understanding" (verse 89, below) is "salvation." But this salvation is as a star compared to the sun, as far as celestial glory is concerned.

The Prophet Joseph Smith used the word "saved" in this sense. He taught (**bold** added for emphasis):

"But except a man be born again, he cannot see the kingdom of God. This eternal truth settles the question of all men's religion. **A man may be saved**, after the judgment, **in the terrestrial kingdom, or in the telestial kingdom, but he can never see the celestial kingdom of God without being born of the water and the Spirit**. He may receive a glory like unto the moon [i. e. of which the light of the moon is typical], or a star [i. e. of which the light of the stars is typical], but he can never come unto Mount Zion, and unto the city of the living God, the heavenly Jerusalem, and to an innumerable company of angels; to the general assembly and Church of the First-born, which are written in heaven, and to God the judge of all, and to the spirits of just men made perfect, and to Jesus the Mediator of the new covenant, unless he becomes as a little child, and is taught by the Spirit of God" (*History of the Church,* 1:283–84).

89 And **thus we saw,** in the heavenly vision [*consisting of verses 19–113*], **the glory of the telestial, which surpasses all understanding** [*which is far more glorious and beautiful that any of us can imagine*];

The last phrase of verse 89, above, is a reminder that our Heavenly Father is merciful and kind. He is going to give even those who qualify only for telestial glory a reward that is far better than any of us can imagine! Elder John A. Widtsoe explained this. He said:

"The book [Doctrine and Covenants] explains clearly that the lowest glory to which man is assigned is so glorious as to be beyond the understanding of man. It is a doctrine fundamental in Mormonism that the meanest sinner, in the final judgment, will receive a glory which is beyond human understanding, which is so great that we are unable to describe it adequately. Those who do well will receive an even more glorious place. Those who dwell in the lower may look wistfully to the higher as we do here. The hell on the other side will be felt in some such way.

"The Gospel is a gospel of tremendous love. Love is at the bottom of it. The meanest child is loved so dearly that his reward will be beyond the understanding of mortal man" (*The Message of the Doctrine and Covenants*, 67).

Even though the main vision of the telestial glory ends with verse 89, there are additional qualifications for the telestial kingdom mentioned in verses 99–101 and 103. As mentioned previously, we will continue the use of **bold** and the numbering relating to telestial glory when we get to these verses. You may wish to look ahead to those verses now and then come back to verse 90 to continue your study of section 76.

90 And no man knows it except him to whom God has revealed it [*perhaps meaning that none can know these details about the three degrees of glory, exaltation, and perdition unless it is given them by revelation*].

91 And thus we saw **the glory of the terrestrial** which **excels in all things the glory of the telestial**, even in glory, and in power, and in might, and in dominion.

92 And thus we saw **the glory of the celestial**, which **excels in all things—where God, even the Father, reigns upon his throne forever and ever;**

93 Before whose throne all things bow in humble reverence, and give him glory forever and ever.

> Verses 94–95, next, refer to exaltation, or, in other words, becoming gods and receiving "all that my father hath" (D&C 84:38).

94 **They who dwell in his presence are the church of the Firstborn** [*another term for exaltation*]; and **they see as they are seen** [*by the Father—verse 92*], **and know as they are known** [*by the Father*], **having received of his fulness and of his grace** [*having become gods*];

95 And **he makes them equal in power, and in might, and in dominion.**

96 And **the glory of the celestial is one** [*degree of glory*], **even as**

the glory of the sun is one.

97 And **the glory of the terrestrial is one** [*degree of glory*], even as the glory of the moon is one.

98 And **the glory of the telestial is one** [*degree of glory*], even as the glory of the stars is one; for as one star differs from another star in glory, even so differs one from another in glory in the telestial world [*the telestial kingdom has many different degrees of glory within it*];

99 For **[3] these are they who are of Paul, and of Apollos, and of Cephas.**

100 **These are they who say they are some of one and some of another**—some **of Christ** and some of **John**, and some of **Moses**, and some of **Elias**, and some of **Esaias** [*an ancient prophet who lived in the days of Abraham; see "Esaias" in the Bible Dictionary and D&C 84:11–13*], and some of **Isaiah**, and some of **Enoch**;

101 But **[4] received not the gospel, neither the testimony of Jesus** [*these two were already numbered in verse 82*], **neither the prophets, neither the everlasting covenant.**

102 Last of all, these all are they who will not be gathered with the saints, to be caught up unto the church of the Firstborn, and received into the cloud.

103 **[5] These are they who are liars, and sorcerers, and adulterers, and whoremongers, and whosoever loves and makes a lie.**

We noted two qualifications for telestial glory as we studied verses 82–83. As you can see, we continued this numbering, beginning with verse 99, above. We will now add notes for items 3–5.

(3) "these are they who are of Paul, and of Apollos, and of Cephas, of Christ, John, Moses, Elias, Esaias, Isaiah, and Enoch"

Paul was, of course, a member of the Church. If you check Acts 18:24 and 19:1, 5, you will see that Apollos and Cephas likewise were faithful followers of Christ. So were the other prophets mentioned in verse 100. So, what is the message here?

Throughout the world's history, there have been various sects and religions who have claimed to believe the Bible, in which the words of Christ and the prophets are taught. Yet their creeds and teachings vary greatly. Also, there have been a number of members of the true Church who have broken away and set up their own false churches (based on the teachings of past prophets), and rejected the teachings of the living prophets.

Thus, many in the telestial kingdom will be those who claimed to believe but who did not live according to the full gospel. In fact, many of these groups have engaged in bloody battles against each other and in wars of hatred and vicious verbal opposition. They are not followers of Christ and have rejected the full gospel of the Savior. Elder James E. Talmage explained this. He said:

"We learn further that the inhabitants of this kingdom [telestial] are to be graded among themselves, comprising as they do the unenlightened among the varied opposing sects and divisions of men, and sinners of many types, whose offenses are not those of utter perdition: 'For as one star differs from another star in glory, even so differs one from another in glory in the telestial world; for these are they who are of Paul, and of Apollos, and of Cephas. These are they who say they are some of one and some of another—some of Christ, and some of John, and some of Moses, and some of Elias, and some of Esaias, and some of Isaiah, and some of Enoch; But received not the gospel, neither the testimony of Jesus, neither the prophets, neither the everlasting covenant'" (*Articles of Faith*, 369).

(4) received not the gospel, neither the testimony of Jesus, neither the prophets, neither the everlasting covenant

These are the wicked who rejected the Savior and His prophets and who refused to enter into the covenants of the gospel that are required of those who desire exaltation. They refused to repent when the principles of righteousness were explained to them and foolishly or blatantly continued in their wicked ways.

(5) These are they who are liars, and sorcerers, and adulterers, and whoremongers, and whosoever loves and makes a lie

As you can see, this verse (verse 103) has several qualifiers for telestial glory. It could be broken down into categories, including

• **Dishonesty** in any form.

• **The occult**, including witchcraft, fortune telling, and so on.

• **Sexual immorality**. The First Presidency said the following about illicit sex: "The doctrine of this Church is that sexual sin—the illicit sexual relations of men and women—stands, in its enormity, next to murder. The Lord has drawn no essential distinctions between fornication, adultery, and harlotry or prostitution. Each has fallen under His solemn and awful condemnation" (Heber J. Grant, J.

Reuben Clark Jr., David O. McKay, general conference, October 11, 1942).

- **Making illicit sex the central focus of life** (whoremongers).

- **Whoever "loves and makes a lie."** Possibilities for this category can include covenant breakers, who, in effect "lie" to God when they break their covenants. It can include those involved in illicit sex who love it and lie to try to cover it up. It can also include people who love gossip and love to pass on lies about others. All these are forms of dishonesty.

In Galatians, we find an expanded list of sins which, unrepented of, will lead to telestial glory. We will include it here for reference (**bold** added for emphasis):

Galatians 5:19–21

19 Now the works of the flesh are manifest, which are these [now here are some of the worldly sins you must avoid]; **Adultery, fornication, uncleanness, lasciviousness** [lustful behavior, thinking and talking and all sexual immorality, including pornography],

20 **Idolatry** [idol worship], **witchcraft, hatred, variance** [disharmony], **emulations** [rivalry and other such behaviors based on jealousy and worldly ambitions], **wrath** [anger, loss of temper], **strife, seditions** [stirring up unrighteous discontent with those in power, including government leaders and church leaders], **heresies** [false doctrines],

21 **Envyings, murders, drunkenness, revellings** [riotous, drunken parties and lifestyles], and such like: of the which I tell you before [I forewarn you], as I have also told *you* in time past, that **they which do such things shall not inherit the kingdom of God** [the celestial kingdom, or the terrestrial kingdom for that matter].

Next, we are taught additional details about those who are consigned to the telestial kingdom.

104 **These are they who suffer the wrath of God on earth.**

105 **These are they who suffer the vengeance of eternal fire** [they will be turned over to Satan to be punished for their own sins, since they refused to repent and thus accept the Savior's payment for them; see verse 106, next; also verses 84–86 and D&C 19:15–17].

106 **These are they who are cast down to hell and suffer the wrath of Almighty God**, until the fulness of times [until the end of the Millennium; see verse 85], when

Christ shall have subdued all enemies under his feet, and shall have perfected his work;

> The question sometimes comes up as to whether the Savior will ever finish up His work assigned to Him by the Father and become a Heavenly Father to His own worlds. The answer is found in verses 107–8, next.

107 When **he** [*Christ*] **shall deliver up the kingdom, and present it unto the Father**, spotless, saying: I have overcome and have trodden the wine-press alone, even the wine-press of the fierceness of the wrath of Almighty God.

108 **Then shall he be crowned with the crown of his glory, to sit on the throne of his power** to reign forever and ever.

> A few more details about the telestial kingdom are given in verses 109–12, next.

109 But behold, and lo, **we saw the glory and the inhabitants of the telestial world, that they were as innumerable as the stars in the firmament of heaven, or as the sand upon the seashore;**

110 And heard the voice of the Lord saying: **These all shall bow the knee, and every tongue shall confess to him** who sits upon the throne forever and ever;

111 For **they shall be judged according to their works**, and every man shall receive according to his own works, his own dominion, in the mansions which are prepared;

112 And **they shall be servants of the Most High; but where God and Christ dwell they cannot come, worlds without end.**

> The question often comes up concerning verse 112, above, as to whether it is possible, after the final Judgment Day, to eventually progress from one degree of glory to another. At the time this study guide went to press, the instruction from the First Presidency and the Quorum of the Twelve Apostles to curriculum writers for the Church was that we do not have sufficient information from the Lord at this point to answer that question either yes or no.

> Verse 113, next, informs us that this is the end of the vision, which started in verse 19.

113 **This is the end of the vision which we saw**, which we were commanded to write while we were yet in the Spirit.

114 But **great and marvelous are the works of the Lord, and the mysteries of his kingdom which he showed unto us, which**

surpass all understanding in glory, and in might, and in dominion;

> We find in verses 115–16, next, that there were many things that Joseph Smith and Sidney Rigdon saw that they were commanded not to write. Also, these brethren tell us that it would be impossible to put into words many of the things they saw.

115 **Which he commanded us we should not write** while we were yet in the Spirit, and are not lawful for man to utter;

116 **Neither is man capable to make them known, for they are only to be seen and understood by the power of the Holy Spirit**, which God bestows on those who love him, and purify themselves before him;

117 **To whom he grants this privilege of seeing and knowing for themselves**;

118 **That through the power and manifestation of the Spirit, while in the flesh, they may be able to bear his presence in the world of glory.**

119 **And to God and the Lamb be glory, and honor, and dominion forever and ever. Amen.**

> We will learn more about the celestial kingdom and exaltation when we get to sections 131 and 132.

SECTION 77

Background

This revelation was given to the Prophet Joseph Smith in Hiram, Ohio, in March 1832 while he was working on the Book of Revelation for the inspired translation of the Bible (*the Joseph Smith Translation*, or JST).

He had begun his inspired translation and revision of the New Testament on March 8, 1831, and would complete his initial work on it in July 1832. He then continued reviewing and revising the translation until February 2, 1833.

Section 77 contains a series of questions and answers about the Apostle John's book of Revelation in the Bible. It provides many answers to questions that arise while striving to understand the vision given to the Apostle John while he was being held in a prison colony on the Isle of Patmos (Revelation 1:9) about A.D. 95 In fact, it serves as a key to unlocking many of the "hidden mysteries" of this marvelous book.

Joseph Smith explained that "John had the curtains of heaven withdrawn, and by vision looked through the dark vista of future ages, and contemplated events that should transpire throughout every subsequent period of time until the final winding up scene—[and] while he gazed upon the glories of the eternal world, saw an innumerable company of angels and heard the voice of God" (in *Manuscript History of the Church*, vol. C-1, Addenda, page 69, josephsmithpapers.org).

One of the main questions that arises among students of the book of Revelation has to do with determining what is symbolic and what is literal when it comes to the imagery used in John's writing. The revealed answers to questions, as given here through Joseph Smith, serve as invaluable keys in this matter.

As we proceed, we will include the verses from Revelation that are referenced in this section. For example, verses 1–3, next, refer to Revelation 4:6.

Revelation 4:6

6 And before the throne there was **a sea of glass** like unto crystal: and in the midst of the throne, and round about the throne, were **four beasts** full of eyes before and behind [*in front and back*].

1 Q. **What is the sea of glass** spoken of by John, 4th chapter, and 6th verse of the Revelation?

A. **It is the earth**, in its sanctified, immortal, and eternal state [*as a celestial planet*].

The Prophet taught more about this. He said:

"While at dinner, I remarked to my family and friends present, that when the earth was sanctified and became like a sea of glass, it would be one great urim and thummim, and the Saints could look in it and see as they are seen" (*History of the Church*, 5:279).

Also, in section 130, he taught:

D&C 130:9

9 This earth, in its sanctified and immortal state [*when it becomes a celestial kingdom*], **will be made like unto crystal and will be a Urim and Thummim to the inhabitants who dwell thereon,** whereby all things pertaining to an inferior kingdom, or all kingdoms of a lower order, will be manifest to those who dwell on it; and this earth will be Christ's.

Brigham Young spoke of this when he said:

"This Earth will become a celestial body—be like a sea of glass, or like a Urim and Thummim; and when you wish to know anything, you can look in this Earth and see all the eternities of God" (*Journal of Discourses*, 8:200).

2 Q. **What are** we to understand by **the four beasts**, spoken of in the same verse?

A. They are **figurative** [*symbolic*] **expressions**, used by the Revelator, John, in describing heaven, the paradise of God, the happiness of man, and of beasts, and of creeping things, and of the fowls of the air; that which is spiritual being in the likeness of that which is temporal; and that which is temporal in the likeness of that which is spiritual; the spirit of man in the likeness of his person, as also the spirit of the beast, and every other creature which God has created.

Did you notice other things also taught in verse 2, above, in addition to the fact that the beasts are symbolic? We will list two of them.

1. Beasts, creeping things, and fowls of the air have the capacity to be happy and will have that capacity eternally (see verse 3, next).

2. Spirit looks like the physical body it inhabits. Bruce R. McConkie spoke of this when he said:

"Man and all forms of life existed as spirit beings and entities before the foundations of this earth were laid. There were spirit men and spirit beasts, spirit fowls and spirit fishes, spirit plants and spirit trees. Every creeping thing, every herb and shrub, every amoeba and tadpole, every elephant and dinosaur—all things—existed as spirits, as spirit beings, before they were placed naturally upon the earth" (*The Millennial Messiah*, 642–43; also quoted in the *Doctrines of the Gospel Student Manual*, 1981, 16).

3 Q. **Are the four beasts limited to individual beasts, or do they represent classes or orders?**

A. **They are limited to four individual beasts, which** were shown to John, to **represent** [*are symbolic of*] **the glory of the classes of beings** in their destined order or sphere of creation, **in the enjoyment of their eternal felicity** [*eternal happiness*].

The Prophet Joseph Smith taught that there are many beasts in heaven that would be entirely strange to us. He said that these animals come from other earths. We will quote the Prophet here:

"I suppose John saw beings there of a thousand forms, that had been saved from ten thousand times ten thousand earths like this,—strange beasts of which we have no conception: all might be seen in heaven. The grand secret was to show John what there was in heaven. John learned that God glorified Himself by saving all that His hands had made, whether beasts, fowls, fishes or men; and He will glorify Himself with them" (*Teachings of the Prophet Joseph Smith*, 291).

As we move on, imagine that

you were reading the book of Revelation with no outside help and were trying to figure out the "eyes and wings" spoken of in Revelation 4:8 ("eyes" are also spoken of in Revelation 4:6, as quoted above). We will give verse 8 here, using **bold** for emphasis:

Revelation 4:8

8 And **the four beasts had each of them six wings** about *him;* **and they were full of eyes** within: and they rest not day and night, saying, Holy, holy, holy [*in Hebrew, such things repeated three times symbolize the superlative, the very best*], Lord God Almighty, which was, and is, and is to come.

Without the revealed word of the Lord, as given in verse 4, next, we wouldn't be able to understand this verse. With it, we are greatly blessed.

4 Q. **What are we to understand by the eyes and wings**, which the beasts had?

A. **Their eyes are a representation** [*are symbolic*] **of light and knowledge**, that is, they are full of knowledge; and **their wings are a representation of power, to move, to act, etc.**

Have you ever wondered why many pictures of angels show them with wings? Verse 4, above, helps us understand that symbolism. In ancient times, the fastest creatures were birds. With their wings, they were able to get from one place to another quickly. Since angels are able to instantly be wherever they are needed, it was logical for artists to picture them with wings, representing their ability to "move, to act" as needed in carrying out the work of God.

Next, verse 5 refers back to three verses in the fourth chapter of Revelation. We will quote them here:

Revelation 4:4, 10–11

4 And round about the throne *were* four and twenty seats: and upon the seats I saw **four and twenty elders sitting, clothed in white raiment** [*symbolic of celestial glory*]; and they had on their heads **crowns of gold** [*symbolic that they had qualified to receive exaltation*].

10 The four and twenty elders fall down before him that sat on the throne, and worship him that liveth for ever and ever, and cast their crowns before the throne, saying,

11 Thou art worthy, O Lord, to receive glory and honour and power: for thou hast created all things, and for thy pleasure

they are and were created.

5 Q. **What are** we to understand by **the four and twenty elders,** spoken of by John?

A. We are to understand that **these** elders whom John saw, **were elders who had been faithful in the work of the ministry and were dead; who belonged to the seven churches** [wards or branches spoken of in Revelation 1:11], **and were then in the paradise of God.**

> As you can see from the Prophet's answer in verse 5, above, in this case, the twenty-four elders were literal. In other words, they were real individuals who lived in the days during or after Christ's mortal mission and belonged to the seven wards or branches spoken of by John the Apostle in Revelation 1:11. It is highly likely that before his arrest and banishment to the prison colony on the Isle of Patmos (some fifty miles off the western coast of Turkey today), John visited these seven wards or branches of the Church located in what is now western Turkey.
>
> Verse 6, next, has reference to Revelation 5:1.

Revelation 5:1

1 AND I saw in the right hand of him that sat on the throne **a book written within and on the backside, sealed with seven seals.**

6 Q. **What are we to understand by the book** which John saw, which was **sealed on the back with seven seals?**

A. We are to understand that **it contains the revealed will, mysteries, and the works of God**; the hidden things of his economy **concerning this earth during the seven thousand years of its** continuance, or its **temporal** [subject to our current time system] **existence.**

> If you were to study Revelation 5, you would discover that "him" in verse 1 (quoted above) refers to the Father. Thus, the "book" could well be termed "the Father's plan"—in other words, the plan of salvation. "Right hand" symbolizes "covenant hand," thus teaching us that the Father's plan for us relies heavily on covenants. It is "sealed" because no one can carry out the Father's plan for us on the earth except Jesus Christ. Again, if you were to study verses 5–7 in Revelation 5, you would find that the "Lamb" (Jesus) is the one who takes the book from the Father's hand (verse 7). In other words, He accepts the mission from the Father to be our Savior and carry out the Atonement and all that goes with it in order to save us, if we accept it.

Did you also notice how long this earth will have, from the Fall of Adam and Eve to the final winding up scenes, concluding with the final judgment? It is seven thousand years. We have already used up about six thousand years, and still need a thousand for the Millennium. Thus, we know that the Second Coming is getting relatively close.

Next, verse 7 refers both to Revelation 5:1, above, and to chapter 6. As you will see, each seal represents one thousand years of the earth's temporal [*our time system*] history.

7 Q. **What are we to understand by the seven seals** with which it was sealed?

A. We are to understand that **the first seal contains the things of the first thousand years**, and **the second also of the second thousand years, and so on until the seventh**.

We will quote enough of Revelation 6 to give the basic idea for the answer given in verse 7, above, using **bold** as usual for emphasis. As you will see, the opening of each "seal" provides a brief sketch of events and conditions in that particular one-thousand-year period of the earth's history.

Revelation 6:1–12

1 AND **I saw when the Lamb opened one of the seals** [*the first seal, 4,000–3,000 B.C.*], and I heard, as it were the noise of thunder, one of the four beasts saying, Come and see.

2 And I saw, and behold a white horse: and he that sat on him had a bow; and a crown was given unto him: and he went forth conquering, and to conquer.

3 And when he had opened **the second seal** [*3,000–2,000 B.C.*], I heard the second beast say, Come and see.

4 And there went out another horse *that was* red: and *power* was given to him that sat thereon to take peace from the earth, and that they should kill one another: and there was given unto him a great sword.

5 And when he had opened **the third seal** [*2,000–1,000 B.C.*], I heard the third beast say, Come and see. And I beheld, and lo a black horse; and he that sat on him had a pair of balances in his hand.

6 And I heard a voice in the midst of the four beasts say, A

measure of wheat for a penny, and three measures of barley for a penny; and *see* thou hurt not the oil and the wine.

7 And when he had opened **the fourth seal** [*1,000–0 B.C.*], I heard the voice of the fourth beast say, Come and see.

8 And I looked, and behold a pale horse: and his name that sat on him was Death, and Hell followed with him. And power was given unto them over the fourth part of the earth, to kill with sword, and with hunger, and with death, and with the beasts of the earth.

9 And when he had opened **the fifth seal** [*A.D. 0–1,000*], I saw under the altar the souls of them that were slain for the word of God, and for the testimony which they held:

10 And they cried with a loud voice, saying, How long, O Lord, holy and true, dost thou not judge and avenge our blood on them that dwell on the earth?

11 And white robes were given unto every one of them; and it was said unto them, that they should rest yet for a little season, until their fellowservants also and their brethren, that should be killed as they *were,* should be fulfilled.

12 And I beheld when he had opened **the sixth seal** [*A.D. 1,000–2,000*], and, lo, there was a great earthquake; and the sun became black as sackcloth of hair, and the moon became as blood;

By the way, Revelation 8–9 and a few other chapters deal with things that will take place during the seventh seal before the Second Coming and the beginning of the Millennium. We will say more about this in a minute.

Next, in verse 8, the Lord gives information to us through His prophet Joseph Smith about the four powerful angels spoken of in Revelation 7:1.

Revelation 7:1

1 AND **after these things I saw four angels standing on the four corners of the earth** [*symbolic of all the inhabitants of the earth*], holding the four winds of the earth, that the wind [*symbolic of destruction*] should not blow on the earth, nor on the sea, nor on any tree.

8 Q. **What are** we to understand by **the four angels**, spoken of in the 7th chapter and 1st verse of Revelation?

A. We are to understand that **they are four angels sent forth from God, to whom is given power** over the four parts of the earth, **to save life and to destroy**; these are **they** who **have the everlasting gospel to commit to every nation, kindred, tongue, and people**; having power to shut up the heavens, to seal up unto life, or to cast down to the regions of darkness.

> From the answer in verse 8, above, we understand, among other things, that there is much going on behind the scenes by way of angelic ministration and involvement in the work of spreading the gospel throughout the earth before the Second Coming.
>
> We will prepare for verse 9, next, by including verse 3 also for context. You will see that the destruction of the wicked in the last days is not to be completed until the gathering of righteous Israel.

Revelation 7:2–3

2 And **I saw another angel ascending from the east,** having the seal of the living God: and he **cried with a loud voice to the four angels, to whom it was given to hurt the earth and the sea,**

3 **Saying, Hurt not the earth, neither the sea, nor the trees,** till we have sealed the servants of our God in their foreheads [*symbolic of loyalty*].

9 Q. What are we to understand by the angel ascending from the east, Revelation 7th chapter and 2nd verse?

A. We are to understand that **the angel ascending from the east is he to whom is given the seal** [*the power and authority*] **of the living God over the twelve tribes of Israel** [*includes all people throughout the earth in the last days who will accept the gospel and make and keep covenants*]; wherefore, he crieth unto the four angels [*he has power over the four angels spoken of in verse 8*] **having the everlasting gospel, saying: Hurt not the earth, neither the sea, nor the trees** [*perhaps meaning, among other things, not to let mankind destroy the earth's ecology before the righteous are successfully gathered*], **till we have sealed the servants of our God in their foreheads** [*until righteous Israel has been gathered; in Bible symbolism, "forehead" means loyalty; therefore, this phrase can mean "until we have gathered those of Israel who will be completely loyal to God"*]. And, **if you will receive it, this is Elias which was to come to gather together the tribes of Israel and restore all things.**

One of the definitions of the word "Elias," in verse 9, above, is "any messenger from God sent to carry out a specific task." You may wish to turn to your Bible Dictionary in the back of your LDS Bible and read definition 3 under "Elias." Thus, the "Elias" in verse 9 could possibly be a "composite" of many different angels and messengers to be sent forth by God to assist with the restoration of the gospel and the gathering of Israel.

As the Prophet answers the question in verse 10, next, we find that the things spoken of in Revelation 7, including the gathering of Israel, are to happen during the sixth seal.

10 Q. What time are the things spoken of in this chapter [*chapter 7 of Revelation*] **to be accomplished?**

A. They are to be accomplished in the sixth thousand years, or the opening of the sixth seal [*which symbolizes the sixth thousand-year period of the earth's history*].

> Just a word of caution. As we consider the seven one-thousand-year periods of the earth's temporal existence, spoken of in the book of Revelation, it is vital that we be careful not to try to exactly superimpose these time periods upon our calendar system. There are many questions as to the accuracy of our calendar system, especially as we go back to the time of the Fall (read "Chronology" in your Bible Dictionary). Therefore, we don't know just where we are in the sixth seal, or, perhaps we are already in the beginning of the seventh seal. We don't know.

Next, we learn of the 144,000 spoken of in Revelation 7:4. The question as to just who these are often comes up. Perhaps you have heard the idea that there will only be 144,000 saved when the Savior comes. This is not true. We have an answer from the Lord through the Prophet Joseph Smith. As you will see, they are high priests from throughout the world, twelve thousand from each tribe of Israel, who will help with the gathering of Israel in the last days.

Revelation 7:4

4 And I heard the number of them which were sealed: *and there were* **sealed an hundred *and* forty *and* four thousand of all the tribes of the children of Israel.**

11 Q. What are we to understand by sealing the one hundred and forty-four thousand, out of all the tribes of Israel—**twelve thousand out of every tribe?**

A. **We are to understand that those who are sealed are high priests**, ordained unto the holy order of God, **to administer the** everlasting gospel; for they are they who are ordained **out of every nation**, kindred, tongue, and people, by the angels to whom is **given power** over the nations of the earth, **to bring as many as will come to the church of the Firstborn** [*to the Church of Jesus Christ, and ultimately to exaltation in the celestial kingdom; see D&C 76:54, 67, 102*].

> Perhaps you have heard at one time or another the attempts of someone to pin down the exact timing of the Second Coming. Often, such people are of the opinion that the Savior's Coming will be at the conclusion of the sixth seal, the end of the sixth thousand-year period.
>
> A careful study of the answer to the question in verse 12, next, shows that this is not the case. Some things will be finished up in the beginning of the seventh seal, before the actual coming of Christ and the beginning of the Millennium. Thus, it would be impossible to calculate the exact timing of the Second Coming (see Matthew 24:36), even if we knew the exact time of the Fall of Adam.
>
> You may wish to read Revelation 8:6–13 in your Bible as background for verse 12, next.

12 Q. What are we to understand by the sounding of the trumpets, mentioned in the 8th chapter of Revelation?

A. We are to understand that as God made the world in six days, and on the seventh day he finished his work, and sanctified it, and also formed man out of the dust of the earth, even so, **in the beginning of the seventh thousand years** will the Lord God sanctify the earth, and complete the salvation of man, and judge all things, and shall redeem all things, except that which he hath not put into his power, when he shall have sealed all things, unto the end of all things; and **the sounding of the trumpets of the seven angels are the preparing and finishing of his work, in the beginning of the seventh thousand years**—the preparing of the way **before the time of his coming**.

> It appears that just in case we didn't get the message in verse 12, above, that the Savior will not come at the end of the sixth thousand years but rather sometime in the beginning of the seventh, it is repeated in verse 13, next.
>
> You may wish to read Revelation chapter 9 in your Bible as background for verse 13, next. There are a great many signs of the times included in this chapter of Revelation.

13 Q. **When are the things** [*signs of the times*] **to be accomplished, which are written in the 9th chapter of Revelation?**

A. They are to be accomplished **after the opening of the seventh seal, before the coming of Christ.**

> While we don't know the answer, it is sometimes interesting to read Revelation 8–9 and wonder whether we might already be in the beginning of the seventh seal.
>
> Many people are puzzled by the "little book" mentioned in Revelation 10 that John is commanded to eat. It would seem a bit difficult to eat a book. We will include the relevant verses of Revelation, chapter 10, here.

Revelation 10:1–2, 8–11

1 AND **I saw another mighty angel come down from heaven**, clothed with a cloud: and a rainbow was upon his head, and his face was as it were the sun, and his feet as pillars of fire:

2 And **he had in his hand a little book** open: and he set his right foot upon the sea, and his left foot on the earth,

8 And **the voice which I heard from heaven spake unto me** [*John the Beloved Apostle*] again, **and said**, Go and **take the little book** which is open in the hand of the angel which standeth upon the sea and upon the earth.

9 And **I went unto the angel, and said unto him, Give me the little book. And he said unto me, Take it, and eat it up**; and it shall make thy belly bitter, but it shall be in thy mouth sweet as honey.

10 And **I took the little book** out of the angel's hand, **and ate it up**; and it was in my mouth sweet as honey: and as soon as I had eaten it, my belly was bitter.

11 And **he said unto me, Thou must prophesy again before many peoples, and nations, and tongues, and kings.**

> With the help of Joseph Smith, we find this imagery easier to understand.

14 Q. **What are we to understand by the little book which was eaten by John, as mentioned in the 10th chapter of Revelation?**

A. **We are to understand that it was a mission**, and an ordinance, **for him to gather the tribes of Israel**; behold, this is Elias, who, as it is written, must come and restore all things.

As with most missions (including ward and stake callings), there are many aspects of it that are "sweet" (Revelations 10:9) and some aspects that tend to make the "belly bitter" (give one indigestion).

Next, in verse 15, we are given key information that helps us understand Revelation 11, in which two "witnesses" (verse 3) "prophesy" for three and a half years among the Jews and then are killed (verse 7). By the way, the word "prophesy" in this context can mean to teach and instruct as well as to predict the future. We will include the relevant verses of Revelation chapter 11 here, with some explanatory notes as background for section 77, verse 15. These notes are taken from *Your Study of the New Testament Made Easier* by David J. Ridges.

Revelation 11:3–13

3 And **I will give power unto my two witnesses** [*two prophets to the Jews in the last days; D&C 77:15*], **and they shall prophesy** [*serve, minister, prophesy, and so on*] **a thousand two hundred and threescore days** [*42 months or 3 1/2 years, about the same length as Christ's ministry*], clothed in sackcloth [*in humility*].

4 **These are the two olive trees** [*olive trees provide olive oil for lamps so people can be prepared to meet Christ; compare with the parable of the ten virgins in Matthew 25:1–13*], **and the two candlesticks** [*hold light so people can see clearly*] standing before the God of the earth.

5 And **if any man will** [*wants to*] **hurt them** [*the two prophets*], **fire** [*the power of God to destroy*] **proceedeth out of their mouth, and devoureth their enemies** [*the two prophets will be protected during their mission*]: and if any man will hurt them, he must in this manner be killed [*he will be killed by the power of God*].

6 **These** [*the two prophets*] **have power to shut heaven** [*have the power of God; compare with the Prophet Nephi in Helaman 10:5–10 and 11:1–6*], **that it rain not in the days of their prophecy: and have power over waters to turn them to blood, and to smite the earth with all plagues** [*to encourage people to repent; to deliver from evil, bondage, as with the plagues in Egypt*], **as often as they will.**

7 And **when they shall have finished their testimony** [*ministry*], **the beast** [*Satan*] that ascendeth out of the bottomless

pit [*Rev. 9:1–2*] **shall make war against them** [*the two prophets*]**, and shall overcome them, and kill them.**

8 And their dead bodies shall lie in the street of the great city [*Jerusalem*]**,** **which spiritually is called Sodom and Egypt** [*is very wicked*]**, where also our Lord was crucified.**

9 And they [*the wicked*] **of the people and kindreds and tongues and nations shall see their dead bodies three days and an half** [*perhaps symbolically tying in with their 3 1/2 year ministry as well as the Savior's three days in the tomb; the Savior was killed, too, by the wicked for trying to save them*]**, and shall not suffer** [*allow*] **their dead bodies to be put in graves** [*many in eastern cultures believed that if the body is not buried, the spirit is bound to wander the earth in misery forever*]**.**

10 And they that dwell upon the earth [*not just people in Jerusalem; implies that knowledge of the death of the two prophets will be known worldwide*] **shall rejoice over them, and make merry, and shall send gifts one to another** [*people all over the world will cheer and send gifts to one another to celebrate the deaths of these two prophets*]**; because these two prophets tormented them** [*the wicked*] **that dwelt on the earth** [*implies that these prophets' influence was felt and irritated the wicked far beyond Jerusalem*]**.**

11 And after three days and an half the Spirit of life from God entered into them [*they are resurrected at this time; see McConkie,* Doctrinal New Testament Commentary, *3:511*]**, and they stood upon their feet; and great fear fell upon them which saw them.**

12 And they [*the wicked who were celebrating*] **heard a great voice from heaven saying unto them** [*the two slain prophets*]**, Come up hither. And they ascended up to heaven in a cloud; and their enemies beheld** [*saw*] **them.**

13 And the same hour [*immediately*] **was there a great earthquake,** **and the tenth part of the city fell, and in the earthquake were slain of men seven thousand: and the remnant were affrighted, and gave glory to the God of heaven** [*perhaps implying that some of the wicked were converted as was the case with* *the Savior's resurrection and also when Lazarus was brought back from the dead; if so, the deaths of the two prophets bore immediate fruit in helping some begin returning to God]*

The question arises from reading the Bible as to whether these "witnesses" are prophets or missionaries, Jewish or LDS, or what? The answer to the question in verse 15, next, clears this up.

15 Q. What is to be understood by the two witnesses, in the eleventh chapter of Revelation?

A. **They are two prophets that are to be raised up to the Jewish nation in the last days, at the time of the restoration, and to prophesy to the Jews after they are gathered and have built the city of Jerusalem in the land of their fathers.**

Thus, we understand that these are to be members of the Church and, in fact, latter-day prophets. We have fifteen "prophets, seers, and revelators" in the Church today. They are the First Presidency and the Quorum of the Twelve Apostles. It appears that two of them, or their successors, will someday fulfill this prophecy.

Elder Bruce R. McConkie taught about these two prophets. He said that they would be "followers of that humble man Joseph Smith, through whom the Lord of Heaven restored the fulness of his everlasting gospel in this final dispensation of grace. No doubt they will be members of the Council of the Twelve or of the First Presidency of the Church" (*Doctrinal New Testament Commentary*, 3:509).

SECTION 78

Background

This revelation was given through the Prophet Joseph Smith in Hiram, Ohio, on March 1, 1832. It deals primarily with the establishment of a "firm," later known as the "United Firm" in order "to manage the Church's storehouses and publishing efforts" (see *Doctrine and Covenants Student Manual*, 2018, chapter 29) and also with the personal righteousness and character traits required to live the law of consecration.

As background for section 78, the student manual quoted above additionally explains:

"In a revelation given in February 1831, the Lord commanded the Saints to establish a storehouse to gather surplus goods and money for the benefit of the poor (see D&C 42:34–35; see also D&C 51:13). Newel K. Whitney's mercantile store in Kirtland, Ohio, operated as one storehouse, and Sidney Gilbert established another in Independence, Missouri (see D&C 57:8–10; 72:8–10). These

SECTION 78

storehouses not only supplied the Saints with needed goods but also generated revenue to purchase land and finance the publication of the Lord's revelations to the Prophet Joseph Smith. Additionally, in November 1831, the Lord appointed Joseph Smith, Oliver Cowdery, John Whitmer, Sidney Rigdon, Martin Harris, and William W. Phelps as 'stewards over the revelations and commandments' (D&C 70:3). This group had the responsibility to oversee the publication of the revelations. For their labors, they were to receive compensation from the profits generated from the sale of the published revelations. The Lord instructed them to place any profits over and above their needs in His storehouse for the benefit of the Saints in Zion (see D&C 70:7–8).

"On March 1, 1832, the Prophet Joseph Smith met with a group of high priests in Kirtland, Ohio, possibly to discuss the Church's mercantile and publication efforts. During the meeting, the Prophet dictated the revelation recorded in Doctrine and Covenants 78. Subsequently, the United Firm was created to better manage the Church's property and financial endeavors, such as the storehouses. The part of the United Firm that managed the Church's publishing efforts was called the Literary Firm."

The Prophet received three other revelations about the same time. He explained: "Besides the work of translating [the translation of the Bible—the JST], previous to the 20th of March, I received the four following revelations: [D&C 78–81]" (*History of the Church*, 1:255).

You may be aware that in earlier editions of the Doctrine and Covenants, substitute names were used for several of the brethren in this section, as well as in section 82, verse 11, and in section 104, verses 26 and 43. Just in case this topic is brought up to you, we will quote Elder Orson Pratt's explanation of it:

"The names that were incorporated when it was printed, did not exist there when the manuscript revelations were given, for I saw them myself. Some of them I copied. And when the Lord was about to have the Book of Covenants given to the world it was thought wisdom, in consequence of the persecutions of our enemies in Kirtland and some of the regions around, that some of the names should be changed, and Joseph was called Baurak Ale, which was a Hebrew word; meaning God bless you. He was also called Gazelam, being a person to whom the Lord had given the Urim and Thummim. He was also called Enoch. Sidney Rigdon was called Baneemy. And the revelation where it read so many dollars into the treasury was changed to talents. And the City of New York was changed to Cainhannoch" (*Journal of Discourses*, 16:156).

Beginning with the 1981 edition of the Doctrine and Covenants, the use of these substitute names was done away with. Joseph Fielding Smith gave additional background for this section. He said (**bold** added for emphasis):

"During the early part of the year 1832, the Prophet and Sidney Rigdon continued the work of the revision of the scriptures [the JST]. At the time the Prophet was still residing in the house of Father John Johnson, at Hiram. It was during this time that this important revelation was given to the members of the Priesthood who were assembled imparting instructions in relation to the plan of **the 'united order'** or 'order of Enoch,' on which the promised Zion should be built. The Lord had revealed that it was only through obedience to his divine will, **the celestial law**, that Zion could be built. The members of the Church rejoiced when the Lord revealed to them the site on which the New Jerusalem, or City of Zion, should be built. Their enthusiasm, however, was not sufficient to carry them through to a conclusion in strict obedience to the divine will. In this revelation (section 78) the Lord reveals his will in words of wisdom to all those holding the High Priesthood" (*Church History and Modern Revelation*, 1:304–5).

As we study this revelation, you will see that unselfishness and charity are essential personal character traits for those who successfully live the "United Order" (see D&C 92:1) under the law of consecration. Such characteristics are part of celestial law (see verse 7). As noted above, this revelation was given to a number of priesthood brethren who had assembled with the Prophet in the John Johnson home. Beginning with verse 1, the Lord addresses these Melchizedek Priesthood holders and teaches them principles relating to the United Order and the law of consecration.

1 THE Lord spake unto Joseph Smith, Jun., saying: **Hearken unto me**, saith the Lord your God, **who are ordained unto the high priesthood of my church, who have assembled yourselves together**;

2 And **listen to the counsel of him who has ordained you from on high**, who shall speak in your ears the words of wisdom, that salvation may be unto you in that thing which you have presented before me, saith the Lord God.

Did you notice, in verse 2, above, that when hands are laid upon our heads by faithful priesthood holders here on earth, it is the same as the Savior Himself doing it?

3 For verily I say unto you, **the time has come, and is now at hand**; and behold, and lo, **it must needs be** [*it is necessary*] **that there be an organization** [*the United Firm; see D&C 92 heading (2013 edition)*] **of my people**, in **regulating and establishing the affairs of the storehouse for the poor of my people**, both in this place [*the Kirtland area*] and in the land of Zion [*in Jackson County, Missouri*]—

4 For a permanent and everlasting establishment and order unto my church, **to advance** the cause, which ye have espoused [*adopted as your own*], to **the salvation of man**, and to the glory of your Father who is in heaven [*compare with Moses 1:39*];

> In verses 5–7, next, the Lord teaches us that in order to be prepared to live comfortably in celestial glory, we must learn to live the celestial laws embedded in the law of consecration and the United Order here on earth.

5 **That you may be equal in the bonds of heavenly things**, yea, **and earthly things** also, **for the obtaining of heavenly things**.

6 For **if ye are not equal in earthly things ye cannot be equal in obtaining heavenly things**;

7 For **if you will that I give unto you a place in the celestial world, you must prepare yourselves by doing the things which I have commanded you and required of you.**

We will take just a moment to review what it means to be "equal in earthly things" (verse 6, above). This must not be interpreted as taking away personality, individuality, individual talents, hobbies, interests, and so forth. President J. Reuben Clark Jr. explained this as follows (**bold** added for emphasis):

"One of the places in which some of the brethren are going astray is this: There is continuous reference in the revelations to equality among the brethren, but I think you will find only one place where that equality is really described, though it is referred to in other revelations. That revelation (D. & C. 51:3) affirms that every man is to be '**equal according to** his **family**, according to his **circumstances** and his **wants** and **needs**.' (See also D. & C. 82:17; 78:5–6.) **Obviously, this is not a case of 'dead level' equality. It is 'equality' that will vary as much as the man's circumstances, his family, his wants and needs, may vary**" (In Conference Report, October 1942, 55).

You may have noticed that through tithing, fast offering, humanitarian aid fund, perpetual education fund, missionary fund, temple construction fund, and so on, and helping one another through compassionate service, service projects, dedicating time and talents to temple work, missionary service, and so forth, we are much closer to living the United Order today than some members might realize. It is all part of the law of consecration.

8 And now, verily thus saith the Lord, **it is expedient** [*necessary*] **that all things be done unto my glory** [*which is bringing exaltation to people; see Moses 1:39*], **by you who are joined together in this order** [*the United Firm which has just been organized at this point in Church history for the poor and needy members in the Kirtland area and Jackson County, Missouri—see verse 3*];

9 Or, in other words, **let my servant Newel K. Whitney** [*who was called to serve as bishop in the Kirtland area; see D&C 72:2, 8*] and my servant **Joseph Smith, Jun.**, and my servant **Sidney Rigdon** sit in **council with the saints which are in Zion** [*help the Saints in Missouri better understand the principles and applications of the United Firm*];

10 **Otherwise Satan seeketh to turn their hearts away from the truth**, that they become blinded and understand not the things which are prepared for them.

11 Wherefore, a commandment I give unto you, to **prepare and organize yourselves by a bond or everlasting covenant that cannot be broken** [*by the Lord; see D&C 82:10—nor by members without very serious consequences*].

As you can see, from verse 11, above, covenants are an integral part of living the United Firm under the law of consecration. The seriousness of breaking covenants made with God is pointed out in verse 12, next.

12 And **he who breaketh it** [*the covenant spoken of in verse 11, above*] **shall lose his office and standing in the church, and shall be delivered over to the buffetings of Satan until the day of redemption.**

Elder Bruce R. McConkie defined what it means to be turned over "to the buffetings of Satan." He said:

"To be turned over to the buffetings of Satan is to be given into his hands; it is to be turned over to him with all the protective power of the priesthood, of righteousness, and of godliness removed, so that Lucifer is free to torment, persecute, and afflict such a person without let or hindrance" (*Mormon Doctrine*, 108).

13 Behold, **this is the preparation wherewith I prepare you**, and the foundation, and the

ensample [*example*] which I give unto you, **whereby you may accomplish the commandments which are given you;**

14 **That through my providence** [*help*], **notwithstanding the tribulation which shall descend upon you** [*a prophecy that the Saints in Ohio and Missouri will yet go through much trial and tribulation*], **that the church may stand independent above all other creatures beneath the celestial world** [*under heaven; a prophecy that the day will come when the Church will grow and be independent of all outside forces*];

> Next, in verse 15, the Lord uses terms meaning exaltation to describe the reward of those who successfully and faithfully live in harmony with the law of consecration.

15 **That you may come up unto the crown** [*symbolic of being a ruler*] **prepared for you** [*exaltation*], and **be made rulers over many kingdoms** [*when they become gods; compare with D&C 132:19–20*], saith the Lord God, the Holy One of Zion [*in other words, Jesus Christ*], who hath established the foundations of Adam-ondi-Ahman [*the place (in Missouri) where Adam met with his posterity to bless them three years before he died; see D&C 107:53–56*];

16 **Who hath appointed Michael** [*Adam*] **your prince**, and established his feet, and set him upon high, **and given unto him the keys of salvation under the counsel and direction of the Holy One** [*Christ*], who is without beginning of days or end of life.

> One of the doctrines taught in verse 16, above, is that Adam stands next to Christ in authority over this earth, having been given the "keys of salvation" under the direction of Christ. This correct view of Adam and his power and authority is a far cry from the commonly held view of him among many other faiths.
>
> Next, the Lord speaks to these men, and to all of us, explaining that we have hardly even begun to see the blessings and advantages of living celestial laws. His kindness and charity are seen as He cheers us on and encourages us to take His hand and be led to celestial glory.

17 Verily, verily, I say unto you, **ye are little children**, and **ye have not as yet understood how great blessings the Father hath in his own hands and prepared for you;**

18 And **ye cannot bear all things now**; nevertheless, **be of good cheer, for I will lead you along. The kingdom is yours** and the

blessings thereof are yours, and the riches of eternity are yours.

> Once again, we see the value and importance of gratitude as taught in verse 19, next. (Compare with D&C 59:21.)

19 And **he who receiveth all things with thankfulness shall be made glorious**; and the things of this earth shall be added unto him, even an hundred fold, yea, more.

20 Wherefore [*therefore*], **do the things which I have commanded you**, saith your Redeemer, even the Son Ahman [*Jesus Christ*], who prepareth all things before he taketh you [*perhaps meaning who has prepared everything in advance in order to successfully "lead us along" the covenant path (verse 18)*];

> The name, "Son Ahman," found near the end of verse 20, above, is also used in D&C 95:17. It means "the Son of God." "Ahman" is the name of God in the pure language. Elder Orson Pratt explained this in some detail. He taught:

> "There is one revelation that this people are not generally acquainted with. I think it has never been published, but probably it will be in the Church History. It is given in questions and answers. The first question is, 'What is the name of God in the pure language?' The answer says, 'Ahman.' 'What is the name of the Son of God?' Answer, 'Son Ahman—the greatest of all the parts of God excepting Ahman'" (*Journal of Discourses*, 2:342).

21 For **ye are the church of the Firstborn**, and he will take you up in a cloud [*symbolic of being taken up to heaven; see Acts 1:9*], and appoint every man his portion.

> The "church of the Firstborn," in verse 21, above, is another term for exaltation. We saw it in D&C 76:54, 67, and 102. Joseph Fielding Smith explained this term as follows:

> "Those who gain exaltation in the celestial kingdom are those who are members of the Church of the Firstborn; in other words, those who keep all the commandments of the Lord (*Doctrines of Salvation*, 2:41).

22 And **he that is a faithful and wise steward shall inherit all things** [*will become a god*]. Amen.

SECTION 79

Background

This revelation was given through the Prophet Joseph Smith in Hiram, Ohio, on March 12, 1832. In the background to section 78 in this book, we mentioned that it was one of four revelations (sections 78–81) that the Prophet

SECTION 79

received prior to March 20, 1832, while residing at the home of John Johnson.

As is the case with all sections of the Doctrine and Covenants, there is at least one message that is of value for us by way of application in our own lives. Even though this section is brief, it has several.

As you can see, this revelation was given to Jared Carter. He was converted to the Church when he first read the Book of Mormon. He was baptized in Colesville, New York, by Hyrum Smith in February 1831 at age thirty. He moved with the Colesville Saints to Ohio. In the fall of 1831, Brother Carter left to serve a mission in the east and preached in Ohio, Pennsylvania, New York, and Vermont for five months. He then returned home to Ohio. Shortly after his return, he visited the Prophet Joseph Smith to ask about his next mission, and on March 12, 1832, he was given this revelation, section 79. In it, he is asked to serve a mission "again into the eastern countries" (verse 1).

1 VERILY I say unto you, that it is my will that my servant **Jared Carter should go again into the eastern countries**, from place to place, and from city to city, in the power of the ordination wherewith he has been ordained, **proclaiming glad tidings of great joy, even the everlasting gospel.**

In verse 2, next, we see two of the many functions of the Holy Ghost.

2 And **I will send upon him the Comforter** [*the Holy Ghost*], **which shall teach him the truth and the way whither he shall go;**

3 And **inasmuch as he is faithful, I will crown him again with sheaves** [*the Lord will give him another bountiful harvest of souls*].

4 Wherefore, **let your heart be glad**, my servant Jared Carter, and **fear not**, saith your Lord, even Jesus Christ. Amen.

Jared Carter left on this mission as instructed on April 25, 1832. This mission lasted six months and two days, and he brought seventy-nine souls into the Church. We will quote again from the 2018 *Doctrine and Covenants Student Manual*, chapter 29, for an inspiring account of John and Elizabeth Tanner, whom he helped bring into the true gospel. The source for this account is the Journal of Jared Carter, typescript, 20, Church History Library, Salt Lake City).

"Among those he helped convert to the restored gospel were John and Elizabeth Tanner. John Tanner was a wealthy businessman whose leg had been afflicted with sores. Jared Carter gave the following account of the healing of John Tanner: 'The Lord had mercy upon a lame man by the name of Tanner, who was so lame that he could not bear his weight . . . on one of his feet. He had been lame for months but we found he was a believer in the Book of Mormon. I asked him to endeavor to walk in the name of Christ [and] he agreed to undertake. I then took him by the hand and commanded him in the name of Christ to walk and by the power of Christ he was enabled to walk' (Journal of Jared Carter, 19). After his conversion, John Tanner moved to Ohio and donated thousands of dollars to pay the debt on the Kirtland Temple site and to finance its construction. This was an answer to the prayers of the Prophet Joseph Smith and other Church leaders."

SECTION 80

Background

This revelation was given to eighteen-year-old Stephen Burnett in Hiram, Ohio, on March 7, 1832. He had joined the Church at age sixteen in Warrensville, Ohio. A year later, he was ordained a high priest by Oliver Cowdery.

Both he and Eden Smith (verse 2) had been previously called to serve missions with different companions on January 25, 1832 (during a conference held at Amherst, Ohio; see D&C 75:35–36). We don't currently know whether or not he fulfilled that call.

1 VERILY, **thus saith the Lord unto** you my servant **Stephen Burnett** [*eighteen years old*]: **Go ye, go ye into the world and preach the gospel to every creature that cometh under the sound of your voice**.

We too are to help spread the gospel to all who come within our sphere of influence. Except when we are serving formally as missionaries, being a good example is often the best way to "preach." In so doing, we "cannot go amiss" (verse 3).

2 And inasmuch as you desire a companion, **I will give unto you my servant Eden Smith** [*about twenty-six years old*].

When we studied D&C 60:5, we mentioned that some decisions in our lives do not have a "right" answer. It "mattereth not" to the Lord. Therefore, we can do whatever we think is best and it will be fine with God. Verse 3, next, describes one such situation.

3 Wherefore, **go ye and preach my gospel, whether to the north or to the south, to the east or to the west, it mattereth not, for ye cannot go amiss** [*you can't go wrong*].

In verse 4, next, we are reminded of the importance of missionaries knowing the gospel and having their own testimony of the things they are teaching.

4 Therefore, **declare the things which ye have heard, and verily believe, and know to be true.**

5 Behold, this is the will of him who hath called you, your Redeemer, even Jesus Christ. Amen.

SECTION 81

Background

This revelation was given through the Prophet Joseph Smith on March 15, 1832, in Hiram, Ohio.

As you can see, the heading and introduction to this section in your Doctrine and Covenants is about as long as the seven verses of the revelation itself. This section is particularly significant because it represents a major step forward in organizing the First Presidency of the Church, which began with organizing the Presidency of the High Priesthood (verse 2). This step is the calling of counselors to serve with the Prophet, thus leading ultimately to the formal organizing of the First Presidency as the leading quorum of the Church (see D&C 107:22).

You can also see, from the information in the heading in your Doctrine and Covenants, that Jesse Gause (about twenty years older than the Prophet) was one of the two men originally called by the Lord to serve as counselors in the First Presidency. However, as noted in the heading, he apostatized and was excommunicated in December 1832. This is a sad reminder that Church leaders can misuse their agency even to the point of losing their membership.

Frederick G Williams was the one who replaced Jesse Gause in January 1833, a few weeks after Jesse Gause was excommunicated. Thus, his name was written into the transcription of this revelation for the first publication of the Doctrine and Covenants in 1835.

Brother Williams was born on October 28, 1787. He was eighteen years older than Joseph Smith (then twenty-six years old) and just over five years older than Sidney Rigdon, the other counselor (D&C 90:6).

By the way, the last half of verse 5 (**bolded** part) is one of the more often quoted verses in the Church. If you don't particularly recognize it now, you will no doubt recognize it in the future because of paying attention to it now.

As we proceed to study this section, we will be taught about the keys of the priesthood held by the First Presidency and will be given counsel that applies to any member of the Church called to serve as a counselor to a president.

1 **VERILY, verily, I say unto you** my servant **Frederick G. Williams:** Listen to the voice of him who speaketh, to the word of

the Lord your God, and **hearken to the calling wherewith you are called,** even **to be a high priest in my church, and a counselor unto my servant Joseph Smith, Jun.;**

2 Unto whom I have given **the keys of the kingdom,** which **belong always unto the Presidency of the High Priesthood** [*which gradually became the First Presidency*]:

> One of the important lessons in verse 3, next, is that the Lord sustains His prophet. So also, should the counselors. So it is with any authorized presidency within the quorums and auxiliaries of the Church.

3 Therefore, verily **I acknowledge him** [*Joseph Smith*] **and will bless him, and also thee, inasmuch as** [*if*] **thou art faithful in counsel,** in the office which I have appointed unto you [*as a counselor*], **in prayer always, vocally and in thy heart, in public and in private,** also in thy ministry in proclaiming the gospel in the land of the living, and among thy brethren.

> We often hear the counsel to "lift where you stand"—in other words, fulfill the calling you currently have to the best of your ability, even if it doesn't put you in the limelight. Verse 4, next, reflects this counsel.

4 And **in doing these things thou wilt do the greatest good unto thy fellow beings, and wilt promote the glory of him who is your Lord.**

> As stated earlier, verse 5, next, contains sweet counsel for counselors, and for all of us as we sustain our leaders.

5 Wherefore, be faithful; stand in the office which I have appointed unto you; **succor the weak, lift up the hands which hang down, and strengthen the feeble knees.**

> In conclusion, verse 6, next, can be seen as another reminder that it is not where we serve but how we serve that counts eternally.

6 And **if thou art faithful unto the end thou shalt have a crown** [*symbolic of exaltation*] **of immortality, and eternal life** [*exaltation*] in the mansions which I have prepared in the house of my Father.

7 Behold, and lo, **these are the words of Alpha and Omega** [*the one in charge of all things, under the direction of the Father*], **even Jesus Christ. Amen.**

SECTION 82

Background

This revelation was given through the Prophet Joseph Smith in Independence, Jackson County, Missouri, on April 26, 1832. We will quote the heading given for this section in the 2013 edition of the Doctrine and Covenants:

*"Revelation given to Joseph Smith the Prophet, in Independence, Jackson County, Missouri, April 26, 1832. The occasion was a council of high priests and elders of the Church. At the council, Joseph Smith was sustained as the President of the High Priesthood, to which office he had previously been ordained at a conference of high priests, elders, and members at Amherst, Ohio, January 25, 1832 (see the heading to section 75). This revelation reiterates instructions given in an earlier revelation (section 78) to establish a firm—known as the **United Firm** (under Joseph Smith's direction, the term "order" later replaced "firm")—to govern the Church's mercantile and publishing endeavors."*

We will quote from the 2018 *Doctrine and Covenants Student Manual*, chapter 30, for additional background for this section. Note that the righteousness, dedication, integrity, and celestial character traits required to keep their covenants as members of the United Firm (see heading above) are the same as needed for successfully living the law of consecration and United Order.

"In 1832 the Church had two centers of growing membership: one in Kirtland, Ohio, and one in Jackson County, Missouri. To assist needy Saints and to generate revenue that could be used to purchase land in Zion (Jackson County) and publish the revelations, a storehouse was established in each location (see D&C 57:8–10; 72:8–10). In November 1831, the Lord appointed a group of Church leaders to be 'stewards over the revelations and commandments' (D&C 70:3) and see to their publication. Later, the Lord commanded that a 'firm' be organized to manage the literary and mercantile endeavors of the Church (see the section headings to D&C 78 and D&C 82).

"The Prophet Joseph Smith and other Church leaders had traveled to Independence, Missouri, in obedience to the Lord's commandment to 'sit in council with the saints which are in Zion' (D&C 78:9). They met to establish a 'firm' or 'order' that would oversee and regulate the mercantile and publishing endeavors of the Church. Church members who were invited to participate in the firm included Joseph Smith, Sidney Rigdon, Newel K. Whitney, and Martin Harris, all of whom resided in Kirtland, Ohio, and Edward Partridge, Sidney Gilbert, John Whitmer, Oliver Cowdery, and William W. Phelps, all of whom resided in Jackson County, Missouri (see D&C 78:9; 82:11). In 1833, two additional members—Frederick G. Williams and John Johnson—were added to the firm by revelation (see D&C 92:1–2; 96:6–9). The objective of the firm was to manage storehouses that would provide goods and money to help the poor as well as to generate revenue to purchase land for Zion and finance the publication of the Lord's revelations to the Prophet. One branch of the firm would operate in Independence and was to be called 'Gilbert, Whitney & Co.,' and one would operate in Kirtland and would be named 'Newel K. Whitney & Co.' (see 'Minutes, 26–27 April 1832,' page 25, josephsmithpapers.org).

"The members of the firm, or order, were to be united with one another in a covenant. Each received a stewardship over part of the business interests of the Church, and each could draw upon the resources of the firm to manage his stewardship. The successful operation of the business endeavors would generate a surplus that was to be kept in the Church's storehouses."

As you know, the law of consecration requires a "Zion" lifestyle and celestial attributes, including a high degree of personal integrity, charity, and righteousness. It is a high goal for any of us to attain, but with the help of the Lord, we can. The members of the United Firm at this time were falling short of the requirements required to successfully carry it out. In section 82, the Master addresses many of these shortcomings and gives direction and encouragement. These personal qualities certainly apply to us if we desire to attain the celestial kingdom.

This section contains a number of familiar quotes often used in talks and gospel conversations—for example, verses 3, 7, and 10.

Verse 1, next, specifically refers to Sidney Rigdon and Bishop Edward Partridge. They'd had a disagreement with each other but had worked things out and made peace with each other by the time of this revelation. In this verse, we are reminded that in order to be forgiven by the Lord, we must forgive each other (Matthew 6:15, D&C 64:9–10).

1 VERILY, verily, I say unto you, my servants, that **inasmuch as you have forgiven one another your trespasses, even so I, the Lord, forgive you.**

Verse 2, next, contains a strict warning by a loving Savior to His people to repent and exercise more self-control and obedience to the commandments.

Remember that these members had just recently come to Missouri where the land was fertile and opportunities for future personal gain were abundant. For some, it was difficult to consecrate potential wealth to the Church. Also, the type of person required to succeed on the frontier of civilization was of necessity strong-willed. Because of this, they sometimes found it difficult to show obedience and loyalty to Church leaders.

2 Nevertheless, **there are those among you who have sinned exceedingly**; yea, even **all of you have sinned**; but verily I say unto you, **beware from henceforth, and refrain from sin** [*they are being given another chance*], **lest sore** [*severe*] **judgments** [*consequences, punishments*] **fall upon your heads.**

Verse 3, next, is much-quoted in the Church. It is, in effect, an equation and reminds us of our greater accountability to be obedient because of the knowledge, testimony, and rich blessings already given us by the Lord.

3 For of him **unto whom much is given much is required**; and he who sins against the greater light shall receive the greater condemnation.

Elder Neil L. Andersen of the Quorum of the Twelve Apostles explained verse 3, above, as follows: "As members of The Church of Jesus Christ of Latter-day Saints, having a witness of His reality not only from the Bible but also from the Book of Mormon; knowing His priesthood has been restored to the earth; having made sacred covenants to follow Him and received the gift of the Holy Ghost; having been endowed with power in His holy temple; and being part of preparing for His glorious return to the earth, we cannot compare what we are to be with those who have not yet received these truths. 'Unto whom much is given much is required' [D&C 82:3]" ("Never Leave Him," *Ensign*, Nov. 2010, 41).

In verse 4, next, the Master Teacher gives us the "why" of verse 3, above.

4 **Ye call upon my name for revelations, and I give them unto you** [*"much is given," including "greater light"*]; **and inasmuch as** [*if*] **ye keep not my sayings**, which I give unto you, **ye become transgressors**; and **justice and judgment are the penalty which is affixed unto my law** [*the law of justice is active for us unless we repent*].

Next, in the first part of verse 5, we are reminded that the counsel and instruction from the Lord in these revelations applies to us all.

5 Therefore, **what I say unto one I say unto all**: Watch, for the adversary [*the devil*] spreadeth his dominions, and darkness [*spiritual darkness*] reigneth;

6 And **the anger of God kindleth against the inhabitants of the earth**; and **none doeth good, for all have gone out of the way** [*everyone has the need and necessity to repent; compare to D&C 49:8, first half*].

Next, in verse 7, we find an important and serious doctrine. It is that if we have repented of certain sins but then commit them again, even years later, the "former sins return." In other words, we have to repent of that type of sin all over again. We have obviously not completely overcome it, or we would not have committed it again.

7 And now, verily I say unto you, I, the Lord, will not lay any sin to your charge; go your ways and sin no more; but **unto that soul who sinneth shall the former sins return**, saith the Lord your God.

Verses 8–15 go together and basically refer to the instruction of the Lord to the brethren mentioned to "bind" themselves by covenant to live in the United Firm in conformity to the law of consecration. See especially verses 11 and 15.

First, in verses 8–9, the Savior gives us a concise lesson in the "why" of obedience to His commandments; namely, that He might bless us.

8 And again, I say unto you, **I give unto you a new commandment**, that you may understand my will concerning you;

9 Or, in other words, **I give unto you directions how you may act before me, that it may turn to you for your salvation.**

Verse 10, next, is perhaps the most well-known in this section and one of the best-known verses in the entire Doctrine and Covenants. It is an absolute guarantee that the Lord will keep His promises to us if we fulfill our part of the contract. You may wish to cross-reference verse 10 in your own Doctrine and Covenants with D&C 130:20–21.

10 **I, the Lord, am bound when ye do what I say; but when ye do not what I say, ye have no promise.**

Verses 11 and 12 go together.

11 Therefore, verily I say unto you, that **it is expedient** [*necessary*] **for** my servants **Edward Partridge** [*the bishop in Missouri*] and **Newel K. Whitney** [*the bishop in Kirtland*], **Sidney Gilbert** and **Sidney Rigdon,** and my servant **Joseph Smith,** and **John Whitmer** and **Oliver Cowdery,** and

W. W. Phelps and Martin Harris to be bound together [*in living the law of consecration in the United Firm in Missouri and Kirtland*] by a bond and covenant that cannot be broken by transgression, except judgment shall immediately follow, in your several stewardships—

12 To manage the affairs of the poor, and all things pertaining to the bishopric both in the land of Zion and in the land of Kirtland;

> Next, in verses 13–14, the Savior explains that while Kirtland will serve as a headquarters for the Church yet for a season (a total of about five years; see D&C 64:21), Zion, Jackson County, Missouri, will "increase" and "her borders" will be enlarged (verse 14).

13 For I have consecrated the land of Kirtland in mine own due time for the benefit of the saints of the Most High, and for a stake to Zion.

14 For Zion must increase in beauty, and in holiness; her borders must be enlarged; her stakes must be strengthened; yea, verily I say unto you, Zion must arise and put on her beautiful garments [*must "put on the priesthood"; compare with D&C 113:7–8*].

We understand verse 14, above, to be a prophecy that the Church will continue to grow from these small and humble beginnings in Kirtland and Missouri until it has filled the entire earth (Daniel 2:35). President Harold B. Lee spoke of this. He taught:

"Zion, as used here, undoubtedly had reference to the Church. At that time there was but a small body of Church members just beginning to emerge as an organization, after having experienced harsh treatment from enemies outside the Church. . . .

"To be worthy of such a sacred designation as Zion, the Church must think of itself as a bride adorned for her husband, as John the Revelator recorded when he saw in vision the Holy City where the righteous dwelled, adorned as a bride for the Lamb of God as her husband. Here is portrayed the relationship the Lord desires in his people in order to be acceptable to our Lord and Master even as a wife would adorn herself in beautiful garments for her husband.

"The rule by which the people of God must live in order to be worthy of acceptance in the sight of God is indicated by the text to which I have made reference. This people must increase in beauty before the world; have an inward loveliness which may be observed by mankind as a reflection in holiness and in those inherent qualities of sanctity. The borders of Zion, where the righteous and pure in heart may dwell, must now begin to be enlarged. The stakes of Zion must be strengthened. All this so that Zion may arise and shine by becoming increasingly diligent in carrying out the plan of salvation throughout the world" ("Strengthen the Stakes of Zion," *Ensign*, July 1973, 3).

15 **Therefore** [*because of what the Lord knows about the future growth of the Church*], I give unto you this commandment, that ye **bind yourselves by this covenant** [*in the "United Firm"*], and it shall be done according to the laws of the Lord [*it must be done according to the rules of the law of consecration*].

16 Behold, **here is wisdom** also in me **for your good.**

> Next, in verses 17–19, the Savior defines what He means by "equal," as it relates to living the law of consecration, as it applies to the United Firm.

17 And you are to be **equal**, or **in other words, you are to have equal claims on the properties** [*held by the United Firm*], for the benefit of managing the concerns of your stewardships, **every man according to his wants and his needs**, inasmuch as his wants are just—

18 And all this for the benefit of the church of the living God, **that every man may improve upon his talent, that every man may gain other talents** [*surplus, above and beyond his wants and needs*], yea, even an hundred fold, **to be cast into the Lord's storehouse** [*the bishop's storehouse*], **to become the common property of the whole church—**

19 **Every man seeking the interest of his neighbor** [*a celestial character trait*], and **doing all things with an eye single to** [*focused on*] **the glory of God** [*whose "work and . . . glory" is to bless and benefit His children, leading them to exaltation; see Moses 1:39*].

20 **This order** [*the United Firm, run according to the law of consecration*] I have appointed to be **an everlasting order** [*the principles of the law of consecration are eternal*] unto you, and unto your successors, inasmuch as you sin not.

21 And **the soul that sins against this covenant, and hardeneth his heart against it, shall be dealt with according to the laws of my church** (see D&C 78:12), and shall be delivered over to the buffetings of Satan until the day of redemption [*see note for D&C 78:12 in this study guide*].

Some years ago, one of our daughters approached me, her scriptures in hand, with a puzzled look on her face. She said, in effect, "Dad, I thought that we were supposed to avoid associating with wicked people and making friends with them for fear of losing our own souls because of their influence on us." She was reading the Doctrine and Covenants and had just read verse 22, next.

22 And now, verily I say unto you, and this is wisdom, **make unto yourselves friends with the mammon of unrighteousness,** and they will not destroy you.

We sat down together, reread the verse, and then discussed the context created by the final phrase in the verse. Obviously, for these early Saints, this counsel was a life-and-death matter. Also, we are counseled not to deliberately provoke those who are enemies to the ways of righteousness. In fact, when we are friendly and kind toward such people, we have a better chance of preserving our own freedoms and way of life in addition to the better likelihood that some of them will desire to know more about the gospel.

You may have noticed on numerous occasions that the leaders of the Church strive to be friendly toward many whose lifestyles do not reflect gospel standards. The Savior spoke of this when He was accused of associating with sinners.

He replied, "They that be whole need not a physician, but they that are sick" (Matthew 9:12).

According to Wikipedia, the word "mammon" in Hebrew means "money" and has been adopted in modern Hebrew to mean "wealth."

Joseph Fielding Smith spoke of the Lord's counsel to "make . . . friends with the mammon of unrighteousness." He taught:

"The commandment of the Lord that the saints should make themselves 'friends with the mammon of unrighteousness' seems to be a hard saying when not properly understood. It is not intended that in making friends of the 'mammon of unrighteousness' that the brethren were to partake with them in their sins; to receive them to their bosoms, intermarry with them and otherwise come down to their level. They were to so live that peace with their enemies might be assured. They were to treat them kindly, be friendly with them as far as correct and virtuous principles would permit, but never to swear with them or drink and carouse with them. If they could allay prejudice and show a willingness to trade with and show a kindly spirit, it might help to turn them away from their bitterness. Judgment was to be left with the Lord" (*Church History and Modern Revelation*, 1:323).

In verse 23, next, the Lord reminds us that He is the final Judge and that He is the one who gives out punishments and rewards. He continues in verse 24 by reminding the Saints that the goal of eternal life can be attained by them.

23 **Leave judgment alone with me**, for it is mine and **I will repay**. Peace be with you; my blessings continue with you.

24 For **even yet the kingdom is yours, and shall be forever, if you fall not from your steadfastness.** Even so. Amen.

SECTION 83

Background

This revelation was given through the Prophet Joseph Smith in Independence, Missouri, on April 30, 1832. At this time, some members of the Church in Missouri were striving to live according to the principles of consecration. It appears that some questions had come up concerning property rights of women whose deceased husbands had consecrated their property to the Church. Whatever the case, this revelation was given to Joseph Smith as he sat in counsel with some of the brethren.

1 VERILY, thus saith the Lord, in addition to the laws of the church **concerning women and children, those who belong to the church, who have lost their husbands or fathers:**

2 **Women have claim on their husbands for their maintenance, until their husbands are taken** [*die*]; **and if they are not found transgressors they shall have fellowship in the church.**

3 And if they are not faithful they shall not have fellowship in the church [*they will lose their membership in the Church*]; **yet they may remain upon their inheritances according to the laws of the land** [*because the United Order includes private ownership of property; see D&C 51:4–5; thus their property belongs to them, not to the Church*].

4 **All children have claim upon their parents for their maintenance** [*for their daily physical needs*] **until they are of age.**

5 And **after that, they have claim upon the church**, or in other words upon the Lord's storehouse [*the bishop's storehouse*], **if their parents have not wherewith to give them inheritances** [*if the family can't help*].

6 And **the storehouse** [*bishop's storehouse*] **shall be kept** [*filled*] **by the consecrations of the church; and widows and orphans shall be provided for, as also the poor.** Amen.

SECTION 84

Background

This revelation was given through the Prophet Joseph Smith at Kirtland, Ohio, on September 22 and 23, 1832. The Prophet called this a revelation on priesthood.

This is one of the major doctrinal sections of the Doctrine and Covenants. Among other topics, it deals with:

- New Jerusalem

- The priesthood line of authority from Adam to Moses

- Melchizedek Priesthood

- Aaronic Priesthood

- The Oath and Covenant of the Priesthood

- The light of Christ

- The condemnation of the Church for not studying the Book of Mormon sufficiently

- Signs that follow believers

- Plagues of the last days

- **What it means to** "sing a new song"

- The Millennium

- The destruction of New York, Albany, and Boston, **if** they reject the gospel

Joseph Smith gave the background to section 84 as follows:

"As soon as I could arrange my affairs, I recommenced the translation of the Scriptures, and thus I spent most of the summer. In July, we received the first number of *The Evening and Morning Star*, which was a joyous treat to the Saints. Delightful, indeed, was it to contemplate that the little band of brethren had become so large, and grown so strong, in so short a time as to be able to issue a paper of their own, which contained not only some of the revelations, but other information also,—which would gratify and enlighten the humble inquirer after truth. . . .

"The Elders during the month of September began to return from their missions to the Eastern States, and present the histories of their several stewardships in the Lord's vineyard; and while together in these seasons of joy, I inquired of the Lord, and received on the 22nd and 23rd of September [1832], the following revelation on Priesthood: [D&C 84]" (*History of the Church*, 1:273, 286–87).

As mentioned at the beginning of the background for this section, this revelation was given over a period of two days. Apparently, as stated in verse 1, six elders were present on September 22 when the revelation began, but additional information from a note in an original handwritten copy of this revelation tells us that ten high priests were there during the latter part of the revelation. (See *The Joseph Smith Papers, Documents,*

Volume 2: July 1831–January 1833, ed. Matthew C. Godfrey and others [2013], 289–90.)

Since section 84 contains many revealed doctrines, we will point out a number of them by placing "**Doctrine**" at the beginning of the relevant verse or verses. These doctrines are examples of what the Savior told us in D&C 10:62–63, when He stated that He would bring back many of His "points of doctrine." They are likewise examples of the fulfillment of the prophecy found in 1 Nephi 13:40, in which the Lord said He would restore the "plain and precious things" that had been taken away from the Bible.

In verses 1–5, the Savior reviews the purposes of the Restoration and gives more detail about New Jerusalem and the temple that will someday be built in Independence, Missouri.

1 **A REVELATION of Jesus Christ** unto his servant Joseph Smith, Jun., and six elders, as they united their hearts and lifted their voices on high.

2 Yea, **the word of the Lord concerning his church, established** in the last days **for the restoration of his people,** as he has spoken by the mouth of his prophets, and **for the gathering of his saints** to stand upon Mount Zion, which shall be **the city of New Jerusalem.**

The temple lot, spoken of in verse 3, next, is currently owned by the Church of Christ Temple Lot, commonly called the Hedrickites—a church established by Granville Hedrick after the martyrdom of the Prophet Joseph Smith. The lot was laid out with corner stones under the direction of Joseph Smith and can easily be seen today. It is just across the parking lot from our visitors' center in Independence, Missouri.

3 **Which city shall be built, beginning at the temple lot**, which is appointed by the finger of the Lord, in the western boundaries of the State of Missouri [see D&C 57:2–3], and **dedicated by the hand of Joseph Smith, Jun., and others** [see D&C 58:57] with whom the Lord was well pleased.

Joseph Smith spoke of the dedication of the land of Zion by Sidney Rigdon and recorded that he, himself, dedicated the site for the temple. He said:

"On the second day of August [1831], I assisted the Colesville branch of the Church to lay the first log, for a house, as a foundation of Zion in Kaw township, twelve miles west of Independence. The log was carried and placed by twelve men, in honor of the twelve tribes of Israel. At the same time, through prayer, the land of Zion was consecrated and dedicated by Elder Sidney Rigdon

SECTION 84

for the gathering of the Saints. It was a season of joy to those present, and afforded a glimpse of the future, which time will yet unfold to the satisfaction of the faithful" (*History of the Church*, 1:196).

"On the third day of August, I proceeded to dedicate the spot for the Temple, a little west of Independence, and there were also present Sidney Rigdon, Edward Partridge, W. W. Phelps, Oliver Cowdery, Martin Harris and Joseph Coe" (*History of the Church*, 1:199).

Doctrine

A city called "New Jerusalem" will be built in Jackson County, Missouri, along with a temple.

4 Verily this is the word of the Lord, that the city New Jerusalem shall be built by the gathering of the saints, **beginning at this place,** even **the place of the temple, which temple shall be reared in this generation.**

5 For verily **this generation shall not all pass away until an house shall be built unto the Lord, and a cloud shall rest upon it, which cloud shall be even the glory of the Lord, which shall fill the house.**

Some critics of the Church have pointed at verses 4–5, above, and claimed that this is one prophecy that failed to come true. They have used it in their attempts to discredit the Prophet Joseph Smith. They claim that since a temple was not built in Independence, Missouri, during that "generation," Joseph Smith is a false prophet.

The interpretation of this aspect of these verses hinges on the definition of the word "generation." There are many different definitions of this word. Among others, it can mean the time from the marriage of a couple to the marriage of their children, or about twenty to thirty years. It is often used in scripture to mean one hundred years, as in the case of the Nephites after the visit of the resurrected Christ to them. They had peace for two generations, or two hundred years (see 4 Nephi 1:22) and were basically destroyed at the end of four generations, or four hundred years.

Another definition of "generation," and perhaps the one that best applies to verses 4–5, above, is the one used in Matthew 24:34, which refers to the signs of the times to be shown before the Second Coming. In this case, "generation" means an indefinite period of time in which prophesied events will take place. This definition of "generation" is also found in Joseph Smith—Matthew 1:34 and surrounding verses.

If we apply this last definition, there is no problem, because New

Jerusalem, including a temple, will indeed be built in Independence, Missouri, in this "generation," meaning in the time period from the restoration of the true Church, through Joseph Smith, up to the Second Coming. It is a true prophecy given through a true prophet of God, Joseph Smith. The faithful will rejoice when this takes place, and the critics of the Church will be disappointed.

We will include a quote from the 2018 *Doctrine and Covenants Student Manual* that summarizes the teachings in verses 2–5, above:

"During the Prophet Joseph Smith's first visit to Jackson County, Missouri, in July 1831, the Lord identified the area as 'the land which I have appointed and consecrated for the gathering of the saints' (D&C 57:1). He continued: 'Wherefore, this is the land of promise, and the place for the city of Zion. . . . The place which is now called Independence is the center place' (D&C 57:2–3). Joseph Smith and Sidney Rigdon soon dedicated the land of Zion and a site for a temple to be built. They were familiar with earlier revelations in which the Lord had indicated that the center place of Zion would be known as the city of the New Jerusalem, where God's people would gather and build a temple and where Jesus Christ would someday come to visit His people (see Ether 13:6, 8; D&C 42:9, 35–36; 45:66–67).

"In the months after Joseph and Sidney dedicated the land, hundreds of Church members arrived and settled in Jackson County. In September 1832, as recorded in Doctrine and Covenants 84, the Lord reaffirmed His will for the Saints to build 'the city of New Jerusalem' (D&C 84:2), beginning with the temple, which the Lord commanded should 'be reared in this generation' (D&C 84:4).

"However, by the end of 1833, the Latter-day Saints had been driven out of Jackson County by their enemies and eventually settled elsewhere. The Saints learned that their own transgressions had contributed to their expulsion from Zion (see D&C 101:1–6; 105:1–6). Neither the city of New Jerusalem nor the temple was built at that time, as commanded in Doctrine and Covenants 84:4–5. Several years later, after the Saints had established themselves in Nauvoo, Illinois, the Lord declared that they were excused from the commandment to build the city of New Jerusalem and the temple (see D&C 124:49–51). Nevertheless, the Lord's promises remain that Zion will one day be redeemed and the New Jerusalem will be built (see D&C 100:13; 105:9; 136:18)."

Next, in verses 6–16, we are given the direct line of authority from Moses back to Adam.

Doctrine, verses 6–16

The priesthood must be passed from one man to another by the laying on of hands. Moses had a direct line of priesthood authority going back to Adam.

We will use **bold** to point out this direct line of priesthood from Moses to Adam. But we need to call your attention to something before we continue. The first phrase of verse 6, next, **"And the sons of Moses,"** is the beginning of a sentence that skips all the way over to verse 31 where it continues with **"—for the sons of Moses and also the sons of Aaron shall offer an acceptable offering and sacrifice in the house of the Lord, which house shall be built unto the Lord in this generation, upon the consecrated spot as I have appointed—"**

Everything between the two quotes given above is parenthetical, like being in parentheses; in other words, it is basically a long explanation that could have a parenthesis at the beginning and one at the end. If you were to place these parentheses in your own scriptures as notes, you would have the following in parentheses, which is the priesthood line of authority for Moses back to Adam:

6 And the sons of Moses, **(according to the Holy Priesthood which he received under the hand of** his father–in–law, Jethro;

. . . and continuing to verse 31 . . .

31 **Therefore, as I said concerning the sons of Moses)**—for the sons of Moses and also the sons of Aaron shall offer an acceptable offering and sacrifice in the house of the Lord, which house shall be built unto the Lord in this generation, upon the consecrated spot as I have appointed—

We will study the words of the Savior within these "parentheses," that is, verses 6 through the first part of verse 31, and then when we get to verse 31, we will study the concept that began with the first phrase of verse 6.

Priesthood Line of Authority of Moses Back to Adam

6 And the sons of **Moses**, according to the Holy Priesthood which he received under the hand [*by the laying on of hands*] of his father–in–law, **Jethro**;

7 And Jethro received it under the hand of **Caleb**;

8 And Caleb received it under the hand of **Elihu**;

9 And Elihu under the hand of **Jeremy**;

10 And Jeremy under the hand of **Gad**;

11 And Gad under the hand of **Esaias**;

12 And Esaias received it under the hand of God.

> We don't know if verse 12, above, means that Esaias received the Melchizedek Priesthood from Abraham (verse 13, next), under the direction of God, or if it means he received it directly from God. We will continue with Abraham.

13 Esaias also lived in the days of **Abraham**, and was blessed of him—

14 Which Abraham received the priesthood from **Melchizedek**, who received it **through the lineage of his fathers** [*ancestors*], **even till Noah**;

> Did you notice a change beginning with verse 14, above? Until that verse, each individual in the line of authority was given, but as of verse 14, we are apparently seeing a summary of many individuals from Melchizedek back to Noah. The same is true with verses 15–16, next.

15 And from **Noah till Enoch**, through the lineage of their fathers;

16 And from **Enoch to Abel**, who was slain by the conspiracy of his brother, who received the priesthood by the commandments of God, by the hand [*the laying on of hands*] of his father **Adam**, who **was the first man—**

Doctrine, verse 16

Adam was the first man.

As you can see, in the last part of verse 16, above, we have an important revealed truth as to the origin of man. The Savior simply says, "Adam . . . was the first man."

As you know, there are numerous theories as to how mankind came to be on this earth. Several years ago, the First Presidency at the time used the revealed word of God in an official statement on this matter. They said (**bold** added for emphasis):

"It is held by some that Adam was not the first man upon this earth, and that the original human being was a development from lower orders of the animal creation. These, however, are the theories of men. The word of the Lord declares that Adam was 'the first man of all men' (Moses 1:34), and we are therefore in duty bound to regard him as the primal [*first*] parent of our race. It was shown to the brother of Jared that all men were created in the beginning after the image of God; and whether we take this to mean the spirit or the body, or both, it commits us to the same conclusion: **Man began life as a human being**, in the likeness of our heavenly Father." (The First Presidency [Joseph F.

Smith, John R. Winder, and Anthon H. Lund], in James R. Clark, *Messages of the First Presidency,* 4:205–6.)

As we continue, we see two more doctrines—that the priesthood is essential to having the true church on earth and that the priesthood is eternal—along with much other instruction about the priesthood.

Doctrine, verse 17

The priesthood must be on earth in order for the Church of Jesus Christ to exist.

Doctrine, verse 17

The priesthood is eternal.

17 Which priesthood continueth in the church of God in all generations [*is always with the true Church when it exists on earth*]**, and is without beginning of days or end of years** [*is eternal*]**.**

18 And the Lord confirmed a priesthood also upon Aaron and his seed [*the Aaronic Priesthood*]**, throughout all their generations, which priesthood also continueth and abideth forever with the priesthood which is after the holiest order of God** [*the Melchizedek Priesthood*]**.**

Next, in verses 19–22, the Savior teaches us about the role and function of the Melchizedek Priesthood. You may wish to bracket these verses in your own scriptures and place a note saying "Melchizedek Priesthood" along the bracket. The Savior will teach more about this in section 107.

Doctrine, verses 19–22

The Melchizedek Priesthood directs the Church and holds the keys of the "spiritual blessings of the church" (see also D&C 107:18).

19 And this greater priesthood [*Melchizedek*] **administereth the gospel and holdeth the key of the mysteries** [*the simple basics of the gospel, which are "mysteries" to most of the world because they do not have the full gospel of Christ; see Bible Dictionary under "Mystery"*] **of the kingdom, even the key of the knowledge of God.**

Joseph Fielding Smith taught the following about the Melchizedek Priesthood as explained in verse 19, above:

"It is the Holy Priesthood that unlocks the door to heaven and reveals to man the mysteries of the Kingdom of God. It is this Divine Authority which makes known the knowledge of God! Is there any wonder that the world today is groping in gross darkness concerning God and the things of his kingdom? We should also remember that these great truths are not made known even to members of the Church unless they place their lives in harmony with the law on which these blessings are predicated. (D. & C. 130:20–21.)" (*Church History and Modern Revelation*, 1:33).

Doctrine, verse 20

Through the ordinances of the Priesthood, "the power of godliness is manifest."

20 Therefore, **in the ordinances thereof, the power of godliness is manifest.**

Elder Todd D. Christofferson taught about "the power of godliness" as follows:

"Our covenant commitment to Him permits our Heavenly Father to let His divine influence, 'the power of godliness' (D&C 84:20), flow into our lives. He can do that because by our participation in priesthood ordinances we exercise our agency and elect to receive it. . . .

"In all the ordinances, especially those of the temple, we are endowed with power from on high. This 'power of godliness' comes in the person and by the influence of the Holy Ghost. . . .

". . . It is also the Holy Ghost, in His character as the Holy Spirit of Promise, that confirms the validity and efficacy of your covenants and seals God's promises upon you" ("The Power of Covenants," *Ensign*, May 2009, 22).

Doctrine, verses 21–22

Without the authority and ordinances of the Melchizedek Priesthood, we cannot be taught the things necessary to bring "the power of godliness" into our lives.

21 And **without the ordinances thereof** [*without the ordinances of the Melchizedek Priesthood*], **and the authority of the priesthood, the power of godliness is not manifest unto men in the flesh;**

22 For **without this** [*perhaps meaning the "power of godliness" (verse 21), which no doubt includes Melchizedek Priesthood ordinances and the personal righteousness arising out of living the gospel of Christ, plus the gift of the Holy Ghost, which comes to all faithful members via a Melchizedek Priesthood ordinance*] **no man can see the face of God, even the Father, and live.**

Next, we are told that Moses tried diligently to get his people to accept and live the gospel, inherent in the Melchizedek Priesthood-based Church of Jesus Christ.

23 Now **this** [*that without Melchizedek Priesthood ordinances and direction, the "power of godliness" is out*

of reach, as is the privilege of seeing God] **Moses plainly taught to the children of Israel** in the wilderness, **and sought diligently to sanctify his people** [to make them holy and fit to be in the presence of God] **that they might behold** [see] **the face of God** [Exodus 19:10–11];

24 **But they hardened their hearts and could not endure his presence** [would have been killed by His glory if they had seen Him]; therefore, the Lord in his wrath, for his anger was kindled against them, swore that they should not enter into **his rest** while in the wilderness, which rest **is the fulness of his glory.**

Doctrine, verse 24

(Last part of verse 24, above.) "Rest" means exaltation or being in the full presence of God (see also Alma 12:34).

Doctrine, verse 25

The Melchizedek Priesthood was taken from the children of Israel.

25 **Therefore, he took Moses out of their midst, and the Holy Priesthood** [Melchizedek Priesthood] **also;**

Doctrine, verses 26–28

A major purpose of the Aaronic Priesthood is that of preparing us for Melchizedek Priesthood ordinances and blessings.

26 And **the lesser priesthood** [Aaronic Priesthood] continued, which priesthood **holdeth the key of the ministering of angels and the preparatory gospel;**

27 Which gospel is **the gospel of repentance and of baptism, and the remission of sins,** and the law of carnal commandments [part of the law of Moses involving rigid rites and laws, designed as a "schoolmaster" (Galatians 3:24) to raise them to the level where they could benefit from the Melchizedek Priesthood], **which the Lord** in his wrath **caused to continue with the house of Aaron** [the descendants of Aaron, brother of Moses] among the children of Israel **until John** [the Baptist], **whom God raised up, being filled with the Holy Ghost from his mother's womb.**

28 For **he** [John the Baptist] **was baptized** while he was yet **in his childhood,** and was **ordained** [not to the priesthood but perhaps blessed or set apart to carry out his earthly mission, possibly similar to

the blessing of babies today] **by the angel of God at the time he was eight days old unto this power, to overthrow the kingdom of the Jews, and to make straight the way of the Lord before the face of his people, to prepare them for the coming of the Lord,** in whose hand is given all power.

As you can see, several important items were brought up in verses 26–28, above. In reference to "ministering of angels," in verse 26, we are taught that angels do much behind the scenes to prepare the way for people to join the Church. We also understand that there is much "ministering" by angels in assisting us in our family history work so that our dead ancestors can have the blessings of repentance and baptism (verse 27, next).

President Dallin H. Oaks, then an Apostle, spoke on the subject of the Aaronic Priesthood and the ministering of angels in the priesthood session of general conference in October 1998 as follows (**bold** added for emphasis):

"The scriptures recite numerous instances where an angel appeared personally. Angelic appearances to Zacharias and Mary (see Luke 1) and to King Benjamin and Nephi, the grandson of Helaman (see Mosiah 3:2; 3 Ne. 7:17–18) are only a few examples. **When I was young, I thought such personal appearances were the only meaning of the ministering of angels.** As a young holder of the Aaronic Priesthood, I did not think I would see an angel, and **I wondered what such appearances had to do with the Aaronic Priesthood.**

"But **the ministering of angels can also be unseen.** Angelic messages can be **delivered by a voice** or merely by **thoughts** or **feelings communicated to the mind.** President John Taylor described 'the action of the angels, or messengers of God, upon our minds, so that the heart can conceive . . . revelations from the eternal world' (*Gospel Kingdom,* sel. G. Homer Durham [1987], 31.)

"Nephi described three manifestations of the ministering of angels when he reminded his rebellious brothers that (1) **they had 'seen an angel,'** (2) **they had 'heard his voice from time to time,'** and (3) also that **an angel had 'spoken unto [them] in a still small voice'** though they were 'past feeling' and 'could not feel his words' (1 Ne. 17:45). The scriptures contain many other statements that angels are sent to teach the gospel and bring men to Christ (see Hebrews 1:14; Alma 39:19; Moroni 7:25, 29, 31–32; D&C 20:35). **Most angelic communications are felt or heard rather than seen.**

"**How does the Aaronic Priesthood hold the key to the ministering of angels?** The answer is the same as for the Spirit of the Lord.

"**In general, the blessings of spiritual companionship and communication are only available to those who are clean**. As explained earlier, **through the Aaronic Priesthood ordinances of baptism and the sacrament, we are cleansed of our sins and promised that if we keep our covenants we will always have His Spirit to be with us. I believe that promise not only refers to the Holy Ghost but also to the ministering of angels**, for 'angels speak by the power of the Holy Ghost; wherefore, they speak the words of Christ' (2 Ne. 32:3.) So it is that **those who hold the Aaronic Priesthood open the door for all Church members who worthily partake of the sacrament to enjoy the companionship of the Spirit of the Lord and the ministering of angels**" ("The Aaronic Priesthood and the Sacrament," *Ensign,* November 1998, 39).

In the last part of verse 27 and in verse 28, next, we find revealed information about John the Baptist. It is not available other than through revelation from the Lord. Questions arise as to whether John had the gift of the Holy Ghost while still in the womb, and whether he was given the priesthood when he was eight days old. We will read a quote from Elder Bruce R. McConkie about these questions and then go on to verse 28. We will use **bold** for emphasis.

"We do know that 'he was **baptized** while he was yet in his childhood [meaning, **when he was eight years of age**], and was **ordained** by the angel of God at the time he was eight days old unto this power [note it well, **not to the Aaronic Priesthood**, but] to overthrow the kingdom of the Jews, and to make straight the way of the Lord before the face of his people, **to prepare them for the coming of the Lord**, in whose hand is given all power.' (D&C 84:24.) **We do not know when he received the Aaronic Priesthood**, but obviously it came to him after his baptism, at whatever age was proper, and before he was sent by one whom he does not name to preach and baptize with water" (*Mortal Messiah,* 384–85).

Next, we are taught some specifics about various Melchizedek and Aaronic Priesthood offices. Keep in mind that this was new information for the members in the beginning stages of the Restoration.

29 And again, the offices of **elder and bishop** [*must be ordained a high priest in order to serve as a bishop*] **are** necessary **appendages belonging unto** [*are categories within*] **the high priesthood** [*Melchizedek Priesthood*].

30 And again, **the offices of teacher and deacon are necessary appendages belonging to the lesser priesthood** [*the Aaronic Priesthood*], **which priesthood was confirmed upon Aaron and his sons.**

> As previously mentioned, the Savior began a sentence at the beginning of verse 6 and then added much parenthetical information (verses 6–30). He now completes that sentence, explaining that "an acceptable offering and sacrifice" will once again be possible in the last days, because of the restoration of the gospel and the priesthood. Without proper priesthood authority, our "offerings" and "sacrifices," our ordinances and covenants, would not be valid. None of our ordinances of exaltation performed in temples would be in effect now or in eternity.
>
> With true priesthood, because of the Restoration, authorized ordinances can once again be performed on earth by both Aaronic and Melchizedek Priesthood holders during this wonderful dispensation of the fullness of times.

Doctrine, verse 31

With the restoration of the priesthood, valid ordinances of salvation and exaltation can once again be performed on earth.

31 Therefore, as I [*the Savior*] said [*at the beginning of verse 6*] concerning the sons of Moses—for **the sons of Moses** [*symbolic of Melchizedek Priesthood holders*] and **also the sons of Aaron** [*Aaronic Priesthood holders*] **shall offer an acceptable offering and sacrifice in the house of the Lord,** which house shall be built unto the Lord in this generation, upon the consecrated spot as I have appointed—

> A most significant phrase, defining who the latter-day "sons of Moses and of Aaron" are, is found in verse 32, next. As you will see, it defines them as our faithful priesthood holders today. There is important symbolism here.

32 And **the sons of Moses and of Aaron** shall be filled with the glory of the Lord, upon Mount Zion in the Lord's house, **whose sons are ye** [*perhaps meaning Joseph Smith and the elders mentioned by the Lord in verse 1 of this section*]; **and also many** [*faithful priesthood holders in the last days*] **whom I have called and sent forth to build up my church.**

> A quote from the 2018 *Doctrine and Covenants Student Manual*, (which is an official publication of the Church and thus has doctrinal reliability) confirms who the sons of Moses and the sons of Aaron

in verses 31 and 32, above, are (**bold** added for emphasis):

"In Doctrine and Covenants 84:31, the Lord continued the discussion that began in Doctrine and Covenants 84:5–6 regarding the role of 'the sons of Moses and also the sons of Aaron . . . in the house of the Lord,' including the latter-day temple that will be built in the city of New Jerusalem. **The sons of Moses are those who hold the Melchizedek Priesthood. The sons of Aaron are those who hold the Aaronic Priesthood**. These priesthood bearers will 'offer an acceptable offering and sacrifice in the house of the Lord' (D&C 84:31)." (For further details about these latter-day offerings, see Isaiah 66:20–21; Omni 1:26; D&C 13:1; 128:24.)

You may wish to cross-reference verse 32, here, with verse 34, below.

In verses 33–42, next, we have what is known as "the Oath and Covenant of the Priesthood." Here, again, you may wish to bracket or otherwise identify these verses and place a note out to the side that says, "Oath and Covenant of the Priesthood."

The Oath and Covenant of the Priesthood

Doctrine

Faithful Melchizedek Priesthood holders make a covenant with God upon accepting and being ordained to the priesthood. The Father makes an "oath" with them that if they serve faithfully, they will receive all that He has (verse 38). This is known as "The Oath and Covenant of the Priesthood."

33 For whoso is faithful unto the obtaining these two priesthoods [*Aaronic and Melchizedek*] of which I have spoken, **and the magnifying their calling, are sanctified** by the Spirit [*are directed and prompted by the Holy Ghost, leading them to sanctification—being made holy and fit to be in the presence of God through the blessings of the Atonement; compare with Moses 6:60*] **unto the renewing of their bodies.**

The "renewing of their bodies," in verse 33, above, can have at least two meanings. One is that they will receive celestial bodies at the time they are resurrected (see D&C 88:28–29). Another possible meaning is that, on occasions when they are weary and tired, they will be carried by the power of the Lord to complete their work. They will know that they have been blessed far beyond their physical and mental capacities.

34 They become the sons of Moses and of Aaron and the seed of

Abraham [*symbolic of exaltation; in effect, the "heirs" of Abraham, who has already become a god; see D&C 132:29, 37*], and **the church and kingdom, and the elect of God.** [*All of these are terms meaning exaltation.*]

We will include two quotes here from the 1981 *Doctrine and Covenants Student Manual* that explain what it means to "become the sons of Moses and of Aaron."

"Who are the sons of Aaron and Levi today? They are, by virtue of the blessings of the Almighty, those who are ordained by those who hold the authority to officiate in the offices of the priesthood. It is written that those so ordained become the sons of Moses and Aaron" (Joseph Fielding Smith, *Doctrines of Salvation,* Bookcraft, 1956, 3:93; see also *Doctrine and Covenants Student Manual,* 1981, 184).

"'Sons of Moses,' and 'sons of Aaron' do not refer to their literal descendants only, for all who are faithful and obtain these Priesthoods, and magnify their calling, are sanctified by the Spirit and become the 'sons' of Moses and of Aaron, and the seed of Abraham, as well as the Church and Kingdom, and the elect of God (verse 34). Paul expresses this thought as follows, 'Know ye therefore that they which are of faith, the same are the children of Abraham' (Gal. 3:7). (Smith and Sjodahl, *Commentary,* 504.)" (*Doctrine and Covenants Student Manual,* 1981, 184).

While verse 35, next, is generally understood to pertain to men as they accept the call to hold the Melchizedek Priesthood, it can, in a very important sense, pertain to all righteous members, male and female, who enter into or "receive" priesthood ordinances and covenants. D&C 132:19 makes it clear that when faithful men and women enter into covenants performed by "him who is anointed, unto whom I have appointed this power and the keys of this priesthood," if they continue to live worthy, they will enter exaltation and become gods (D&C 132:20).

In verses 35–38, the Master shows us a beautiful "progression" of steps leading to exaltation.

35 And also **all they who receive this priesthood receive me**, saith the Lord;

36 For **he that receiveth my servants receiveth me**;

37 And **he that receiveth me receiveth my Father**;

Doctrine, verse 38

It is possible to become gods.

38 And **he that receiveth my Father receiveth my Father's kingdom**; therefore [*for this*

reason] **all that my Father hath shall be given unto him.**

Next, in verse 39, we find the wording that leads to the term "Oath and Covenant of the Priesthood."

39 And this is according to **the oath and covenant which belongeth to the priesthood.**

40 Therefore, **all those who receive the priesthood, receive this oath and covenant of my Father, which he cannot break,** neither can it be moved [*compare with D&C 82:10*].

From verse 40, above, we learn that the "oath" is what the Father promises. His "oath and covenant" is to give those who "receive the priesthood" all that He has.

It doesn't take much analyzing to see that when we give our "all" and qualify to receive the Father's "all," we get the better bargain.

President Henry B. Eyring taught what it means to receive this oath and covenant. He said:

"Rising to the possibilities of the oath and covenant brings the greatest of all the gifts of God: eternal life [*exaltation*]. That is a purpose of the Melchizedek Priesthood. Through keeping the covenants as we receive the priesthood and renewing them in the temple ceremonies, we are promised by an oath made by our Heavenly Father, Elohim, that we will gain the fulness of His glory and live as He lives. We will have the blessing of being sealed in a family forever with the promise of eternal increase . . .

". . . The very fact that you have been offered the oath and covenant is evidence that God has chosen you, knowing your power and capacity. He has known you since you were with Him in the spirit world. With His foreknowledge of your strength, He has allowed you to find the true Church of Jesus Christ and to be offered the priesthood. You can feel confidence because you have evidence of His confidence in you" ("Faith and the Oath and Covenant of the Priesthood," *Ensign*, May 2008, 61–62).

Verse 41, next, explains the seriousness of violating the covenants we make when accepting the Melchizedek Priesthood. President Marion G. Romney explained this verse as follows:

"Now, I do not think this means that all who fail to magnify their callings in the priesthood will have committed the unpardonable sin, but I do think that priesthood bearers who have entered into the covenants that we enter into—in the waters of baptism, in connection with the law of tithing, the Word of Wisdom, and the many other covenants we make—and then refuse to live up to these covenants will stand in jeopardy of losing the promise of eternal life" ("The Covenant of the Priesthood," *Ensign*, July 1972, 99).

41 But **whoso breaketh this covenant after he hath received it, and altogether turneth therefrom, shall not have forgiveness of sins in this world nor in the world to come.**

> Because of the seriousness of this covenant, as stated in verse 41, above, it may be that some will decide not to enter into it. It appears that verse 42, next, addresses such persons, likely meaning both men and women who intentionally avoid the highest priesthood ordinances available in the temple because of the seriousness and accountability that accompany ordinances of exaltation.

42 And **wo unto all those who come not unto this priesthood** which ye have received, which I now confirm [*perhaps meaning "reconfirm," reassure that it is in force in your behalf*] upon you who are present this day [*Joseph Smith and the elders mentioned in verse 1*], by mine own voice out of the heavens; and even I have given the heavenly hosts and mine angels charge concerning you [*another reminder that there is much done for us, behind the scenes, by angels*].

> In verses 43–44, next, we are counseled not to let our guard down and to carefully live by the revealed word of God.

43 And I now give unto you a commandment to **beware concerning yourselves, to give diligent heed to the words of eternal life** [*exaltation*].

44 For you shall **live by every word that proceedeth forth from the mouth of God.**

> Some major functions of the Light of Christ are explained in verses 45–47, next.

Doctrine, verses 45–47

Everyone born into the world is given the Spirit of Christ, sometimes called the Light of Christ. A major function of the Light of Christ (also sometimes called "conscience") is to lead all who will follow it to the gospel of Jesus Christ. If they listen and follow until they become members of the Church, they will receive the greater light and help of the gift of the Holy Ghost. It will, in turn, lead them home to the Father if they live according to its promptings.

45 For the word of the Lord is **truth,** and whatsoever is **truth is light** [*among other things, truth*

brings "light" and understanding into our souls], and whatsoever is **light is Spirit** [*includes the fact that truth and light come to us from the Spirit of Christ*], even **the Spirit of Jesus Christ** [*often referred to as the Light of Christ*].

46 And **the Spirit giveth light to every man that cometh into the world; and the Spirit enlighteneth every man through the world, that hearkeneth to the voice of the Spirit** [*those who listen to the Spirit of Christ will receive enlightenment*].

47 And **every one that hearkeneth to the voice of the Spirit cometh unto God, even the Father** [*those who heed the promptings of the Spirit of Christ will be led home to the Father by eventually joining the Church of Jesus Christ and living the gospel*].

Elder Richard G. Scott taught about the Light of Christ as follows:

"The Light of Christ is that divine power or influence that emanates from God through Jesus Christ. It gives light and life to all things. It prompts all rational individuals throughout the earth to distinguish truth from error, right from wrong. It activates your conscience. Its influence can be weakened through transgression and addiction and restored through proper repentance. The Light of Christ is not a person. It is a power and influence that comes from God and when followed can lead a person to qualify for the guidance and inspiration of the Holy Ghost" ("Peace of Conscience and Peace of Mind," *Ensign,* November 2004, 15.)

Verse 48, next, teaches us the result of following the Light of Christ. This result is available to all people. If they follow the Spirit of Christ, it will lead them to the true Church. If they join, they will be taught about the "covenant," which, in this context, includes the full gospel of Jesus Christ, with its attending covenants and ordinances.

48 And **the Father teacheth him** [*those who follow the Spirit of Christ and are led to the true Church*] **of the covenant which he has renewed and confirmed upon you** [*through the restoration of the gospel*], which is confirmed upon you for your sakes, and **not for your sakes only, but for the sake of the whole world** [*the restored gospel will ultimately be made available to all*].

Next, the Savior reviews the need for all to heed the influence of the Spirit of Christ upon them and come to the restored gospel.

49 And **the whole world lieth in sin, and groaneth under darkness** [*spiritual darkness*] **and**

under the bondage [*captivity*] of sin.

50 And by this you may know they are under the bondage of sin, because they come not unto me.

> Did you notice the "equation" given in verse 50, above? Those who are not with Christ are being held captive by sin, whether they know it or not. It is just that simple.

51 For whoso cometh not unto me is under the bondage of sin.

> Sometimes people are disturbed by the use of the term "wicked" (verse 53) in reference to the people in spirit prison. This is because they know that there are some wonderful and good people there (in the spirit prison, which I prefer to call the "spirit world mission field") who have not yet been taught the gospel, and they don't like to hear them referred to as wicked. Verses 52–53, next, show us that there is another scriptural meaning for the word "wicked" in addition to its use as a term for those involved in sin and gross evil. As you will see, "wicked" is sometimes used in scripture to refer to those who have not yet been taught the gospel.

52 And whoso receiveth not my voice **is not acquainted with my voice, and is not of me.**

53 And by this you may know the righteous from the wicked, and that the whole world groaneth under sin and darkness even now.

> Next, in verses 54–59, an extremely serious matter is explained by the Savior. It is that the Saints have not treated seriously enough the things He has already given them. As you will see, this includes the Book of Mormon. We would do well to pay close attention ourselves to His words of reprimand and counsel.

54 And your minds in times past have been darkened because of unbelief, and **because you have treated lightly the things you have received—**

55 Which vanity and unbelief have brought the whole church under condemnation.

56 And this condemnation resteth upon the children of Zion [*the members in Missouri at this time*]**, even all.**

57 And they shall remain under this condemnation until they repent and remember the new covenant, even the Book of Mormon and the former commandments which I have given them, not only to say, but to do according to that which I have written—

President Ezra Taft Benson spoke of the importance of the Book of Mormon in each of our lives. He said:

"Every Latter-day Saint should make the study of this book a lifetime pursuit. Otherwise he is placing his soul in jeopardy and neglecting that which could give spiritual and intellectual unity to his whole life" ("The Book of Mormon Is the Word of God," *Ensign*, May 1975, 65).

58 That they may bring forth fruit meet for [*worthy of*] **their Father's kingdom; otherwise there remaineth a scourge and judgment to be poured out upon the children of Zion.**

The Saints who were settling in Missouri at the time of this revelation fully expected that the Church would be established there, never to be removed, and that it would continue to grow and flourish in Jackson County until the Second Coming.

As you can see, in verses 58 and 59, there is a stern warning from the Lord that if they do not "bring forth fruit meet for their Father's kingdom" (verse 58)—in other words, if they do not live in harmony with the celestial laws incorporated in the gospel, including the oath and covenant of the priesthood, they will be "scourged" (driven and plundered).

59 For shall the children of the kingdom pollute my holy land [*by their disobedience and lack of diligence in living the gospel*]**? Verily, I say unto you, Nay.**

Next, in verses 60–61, the Savior assures these brethren that if they heed the counsel and warning He has just given, and follow the counsel He gives next, they will be forgiven. In a way, this is a formula for spiritual success and applies to all of us.

60 Verily, verily [*a scriptural term meaning that what comes next is of key importance*]**, I say unto you who now hear my words,** which are my voice, **blessed are ye inasmuch as you** [*if you will*] **receive these things;**

61 For I will forgive you of your sins with this commandment— that you remain steadfast in your minds in solemnity and the spirit of prayer, in bearing testimony to all the world of those things which are communicated unto you.

We do not know who the men are that are with the Prophet as this revelation is given. It appears from the context that they were some of the leading brethren at the time. We learn from verse 62, next, that they are to continue preaching the gospel themselves and enlist the aid of others to continue taking the gospel to all the world. The General Authorities of the Church are continuing this same pattern of missionary work today.

62 Therefore, **go ye into all the world**; and **unto whatsoever place ye cannot go ye shall send** [*send others on missions to those places*], **that the testimony may go from you into all the world unto every creature.**

63 And **as I said unto mine Apostles, even so I say unto you, for you are mine Apostles, even God's high priests**; ye are they whom my Father hath given me; **ye are my friends**;

> We don't want to miss what just happened at the end of verse 63, above. The Savior called them His "friends." From this point on in the Doctrine and Covenants, the Master will refer to these and other humble followers as "friends." This is a term of endearment and closeness that signifies a change in relationship as they become more righteous and faithful.

64 Therefore, **as I said unto mine Apostles I say unto you** again, that **every soul who believeth on your words, and is baptized by water for the remission of sins, shall receive the Holy Ghost.**

Next, in verses 65–73, the Savior tells us of many of the miracles that will be evident in His church. While we understand these to be literal, there is value in also seeing spiritual symbolism in each of them. If you learn to see such symbolism, then you will often see the spiritual counterpart for literal healings. As you know, spiritual healing has eternal benefits that reach far beyond the literal healing of the physical body and mind. We will designate these spiritual counterparts to literal healings through notes in brackets.

Doctrine, verses 65–73

This is a day of miracles. Miracles, signs, and wonders are a quiet and sweet part of the gospel of Christ.

65 And **these signs shall follow them that believe—**

66 **In my name they shall do many wonderful works;**

67 In my name **they shall cast out devils** [*literal; symbolically could include that the pure gospel of Christ "casts out" evil thoughts, damaging philosophies, fears, confusion as to the purpose of life, and so forth*];

68 **In my name they shall heal the sick** [*literal; symbolically could include the healing of spiritual darkness and confusion, remorse and guilt, anger and hatred*];

SECTION 84

69 **In my name they shall open the eyes of the blind** [*literal; often means healing the spiritually "blind"*], and **unstop the ears of the deaf** [*including the spiritually deaf*];

70 And **the tongue of the dumb** [*those who can't speak*] **shall speak** [*can also refer to the power of the Holy Ghost to help us express ourselves more effectively as we discuss the gospel with others, as well as when we speak and teach in church*];

71 And if any man shall administer **poison** unto them it **shall not hurt them** [*symbolically, "poison" could include false philosophies, false doctrines, confusing false political theories, and so forth*];

72 And the **poison of a serpent** [*can also be symbolic of the false doctrines put forth by Satan (the "serpent"), including Internet content that is leading some away from the Church today*] **shall not have power to harm them.**

Sacred experiences, including miracles, are often for our own private blessing and benefit and are usually best kept to ourselves or within a small number of family or close friends. They are not to be used for building ourselves up in the eyes of others. This is a real danger against which the Lord warns in verse 73, next.

73 But a commandment I give unto them, that **they shall not boast themselves of these things, neither speak them before the world**; for **these things are given unto you for your profit and for salvation.**

In verses 74–76, next, we are once again reminded of the importance of our sharing the gospel with others, and of their responsibility to accept it when they know it is true.

74 Verily, verily, I say unto you, **they who believe not on your words, and are not baptized in water in my name, for the remission of their sins, that they may receive the Holy Ghost, shall be damned** [*stopped in spiritual progress*], **and shall not come into my Father's kingdom** [*celestial glory*] **where my Father and I am.**

75 And **this revelation** unto you, **and commandment, is in force** from this very hour **upon all the world,** and **the gospel is unto all who have not received it** [*the gospel is to be taken to all the world*].

76 But, verily I say **unto all those to whom the kingdom has been given** [*all the members of the Church*]—**from you it must be preached unto them** [*Church

leaders are to continue preaching the gospel to the members], **that they shall repent of their former evil works**; for they are to be upbraided [*scolded, chastised*] for their evil hearts of unbelief, and your brethren in Zion [*in Missouri*] for their rebellion against you at the time I sent you.

> We will do one more thing with verse 76, above. The word "upbraided" may be familiar to you. "Upbraideth not" is used in James 1:5, which young Joseph Smith read in the Bible before going into the grove to pray. It comes from the ancient practice of jerking a child's braid upward as a means of scolding or disciplining. Thus, the word came to mean to "scold or chastise."

> Again, in verse 77, next, the Savior refers to these men as His friends. He then goes on to tell them that they are getting the same advice as His disciples of old.

77 And again I say unto you, **my friends** (see also verse 63), for **from henceforth** [*from now on*] **I shall call you friends**, it is expedient [*necessary*] that I give unto you this commandment [*to continue teaching the gospel to the members of the Church, as well as to the world*], that ye become even as my friends [*disciples*] in days when I was with them [*during the Savior's mortal ministry*], traveling to preach the gospel in my power;

78 **For I suffered** [*allowed*] **them not to have purse** [*a money bag*] **or scrip** [*a bag for carrying food; see Bible Dictionary under "Scrip"*], **neither two coats.**

79 Behold, **I send you out to prove the world** [*to test the world by teaching them the gospel so that they can use their moral agency and be accountable for their actions*], and **the laborer is worthy of his hire** [*those who preach the gospel earn their blessings through hard work*].

> In verses 80–91, next, the Savior informs these early brethren that He will take care of those who go forth to preach the gospel. They will be fed, clothed, and assisted financially by people as they pursue their missionary journeys (verses 89–90). This required great faith on the part of these missionaries, and there was much success in bringing converts into the Church. Because of the success of these missionary efforts, the Church was greatly strengthened by the large influx of converts and positioned for significant continued missionary efforts into all the world.

> For the most part, these verses must be understood in the context of these early missionary efforts. Otherwise, we would have missionaries going out today without

proper preparation for taking care of their physical needs.

80 And **any man that shall go and preach** this gospel of the kingdom, **and fail not to continue faithful in all things, shall not be weary in mind, neither darkened** [*spiritually*], **neither in body, limb, nor joint**; and **a hair of his head shall not fall to the ground unnoticed** [*the Lord is watching over them*]. And **they shall not go hungry, neither athirst** [*this aspect of missionary work is taken care of today by the funds of the Church as well as by the financial support of family and friends of missionaries*].

> Verses 81–84, next, are similar to Matthew 6:25–36, which, according to JST Matthew 6:25–27 and 3 Nephi 13:25–34, were addressed to the Savior's Apostles.

81 **Therefore, take ye no thought for the morrow**, for what ye shall eat, or what ye shall drink, or wherewithal ye shall be clothed.

82 **For, consider the lilies of the field,** how they grow, they toil not, neither do they spin; and the kingdoms of the world, in all their glory, are not arrayed like one of these.

83 **For your Father, who is in heaven, knoweth that you have need of all these things.**

84 Therefore, **let the morrow take thought for the things of itself.**

85 **Neither take ye thought beforehand what ye shall say; but treasure up in your minds continually the words of life** [*keep studying the gospel*], **and it shall be given you in the very hour that portion that shall be meted unto every man** [*with proper preparation, you will qualify to have the help of the Holy Ghost in determining what to teach to each person you meet*].

86 Therefore, **let no man among you,** for this commandment is unto all the faithful who are called of God in the church unto the ministry, **from this hour take purse or scrip,** that goeth forth to proclaim this gospel of the kingdom.

> As previously mentioned, some could understand, based on verse 86, above, that none of our missionaries or general Church leaders today should take money and supplies with them as they go forth to preach the gospel. However, as you know, we believe in continuous revelation. Thus, this advice no longer applies. The Lord does not require that His servants today go without "purse or scrip," depending on the kindness and generosity of people throughout the world to travelers and missionaries. Rather,

funds are made available to take care of their needs.

As the Savior continues teaching these brethren, we see that the message of the gospel as taught by the missionaries is to make people accountable and to provide them the option of using their agency wisely.

87 Behold, I send you out to reprove the world of all their unrighteous deeds [*to call the people of the earth to repentance*]**, and to teach them of a judgment which is to come** [*to teach them that they will someday face God on Judgment Day*]**.**

Verse 88, next, is a favorite of missionaries, including senior missionaries, as they go forth into the unknown to serve. You may wish to mark it in your own scriptures.

88 And whoso receiveth you, there I will be also, for **I will go before your face. I will be on your right hand and on your left, and my Spirit shall be in your hearts, and mine angels round about you, to bear you up.**

89 Whoso receiveth you receiveth me; and the same will feed you, and clothe you, and give you money.

90 And **he who feeds you, or clothes you, or gives you money, shall in nowise lose his reward.**

Verse 91, next, seems to refer more to members of the Church than to nonmembers. The message is clear. If we pay our tithes and offerings, which serve to help spread the gospel to all the world, we are true disciples (followers) of Christ. If we don't, we are not!

91 And **he that doeth not these things is not my disciple; by this you may know my disciples.**

Verses 92–95 are sensitive and must be kept in context. The context here appears to be that of a testimony that they tried to preach the gospel to the person or to the people but were rejected. Based on what we understand in the overall context of the scriptures, the Lord continues to reach out to people throughout their lives. See, for example, Jacob 6:4–5. You probably know several people who have come into activity later in life after having been less active or who had rejected earlier efforts to teach them the gospel. They are now faithful, committed Saints.

92 **He that receiveth you not, go away from him alone by yourselves** [*so you don't cause unnecessary trouble*]**, and cleanse your feet** even with water, pure water, whether in heat or in cold, and **bear testimony of it unto your Father** which is in heaven, and

return not again unto that man.

> See section 60, verse 15, in this study guide for more concerning the washing of feet as mentioned in verse 92, above.

93 And in whatsoever village or city ye enter, do likewise.

> Verse 94, next, seems to imply that some missionaries could be tempted to simply wash their feet a lot, thus getting off somewhat easy, rather than going to every effort to find and teach the honest in heart.

94 **Nevertheless, search diligently** [*for people who will listen to you*] **and spare not** [*don't spare any effort*]; **and wo unto that house, or that village or city that rejecteth you, or your words, or your testimony concerning me.**

95 **Wo** [*trouble*], I say again, **unto that house, or that village or city that rejecteth you, or your words, or your testimony of me;**

> One of the signs of the times is given in verses 96–97, next. It is that, in the last days, as people reject the quiet, humble, gentle approach of the missionaries who are sent throughout the world to preach the gospel (see D&C 88:88–90), the Lord will "turn up the volume" via plagues, natural disasters, and so forth in order to get people's attention. Such things are the natural consequence, decreed by God, for mass wickedness among the inhabitants of the earth.

Doctrine, verses 96–97
Things will continue to get worse until the Second Coming.

96 For **I, the Almighty, have laid my hands upon the nations, to scourge them for their wickedness.**

97 And **plagues shall go forth, and they shall not be taken from the earth until I have completed my work**, which shall be cut short in righteousness [*perhaps meaning that Christ will come a little sooner than expected (Joseph Smith—Matthew 1:47–48; could also mean that if the last days were not cut short by the Second Coming, none of the righteous would survive—compare with Matthew 24:22*]—

> A major transition takes place between verse 97 and verse 98. The Savior now takes us from the plagues, pestilences, and devastations of the last days into the Millennium. Verse 98 teaches us that the time will come during the Millennium when virtually all people will have joined the Church and will live the gospel.
>
> "Virtually all," for all practical

purposes, means "everyone." The reason we don't say "all people" is that, because of agency, a few will turn to wickedness even during the Millennium as stated by Isaiah in Isaiah 65:20.

Doctrine, verse 98

During the Millennium, the time will come when virtually all people on earth will accept and live the gospel.

98 Until all shall know me, who remain [*who were not destroyed by the Second Coming; see 2 Nephi 12:10, 19, 21, and who live during the Millennium*], even from the least unto the greatest, **and shall be filled with the knowledge of the Lord, and shall see eye to eye** [*will live in peace and harmony one with another*], **and shall** lift up their voice, and with the voice together **sing this new song**, saying:

Verses 99–103 describe conditions that will exist during the Millennium. But before we continue, we will take a moment to consider the phrase "sing this new song" at the end of verse 98, above.

Singing a "new song" can mean rejoicing about something that could not be celebrated before because it had not yet taken place. Symbolically, new converts could "sing a new song," rejoicing that they now belong to the true Church. First-time parents could "sing a new song" that they are now parents. Missionaries could "sing a new song," rejoicing that they are now finally on their mission.

In this case, those who are present at the beginning of the Millennium can "sing a new song" of rejoicing that the Savior is finally here on earth and that millennial conditions of peace and harmony prevail.

On a personal note, some years ago as I entered the freeway on my way to teach my evening Book of Mormon class at the institute, a "new song" came into my mind—beautiful music I had never heard before (or since). It continued playing in my mind for about fifteen minutes. I enjoyed it but had no idea what it meant. That evening, during class, I noticed a new student sitting toward the back of the room in a rather large class. The Spirit was strong, and I taught a number of things I had not specifically prepared.

After class, the young lady came up, introduced herself to me, and said that I had been talking directly to her during the class and had specifically addressed her concerns about joining the Church. She was not a member but was investigating the Church. With her questions answered, she was determined to be baptized and asked me to confirm her, which I did two weeks later at her baptism conducted by the full-time missionaries.

As I traveled home after class, it occurred to me that the reason I'd had the "new song" playing in my mind before class was that the young investigator was soon going to be able to "sing a new song" in her life; namely, a song of rejoicing that she had found the true gospel of Jesus Christ and had become a member.

We will continue now with verses 99–102, which constitute "singing a new song" in celebration of the arrival of the Millennium, and describe some millennial conditions.

We will provide some possible explanatory notes. You could no doubt see additional possibilities and interpretations.

Doctrine, verses 99–102

The Millennium will come as prophesied.

99 The Lord hath brought again Zion [*the Lord's kingdom has finally come again*];

The Lord hath redeemed his people, Israel [*righteous Israel have been set free from Satan and sin, and the thousand years of peace have been ushered in*],

According to the election of grace [*as prophesied because of the divine help of Christ and His Atonement*],

Which was brought to pass by the faith

And covenant of their fathers [*their ancestors*].

100 The Lord hath redeemed his people;

And **Satan is bound** [*not allowed to tempt at all; see D&C 101:28*] **and time is no longer** [*we don't have to wait any longer for the Millennium because it is here*].

The Lord hath gathered all things in one [*all things have been restored*].

The Lord hath brought down Zion [*the kingdom of heaven has come down upon the earth; see D&C 65:6*] **from above.**

The Lord hath brought up Zion [*the kingdom of God on earth; see D&C 65:6*] **from beneath** [*from the earth; in other words, the Church in heaven is now combined with the Church on earth*].

101 The earth hath travailed and brought forth her strength [*symbolically, the earth has gone into labor (as in childbirth) and has finally succeeded in bringing forth a righteous people; compare with 1 Nephi 21:18–21, where Isaiah prophesies that righteous people will cover the earth*];

And **truth is established in her bowels** [*the entire earth is filled with the truths of the gospel*];

And **the heavens have smiled upon her** [*mother earth finally has the satisfaction of resting from the wickedness that has been upon her for so long; compare with Moses 7:48*];

And **she is clothed with the glory of her God** [*mother earth is wrapped with the warmth and glory of the Savior*];

For **he stands in the midst of his people** [*Jesus Christ rules and reigns among His people for a thousand years*].

> The final "verse" of this "new song" (verse 102) is a song of gratitude to God.

102 **Glory, and honor, and power, and might,**

Be ascribed [*given*] **to our God; for he is full of mercy,**

Justice, grace and truth, and peace,

Forever and ever, Amen.

> Verses 103–8, next, give practical instructions on how to share resources, including money given to them as they travel and preach.

103 And again, verily, verily, I say unto you, **it is expedient** [*wise, necessary*] that **every man who goes forth to proclaim mine everlasting gospel, that inasmuch as** [*if*] **they have families, and receive money by gift, that they should send it unto them** [*their families back home*] **or make use of it for their benefit** [*or use it themselves*], **as the Lord shall direct them,** for thus it seemeth me good.

104 And **let all those** [*missionaries*] **who have not families, who receive money** [*who receive donations from people in their mission fields*], **send it up unto the bishop in Zion** [*send it to Bishop Edward Partridge, in Jackson County, Missouri*], **or unto the bishop** [*Bishop Newel K. Whitney*] **in Ohio,** that it may be consecrated **for the bringing forth of the revelations** [*the Book of Commandments—the predecessor to the first Doctrine and Covenants*] **and the printing thereof, and for establishing Zion** [*and for building up the Church in Missouri*].

> Verse 105, next, describes the purpose of our current Deseret Industries and of the Humanitarian Fund.

105 And **if any man shall give unto any of you a coat, or a suit,**

take the old [*your old coat or suit*] and cast [*give*] it unto the poor, and go on your way rejoicing.

> The principle given in verse 106, next, is often seen in missionary companionships as well as in the assigning of ministering companionships.

106 And **if any man among you be strong in the Spirit, let him take with him that is weak, that he may be edified** [*strengthened and taught*] **in all meekness, that he may become strong also.**

> The use of Aaronic Priesthood holders to assist and learn under the direction of Melchizedek Priesthood holders is exemplified in verse 107, next.

107 Therefore, **take with you those who are ordained unto the lesser priesthood** [*Aaronic Priesthood*]**, and send them before you to make appointments, and to prepare the way, and to fill appointments that you yourselves are not able to fill.**

108 Behold, **this is the way that mine Apostles, in ancient days, built up my church unto me.**

> Verses 109–10, next, teach the importance of each member of the Church fulfilling his or her calling, and of all working in peace and harmony with each other. Every member is needed in the Church. You have likely heard this as a theme of a number of gospel sermons over the years.

109 Therefore, **let every man stand in his own office, and labor in his own calling; and let not the head say unto the feet it hath no need of the feet; for without the feet how shall the body be able to stand?**

110 Also **the body** [*the Church, the kingdom of God*] **hath need of every member, that all may be edified** [*strengthened and built up*] **together, that the system may be kept perfect.**

> The last phrase of verse 110, above, is interesting. Perhaps you've noticed that the Lord does a "perfect" work (saving souls) using imperfect people, backed up by the "perfect" gospel in the "perfect system"—in other words, the Church.

> Next, we see specific instructions relating to the duties of various priesthood offices.

111 And behold, the **high priests should travel, and also the elders, and also the lesser priests** [*priests in the Aaronic Priesthood*]; **but the deacons and teachers should be appointed to watch over the church, to be standing ministers unto the church** [*deacons and teachers should stay at*

home and function in the local wards and branches].

> When I was a new bishop, I was told that it was my responsibility not only to wisely assist the poor and needy who approached me for help but also that I was to <u>seek out the poor and assist them</u> if appropriate. That caught me a bit by surprise. Verse 112, next, is the scriptural basis for that advice to me. I followed the counsel.

112 And **the bishop,** Newel K. Whitney, also **should travel round about and among all the churches, searching after the poor to administer to their wants** by humbling the rich and the proud [*the rich are often vulnerable to becoming prideful, and giving to the poor can help keep them humble*].

> Verse 113, next, provides a basis for having some full- and part-time employees to help operate bishops' storehouses, Welfare Square, Deseret Industries, and so forth.

113 **He should also employ an agent** to take charge and to do his secular business as he shall direct.

> While I was serving as a stake president, a member of my stake came to me one day, concerned about whether she should warn her relatives in New York to move elsewhere. She had just read verses 114–15, next, and was sincerely concerned for their safety. I pointed out to her that the word "if" was contained in both verses, and I asked if she had noticed that. She hadn't and was greatly relieved, realizing that there are many in these cities who have accepted the gospel. In fact, we now have temples in these areas!

114 Nevertheless, **let the bishop go unto the city of New York,** also to the city of **Albany,** and also to the city of **Boston, and warn the people of those cities** with the sound of the gospel, with a loud voice, **of the desolation and utter abolishment which await them <u>if</u> they do reject these things.**

115 For <u>if</u> **they do reject these things** the hour of their judgment is nigh, and their house shall be left unto them desolate.

> The "if . . . then" nature of the above prophecy about New York, Albany, and Boston bears looking at a bit closer. As you read the scriptures, you will come across a number of such prophecies. One of them was the preaching of Jonah to the wicked city of Nineveh (Jonah 3). He told the wicked citizens of Nineveh that they would be destroyed in forty days (Jonah 3:4). If you read this chapter of Jonah in your Latter-day Saint Bible and pay close

attention to the JST changes in the footnotes, you will see that the people repented after being warned by Jonah.

This was quite a disappointment to him (see Jonah 4). Apparently, he didn't understand the "if . . . then" principle of prophecy. The Lord explained it to him in Jonah 4:4–11.

Next, the Lord reassures Bishop Newel K. Whitney that He will watch over him as he goes on his mission to the east.

116 Let him trust in me and he shall not be confounded [*he won't be stopped from carrying out this assignment*]; **and a hair of his head shall not fall to the ground unnoticed.**

The Lord brings this revelation to a close by encouraging the missionaries to go forth and preach as He has instructed, pointing out that they are to warn the inhabitants of the earth of the destructions and devastations that will come in the last days. In verse 119, we see that as these signs of the times are fulfilled, they can strengthen our testimonies.

117 And verily I say unto you, the rest of my servants, go ye forth as your circumstances shall permit, in your several callings, unto the great and notable cities and villages, **reproving the world in righteousness** [*standing as righteous witnesses against the wicked world*] **of all their unrighteous and ungodly deeds, setting forth clearly and understandingly the desolation of abomination in the last days.**

The phrase "desolation of abomination," found at the end of verse 117, above, is similar to the phrase "abomination of desolation" found in Joseph Smith—Matthew 1:12, 32. The Bible Dictionary defines this term as it applies to verse 117. We will quote it here:

Bible Dictionary: Abomination of Desolation

"Daniel spoke prophetically of a day when there would be 'the abomination that maketh desolate' (Dan. 11:31; 12:11), and the phrase was recoined in New Testament times to say 'the abomination of desolation, spoken of by Daniel the prophet' (Matt. 24:15).

"Conditions of desolation, born of abomination and wickedness, were to occur twice in fulfillment of Daniel's words. The first was to be when the Roman legions under Titus, in A.D. 70, laid siege to Jerusalem (Matt. 24:15; JS—M 1:12).

"Speaking of the last days, of the days following the Restoration of the gospel and its declaration 'for a witness unto all nations,' our Lord said: 'And again shall the abomination of desolation, spoken of by Daniel the prophet, be fulfilled' (JS—M 1:31–32). That is, Jerusalem again will be under siege.

"In a general sense, abomination of desolation also describes the latter-day judgments to be poured out upon the wicked wherever they may be. And so that the honest in heart may escape these things, the Lord sends His servants forth to raise the warning voice, to declare the glad tidings of the Restoration, lest 'desolation and utter abolishment' come upon them. The elders are commanded to reprove 'the world in righteousness of all their unrighteous and ungodly deeds, setting forth clearly and understandingly the desolation of abomination in the last days' (D&C 84:114, 117; 88:84–85)."

Continuing, we see that everyone in the world will have a chance to recognize and acknowledge the Lord because of the signs of the times that will be shown by nature in the last days.

118 For, with you saith the Lord Almighty, **I will rend their kingdoms; I will not only shake the earth, but the starry heavens shall tremble.**

119 For **I, the Lord, have put forth my hand to exert the powers of heaven;** ye cannot see it now, **yet a little while and ye shall see it, and know that I am, and that I will come and reign with my people.**

120 **I am Alpha and Omega,** the beginning and the end. Amen.

SECTION 85

Background

This is a revelation given through the Prophet Joseph Smith on November 27, 1832, at Kirtland, Ohio.

The heading to section 85 in the 2013 edition of the Doctrine and Covenants, given here, gives helpful additional background compared to the heading in the 1981 edition:

*Revelation given through Joseph Smith the Prophet, at Kirtland, Ohio, November 27, 1832. This section is an extract from a letter of the Prophet to William W. Phelps, who was living in Independence, Missouri. It answers questions about those Saints who had moved to Zion **but who had not followed the commandment to consecrate their properties** and had thus not received their inheritances according to the established order in the Church.*

A quote from the 2018 *Doctrine and Covenants Student Manual* gives valuable background information for this section:

SECTION 85

"By November 1832, more than 800 Latter-day Saints had gathered to the land of Zion in Jackson County, Missouri (see *The Joseph Smith Papers, Documents, Volume 2: July 1831–January 1833*, ed. Matthew C. Godfrey and others [2013], 315). It was expected that Church members who settled in Zion would live according to the system of consecration commanded by the Lord (see D&C 42:30–36; 57:4–7; 58:19, 34–36; 72:15). This meant that a member would consecrate or dedicate property and resources to the Lord through a legal deed that was signed by both the member and the bishop. In return, the member was given, through another legal deed, property and resources called an 'inheritance' or 'stewardship' according to the needs and wants of the member's family. Saints who settled in Jackson County, Missouri, and were obedient to the law of consecration received an inheritance of land that had been purchased by Church agents" (*Doctrine and Covenants Student Manual*, 2018, chapter 32).

Some of the brethren living in Missouri wrote to the Prophet to ask him for counsel regarding the fact that some members who had moved to Jackson County were not living according to the law of consecration. Joseph Smith wrote a letter addressed to William W. Phelps, then living in Independence, Missouri, in which he answered this and other questions. Section 85 is an extract from this letter. The Prophet introduced this letter as follows (**bold** used to point out the problem of not receiving deeds):

"In answer to letters received from the brethren in Missouri, I wrote as follows:

"*Kirtland, Nov. 27th, 1832.*

"Brother William W. Phelps:

"... While I dictate this letter, I fancy to myself that you are saying or thinking something similar to these words:—'My God, great and mighty art Thou, therefore **show unto Thy servant what shall become of those who** are essaying [*attempting*] to **come up unto Zion**, in order to keep the commandments of God, **and yet receive not their inheritance by consecrations, by order of deed from the Bishop**, the man that God has appointed in a legal way, agreeably to the law given to organize and regulate the Church, and all the affairs of the same'" (*History of the Church*, 1:297).

First of all, in verse 1, next, the Prophet confirms that accurate records must be kept of the activities of the Church in Zion, including records of the consecration of property, and the redistribution of property to those living the law of consecration in Missouri. Clerks were appointed to keep such records. As you know, we have ward and stake clerks today, with similar responsibilities to keep accurate records.

1 IT is the duty of the Lord's clerk, whom he has appointed, to keep a history, and a general church record of all things that transpire in Zion, and of all those who consecrate properties, and receive inheritances legally [*according to the laws of the land, including written deeds that gave private ownership of property*] from the bishop [*from Bishop Partridge*];

2 And also their manner of life, their faith, and works; and also of the apostates [*people who leave the Church*] who apostatize after receiving their inheritances [*after having property deeded to them—compare with D&C 51:5*].

> If you go back and read D&C 51:5, you will see that apostates would still own the land that had been deeded to them under the law of consecration.
>
> Next, in verses 3–5, the Lord instructs that members moving to Missouri who were not willing to participate in the law of consecration were not to have their names entered in the records of the faithful in Zion. It appears also that no genealogies were to be kept of these people and their families, through which someone might try to make a legal claim on property owned by the Church.

3 **It is contrary to the will and commandment of God that those who receive not their inheritance by consecration** [*those who refuse to participate in the law of consecration*], **agreeable to his law**, which he has given, that he may tithe his people, to prepare them against the day of vengeance and burning, **should have their names enrolled with the people of God.**

4 **Neither is their genealogy to be kept, or to be had where it may be found on any of the records or history of the church.**

5 **Their names shall not be found, neither the names of the fathers, nor the names of the children written in the book of the law of God** [*the official tithing record of the Church; see October 1899 general conference explanation by Joseph F. Smith*], **saith the Lord of Hosts.**

> In verse 6, next, Joseph Smith explains that he is receiving this revelation from the Holy Ghost. It reminds us that we sometimes feel the help and witness of the Holy Ghost in "every fiber of our being."

6 Yea, thus saith **the still small voice, which whispereth through and pierceth all things, and oftentimes it maketh my bones to quake while it maketh manifest,** saying:

SECTION 85

It helps to have a bit of history in advance before reading verses 7 and 8, next. In verse 8, Bishop Edward Partridge is told that he will be replaced if he doesn't repent and start following the program set up by the Lord, rather than trying to tell the leaders of the Church how to run things. If he doesn't repent, then one "mighty and strong" (verse 7) will be sent to replace him. Bishop Partridge repented, and so no one was needed to replace him.

7 And it shall come to pass that **I, the Lord God, will send one mighty and strong**, holding the scepter of power in his hand, clothed with light for a covering, whose mouth shall utter words, eternal words; while his bowels shall be a fountain of truth, **to set in order the house of God** [*in Missouri*]**, and to arrange by lot the inheritances of the saints** [*to distribute consecrated property fairly, by written deed*] **whose names are found, and the names of their fathers, and of their children, enrolled in the book of the law of God** [*whose names are properly recorded by the clerk (verse 1) in the records of the Church in Missouri, as those who are participating in the law of consecration*];

8 While **that man** [*Bishop Edward Partridge*]**, who was called of God and appointed** [*to be the Presiding Bishop of the Church and to handle the law of consecration in Missouri*]**, that putteth forth his hand to steady the ark of God** [*who is trying to tell the Prophet and other Church leaders how to run the Church—in other words, is telling the Lord how to run things*]**, shall fall by the shaft of death, like as a tree that is smitten by the vivid shaft of lightning.**

We will include a rather lengthy official statement from the First Presidency of the Church (Joseph F. Smith, John R. Winder, and Anthon H. Lund) in 1905 explaining verses 7–8, above. We will add **bold** for emphasis. They wrote:

"It is to be observed first of all that the subject of **this whole letter** [the letter from Joseph Smith to W. W. Phelps, from which section 85 is taken], as also the part of it subsequently accepted as a revelation, **relates to the affairs of the Church in Missouri**, the gathering of the Saints to that land **and obtaining their inheritances under the law of consecration and stewardship**; and **the Prophet deals especially with the matter of what is to become of those who fail to receive their inheritances by order or deed from the bishop**....

"It was while these conditions of rebellion, jealousy, pride, unbelief and hardness of heart prevailed among the brethren in Zion—

Jackson county, Missouri—in all of which Bishop Partridge participated, that the words of the revelation taken from the letter to William W. Phelps, of the 27th of November, 1832, were written. The 'man who was called and appointed of God' to 'divide unto the Saints their inheritance'—**Edward Partridge—was at that time out of order, neglecting his own duty, and putting 'forth his hand to steady the ark'**; hence, he was warned of the judgment of God impending, and the prediction was made that **another, 'one mighty and strong,' would be sent of God to take his place**, to have his bishopric—one having the spirit and power of that high office resting upon him, by which he would have power to 'set in order the house of God, and arrange by lot the inheritance of the Saints'; in other words, one who would do the work that Bishop Edward Partridge had been appointed to do, but had failed to accomplish. . . .

"And inasmuch as **through his repentance and sacrifices and suffering, Bishop Edward Partridge undoubtedly obtained a mitigation of the threatened judgment against him** of falling 'by the shaft of death, like as a tree that is smitten by the vivid shaft of lightning,' so the occasion for sending another to fill his station—'one mighty and strong to set in order the house of God, and to arrange by lot the inheritances of the Saints'—may also be considered as having passed away and the whole incident of the prophecy closed" (Clark, *Messages of the First Presidency,* 4:112, 115, 117).

"This much, then, we have learned, viz., that Edward Partridge, the Bishop of the Church, was the one 'called and appointed, to divide by lot unto the Saints their inheritances.' But was Edward Partridge the one in 1832 who was 'putting forth his hand to steady the ark,' and threatened with falling 'by the shaft of death like as a tree that is smitten by the vivid shaft of lightning'? Undoubtedly. The brethren in those days were limited in their experience. The Church had been organized but as yesterday. The order of the Priesthood was not understood then, as it is understood today. The brethren composing it had been but recently brought together. Some of them were often in rebellion against the Prophet and the order of the Church because of these conditions; and it required instruction and time and experience to enable men to understand their duties and preserve their right relationship to each other as officers of the Church.

"Bishop Partridge was one of the brethren, who—though a most worthy man, one whom the Lord loved, and whom the Prophet described as 'a pattern of piety,' and 'one of the Lord's great men'—at times arrayed himself in opposition to the Prophet in those early days, and sought to correct him in his administrations of the affairs of the Church; in other words, 'put forth his hand to steady the ark'" (Clark, *Messages of the First Presidency,* 4:113).

We will explain the phrase "to steady the ark." We read about this in 2 Samuel 6:6–7. First, though, a bit more background. In Old Testament days, the Ark of the Covenant normally resided in the Tabernacle's Holy of Holies in Israel. It symbolized the earthly dwelling place of God. When it was in the Tabernacle, only the high priest could approach it. No other priests were allowed to.

It was taken from Israel by the Philistines (1 Samuel 4:10–11), but they sent it back to Israel because of troubles encountered while they possessed it (1 Samuel 5–6). King David arranged to have it picked up after the Philistines returned it and to have it carried by authorized priests back to its proper place. It was expressly forbidden for the Ark of the Covenant to be touched by an unauthorized person.

As it was being transported to another location, the cart upon which it was being transported passed over rough ground and the Ark started to tip. Uzzah tried to "steady the ark" and was struck dead (2 Samuel 6:6–7). Obviously, there is much more to the story. But for our purposes here, the point is that this phrase came to mean "one who tries to take things into his own hands" or "one who feels that the proper authorities of the Church are not doing their job correctly, therefore he takes it upon himself to straighten them out or take over their responsibilities."

On a sad note, several apostates from the Church, who have attempted to set up their own churches, have claimed that they were the "one mighty and strong" mentioned in verse 7 of this section sent by the Lord to get the church back on track.

We will now proceed with verse 9, next. You will see the phrase "book of remembrance." In the Topical Guide in our Latter-day Saint Bible, "book of remembrance" is cross-referenced with "book of life," which is mentioned in Revelation 3:5 as the record kept in heaven in which the names of those who receive exaltation are recorded.

9 And **all they who are not found written in the book of remembrance shall find none inheritance in that day** [*perhaps referring to Judgment Day*], **but they shall be cut asunder** [*destroyed*], **and their portion** [*reward*] **shall be appointed them among unbelievers, where are wailing and gnashing** [*grinding in agony*] **of teeth** [*see D&C 19:5; a description of*

those who receive the punishments of God reserved for the wicked].

Next, the Prophet Joseph Smith assures W. W. Phelps (to whom this revelation is being written) that he is not just giving his opinion but rather is giving the word of the Lord concerning the situation in Zion.

10 These things I say not of myself; therefore, as the Lord speaketh, he will also fulfil.

Verse 11, next, reminds us that there is no "privilege" in the Church of Jesus Christ because of position or rank in authority. None who fail to qualify will receive land in Missouri, symbolic of receiving "an inheritance" in celestial glory.

11 And **they** who are of the High Priesthood, **whose names are not found written in the book of the law** [*see verse 5, above*], or that are found to have **apostatized**, or to have been **cut off from the church**, as well as the lesser priesthood, or the members, in that day **shall not find an inheritance among the saints of the Most High**;

12 Therefore, it shall be done unto them as unto the children of the priest, as will be found recorded in the second chapter and sixty-first and second verses of Ezra.

We will include the above-mentioned verses of Ezra here. As you will see, they emphasize the importance of worthily having your name on the official records of the Church. We will add **bold** for emphasis:

Ezra 2:61–62

61 **And of the children of the priests**: the children of Habaiah, the children of Koz, the children of Barzillai; which took a wife of the daughters of Barzillai the Gileadite, and was called after their name:

62 **These sought their register** *among* those that were reckoned by genealogy, **but they were not found: therefore** were they, as polluted, **put from the priesthood**. [*In other words, their names were not on the records of the Church, therefore they could not hold the priesthood or have the blessings thereof.*]

SECTION 86

Background

This revelation was given through the Prophet Joseph Smith on December 6, 1832, in Kirtland, Ohio. It is a direct result of his work on the translation of the Bible (the JST). Verses 1–7 deal with the parable of the wheat and the tares. Verses 8–11 deal with the blessings of the priesthood, particularly the blessings promised in Abraham 2:9–11.

In Matthew 13:24–30, 36–43, Jesus gave the parable of the wheat and the tares. It helps to understand that tares are a weed that in its early and intermediate stages of growth looks like wheat. We read the following about tares in the Bible Dictionary:

Tares

"Matt. 13:25. The word denotes darnel grass, a poisonous weed, which, until it comes into ear, is similar in appearance to wheat."

Before studying this section, you may wish to read the parable of the wheat and the tares in your Bible. As mentioned above, it is found in Matthew 13:24–30, 36–43.

We will now study verses 1–7 verse by verse.

1 VERILY, **thus saith the Lord** unto you my servants, **concerning the parable of the wheat and of the tares:**

2 Behold, verily I say, **the field was the world,** and **the Apostles were the sowers** of the seed [*the Savior's Apostles planted the seeds of the gospel abroad*];

> Verse 2, above, is different than Matthew 13:37, which says that the sower is the "Son of man," meaning Jesus. There is no problem here because Jesus is in charge and His Apostles "sow" under His direction. "Whether by mine own voice or by the voice of my servants, it is the same" (D&C 1:38).

3 And **after they have fallen asleep** [*after the Apostles had died*] **the great persecutor of the church** [*Satan*], **the apostate, the whore** [*Satan; Satan's kingdom (1 Nephi 14:10–11); one who perverts that which is pure and righteous for evil purposes*], even **Babylon** [*the kingdom of the devil; the wicked of the earth*], **that maketh all nations to drink of her cup** [*who spreads evil throughout the world*], **in whose hearts the enemy, even Satan, sitteth to reign**—behold **he soweth the tares** [*plants evil and wickedness throughout the world; often disguises evil ("tares") to make it look good (makes it look like "wheat")*]; wherefore, **the tares choke the wheat** and **drive the church into the wilderness** [*symbolic of the apostasy that took place after the crucifixion and resurrection of Christ and the death of His Apostles*].

> From verse 3, above, to verse 4, next, we see the transition from the apostasy and dark ages after Christ's mortal ministry to the restoration of the gospel through Joseph Smith. Then, in verse 5, we are told that angels are

now anxious to begin the final destruction of the wicked. But in verses 6–7, the Lord requires them to wait until the time is right.

4 But behold, **in the last days, even now** [*in Joseph Smith's day*] while the Lord is beginning to bring forth the word [*in the early beginnings of the Restoration*], and the blade is springing up and is yet tender [*the gospel has been restored and the converts are like tender plants, with much to learn*]—

5 Behold, verily I say unto you, **the angels are crying unto the Lord day and night**, who are ready and waiting **to be sent forth to reap down the fields** [*the angels want to destroy the wicked now*];

> There is much symbolism in verse 6, next, including that all of us have both "wheat" and "tares" growing within us. The Lord is kind not to root out all of our sins, weaknesses, imperfections, and so forth all at once, which would completely overwhelm us (compare with Jacob 5:65–66 in the Book of Mormon). Rather, with patience and kindness, He allows us to grow "line upon line, precept upon precept" (see 2 Nephi 28:30).

6 But the Lord saith unto them, **pluck not up the tares while the blade is yet tender** (for verily your faith is weak [*in other words, the members of the Church have much growing yet to do*]), **lest you destroy the wheat also.**

Another important insight we gain from verse 6, above, is that the Lord, in His mercy, doesn't show us all of our weaknesses at the same time. Rather, He has the Holy Ghost point out some weakness now, and then when we have improved sufficiently on those matters, He points out additional things for us to work on. This approach is briefly mentioned at the end of Revelation 2:24, at the conclusion of encouragement and warnings given to the early Saints in Thyatira.

Revelation 2:24

24 But unto you I say, and unto the rest in Thyatira, as many as have not this doctrine, and which have not known the depths of Satan, as they speak; **I will put upon you none other burden.**

Among the many things we learn from verse 7, next, is that at the time of the Second Coming, the righteous will be taken up first and then the wicked will be burned. This is a different order than given in Matthew 13:30, where the tares are burned and then the wheat is gathered.

In other words, the correct order is that the righteous will be taken up at the time of the Second Coming, and then the wicked will be burned and the earth cleansed in preparation for the Millennium.

7 Therefore, **let the wheat and the tares grow together until the harvest is fully ripe**; then ye shall **first gather out the wheat** from among the tares, and after the gathering of the wheat, behold and lo, **the tares are bound in bundles, and the field remaineth to be burned**.

Perhaps you have noticed that there are "wheat" and "tares" in almost every branch and ward in the Church. This will continue to be the case until the Second Coming, when there will be a complete separation of the righteous from the wicked. In the meantime, through kindness and patience on the part of the members, and with the help of the Holy Ghost, some "tares" will become converted and become "wheat."

The last four verses of this revelation deal with encouragement for these brethren and others, including us, no doubt, to press forward with faith in continuing the restoration of the gospel and the carrying of it to all the world.

President Russell M. Nelson, then of the Quorum of the Twelve Apostles, helps us understand verses 8–10, next, with the following quote (**bold** added for emphasis):

"You are one of God's noble and great spirits, held in reserve to come to earth at this time. (See D&C 86:8–11.) In your premortal life you were appointed to help prepare the world for the great gathering of souls that will precede the Lord's second coming. **You are one of a covenant people. You are an heir to the promise that all the earth will be blessed by the seed of Abraham and that God's covenant with Abraham will be fulfilled through his lineage in these latter days**. (See 1 Ne. 15:18; 3 Ne. 20:25.)" ("Choices," *Ensign*, Nov. 1990, 73).

8 Therefore, **thus saith the Lord unto you, with whom the priesthood hath continued through the lineage of your fathers** [*meaning that the direct line of priesthood authority, which came from your "fathers," meaning Abraham, Isaac, Jacob, and so forth, was interrupted by the apostasy after Christ's death and now continues with you*]—

9 **For ye are lawful heirs** [*you have the right to the priesthood of Abraham, Isaac, and Jacob, as members of the house of Israel; see Abraham 2:9–11*], **according to the flesh** [*here in mortality as descendants of Abraham*], and have been hid from the world with Christ in God—

10 **Therefore your life and the priesthood have remained, and**

must needs remain through you and your lineage until the restoration of all things spoken by the mouths of all the holy prophets since the world began.

11 Therefore, **blessed are ye if ye continue in my goodness** [*they will receive many blessings and much happiness if they continue faithful*], **a light unto the Gentiles** [*they will be a light to all nonmembers in the world*], and **through this priesthood, a savior unto my people Israel** [*through performing valid priesthood ordinances, modern priesthood holders (along with the sisters who do work for the dead) become "saviors," and all people on earth can join the Church and become part of covenant Israel*]. The Lord hath said it. Amen.

SECTION 87

Background

This revelation was given at or near Kirtland, Ohio, on Christmas day, December 25, 1832, through the Prophet Joseph Smith.

If you have ever wanted "proof" to show others that Joseph Smith was indeed a true prophet of God, this section is an excellent choice.

Verse one is a prophecy that the Civil War would start with the rebellion of South Carolina. If you look again at the date it was given, December 25, 1832, and then do a little research, you'll find that the Civil War was begun by South Carolina as Union troops housed in Fort Sumter, South Carolina, were fired upon on April 12, 1861. This specific prophecy was given about twenty-eight years before it was fulfilled! Joseph Smith was a prophet of God!

As we proceed to study this section, you will see that it covers much in addition to the Civil War. It is a prophecy on wars, and it covers the time from the beginning of the Civil War right up to the Second Coming. It foretells the rebellion and rising up of oppressed people everywhere, and the wars and bloodshed that will eventually be poured out upon the entire earth prior to the Millennium.

Please note in verse 1 that as the Lord reveals these things through Joseph Smith, He speaks of "wars" (plural), beginning with the Civil War (1861–1865).

1 VERILY, thus saith the Lord **concerning the wars that will shortly come to pass, beginning at the rebellion of South Carolina**, which will eventually terminate in the death and misery of many souls;

2 And the time will come that **war will be poured out upon all nations, beginning at this place** [*South Carolina*].

Note the incredible specifics given in verse 3, next. We will give one possible interpretation for the last half of the verse.

3 For behold, **the Southern States shall be divided against the Northern States**, and **the Southern States will call on other nations, even the nation of Great Britain**, as it is called [*plus France, Holland, and Belgium; at this point, it appears to begin a transition into World Wars I and II*], **and they** [*probably meaning Great Britain, France, Holland, Belgium, and so on*] **shall also call upon other nations** [*including the United States*], **in order to defend themselves against other nations** [*including Germany*]; and **then war shall be poured out upon all nations** [*likely meaning that after World War II, war will continue to be poured out upon the whole world until the Savior comes*].

Next, this prophecy indicates that "slaves" will rebel against their "masters." To think that this applies only to the slaves during the period of slavery in the Southern states would be far too narrow. There are "slaves" or oppressed people, cultures, and nations throughout the world who are rebelling against the shackles of tyranny and unrighteous dominion.

4 And it shall come to pass, after many days, **slaves shall rise up against their masters**, who shall be marshaled and disciplined for war [*there will be many rebellions and uprisings leading to fighting, civil wars, and so on as people struggle to gain basic civil rights*].

The word "remnants" is used in verse 5, next. "Remnant," as used in the scriptures, always refers to segments or portions of the house of Israel. You can verify this by looking through the references given in the Topical Guide, under "Remnant."

The reason we mention this is that some interpret verse 5 as being a prophecy about the Lamanites on the Western Hemisphere. No doubt it refers to many "remnants" of Israel including the Lamanites, but it is not limited to them. Thus, it appears that verse 5, among other possibilities, can be a prophecy that remnants of Israel throughout the world will become restless and will yearn for basic freedoms, thus "vexing" those in oppressive authority over them as part of their preparation to be gathered to the gospel.

5 And it shall come to pass also that **the remnants** [*of Israel*] **who are left** of the land **will marshal themselves** [*will organize themselves*], and **shall become exceedingly angry, and shall vex the Gentiles** [*their oppressors*] **with a sore vexation** [*will cause much*

trouble for the Gentiles who attempt to suppress them].

Verse 6, next, is a prophetic summary of the wars and turbulence among mankind as well as in nature, which will continue to increase in intensity until the Second Coming. These things will bear witness of the displeasure of God at the wickedness that continues to increase upon the earth. The wise will note this and seek God.

6 And **thus, with the sword** and by **bloodshed** the inhabitants of the earth shall mourn; and with **famine**, and **plague**, and **earthquake**, and the **thunder** of heaven, and the fierce and vivid **lightning** also, **shall the inhabitants of the earth be made to feel the wrath, and indignation, and chastening** [*scolding, punishing*] **hand of an Almighty God, until the consumption decreed** [*until the prophesied devastations*] **hath made a full end of all nations** [*until all man-made governments cease to exist and the Savior's millennial government takes over in conjunction with the Second Coming*];

Many people wonder why the "justice of God" doesn't fall upon the wicked sooner than it generally does. One of the reasons the Lord puts off the destruction of the wicked as long as possible is that He may be able to save more of them. See D&C 64:21, last of the verse. That the wicked who have killed the Saints and stood in the way of the work of the Lord will eventually be caught up with if they don't repent is evidenced by verse 7, next. It gives the basic reason for the fulfilling of the signs of the times given in verse 6, above.

7 **That the cry of the saints, and of the blood of the saints, shall cease to come up into the ears of the Lord** of Sabaoth [*the Savior; "the creator of the first day"; see D&C 95:7*], **from the earth, to be avenged of their enemies** [*to have the law of justice put in force to punish the wicked*].

The word "Sabaoth" (verse 7, above) is defined in the Bible Dictionary in your Latter-day Saint Bible. We will include that definition here:

Sabaoth

"*Hosts*. The Lord of Sabaoth was a title of Jehovah; the hosts were the armies of Israel (1 Sam. 17:45), but also included the angelic armies of heaven (cf. Judg. 5:20; 2 Kgs. 6:17; Rom. 9:29; James 5:4; see also D&C 87:7; 88:2; 95:7; 98:2)."

Next, in verse 8, the Savior tells us what to do to be spiritually safe as the plagues and devastations of the last days sweep the earth.

8 Wherefore, **stand ye in holy**

places, and be not moved, until the day of the Lord come; for behold, it cometh quickly, saith the Lord. Amen.

"Holy places," no doubt include righteous homes, temples, sacrament meetings, other church meetings and classes, seminary and institute classes, the settings in which you study your scriptures and say your private prayers, and so forth.

SECTION 88

Background

Verses 1–126 of this revelation were given through the Prophet Joseph Smith at Kirtland, Ohio, over the course of a two-day conference held on December 27–28, 1832. Verses 127–37 were given on January 3, 1833. Verses 138–141 were added during the publication of the first Doctrine and Covenants in 1835.

We will include a quote from the 2018 *Doctrine and Covenants Student Manual* for background to section 88:

"On December 27, 1832, the Prophet Joseph Smith met with several Church leaders and other members in the 'translating room,' located upstairs in Newel K. Whitney's store in Kirtland, Ohio. He desired further divine instruction about the elders' duties and about how to build up Zion. As this meeting, or conference, began, the Prophet explained that in order for revelation to be received, each person in the assembled group should exercise faith in God and be of one heart and mind. He proceeded to invite each person to take a turn praying aloud to know the Lord's will. The ensuing revelation was then dictated by Joseph Smith until 9:00 p.m. that evening, at which time they stopped for the night. The next morning the group reassembled and prayed, and the remainder of the revelation was received. Later, on January 3, 1833, the Prophet received additional revelation that was later added to the revelation he had received in December (see D&C 88:127–37). Beginning with the 1835 edition of the Doctrine and Covenants, the revelation that was given on January 3, 1833, was added to the one received on December 27–28, 1832, along with four more verses that were added at the end (see D&C 88:138–41).

"For many months before January 1833, Church leaders in Missouri had directed accusations and expressed unkind feelings toward Church leaders in Ohio. On January 11, 1833, Joseph Smith sent a letter to William W. Phelps in Independence, Missouri, and included a copy of the revelation recorded in Doctrine and Covenants 88:1–126 (and perhaps the portion in verses 127–37) and explained: 'I send you the olive leaf which we have plucked from the tree of

Paradise, the Lord's message of peace to us; for though our Brethren in Zion indulge in feelings towards us, which are not according to the requirements of the new covenant, yet we have the satisfaction of knowing that the Lord approves of us and has accepted us, and established His name in Kirtland for the salvation of the nations. . . . Let me say to you, seek to purify yourselves, and also all the inhabitants of Zion, lest the Lord's anger be kindled to fierceness. . . . The Brethren in Kirtland pray for you unceasingly, for knowing the terrors of the Lord, they greatly fear for you' (in *The Joseph Smith Papers, Documents, Volume 2: July 1831–January 1833*, ed. Matthew C. Godfrey and others (2013), 365, 367; capitalization, spelling, and punctuation standardized)."

This revelation is a "high mountain" experience for faithful members of the Church who desire to do right and strive to retain spirituality despite opposing forces all around them. It holds many keys for achieving spiritual peace.

Just a bit more about "high mountain" experiences. Many prophets throughout history have been taken up into a "high mountain" (example: 1 Nephi 11:1) where they have been shown many things from the Lord's perspective. The Holy Ghost and the scriptures can do similar things for us. When we see things as the Lord sees them, it makes it much easier for us to successfully pass the tests and learn the lessons set out for us in our mortal "curriculum."

Joseph Smith had several "high mountain" experiences, including the First Vision, the visits and instructions of Moroni, the vision of the three degrees of glory and perdition (section 76), the appearance of Christ, Moses, Elias, and Elijah in the Kirtland Temple (section 110), and so forth. Yet, between these marvelous manifestations, he had to deal with the details, trials, and decisions of daily living as a husband, father, and friend, in addition to the responsibilities of being the Lord's prophet.

The Saints at this time in history were facing difficult times and were yet to have more intense opposition as enemies within and outside of the Church mounted persecution against them. The doctrines and perspectives given in section 88 served as a "high mountain" experience for them, enabling them to face their trials with intelligence and knowledge of the "big picture" as the Savior sees things, and thus they were empowered to succeed in their mortal missions. Section 88 can do the same thing for us.

As this section takes you up on this "high mountain," you will see that the Savior teaches a great many specific doctrines in the course of this revelation. We will point out a number of them as we go along.

First, in verses 1–2, Jesus tells these men, including the Prophet, that it pleases Him when His followers sincerely desire to know His will concerning them. This certainly applies to us also.

1 VERILY, **thus saith the Lord unto you who have assembled yourselves together to receive his will concerning you:**

2 Behold, **this is pleasing unto your Lord,** and **the angels rejoice over you**; the alms of **your prayers** [*prayers are "offerings" or "alms" to the Lord*] have come up into the ears of the Lord of Sabaoth [*the Savior; see notes for D&C 87:7 in this study guide*], and **are recorded in the book of the names of the sanctified** [*the Book of Life in which the names of the righteous are recorded in heaven; Revelation 3:5*], **even them of the celestial world.**

Next, in verses 3–4, the Savior explains that a major function of the Holy Ghost is to lead us to exaltation in the celestial kingdom.

3 Wherefore, **I now send** upon you **another Comforter,** even upon you my friends, that it may abide in your hearts, even **the Holy Spirit of promise** [*the Holy Ghost; the "Holy Spirit that was promised" by the Savior to his disciples; see Acts 1:5*]; which **other Comforter** is the same that I promised unto my disciples, as is recorded in the testimony of John.

Quoting from the 2018 *Doctrine and Covenants Student Manual* regarding "The Holy Spirit of Promise," referred to in verse 3, above:

"President Joseph Fielding Smith (1876–1972) explained: 'The Holy Spirit of Promise is not the Second Comforter. The Holy Spirit of Promise is the Holy Ghost who places the stamp of approval upon every ordinance that is done righteously; and when covenants are broken he removes the seal' (*Doctrines of Salvation* 1:55).

"While each of those who were present had previously received the gift of the Holy Ghost, they were then being promised that they could receive an assurance of eternal life through a manifestation of the Holy Ghost (see Ephesians 1:13–14; D&C 76:51–54; 132:7). The Holy Spirit of Promise is an assurance from the Holy Ghost that the ordinances and covenants necessary for salvation have been properly entered into and have been kept. In essence, it is a witness from the Spirit that a person has the promise of eternal life."

Doctrine, verse 4

A major function of the gift of the Holy Ghost is that of leading us to celestial exaltation.

4 This Comforter [*the Holy Ghost*] **is the promise which I give unto you of eternal life** [*the help they were promised that, when followed, leads to eternal life, which is another term for exaltation*], **even the glory of the celestial kingdom;**

> Next, in verse 5, we are taught that the celestial kingdom is the highest glory, that exaltation is within that kingdom, and that God the Father lives in celestial glory.

Doctrine, verse 5

God the Father lives in celestial glory.

5 Which glory [*the celestial kingdom—verse 4, above*] **is that of the church of the Firstborn** [*means exaltation; see D&C 76:54, 67*], **even of God, the holiest of all** [*the Father*], **through Jesus Christ his Son** [*the Holy Ghost (verse 4) leads us to celestial glory through Jesus Christ and the Atonement*]—

> Having been taught the role of the Holy Ghost in leading us to celestial glory through Christ, we will now be taught more about the Savior Himself. You have often seen Christ introduced as "Alpha and Omega" (example: D&C 84:120) and have had it explained that Alpha and Omega are the first and last letters of the Greek alphabet. The symbolism is that all things fall under Christ's direction and power.
>
> Verse 6, next, exemplifies this as it describes Christ's overcoming of all things in order to serve as our Redeemer.

6 He that **ascended up on high**, as also **he descended below all things** [*D&C 122:8*], in that **he comprehended all things** [*He encompassed and overcame all things necessary in order to save us*], **that he might be in all and through all things** [*that He might provide an infinite Atonement*], **the light of truth** [*Jesus is the "light of truth"*];

> Perhaps you have wondered what holds all the planets and stars in their orbits such that they don't crash into each other and create total chaos in the universe. Verses 6–13, next, inform us that Jesus is the power that holds all things, both in the macrocosm as well as in the microcosm, in their proper orbits and relationships with each other. He not only created them, but His power also controls them and keeps them orderly.

Doctrine, verses 6–13

The Light of Christ is the power that holds all planets, stars, electrons, atomic particles, and so forth in their proper orbits and relationships with each other, thus preventing chaos in the universe. It controls all matter and energy in the universe.

7 Which truth shineth. This is the light of Christ. As also **he is in the sun** [*His power is evidenced by the performance of the sun*], and **the light of the sun, and the power thereof by which it was made.**

8 As also **he is in the moon,** and **is the light of the moon,** and **the power thereof by which it was made;**

9 As also **the light of the stars,** and **the power thereof by which they were made;**

10 And **the earth** also, and **the power thereof,** even the earth upon which you stand.

11 And **the light which shineth, which giveth you light, is through him who enlighteneth your eyes,** which is **the same light that quickeneth** [*increases, sharpens*] **your understandings;**

12 **Which light proceedeth forth from the presence of God to fill the immensity of space** [*the Light of Christ influences all things in space*]—

13 **The light which is in all things,** which **giveth life to all things,** which is **the law by which all things are governed,** even **the power of God** who sitteth upon his throne, who is in the bosom of eternity, who is in the midst of all things.

Joseph Fielding Smith taught about the Light of Christ. He said that the "Light of Christ is not a personage. It has no body. I do not know what it is as far as substance is concerned; but it fills the immensity of space and emanates from God. It is the light by which the worlds are controlled, by which they are made. It is the light of the sun and all other bodies. It is the light which gives life to vegetation. It quickens the understanding of men, and has these various functions as set forth in these verses.

"It is: 'The light which is in all things, which giveth life to all things, which is the law by which all things are governed, even the power of God who sitteth upon his throne, who is in the bosom of eternity, who is in the midst of all things.'

"This is our explanation in regard to the Spirit of Christ, or Light of Truth, which every man receives and is guided by. Unless a man had the blessings that come from this Spirit, his mind would not be quickened; there would be no vegetation grown; the worlds would not stay in their orbits; because it is through this Spirit of Truth, this Light of Truth, according to this revelation, that all these things are done.

"The Lord has given to 'every man that cometh into the world,' the guidance of the Light of Truth, or Spirit of Jesus Christ, and if a man will hearken to this Spirit he will be led to the truth and will recognize it and will accept it when he hears it" (*Doctrines of Salvation*, 1:52–53).

Having been shown the all-encompassing role of the Light of Christ, which, as you can see, is much more than our "conscience" (although that is a vital role of the Light of Christ), our attention is next turned to the Savior's role as Redeemer.

First, in verses 14–17, we see the Savior's role in providing resurrection for us.

14 Now, verily I say unto you, that **through the redemption which is made for you is brought to pass the resurrection from the dead.**

Doctrine, verse 15

The strict gospel definition of "soul" is the spirit and the body together.

15 And **the spirit and the body are the soul of man.**

Remember also that the spirit itself is composed of two things; namely, intelligence (D&C 93:29), and the spirit body, which is composed of spirit matter (D&C 131:7–8).

16 And **the resurrection from the dead is the redemption of the soul** [*the "soul," composed of the spirit and the physical body, is put back together, so to speak, at the time of resurrection*].

17 And **the redemption of the soul** [*the resurrection*] **is through him** [*Christ*] **that quickeneth all things** [*who gives life to all things as taught in verses 6–13, above*], in whose bosom [*in whose tender heart*] it is decreed that **the poor and the meek of the earth shall inherit it** [*the earth*].

Did you notice the doctrine taught at the end of verse 17, above? We will list it next.

Doctrine, verse 17

Those from this earth who earn celestial glory will live on it when it is glorified and becomes our celestial planet. See also D&C 130:9–11.

Next, beginning with verse 18, we will be taught what must happen to the earth in order for it to become a celestial planet, the celestial kingdom for those of us who attain celestial glory.

18 Therefore, **it must needs be sanctified from all unrighteousness** [*it has to be cleansed from all wickedness*], **that it may be prepared for the celestial glory** [*that it may become the celestial kingdom for us*];

19 For **after it hath filled the measure of its creation** [*after it has finished its work of hosting mankind, through the end of the Millennium and to the end of the "little season" after the Millennium; see D&C 88:111*], **it shall be crowned with glory** [*it will become a celestial planet*], **even with the presence of God the Father;**

> Joseph Smith taught that this earth "will be rolled back into the presence of God, and crowned with celestial glory" (*Teachings of the Prophet Joseph Smith*, 181).

20 **That bodies** [*in order that people who receive celestial bodies at the time of resurrection; see D&C 88:28–29*] **who are of the celestial kingdom may possess it forever and ever** [*so that resurrected mortals who are worthy of celestial glory can live on it forever*]; **for, for this intent was it made and created** [*this is the reason the earth was created in the first place*], **and for this intent are they sanctified** [*made clean, pure, holy, and fit to be in the presence of God through the Atonement*].

Doctrine, verse 21

Those who do not qualify for celestial glory will have to live on other planets, terrestrial and telestial, which will be prepared for them.

21 And **they who are not sanctified through the law** [*those who refuse to be made pure and holy, fit to live in the presence of God through the laws and covenants of the gospel and Atonement of Christ*] which I have given unto you, **even the law of Christ, must inherit another kingdom** [*another planet*], even that of **a terrestrial kingdom, or that of a telestial kingdom.**

> Joseph Fielding Smith taught that "other earths, no doubt, are being prepared as habitations for terrestrial and telestial beings, for there must be places prepared for those who fail to obtain celestial glory, who receive immortality but not eternal life" (*Doctrines of Salvation*, 1:72).

Doctrine, verse 22

Those who have not qualified for celestial glory would be miserable if placed in the celestial kingdom.

22 For **he who is not able to abide** [*not able to live*] **the law of a celestial kingdom cannot abide** [*can't stand; would not be comfortable in*] **a celestial glory.**

Doctrine, verse 23

Those who have lived beneath the standards of terrestrial glory would be miserable if placed in the terrestrial kingdom.

23 And **he who cannot abide** [*live*] **the law of a terrestrial kingdom cannot abide a terrestrial glory.**

Doctrine, verse 24

Sons of perdition could not stand to live in a kingdom of glory.

24 **And he who cannot abide the law of a telestial kingdom cannot abide a telestial glory; therefore he is not meet** [*suited*] **for a kingdom of glory. Therefore** [*for this reason*] **he must abide a kingdom which is not a kingdom of glory** [*in other words, must live in outer darkness with Satan and the other sons of perdition*].

Next, we are taught that the earth is living the laws that will lead her to celestial glory. You may wish to read Moses 7:48–49, 58, and 61 to get the feel for the earth's desire to be a celestial planet. This brings up many interesting questions that will yet have to be answered, perhaps at the beginning of the Millennium, when "all things" shall be revealed (D&C 101:32–34).

25 And again, verily I say unto you, **the earth abideth** [*obeys*] **the law of a celestial kingdom**, for **it filleth the measure of its creation** [*it is fulfilling the purposes for which it was created*], and **transgresseth not the law—**

Doctrine, verse 26

The earth will die and will be resurrected to celestial glory.

26 **Wherefore** [*this is why*], **it shall be sanctified** [*it will be cleansed from the wickedness upon it, and be made pure and holy, a fit dwelling place for Christ and those from this earth who qualify for celestial glory; see D&C 130:9*]; yea, notwithstanding **it** [*the earth*] **shall die**, **it shall be quickened again** [*it will be resurrected*], **and shall abide the power by which it is quickened** [*it will be celestialized*], and **the righteous shall inherit it.**

The topic now turns to the righteous who will inherit the earth (end of verse 26, above).

27 For **notwithstanding** [*even though*] **they** [*all mortals*] **die**,

they also [*just like the earth does*] **shall rise again, a spiritual body** [*a resurrected body, consisting of intelligence, spirit, and physical body, permanently combined for eternity*].

Next, we are taught that there will be differences in resurrected bodies depending on whether they are celestial, terrestrial, telestial, or sons of perdition.

Doctrine, verses 28–32

There will be significant differences between the resurrected bodies of celestials, terrestrials, telestials, and sons of perdition.

28 They who are of a celestial spirit [*those who have lived worthy of celestial glory*] **shall receive the same body** [*the same type of body that they had on earth, with all the capabilities, including the powers of procreation*] which was **a natural body; even ye shall receive your bodies,** and **your glory shall be that glory by which your bodies are quickened** [*the type of resurrected body you receive will depend on which degree of glory you receive, or outer darkness*].

Some people have expressed a bit of concern that they really don't want to get their body ("your bodies"—verse 28, above) back in the resurrection because they had hoped for a better one. Alma 40:23 assures us that our bodies will be perfect in the resurrection, that everything will be "perfect and proper." It is thus obvious that we will be delighted with what we get if we attain celestial resurrection.

Verse 29, next, continues the description of celestial, resurrected bodies.

29 Ye who are quickened [*resurrected*] **by a portion of the celestial glory** [*according to the laws of celestial glory*] **shall then receive of the same** [*will receive a celestial body*], **even a fulness** [*the kind of celestial, resurrected bodies that our Heavenly Parents have*].

Next, in verses 30–32, we are taught that terrestrials, telestials, and sons of perdition will receive resurrected bodies that will match their final destination on Judgment Day.

30 And they who are quickened [*resurrected*] **by a portion of** [*according to the laws of*] **the terrestrial glory shall then receive of the same, even a fulness** [*their resurrected bodies will have a "fullness" of terrestrial glory*].

31 And also they who are quickened [*resurrected*] **by a portion of** [*according to the laws of*] **the telestial glory** shall then **receive of the same, even a fulness** [*their* resurrected bodies will reflect the completeness of telestial glory].

32 And **they who remain** [*mortals who become sons of perdition*] **shall also be quickened** [*will also be resurrected*]; nevertheless, **they shall return again to their own place** [*will be cast out with Satan and his evil spirits; see D&C 88:114*], to enjoy that which they are willing to receive, **because they were not willing to enjoy that which they might have received.**

Joseph Fielding Smith taught about the differences between resurrected bodies depending on which kingdom of glory people attain. He said:

"In the resurrection there will be different kinds of bodies; they will not all be alike. The body a man receives will determine his place hereafter. There will be celestial bodies, terrestrial bodies, and telestial bodies, and these bodies will differ as distinctly as do bodies here . . .

"Elder Orson Pratt many years ago in writing of the resurrection and the kind of bodies which would be raised in these kingdoms said: 'In every species of animals and plants, there are many resemblances in the general outlines and many specific differences characterizing the individuals of each species. So in the resurrection. There will be several classes of resurrected bodies; some celestial, some terrestrial, some telestial, and some sons of perdition. Each of these classes will differ from the others by prominent and marked distinctions . . .

"Some will gain celestial bodies with all the powers of exaltation and eternal increase. These bodies will shine like the sun as our Savior's does, as described by John. Those who enter the terrestrial kingdom will have terrestrial bodies, and they will not shine like the sun, but they will be more glorious than the bodies of those who receive the telestial glory.

"In both of these kingdoms there will be changes in the bodies and limitations. They will not have the power of increase, neither the power or nature to live as husbands and wives, for this will be denied them and they cannot increase.

"Some of the functions in the celestial body will not appear in the terrestrial body, neither in the telestial body, and the power of procreation will be removed" (*Doctrines of Salvation,* 2:286–88).

Verse 33, next, continues with the thought at the end of verse 32, above, in which we were taught that sons of perdition "were not willing to enjoy that which they might have received."

33 For **what doth it profit a man if a gift is bestowed upon him, and he receive not the gift?**

Behold, **he rejoices not in that which is given unto him, neither rejoices in him who is the giver of the gift.**

> Verses 34–35, next, explain why those who refuse to live according to the laws of celestial glory cannot be cleansed by the Atonement of Christ. They serve as a brief course in the importance of having and understanding eternal law.

34 And again, verily I say unto you, **that which is governed by law is also preserved by law and perfected and sanctified** [*cleansed and made fit to dwell in the presence of God*] **by the same.**

35 **That which breaketh a law, and abideth not by** [*does not live according to*] **law, but seeketh to become a law unto itself** [*determines to make his or her own rules contrary to the laws of God*]**, and willeth** [*desires*] **to abide in sin, and altogether abideth in sin, cannot be sanctified by law, neither by mercy, justice, nor judgment. Therefore, they must remain filthy still.**

> Perhaps you have wished at times that the Lord would explain more about how He creates things and organizes the universe. In verses 36 through 45, next, He does. He will, in effect, invite us into His "classroom" as He teaches us some laws and principles of creation.
>
> Unless you are different from most, you probably will not quite understand it all. Therefore, He will pause at the end of verse 45, and in verse 46, He will ask us what He could compare these things to, which might make it easier for us to understand.
>
> He begins with the basics.

36 **All kingdoms have a law given;**

37 **And there are many kingdoms; for there is no space in the which there is no kingdom** [*scientists are discovering more about this, that there is no such thing as "empty space"; rather, there are cosmic particles and forms of energy in what was once thought of as empty space*]**; and there is no kingdom in which there is no space, either a greater or a lesser kingdom.**

38 And **unto every kingdom** [*perhaps meaning that in every "domain," whether macroscopic or microscopic, whether referring to a planet, moon, solar system, galaxy atom, cell, or whatever*] **is given a law** [*all things are governed by the laws of God*]**; and unto every law there are certain bounds also and conditions** [*there are rules*

that govern the application of all laws]*.

39 All beings who abide not in those conditions [*who don't keep the laws and commandments of God*] **are not justified** [*ratified and approved to return to God's presence and live there forever in celestial glory*].

One thing that can help us understand the word "justified" as found in verse 39, above, is the use of the term as it relates to computers and word processing. "Justify," in document terminology, means to have the word processing software line up one or both margins of a document in a perfectly straight, vertical line.

In gospel terminology, "justify" can mean to be "lined up in perfect harmony with God." The Holy Ghost assists us in this endeavor, prompting us to do the things necessary to access the Atonement's cleansing and healing power so that we are ultimately "justified" or living in harmony with the laws of God and can thus enter His presence for eternity.

Next, in verse 40, we are taught more about celestial qualities and attributes. We are shown why celestials like to associate with celestials. In a sense also, it shows us why wicked people could not be happy in celestial glory.

We are shown that if we are honest, we love honesty. If we are virtuous, we love virtue. If we are merciful, we love to associate with those who are merciful. If we use clean language, we prefer to associate with those who use clean language themselves. If we love the light of the gospel, we choose friends who likewise respect and love the gospel.

The qualities listed are qualities that thrive in celestial glory and typify the attributes of God. Remember that those whose lifestyles and thinking reflect the opposites of these celestial traits could not be happy eternally with God. This is basic eternal law.

40 For **intelligence cleaveth unto intelligence; wisdom receiveth wisdom; truth embraceth truth; virtue loveth virtue; light cleaveth unto light; mercy hath compassion on mercy and claimeth her own; justice continueth its course and claimeth its own** [*the law of justice will rule over those who fail to qualify for the law of mercy; see Alma 42*]; **judgment goeth before the face of him** [*God*] **who sitteth upon the throne and governeth and executeth all things.**

41 He [*God*] **comprehendeth** [*encompasses*] **all things** [*the theme of verses 6–13, 36–45*], **and all**

things are before him, and **all things are round about him**; and **he is above all things, and in all things, and is through all things, and is round about all things; and all things are by him, and of him, even God**, forever and ever.

42 And again, verily I say unto you, **he hath given a law unto all things, by which they move in their times and their seasons**;

43 And **their courses** [*orbits*] **are fixed**, even **the courses of the heavens and the earth**, which comprehend the earth **and all the planets**.

44 And **they give light to each other in their times and in their seasons, in their minutes, in their hours, in their days, in their weeks, in their months, in their years—all these are one year with God, but not with man** [*God has a different time system than man does*].

> Verse 45, next, summarizes the fact that the creations of God influence every aspect of our lives and bear witness of the existence of God to all who will pay attention (see verse 47; also see Moses 6:63).

45 **The earth rolls upon her wings**, and **the sun giveth his light by day**, and **the moon giveth her light by night**, and **the stars also give their light, as they roll upon their wings in their glory, in the midst of the power of God.**

> As mentioned previously, the Savior now pauses to ask these brethren what He could compare these things to in order for them to better understand.

46 **Unto what shall I liken these kingdoms, that ye may understand?**

> The answer to the question posed by the Master, in verse 46, above, is given by Him in verse 47, next, and also in the parable given in verses 51–61.

47 Behold, all these are kingdoms [*all God's creations are "kingdoms" with their "bounds . . . and conditions" (verse 38), as set by God*], and **any man who hath seen any or the least of these** [*of God's creations*] **hath seen God moving in his majesty and power.** [*In other words, if we have seen His creations, we have, in effect, seen Him, implying that until we become more like Him, this will give us at least a start as far as comprehending how He does things is concerned.*]

48 **I say unto you, he hath seen him**; nevertheless, he [*Christ*] who came unto his own [*came to earth*] was not comprehended.

In verses 49–50, next, He encourages us by informing us that (if we are faithful) the day will come that we will be able to actually comprehend Him!

Doctrine, verses 49–50

Through personal faithfulness and worthiness, we can look forward to the day when we will actually comprehend God.

49 The light shineth in darkness [*in spiritual darkness on earth*], and the darkness comprehendeth it not; nevertheless, **the day shall come when you shall comprehend even God**, being quickened in him and by him.

50 **Then shall ye know that ye have seen me, that I am, and that I am the true light that is in you, and that you are in me; otherwise ye could not abound.**

The Master now gives a parable, in answer to the question He asked in verse 46, above, comprising verses 51–61. In this parable, He teaches that He will visit each of the many worlds He has created, and the worthy inhabitants of each will have the privilege of seeing Him. This does not mean that He will be born, live, be crucified, and then be resurrected on each of these other worlds. Rather, it means that He will visit them from time to time. This parable ties in nicely with D&C 76:24, which informs us that the inhabitants of all of the Father's worlds are saved by the Atonement performed by the Savior on our world.

This parable has twelve worlds (verse 55), but they are symbolic of all the worlds Christ has and will create (see verse 61). It is interesting to note that in biblical symbolism, the number twelve represents God's perfect work.

51 **Behold, I will liken these kingdoms** [*the worlds He has created for the Father*] **unto a man** [*God*] **having a field** [*a world*], **and he sent forth his servants** [*His prophets and faithful members*] **into the field to dig in the field** [*to cultivate the gospel in that world*].

52 And **he** [*Christ*] **said unto the first** [*the servants on the first world*]: Go ye and labor in the field, and **in the first hour I will come unto you, and ye shall behold the joy of my countenance** [*in other words, Christ will visit them*].

53 **And he said unto the second** [*the prophets and faithful members on the second world*]: Go ye also into the field, and **in the second hour I will visit you with the joy of my countenance.**

54 And **also unto the third, saying: I will visit you;**

55 And **unto the fourth, and so on unto the twelfth** [*not a set number, twelve, but, among other things, symbolic of the perfect gospel of Jesus Christ upon all the Father's worlds*].

56 And **the lord of the field** [*Christ*] **went unto the first** [*man (verse 52), world, prophets, faithful members there*] **in the first hour, and tarried with him all that hour** [*perhaps implying that the Savior will visit them for their Millennium*], and he was made glad with the light of the countenance of his lord.

57 And **then he withdrew from the first that he might visit the second also, and the third, and the fourth, and so on unto the twelfth.**

58 **And thus they all received the light of the countenance of their lord, every man in his hour, and in his time, and in his season—**

59 **Beginning at the first, and so on unto the last**, and from the last unto the first, and from the first unto the last [*none will be left out*];

60 **Every man in his own order, until his hour was finished**, even according as his lord had commanded him, **that his lord might be glorified in him, and he in his lord, that they all might be glorified.**

61 Therefore, **unto this parable I will liken** [*compare*] **all these kingdoms** [*all the Father's worlds*], **and the inhabitants thereof** [*and all the inhabitants of these worlds; compare with D&C 76:24*]—**every kingdom in its hour, and in its time, and in its season** [*every one will get its turn as determined by God*], even according to the decree which God hath made.

At this point, the Savior does what He did with the Nephites in 3 Nephi 17:2–3, wherein He told the Nephites to go home and ponder overnight the things He had just told them. Here, likewise, He is, in effect, saying that it was obviously difficult for these brethren to comprehend what He had been teaching them, therefore, He invites them to think these things over and ponder them in their hearts. Perhaps you find yourself in the same situation, needing to think more about these wonderful insights that you can't comprehend completely. Don't miss the commandment that He gives at the end of verse 62, next, and the counsel in verses 63–64, to continue to pray and learn and grow toward the ability to comprehend these things.

62 And again, verily I say unto you, **my friends, I leave these sayings with you to ponder in your hearts, with this commandment which I give unto

you, that ye shall call upon me while I am near—

63 Draw near unto me and I will draw near unto you; seek me diligently and ye shall find me; ask, and ye shall receive; knock, and it shall be opened unto you.

64 Whatsoever ye ask the Father in my name it shall be given unto you, that is expedient for you [*that will be necessary and good for you at this point in your growth and progression*];

65 And **if ye ask anything that is not expedient** [*good, wise, necessary*] **for you, it shall turn unto your condemnation** [*it will stop your progress*].

Just another comment about verse 65, above, before we move on. Perhaps you have met someone who has become caught up in the "mysteries" of the gospel and has forgotten to nourish the basics of faith and simplicity in living it. It is not uncommon for such people to eventually end up in apostasy. Perhaps this is a basic meaning of the wording in verse 65 in which the Savior warns not to "ask anything that is not expedient."

Next, in verses 66–68, after warning us not to get caught up in asking for things we ought not to, verse 65, above (the Holy Ghost will help you know what to pray for; see D&C 46:30; 50:30), the Lord instructs us how to prepare spiritually to understand and comprehend these things of God to a greater and greater extent.

We are taught that, while we are generally not allowed to see the Savior directly, at this point, we are nevertheless allowed to hear His "voice" through the Spirit and can thus learn and understand His teachings and thrive in our gospel growth.

66 Behold, **that which you hear is as the voice of one crying in the wilderness** [*perhaps meaning, among other things, a voice teaching truth in an apostate world*]—in the wilderness, because **you cannot see him**—my voice, because **my voice is Spirit; my Spirit is truth; truth abideth** [*lasts*] and hath no end [*there are absolute truths in the gospel that are not subject to the whims and fancies of men or to the limits of time*]; and if it [*perhaps meaning the Spirit*] be in you it [*truth*] shall abound [*flourish in you as you grow toward exaltation*].

The eye tends to focus the attention and resources of the mind and body. Therefore, the symbolism of the "eye" in verse 67, next, can mean that if you focus your spiritual "eye" on the things of God, you will continue to grow in spiritual knowledge and understanding until you become a god

SECTION 88

(compare with D&C 132:20).

67 And **if your eye be single to my glory** [*if you focus on the things of God*], **your whole bodies shall be filled with light** [*light and truth of the gospel*], and **there shall be no darkness in you; and that body which is filled with light comprehendeth all things** [*has become like God*].

68 **Therefore, sanctify** [*cleanse and purify*] **yourselves that your minds become single to God** [*so that the things of God are top priority in your lives*], **and the days will come that you shall see him; for he will unveil his face unto you**, and it shall be **in his own time, and in his own way, and according to his own will.**

> The final three phrases of verse 68, above, deal with the privilege of literally seeing the Savior or the Father. That "he will unveil his face unto you." Did you notice that it does not necessarily happen when a person wants it but rather when it is wise and appropriate in the eyes of God? This appearance is sometimes referred to as the "other comforter."
>
> Joseph Smith taught (**bold** added for emphasis):
>
> "There are **two Comforters** spoken of. **One is the Holy Ghost**, the same as given on the day of Pentecost, and that all Saints receive after faith, repentance, and baptism. This first Comforter [is the] Holy Ghost. . . . **The other Comforter** spoken of is a subject of great interest and perhaps understood by few of this generation. After a person hath faith in Christ, repents of his sins, and is baptized for the remission of his sins, and receives the Holy Ghost, (by the laying on of hands), which is the first Comforter, then let him continue to humble himself before God, hungering and thirsting after righteousness, and living by every word of God, and the Lord will soon say unto him, Son, thou shalt be exalted. . . . When the Lord has thoroughly proved him, and finds that the man is determined to serve Him at all hazard, then the man will find his calling and election made sure, then it will be his privilege to receive the other Comforter. . . . Now what is this other Comforter? It **is no more or less than the Lord Jesus Christ Himself**; and this is the sum and substance of the whole matter, that **when any man obtains this last Comforter, he will have the personage of Jesus Christ to attend him or appear unto him from time to time, and even He will manifest the Father unto him**, and They will take up their abode with him, and the visions of the heavens will be opened unto him and the Lord will teach him face to face, and he may have a perfect knowledge of the mysteries of the kingdom of God" (in *Manuscript History of*

the Church, vol. C-1, pages 8–9 [addenda], josephsmithpapers.org; spelling, punctuation, and capitalization standardized).

69 Remember the great and last promise which I have made unto you [*perhaps referring to the promise made in verse 68, above, that they would eventually be privileged to see God*]; **cast away your idle thoughts** [*perhaps referring to inappropriate thoughts that tend to slip into an idle mind*] **and your excess of laughter** far from you.

"Excess of laughter" generally means not taking important things seriously. This could easily be the meaning in verse 69, above. Certainly, we see pleasant examples of delightful humor and deep laughter on occasions in the talks and comments of our Prophet and other General Authorities today as well as in times past.

There seems to be a transition now from the Savior's "classroom" to practical instructions for these brethren in conducting the business of the Church in the Kirtland area. Remember, as background for these next verses, that these men have been doing much traveling on the Lord's errand. Next, He asks them to stay in Kirtland for a season.

70 Tarry ye [*stay*], tarry ye **in this place** [*Kirtland*], and **call a solemn assembly** [*hold a conference*], even **of** those who are **the first laborers** [*of the first workers who are laying the foundation of the Church; see D&C 58:7*] **in this last kingdom** [*the dispensation of the fullness of times; the gospel has been restored for the last time, and the Church will continue until the Second Coming when the Savior will take over as "King of Kings and Lord of Lords." See Revelation 19:16*].

71 And **let those whom they have warned in their traveling** [*while on their missions and other travels*] call on the Lord, and **ponder the warning in their hearts which they have received**, for a little season.

Looking at the last half of verse 71, above, we see something that often happens to people after the missionaries have talked with them. They "feel" something in their hearts. The Holy Ghost is testifying to them. There is something different about the missionaries or the member who chatted with them about the gospel. We see at the end of verse 71 that this feeling often lasts for "a little season," but if they do not act upon it, it often dissipates and disappears.

In verses 118–41 of this section, the Lord will give instructions for establishing the School of the Prophets (verse 127), as it was called. It will begin on January 23, 1833, at Kirtland, Ohio. A number of the brethren came to Kirtland to attend the school. They were taught many things that would be helpful in carrying out their duties with their congregations, missionary work, and such, including the gospel, languages, history, and politics.

It appears that verse 72, next, may address their concerns about leaving their families and branches of the Church to attend this schooling, as well as the solemn assembly spoken of in verse 70, above. The Lord will provide people to watch over their "flocks" while they are gone.

72 Behold, and lo, **I will take care of your flocks, and will raise up elders and send unto them.**

73 **Behold, I will hasten my work in its time** [*the Lord will speed the growth of the Church along as appropriate, and this solemn assembly and other schooling is part of that process*].

As you no doubt have noticed, as stated in verse 73, the Lord is indeed "hastening" His work "in its time." It is happening all around us and at every turn!

As you will see, verses 74–80, next, provide more instruction about gathering together and teaching one another.

74 And **I give unto you, who are the first laborers in this last kingdom** [*the dispensation of the fulness of times*] **a commandment** that you **assemble yourselves together,** and **organize yourselves,** and **prepare yourselves,** and **sanctify yourselves;** yea, **purify your hearts,** and **cleanse your hands and your feet before me, that I may make you clean;**

75 **That I may testify unto your Father, and your God, and my God, that you are clean from the blood of this wicked generation;** that I may fulfil this promise, this great and last promise [*possibly referring to the promise in verse 68 that the day would come when they would be privileged to see God*], which I have made unto you, **when I will** [*when the time and circumstances are right, according to God's will*].

76 **Also, I give unto you a commandment that ye shall continue in prayer and fasting** from this time forth.

Verses 77–80, next, could be considered to be the "curriculum" guide for the schooling that these brethren are to organize.

77 And I give unto you a commandment that you shall **teach one another the doctrine of the kingdom.**

78 **Teach ye diligently and my

grace shall attend you, that you may be instructed more perfectly **in theory**, in **principle**, in **doctrine**, in the **law of the gospel**, in **all things that pertain unto the kingdom of God**, that are expedient [*necessary*] for you to understand;

79 **Of things both in heaven and in the earth**, and **under the earth**; things **which have been**, things **which are**, things **which must shortly come to pass**; things **which are at home**, things which are **abroad**; the **wars** and the **perplexities of the nations**, and the **judgments which are on the land**; and a **knowledge also of countries and of kingdoms**—

The importance of this education and schooling is pointed out in verse 80, next.

80 **That ye may be prepared in all things** when I shall send you again to magnify the calling whereunto I have called you, and the mission with which I have commissioned you.

The last half of verse 81, next, is often quoted in gospel discussions and sermons. It is a basic missionary scripture applied to "every member a missionary." "Warned" in this case could also be interpreted to mean "taught."

81 Behold, I sent you out to testify and warn the people, and **it becometh every man who hath been warned to warn his neighbor.**

Verse 82, next, emphasizes the principle of accountability.

82 **Therefore** [*after they have been taught and warned*], **they are left without excuse, and their sins are upon their own heads.**

Verse 83, next, teaches that the Savior is anxious to save souls and is readily available to help and bless us. It also reminds us of the importance of not waiting until it is too late to become involved in the gospel.

83 **He that seeketh me early shall find me, and shall not be forsaken** [*left without help*].

84 **Therefore, tarry ye** [*stay in Kirtland and study and prepare, as instructed in verses 77–80*], and **labor diligently, that you may be perfected in your ministry to go forth among the Gentiles for the last time** [*another reminder that this is the last dispensation before the Second Coming of Christ*], as many as the mouth of the Lord shall name [*the Lord will name those who are to participate in the School of the Prophets*], **to bind up the law and seal up the testimony** [*to preach the gospel and bear*

witness of God; compare with Isaiah 8:16–17], **and to prepare the saints for the hour of judgment which is to come** [*the punishments of God which are soon to come upon the world*];

85 **That their souls may escape the wrath of God, the desolation of abomination** [*the destruction of gross evil and punishment of God*] which awaits the wicked, **both in this world and in the world to come.** Verily, I say unto you, let those who are not the first elders [*the leading elders in the Church*] continue in the vineyard [*not come in to attend the School of the Prophets*] until the mouth of the Lord shall call them, **for their time is not yet come; their garments are not clean from the blood of this generation** [*they have not yet finished warning and preaching to the people to whom they were sent.*]

> For more regarding the "desolation of abomination" mentioned in verse 85, above, see the notes for section 84, verse 117 in this study guide.
>
> Once a person has been cleansed from sin and "set free" from past follies and evil through the Atonement of Christ, it is extremely important that he or she does not revert back to a life of sin as pointed out in verse 86, next.

86 **Abide ye in the liberty wherewith ye are made free; entangle not yourselves in sin, but let your hands be clean, until the Lord comes.**

> Beginning with verse 87 and continuing through verse 116, we will be given much prophecy and detail about the final events leading up to the Second Coming; the taking up of the righteous to meet the coming Lord; the first, second, third, and fourth resurrections; the Millennium; the final battle after the Millennium; and the end of the War in Heaven as Satan and his evil followers are cast out completely.
>
> These are "high mountain doctrines" that allow us to see things from the Lord's perspective. As mentioned in the notes at the beginning of this section, such perspectives provide strength, encouragement, and purpose as we press forward in our daily lives, sometimes battling discouragement and opposition to personal righteousness.
>
> We begin with a summary of some signs of the times that will be fulfilled shortly before the Savior comes. Verse 87 seems to be a summary, and then, beginning with verse 88, we see a sequence.

87 For **not many days hence** and [*it won't be long before*] **the earth shall tremble and reel to and fro as a drunken man; and the sun shall**

hide his face, and** shall **refuse to give light;** and **the moon shall be bathed in blood;** and **the stars shall become exceedingly angry,** and **shall cast themselves down as a fig that falleth from off a fig-tree.**

> One of the first stages of the wind-up scenes before the Second Coming is the preaching of the gospel by missionaries. They will be sent to all the world. This is the gentle approach.
>
> Then, as people become more and more wicked and violent, rejecting the gentle message and invitation of the missionaries, the Lord will "turn up the volume" so to speak and have nature "speak up" in order to get people's attention and save more souls.

88 And **after your testimony cometh wrath and indignation upon the people.**

89 **For after your testimony cometh the testimony of earthquakes,** that shall cause **groanings** in the midst of her [*probably meaning the earth*], and **men shall fall upon the ground and shall not be able to stand.** [*This will, of course, be terrifying, and will cause some to turn to God or back to God.*]

90 And **also cometh the testimony of** the voice of **thunderings,** and the voice of **lightnings,** and the voice of **tempests,** and the voice of **the waves of the sea heaving themselves beyond their bounds.**

91 And **all things** [*including nature, politics, breakdown of the family, uprisings, war, and personal wickedness*] **shall be in commotion;** and surely, **men's hearts shall fail them** [*people will give up hope; there will be much depression and despair*]; **for fear shall come upon all people.**

> As we read verse 92, next, we see that the inhabitants of the earth will be unmistakably alerted that the Second Coming and destruction of the wicked are here when that time arrives.

92 And **angels shall fly through the midst of heaven, crying with a loud voice, sounding the trump of God, saying: Prepare ye, prepare ye, O inhabitants of the earth; for the judgment** [*the prophesied punishments*] **of our God is come.** Behold, and lo, **the Bridegroom** [*the Savior*] **cometh; go ye out to meet him** [*a reference to the Parable of the Ten Virgins, given in Matthew 25:1–13, especially verse 6*].

> We will include a quote here from the 2018 *Doctrine and Covenants Student Manual* regarding the "angels . . . sounding the trump

SECTION 88

of God" mentioned in verse 92, above:

"Seven trumpets, each sounded by a different angel, will signal key events surrounding the Second Coming of Jesus Christ. Among these events are the fall of "the mother of abominations" (see D&C 88:94, 105), the orderly resurrection of the dead (see D&C 88:95–102), the announcement that "the hour of [God's] judgment is come" (see D&C 88:103–4), and the proclamation that God's work is finished (see D&C 88:106). The seven angels will sound their trumpets a second time, and each will announce a review of 1,000 years of the earth's history, from the Fall of Adam to the Millennium (see D&C 88:108–10).

We do not know what the "great sign in heaven" will be, as spoken of in verse 93, next. But we do know that everyone will see it at the same time.

93 And **immediately there shall appear a great sign in heaven,** and **all people shall see it together** [*everyone will see it at the same time*].

The Prophet Joseph Smith spoke of the "sign in heaven," referred to in verse 93, above. He said:

"Then will appear one grand sign of the Son of Man in heaven. But what will the world do? They will say it is a planet, a comet, etc. But the Son of man will come as the sign of the coming of the Son of Man, which will be as the light of the morning cometh out of the east" (*Teachings of the Prophet Joseph Smith,* 286; *Teachings of Presidents of the Church: Joseph Smith,* 252–53).

Next, in verse 94, the complete destruction of the wicked is foretold. As you can see, there is much use of scriptural symbolism in this verse. There are many different terms and phrases that mean Satan, his kingdom, his temptations, and so on. The sounding of the "trump" is a reminder that all will hear and no one will miss this.

94 And **another angel shall sound his trump,** saying: **That great church** [*the church of the devil; see 1 Nephi 14:10; the kingdom of the devil; 1 Nephi 22:22*]**, the mother of abominations** [*Satan and his evil kingdom*]**, that made all nations drink of the wine of the wrath of her fornication** [*which provided temptation toward sin, wickedness, and sexual sin for all in the world to partake of*]**, that persecuteth the saints of God,** that **shed their blood—she** [*Satan's kingdom, the "whore of all the earth"; 1 Nephi 14:10*] **who sitteth upon many waters, and upon the islands of the sea** [*1 Nephi 14:11*]**—behold, she is the tares of the earth** [*the deceiving false doctrines, philosophies, counterfeits of*

God's work, and so on; see notes for section 86 in this study guide]; **she** [*Satan's kingdom; the wicked of the world*] **is bound in bundles** [*prepared for burning*]; **her bands are made strong** [*God has decreed it, there is no escape*], **no man can loose them; therefore, she is ready to be burned.** And **he** [*the angel at the beginning of this verse*] **shall sound his trump both long and loud, and all nations shall hear it** [*everyone on earth will know that this is taking place*].

We do not know what the "silence in heaven for the space of half an hour" is, spoken of in verse 95, next. We do know that silence is an excellent attention getter (compare with 3 Nephi 10:1–2).

Some have thought that the "half an hour" might be in the Lord's time system (one thousand years on earth equals one day in heaven; see 2 Peter 3:8), which would make the "half an hour" into about twenty-one years of our time. They further speculate that during this twenty-one-year period there would be no revelation because of the "silence in heaven."

Suggesting that there would be no revelation is contrary to the fact that the Church will not go into apostasy again (Daniel 2:44–45). It will continue to spread throughout the world, with prophets, seers and revelators at the helm, right up until the kingdom of God (the Church on earth) meets the kingdom of heaven (the Savior and the hosts of heaven) at the Second Coming; see D&C 65:6).

Thus, we are probably best off to consider the "half an hour" to be in our current time system unless told otherwise by a prophet.

95 And **there shall be silence in heaven for the space of half an hour**; and **immediately after shall the curtain of heaven be unfolded** [*the veil will be removed*], as a scroll is unfolded after it is rolled up, **and the face of the Lord shall be unveiled** [*everyone will see the coming Christ*];

Revelation 1:7 informs us that everyone will see the Savior at this time, including those who crucified Him.

Revelation 1:7

7 **Behold, he cometh with clouds; and every eye shall see him, and they *also* which pierced him**: and all kindreds of the earth shall wail because of him. Even so, Amen.

Elder Orson Pratt explained that everyone, including the dead, will see the Savior when He comes. He taught (**bold** added for emphasis):

"The second advent of the Son of God is to be something altogether of a different nature from anything that has hitherto transpired on the face of the earth, accompanied with great power and glory, something that will not be done in a small portion of the earth like Palestine, and seen only by a few; but **it will be an event that will be seen by all**—all flesh shall see the glory of the Lord; when he reveals himself the second time, **every eye, not only those living at that time in the flesh**, in mortality on the earth, **but also the very dead themselves**, they also who pierced him, those who lived eighteen hundred years ago, who were engaged in the cruel act of piercing his hands and his feet and his side, will also see him at that time" (In *Journal of Discourses*, 18:170).

Next, we are told that the righteous, faithful Latter-day Saints who are alive upon the earth at the time will be taken up to meet the coming Lord. They will need to be "quickened" or "transfigured" (see Moses 1:11) by the power of the Holy Ghost in order for their mortal bodies to withstand the presence of the Son of God, who will come in all His glory. By the way, it will be His glory that will destroy the wicked; see D&C 5:19; 2 Nephi 12:10, 19, 21.

Doctrine, verse 96

Faithful Saints who are alive on earth at the time of the Savior's coming will be transfigured and taken up to meet Him.

96 And the saints that are upon the earth, who are alive [*who are still mortal*], **shall be quickened and** be **caught up to meet him**.

Next, in verses 97–98, we are taught that the dead who are worthy of celestial glory (verse 98) will be resurrected and also caught up to meet Him. This is sometimes referred to as the "morning of the first resurrection."

By the way, a large group of the dead, who were worthy of celestial resurrection, was resurrected with the Savior at the time of His resurrection. This would have included Adam and Eve and all the righteous Saints down to the time of Christ's resurrection, including John the Baptist. See D&C 133:54–55.

Doctrine, verse 97

The righteous who died after the resurrection of Christ, who lived worthy of celestial glory, will be resurrected and taken up to meet the coming Lord.

97 And they who have slept in their graves shall come forth [*will be resurrected*], for their graves shall be opened; and **they also shall be caught up to meet him** in the midst of the pillar of heaven—

Verse 98, next, speaks of another

beautiful privilege for the faithful Saints, living and dead. Not only will they be caught up to meet the coming Savior, but they also will have the privilege of descending to the earth with Him as He comes to usher in the Millennium and begin His thousand-year reign on earth. Next time you see a painting of the coming of the Lord, you might picture yourself as one of the beings in the background who are coming down with Him.

At this point, those Saints who are still mortal will continue living on earth until they reach a hundred years of age (Isaiah 65:20). The Saints who are resurrected at this time will begin ruling and reigning with the Savior, as taught in Revelation 20:4.

Doctrine, verses 96–98

The living Saints at the time of the Second Coming, as well as the righteous who are still in the grave and who are resurrected at this time, will have the privilege of meeting the Savior as He comes and then descending to the earth with Him.

98 They [*both the living "saints" in verse 96 and the righteous dead who "have slept in their graves" in verse 97*] **are Christ's**, the first fruits, they **who shall descend with him** first, and they who are on the earth and in their graves, **who are first caught up to meet him**; and all this by the voice of the sounding of the trump of the angel of God [*as announced to the world by the angel blowing his horn*].

Verse 99, next, informs us that those who are worthy of terrestrial glory, who have already died, will be resurrected near the first of the Millennium, but after the celestial dead have been resurrected. This terrestrial resurrection is sometimes referred to as the "afternoon of the first resurrection." No terrestrials have yet been resurrected.

Doctrine, verse 99

Those who lived from the time of Adam and Eve up to the time of the Second Coming, who have already died and who earned terrestrial glory, will be resurrected sometime near the beginning of the Millennium but not until the celestial resurrection spoken of in verse 97, above, has taken place. No terrestrials from this earth have been resurrected yet.

99 And after this [*the events spoken of in verses 96–98*] another angel shall sound, which is the second trump; and then **cometh the redemption of those who are Christ's at his coming; who**

have received their part in that prison [*the spirit prison, as spoken of in D&C 76:73 during the vision of those who receive terrestrial glory (D&C 76:71–80)*] **which is prepared for them**, that they might receive the gospel, and be judged according to men in the flesh.

Verses 100–101, next, teach us that those who have earned telestial glory will not be resurrected until the end of the Millennium. Therefore, no telestials have been resurrected yet.

Doctrine, verses 100–101

Those who qualify for telestial glory will not be resurrected until the end of the Millennium. No telestials from this earth have been resurrected yet.

100 And again, another trump shall sound, which is the third trump; and then come the spirits of men who are to be judged, and are found under condemnation [*will be assigned to the telestial kingdom*];

101 And these are the rest of the dead; and **they live not again until** [*they will not be resurrected until*] **the thousand years are ended**, neither again, until the end of the earth.

There is one more resurrection, the very last one. It is spoken of in verse 102 and is the resurrection of mortals who become sons of perdition.

Doctrine, verse 102

Mortals from this earth who become sons of perdition will be the last to be resurrected.

102 And another trump shall sound, which is **the fourth trump**, saying: **There are found among those who are to remain** until that great and last day, even the end, **who shall remain filthy still**.

Verses 103–5, next, summarize the triumph of God over Satan as the kingdom of the devil, often referred to as "Babylon," falls at the time of the Second Coming.

103 And **another trump shall sound**, which is **the fifth trump**, which is **the fifth angel** who committeth the everlasting gospel—flying through the midst of heaven, unto all nations, kindreds, tongues, and people;

104 And **this shall be the sound of his trump** [*this is his message*], **saying to all people**, both in heaven and in earth, and that are under the earth—**for every ear shall hear it, and every knee shall bow, and every tongue**

shall confess [*ultimately, everyone, including those who follow Satan into perdition, sometimes referred to as outer darkness, will acknowledge that Jesus is the Christ; this does not necessarily mean that they will accept His gospel, rather that they will ultimately have to admit that He is who He says He is*], **while they hear the sound of the trump, saying: Fear God, and give glory to him who sitteth upon the throne, forever and ever; for the hour of his judgment is come.**

105 And again, **another angel shall sound his trump, which is the sixth angel, saying: She** [*Babylon, Satan's kingdom, the church of the devil, "the whore of all the earth"; see 1 Nephi 14:10*] **is fallen** who made all nations drink of the wine of the wrath of her fornication [*who spread gross wickedness throughout the whole world*]; **she is fallen, is fallen!** [*In other words, the wicked are finally destroyed and the thousand years of peace can begin!*]

> You may wish to cross-reference verses 106–7, next, with D&C 76:106–8 in your own scriptures. These verses teach that Christ will ultimately finish His work with this world after the Millennium, the little season, and the final judgment and will turn it back over to the Father.

106 And again, **another angel shall sound his trump**, which is **the seventh angel** [*this is Adam; see verse 112; the number seven in scriptural symbolism represents completeness, perfection*], **saying: It is finished**; it is finished! [*Everything with respect to this world is complete*]. **The Lamb of God** [*Christ*] **hath overcome** [*has triumphed*] and **trodden the wine-press alone** [*Christ was the only one who could carry out the Atonement; thus, He had to do it alone*], even **the wine-press** [*symbolic of the terrible burden and pressure of suffering for all our sins*] **of the fierceness of the wrath of Almighty God** [*to satisfy the demands of the law of justice*].

107 And **then** [*after the world is finished up*] **shall the angels be crowned with the glory of his might, and the saints shall be filled with his glory, and receive their inheritance and be made equal with him** [*will receive exaltation, be made gods*].

> Having been shown the final finish-up scenes for this world in the above verses, we are now taken back in time and given additional details about the final scenes, including the binding of Satan at the beginning of the Millennium, the "little season" after the Millennium is over, during which the battle of

SECTION 88

Gog and Magog takes place (see Bible Dictionary under "Gog"), and the final banishing of Satan and his followers.

First, in verses 108–9, we are shown a bit more about how judgment will take place. Note how well-organized all of this is.

108 And then shall the first angel again sound his trump in the ears of all living, and **reveal the secret acts of men, and the mighty works of God in the first thousand years.**

109 And then shall the second angel sound his trump, and **reveal the secret acts of men, and the thoughts and intents of their hearts, and the mighty works of God in the second thousand years—**

110 And so on, until the seventh angel [*Michael—in other words, Adam; see verse 112*] **shall sound his trump**; and **he shall stand forth upon the land and upon the sea** [*symbolic of Adam's position and authority over the whole earth, under the Savior*], **and swear** [*promise, covenant*] **in the name of him who sitteth upon the throne** [*in other words, he promised in the name of Jesus Christ; see verse 115*], **that there shall be time no longer** [*that there will be no more delay, the Millennium will now begin*]; and **Satan shall be bound** [*will not be allowed to tempt and interfere on earth during the Millennium—compare with D&C 101:28*], that old serpent, who is called the devil, **and shall not be loosed for the space of a thousand years.**

Next, in verses 111–13, we are shown the preparations for the final battle, the Battle of Gog and Magog, during which the war for our loyalty, which began with the War in Heaven, will be brought to a close.

By the way, Gog was the wicked king of Magog in ancient times who attacked Israel. Over time, "Gog and Magog" came to symbolize the forces of evil that fight against God. We will quote from the Bible Dictionary for a bit more about this.

Gog

"(1) A Reubenite (1 Chr. 5:4).

"(2) King of Magog, whose invasion of Israel was prophesied by Ezekiel (Ezek. 38; 39). The prophecy points to a time when the heathen nations of the north would set themselves against the people of God and would be defeated and led to recognize Jehovah as King. **All this appears to be at the second coming** of the Lord. **Another battle, called the battle of Gog and Magog, will occur at the end of the 1,000 years.** This is described by John

111 **And then he shall be loosed for a little season**, that he may **gather together his armies.**

> Joseph Fielding Smith taught that there will be many mortals who will become sons of perdition at this time because they will know the Savior personally, having lived on earth with Him during the final years of the Millennium, and then turning wicked and joining forces with Satan when he is let loose after the Millennium is over.
>
> Elder Smith said:
>
> "After the thousand years Satan will be loosed again and will go forth again to deceive the nations. Because men are still mortal, Satan will go out to deceive them. Men will again deny the Lord, but in doing so they will act with their eyes open and because they love darkness rather than light, and so they become sons of perdition. Satan will gather his hosts, both those on the earth and the wicked dead who will eventually also be brought forth in the resurrection. Michael [Adam], the prince, will gather his forces and the last great battle will be fought. Satan will be defeated with his hosts. Then will come the end. Satan and those who follow him will be banished into outer darkness" (*Doctrines of Salvation*, 1:87).

112 And **Michael**, the seventh angel, even the archangel, **shall gather together his armies**, even the hosts of heaven.

113 And **the devil shall gather together his armies**; even the hosts of hell, **and shall come up to battle against Michael and his armies.**

> We see the final outcome of this battle in verses 114–15, next.

114 And **then cometh the battle of the great God** [*the Battle of Gog and Magog*]; and **the devil and his armies shall be cast away into their own place** [*outer darkness; perdition*]**, that they shall not have power over the saints any more at all.**

115 For **Michael** shall fight their battles, and **shall overcome him** [*Lucifer, Satan*] who **seeketh the throne of him who sitteth upon the throne, even the Lamb.**

> Did you notice Lucifer's basic motivation for all the evil he has caused as mentioned in the last half of verse 15, above? He wanted to be the Redeemer, as stated also in Moses 4:1–3.

116 **This is the glory of God** [*as stated also in Moses 1:39*], and **the sanctified** [*those who obtain celestial glory*]; and they **shall not any more see death** [*perhaps meaning spiritual death, resulting from the*

influence of Satan and his angels; compare with Alma 12:16].

Verse 117, next, provides a transition between the "high mountain" doctrines given in the previous verses and specific instructions for setting up and running the "school of the prophets" (verse 127), which constitute verses 118–41.

117 Therefore, verily I say unto you, my friends, **call your solemn assembly** [*see verses 70–75*]**, as I have commanded you.**

Some are of the opinion that the "solemn assembly" referred to in verse 117, above, as well as in previous verses, is the same thing as the School of the Prophets. In any case, we will use **bold** along with just a few notes, letting the scriptures speak for themselves as we read the Lord's instructions for this School of the Prophets.

By the way, the brethren began meeting in this school on January 23, 1833. They met in an upper room of the Newel K. Whitney Store in Kirtland, Ohio, and had many marvelous manifestations and spiritual discussions there. Also, because many of these men chewed or smoked tobacco and Emma Smith had to clean up after them, this will provide the setting for the receiving of the Word of Wisdom, which we will study next in section 89.

You will likely recognize some of the next verses as often-quoted in lessons and sermons.

118 **And as all have not faith, seek ye diligently and teach one another words of wisdom**; yea, **seek ye out of the best books words of wisdom; seek learning, even by study and also by faith.**

An important caution is given at the end of verse 118, above. It is that there is danger in basing one's studies solely upon the precepts, philosophies, theories, and teachings of men without the gospel as an anchor to the soul. Many have gone into intellectual apostasy because they failed to include faith in their studies.

119 **Organize yourselves; prepare every needful thing;** and **establish** a house, even **a house of prayer**, a house of **fasting**, a house of **faith**, a house of **learning**, a house of **glory**, a house of **order, a house of God;**

120 That your incomings may be in the name of the Lord; that your outgoings may be in the name of the Lord; that all your salutations may be in the name of the Lord, with uplifted hands unto the Most High [*in other words, that everything you do might be done under the direction and influence of the Spirit of the Lord*].

121 Therefore, **cease from all your light speeches, from all laughter, from all your lustful desires,**

from all your pride and light-mindedness, and from all your wicked doings.

> Verse 121, above, is context sensitive. It contains instructions for conducting sessions of the School of the Prophets. While the instruction to avoid "lustful desires," "pride," "light-mindedness" (not taking serious things seriously), and "all your wicked doings" applies to all situations and settings, the instruction regarding "light speeches" and "laughter" would apply to sacred and serious settings where funny speeches and inappropriate laughter would ruin the spirit of the occasion. For example, this would apply to our temple worship. Our living prophets are marvelous examples of proper use of humor.
>
> President Joseph F. Smith taught the following:
>
> "The Lord has called upon us to be a sober-minded people, not given to much laughter, frivolity and light-mindedness, but to consider thoughtfully and thoroughly the things of his kingdom that we may be prepared in all things to understand the glorious truths of the gospel, and be prepared for blessings to come. . . .
>
> ". . . I believe that it is necessary for the Saints to have amusement, but it must be of the proper kind. I do not believe the Lord intends and desires that we should pull a long face and look sanctimonious and hypocritical. I think he expects us to be happy and of a cheerful countenance, but he does not expect of us the indulgence in boisterous and unseemly conduct and the seeking after the vain and foolish things which amuse and entertain the world. He has commanded us to the contrary for our own good and eternal welfare" (In Conference Report, October 1916, 70).

122 **Appoint** among yourselves **a teacher,** and **let not all be spokesmen at once**; but **let one speak at a time** and **let all listen unto his sayings**, that when all have spoken that all may be edified of all [*so that you can learn from each member of the class*], and that every man may have an equal privilege.

123 See that ye **love one another; cease to be covetous; learn to impart one to another as the gospel requires.**

124 **Cease to be idle; cease to be unclean; cease to find fault one with another; cease to sleep longer than is needful; retire to thy bed early, that ye may not be weary; arise early, that your bodies and your minds may be invigorated.**

125 And above all things, **clothe yourselves with the bond of**

charity, as with a mantle, which is **the bond of perfectness and peace**.

126 **Pray always, that ye may not faint** [*become overly discouraged*], until I come. Behold, and lo, I will come quickly, and receive you unto myself. Amen.

127 And again, **the order of** the house prepared for the presidency **of the school of the prophets, established for their instruction in all things that are expedient** [*important and necessary*] **for them**, even for all the officers of the church, or in other words, those who are called to the ministry in the church, beginning at the high priests, even down to the deacons—

128 And **this shall be the order of the house of the presidency** of the school: **He that is appointed to be president, or teacher, shall be found standing in his place**, in the house which shall be prepared for him.

129 Therefore, **he shall be first** in the house of God, **in a place that the congregation in the house may hear his words carefully and distinctly**, not with loud speech.

130 And when he cometh into the house of God, for **he should be first** in the house—behold, this is beautiful, **that he may be an example—**

131 **Let him offer himself in prayer** upon his knees before God, in token or remembrance of the everlasting covenant.

132 And when any shall come in after him, let the teacher arise, and, with uplifted hands to heaven, yea, even directly, salute his brother or brethren with these words:

133 Art thou a brother or brethren? I salute you in the name of the Lord Jesus Christ, in token or remembrance of the everlasting covenant, in which covenant I receive you to fellowship, in a determination that is fixed, immovable, and unchangeable, to be your friend and brother through the grace of God in the bonds of love, to walk in all the commandments of God blameless, in thanksgiving, forever and ever. Amen.

134 And **he that is found unworthy of this salutation** [*the greeting given in verse 133, above*] **shall not have place among you**; for **ye shall not suffer that mine house shall be polluted by him**.

135 And he that cometh in and is faithful before me, and is a brother, or if they be brethren, they shall salute [*greet*] the president or teacher with uplifted hands to heaven, with this same prayer and covenant, or by saying Amen, in token of the same.

136 Behold, verily, I say unto you, **this is an ensample** [*example*] **unto you for a salutation to one another in the house of God, in the school of the prophets.**

137 And ye are called to **do this by prayer and thanksgiving** [*with gratitude*]**, as the Spirit shall give utterance in all your doings in the house of the Lord, in the school of the prophets, that it may become a sanctuary, a tabernacle of the Holy Spirit to your edification.**

138 **And ye shall not receive any among you into this school save he is clean from the blood of this generation**;

139 And **he shall be received by the ordinance of the washing of feet,** for **unto this end** [*purpose*] **was the ordinance of the washing of feet instituted.**

140 And again, **the ordinance of washing feet is to be administered by the president, or presiding elder of the church**.

141 **It is to be commenced with prayer**; and **after partaking of bread and wine** [*the sacrament*], he is to gird [*dress*] himself according to the pattern given in the thirteenth chapter of John's testimony concerning me. Amen.

SECTION 89

Background

This revelation was given through the Prophet Joseph Smith at Kirtland, Ohio, on February 27, 1833. It is known as the Word of Wisdom.

President Brigham Young gave the background for this revelation as follows:

"I think I am as well acquainted with the circumstances which led to the giving of the Word of Wisdom as any man in the Church, although I was not present at the time to witness them. The first School of the Prophets was held in a small room situated over the Prophet Joseph's kitchen, in a house which belonged to Bishop Whitney. . . . The brethren came to that place for hundreds of miles to attend school in a little room probably no larger than eleven by fourteen. When they assembled together in this room after breakfast, the first they did was to light their pipes and, while smoking, talk about the great things of the kingdom and spit all over the room, and as soon as the pipe was out of their mouths a large chew of tobacco would then be taken. Often when the Prophet entered the room to give the school instructions he would find himself in a cloud of tobacco smoke. This, and the complaints of his wife at having to clean so filthy a floor, made the Prophet think upon the matter, and he inquired of the Lord relating to the conduct of the Elders in using tobacco, and the revelation known as the Word of Wisdom was the result of his inquiry. You know what it is and can read it at your leisure" (*Journal of Discourses*, 12:158).

There are many important aspects to this revelation. For instance, as you study it you would do well to note that there are more "dos" than "don'ts" contained in it. Also, pay careful attention to the fact that it is not a system of vegetarianism. In fact, if you look at the verse summaries after the heading to section 89 in your Doctrine and Covenants, you will see that meat is clearly permitted (**bold** added for emphasis):

*10–17, Herbs, fruits, **flesh**, and grain are ordained for the use of man and of animals;*

We will deal more with this when we get to verses 12–13.

As you will see, in verse 2, the Word of Wisdom was not a commandment when it was first given. However, in a general conference of the Church held on September 9, 1851, President Brigham Young presented it to the members as a commandment. Still, many did not comply, perhaps not considering it to be as serious and important as other commandments. Finally, in 1919, under the direction of President Heber J. Grant (see 2018 *Doctrine and Covenants Student Manual*, chapter 35), the Word of Wisdom became a temple recommend item and thus began to be "locked in" as a vital part of being a faithful Saint. It has now become a commandment in the full sense of the word, just in time to protect us from "evils and designs which do and will exist in the hearts of conspiring men" (verse 4), such as the rampant drug culture, alcohol addiction, and sexual immorality, which often go with smoking and drinking.

President Joseph F. Smith explained why the Word of Wisdom was not given as a commandment at first. He said: "At that time, . . . if [the Word of Wisdom] had been given as a commandment it would have brought every man, addicted to the use of these noxious things, under condemnation; so the Lord was merciful and gave them a chance to overcome, before He brought them under the law" (in Conference Report, Oct. 1913, 14).

We will now proceed with our verse-by-verse study.

1 **A WORD OF WISDOM, for the benefit of the council of high priests** [*the School of the Prophets*], **assembled in Kirtland, and the church,** and **also the saints in Zion** [*the members at that time in Jackson County, Missouri*]—

2 To be **sent greeting; not by commandment or constraint** [*see background notes above for this section for when it became a commandment*], **but by revelation and the word of wisdom, showing forth the order and will of God in the temporal** [*physical*] **salvation of all saints in the last days**—

3 Given for **a principle with promise** [*explained in verses 18–21*], **adapted to the capacity of the weak and the weakest of all saints** [*in other words, there is ultimately no excuse for not living the Word of Wisdom*], **who are or can be called saints.**

Even though the Word of Wisdom serves as a law of health, some wonder why we are required to abstain completely from the harmful substances included in the Word of Wisdom rather than being allowed to use them with moderation. The Lord gives the reason next in verse 4. Perhaps you have noticed that, in many cases, the forbidden substances in the Word of Wisdom serve as a gateway to more harmful substances.

4 Behold, verily, thus saith the Lord unto you: **In consequence of evils and designs which do and will exist in the hearts of conspiring men in the last days, I have warned you, and forewarn you,** by giving unto you this word of wisdom by revelation—

President Ezra Taft Benson explained the warning given in verse 4, above:

"There is another part of this revelation [D&C 89] that constitutes a pertinent warning to this modern generation. 'In consequence of evils and designs which do and will exist in the hearts of conspiring men in the last days, I have warned you, and forewarn you, by giving unto you this word of wisdom by revelation.' (D&C 89:4.)

"The Lord foresaw the situation of today when motives for money would cause men to conspire to entice others to take noxious substances into their bodies. Advertisements which promote beer, wine, liquors, coffee, tobacco, and other harmful substances are examples of what the Lord foresaw. But the most pernicious example of an evil conspiracy in our time is those who induce young people into the use of drugs.

"My young brothers and sisters, in all love, we give you warning that Satan and his emissaries will strive to entice you to use harmful substances, because they well know if you partake, your spiritual powers will be inhibited and you will be in their evil power. Stay away from those places or people which would influence you to break the commandments of God. Keep the commandments of God and you will have the wisdom to know and discern that which is evil" ("A Principle with a Promise," *Ensign*, May 1983, 54–55).

5 That **inasmuch as any man drinketh wine or strong drink among you, behold it is not good, neither meet** [*proper; wise*] **in the sight of your Father**, only [*except*] in assembling yourselves together to offer up your sacraments before him [*in other words, except for use with the sacrament; and, as you know, we no longer use wine but rather water; compare with D&C 27:2*].

6 And, behold, **this should be wine, yea, pure wine of the grape of the vine, of your own make**.

7 And, again, **strong drinks are not for the belly**, but for the washing of your bodies.

Regarding the wine to be used for the sacrament at the time of this revelation, if you carefully read the heading to D&C 27 and verses 3 and 4, you will see that the wine they were to use was not to be "strong drink"; it was to be "new"—in other words, fresh juice, not fermented (see 2018 *Doctrine and Covenants Student Manual*, chapter 35).

8 **And again, tobacco is not for the body, neither for the belly, and is not good for man**, but is an herb for bruises and all sick cattle, to be used with judgment and skill.

The question is often asked as to where the words "tea" and "coffee" are found in the Word of Wisdom. The answer is "hot drinks" in verse 9, next.

9 And again, **hot drinks** are not for the body or belly.

The Joseph Smith Papers Project helps us understand what is meant by "hot drinks" in verse nine, above. We will quote from the 2018 *Doctrine and Covenants Student Manual*:

"The Prophet Joseph Smith and Hyrum Smith were reported to have specifically identified coffee and tea as the "hot drinks" mentioned in the Word of Wisdom, and President Brigham Young later confirmed this explanation (see *The Joseph Smith Papers, Documents, Volume 3: February 1833–March 1834*, 14)."

You can also read on page 186 of *True to the Faith*, published by the Church in 2004, that "the term 'hot drinks' refers to tea and coffee." You can also read on the same page that "Anything harmful that people purposefully take into their bodies is not in harmony with the Word of Wisdom. This is especially true of illegal drugs, which can destroy those who become addicted to them. Stay entirely away from them."

Another thing regarding the term "hot drinks" is that some members tend to think that since the word "hot" is used, it may be permissible to drink these products cold or iced. This is not so. Also, some members tend to believe that any hot drink, including hot chocolate, is against the Word of Wisdom. This also is not the case. Of course, any drink that is too hot and burns when you drink it is against the law of common sense, but it is not a matter of temple worthiness.

We must be careful not to add things to the Word of Wisdom that neither the Lord nor His prophets have added. For example, some add cola drinks and other caffeine drinks to the Word of Wisdom. While these might fit into the statement of the Brethren about "anything harmful" taken into our bodies, quoted above, we must be careful not to go beyond what the Lord has said by making these a matter of temple worthiness and imposing our own interpretations upon others.

Beginning with verse 10 and continuing through verse 17, we see many "dos" that, when followed, will provide better health.

10 And again, verily I say unto you, **all wholesome herbs** [*a word meaning "vegetables and plants" in Joseph Smith's day*] God hath ordained for the constitution, nature, and use of man—

11 **Every herb in the season thereof**, and **every fruit in the season thereof**; all these to be used with prudence and thanksgiving.

12 Yea, **flesh also of beasts and of the fowls of the air**, I, the Lord, have ordained [*authorized*] for the use of man with thanksgiving; **nevertheless they are to be used sparingly** [*"sparingly" seems to be the key word, here*];

Verse 13, next, is sometimes used to claim that the Word of Wisdom is a system of vegetarianism. We will quote from Elder John A. Widtsoe. He said:

"The Word of Wisdom is not a system of vegetarianism. Clearly, meat is permitted [see D&C 49:18]" (Widtsoe, *Evidences and Reconciliations*, 3:156–57; quoted in the *Doctrine and Covenants Student Manual*, 1981, 210).

If you will read D&C 49:18–19 and footnote 18a that was placed there by our Church leaders, you will again see that meat is not prohibited by the Word of Wisdom. You may also wish to read D&C 59:16–19, which likewise confirms this.

What, then, do we do with verse 13, next, which seems to say that meat should only be used in times of famine or cold? Let's read it first and then do a bit more with it.

13 **And it is pleasing unto me that they should not be used, only in times of winter, or of cold, or famine.**

Since we already have the answers, above, revealed through the Brethren that the Word of Wisdom is not a system of vegetarianism, we can take another look at verse 13 and see if we are reading it correctly.

At the time this revelation was given, there were groups in the Kirtland, Ohio, area who advocated not eating meat. One of these was the Shaking Quakers, all of whom avoided eating pork as a matter of religion, and many of whom likewise made abstinence from all meat a matter of religious belief. See heading to section 49. With this in mind, we might read verse 13, above, as follows:

"And it is pleasing unto me that they [*the flesh of beasts and . . . fowls—verse 12*] should not be used only in times of winter, or cold, or famine as Ann Lee and the Shaking Quakers teach. Rather, they are to be used sparingly."

Whatever the case, we are wise if we follow our Church leaders on this matter. Of course, those whose bodies function best on a meat-free diet are welcome to follow such eating habits. But they must be cautious not to impose their preferences upon other members as the will of the Lord and the doctrine of the Church.

14 **All grain is ordained** [*approved*] **for the use of man and of beasts, to be the staff of life**, not only **for man** but **for the beasts of the field** [*domestic animals*], and **the fowls of heaven**, and **all wild animals** that run or creep on the earth;

15 And **these** [*perhaps meaning the wild animals mentioned in verse 14, above—we don't know for sure*] **hath God made for the use of man only in times of famine and excess of hunger.**

16 **All grain is good for the food of man**; as **also the fruit of the vine**; that which yieldeth fruit, **whether in the ground** [*such as potatoes, radishes, carrots, and so forth*] **or above the ground—**

It is interesting that modern animal science studies have verified that the grains recommended for specific animals, in verse 17, next, are correct.

17 Nevertheless, wheat for man, and **corn for the ox,** and **oats for the horse,** and **rye for the fowls and for swine, and for all beasts of the field** [*domestic animals*], and **barley for all useful animals**, and for mild drinks, as also other grain.

In verse 3, above, we were told that the Word of Wisdom is "a principle with promise." The promised blessings are given in verses 18–21, next. This is an important part of the Word of Wisdom that unfortunately is often left out of discussions and conversations about it.

18 **And all saints who remember to keep and do these sayings, walking in obedience to the commandments** [*an additional stipulation for receiving these blessings*], **shall receive health in their navel and marrow to their bones** [*a biblical phrase meaning "the support and blessings of the Lord," as was the case with Daniel and his three companions; see Daniel 1:6–20; see also Proverbs 3:7–10*];

19 **And shall find wisdom and great treasures of knowledge, even hidden treasures** [*meaning, among other things, will have better knowledge and stronger testimonies of the gospel*];

It is not uncommon for people who have physical limitations and disabilities, who faithfully keep the Word of Wisdom, to be a bit disappointed when they read verse 20, next. While better health and strength are obviously a major benefit of keeping the Word of Wisdom, verse 20 has a symbolic meaning that applies to all the faithful and that is even more important eternally than mortal strength and stamina. We will add it as a note to the end of the verse.

20 **And shall run and not be weary, and shall walk and not faint.** [*They will be strengthened by the Lord and will not be stopped in pursuing the path to exaltation. Compare with Isaiah 40:28–31.*]

Verse 20, above, should be read in the context of verse 21, next.

21 **And I, the Lord, give unto them a promise, that the destroying angel shall pass by them, as the children of Israel, and not slay them.** Amen.

President J. Reuben Clark Jr. spoke of these promises as follows (**bold** added for emphasis):

"This does not say and this does not mean, that to keep the Word of Wisdom is to insure us against death, for death is, in the eternal plan, coequal with birth. This is the eternal decree. [1 Cor. 15:22; 2 Nephi 9:6.] But it does mean that the destroying angel, he who comes to punish the unrighteous for their sins, as he in olden time afflicted the corrupt Egyptians in their wickedness [Ex. 12:23, 29], shall pass by the Saints, 'who are walking in obedience to the commandments,' and who 'remember to keep and do these sayings.' **These promises do mean that all those who qualify themselves to enjoy them will be permitted so to live out their lives that they may gain the full experiences and get the full knowledge which they need in order to progress to the highest exaltation in eternity**, all these will live until their work is finished and God calls them back to their eternal home, as a reward" (In Conference Report, October 1940, 17–18).

SECTION 90

Background

This revelation was given to the Prophet Joseph Smith on March 8, 1833, in Kirtland, Ohio. In this revelation (see verse 6), the Lord instructed that Sidney Rigdon and Frederick G. Williams were to be "equal with thee (Joseph Smith) in holding the keys of this last kingdom." As a result, ten days later, on March 18, 1833, they were ordained as counselors in the Presidency of the High Priesthood (which later became known as the First Presidency). Joseph Smith described how this took place:

"I laid my hands on Brothers Sidney and Frederick, and ordained them to take part with me in holding the keys, of this last kingdom, and to assist in the presidency of the high priesthood, as my counselors; after which, I exhorted the brethren to faithfulness, and diligence in keeping the commandments of God, and gave much instruction for the benefit of the saints, with a promise, that the pure in heart should see a heavenly vision; and, after remaining a short time in secret prayer, the promise was verified; for many present had the eyes of their understanding opened by the Spirit of God so as to behold many things. . . .

"After [partaking of the sacrament] many of the brethren saw a heavenly vision of the Savior, and concourses of angels, and many other things, of which each one has a record of what he saw" (in *Manuscript History of the Church*, vol. A-1, page 281, josephsmithpapers.org; spelling standardized).

The "Presidency of the High Priesthood" became known as the "First Presidency" by 1835. (See *The Joseph Smith Papers, Documents, Volume 3: February 1833–March 1834*, 26).

In verse one, we see that the humble Prophet of the Restoration, Joseph Smith Jr., had been feeling his inadequacies and had pled with the Lord for forgiveness of his sins.

1 **THUS saith the Lord,** verily, verily **I say unto you my son** [*a term of closeness and endearment*], **thy sins are forgiven thee, according to thy petition,** for **thy prayers and the prayers of thy brethren have come up into my ears.**

In verses 2–3, next, we are told once more that this is the last time the gospel will be restored again before the Second Coming. This is significant because every other time throughout the history of the earth that the gospel was restored, the Church eventually went into apostasy and had to be restored again. It will not happen this time (see Daniel 2:45–46).

Joseph Smith and his successors hold the priesthood keys of authority to administer and direct the Church, and will continue to hold them until they turn them over to the Savior at the council at Adam-ondi-Ahman, shortly before the Second Coming; see Daniel 7:14.

2 Therefore, **thou art blessed from henceforth that bear the keys of the kingdom** given unto you; **which kingdom is coming forth for the last time.**

3 Verily I say unto you, **the keys of this kingdom shall never be taken from you, while thou art in the world, neither in the world to come;**

The word "oracles," as used in verses 4–5, next, means both "revelations" and "the prophets through whom revelations are received." Verse 5 emphasizes the accountability of all who receive the revelations of God through His living oracles.

4 Nevertheless, **through you shall the oracles be given** to another, yea, even **unto the church.**

5 And **all they who receive the oracles of God, let them beware how they hold them** [*respond to them*] **lest they are accounted as a light thing, and are brought under condemnation thereby,** and stumble and fall when the storms descend, and the winds blow, and the rains descend, and beat upon their house [*in other words, when the temptations of the devil try to steer them away from following the revelations of God through His prophets*].

Sidney Rigdon and Frederick G. Williams are addressed, beginning in verse 6, next.

6 And again, verily **I say unto** thy brethren, **Sidney Rigdon and Frederick G. Williams, their sins are forgiven them also,** and they are accounted as **equal with thee in holding the keys of this last kingdom;**

These brethren, along with the

Prophet, now form what we know as the "Quorum of the First Presidency." The two counselors function under the direction of the Prophet, but not independently. When the Prophet dies, the Quorum of the First Presidency is dissolved.

In order to understand the last phrase of verse 6, above, it is helpful to know that each new Apostle is given all the keys of the priesthood at the time he is ordained an Apostle and set apart to serve in the Quorum of the Twelve. Thus, each of the fifteen "prophets, seers, and revelators" who serve as the First Presidency and the Twelve today holds all of the priesthood keys. However, only the Prophet has the authority to exercise all of the keys. They are dormant in the others until if and when they become the President of the Church. Otherwise, there would be no one on earth to give the new Prophet the keys after the previous President of the Church has passed away.

Next, beginning with verse 7, these counselors to the Prophet are given more on-the-job training, including instructions about the purposes of the School of the Prophets.

7 As **also through your administration the keys of the school of the prophets** [see D&C 88:118–141], **which I have commanded to be organized;**

8 **That thereby they** [*the brethren chosen to attend the School of the Prophets*] **may be perfected in their ministry** for the salvation of Zion, and of the nations of Israel, and of the Gentiles, as many as will believe;

9 That **through your administration they may receive the word** [*you are to teach them*], and through their administration [*they are to teach others*] the word may go forth unto the ends of the earth, unto the Gentiles first, and then, behold, and lo, they shall turn unto the Jews.

Next, the Savior gives these men an overview of the impact that their work will have upon the world.

10 And **then cometh the day when the arm of the Lord shall be revealed in power in convincing the nations, the heathen nations, the house of Joseph, of the gospel of their salvation.**

11 For it shall come to pass **in that day**, that **every man shall hear the fulness of the gospel in his own tongue**, and **in his own language**, through those who are ordained unto this power, **by the administration of the Comforter** [*all will be given a chance to be taught under the direction and power of the Holy Ghost*], **shed forth**

upon them for the revelation of Jesus Christ [*to bear testimony to them that Jesus is the Christ*].

The message given in verse 11, above, is of tremendous importance. Among other things, it certifies that God is completely fair. It states basically that every individual who ever comes to earth, who lives beyond the years of accountability (D&C 68:25–28, 137:10), will have the opportunity to hear and understand the gospel under the direction and power of the Holy Ghost, who will bear witness to them that Jesus is the Christ. Whether this happens for them in this life or in the spirit world mission field, the outcome is the same.

Once they have received this completely fair opportunity to hear and understand the gospel of Jesus Christ, under the direction and influence of the Holy Ghost, they are then free to accept it or reject it.

Knowing this is comforting to those who worry about whether a loved one has had a fair chance to understand the gospel.

Verses 12–18, next, appear to be directed specifically to the First Presidency.

12 And now, verily I say unto you, I give unto you a commandment that you **continue in the ministry and presidency.**

13 And **when you have finished the translation of the prophets** [*the JST work on the Old Testament*], **you shall from thenceforth preside over the affairs of the church and the school** [*the School of the Prophets*];

14 And **from time to time**, as shall be manifested by the Comforter, **receive revelations to unfold the mysteries of the kingdom;**

15 And **set in order the churches** [*supervise the wards and branches of the Church*], and **study and learn, and become acquainted with all good books, and with languages, tongues, and people.**

16 And **this shall be your business and mission in all your lives, to preside in council, and set in order all the affairs of this church and kingdom.**

Next, these brethren are reminded that they are still subject to temptation and must humbly strive to live the gospel themselves. Position does not give privilege as far as yielding to sin and temptation are concerned.

17 **Be not ashamed** [*don't be embarrassed to do what is right*], **neither confounded** [*stopped from performing your duties*]; **but be admonished** [*accept correction*] **in all your high-mindedness and**

pride, for it bringeth a snare upon your souls.

18 Set in order your houses; keep slothfulness and uncleanness far from you.

> Unfortunately, both Sidney Rigdon and Frederick G. Williams eventually apostatized and left the Church, both having been trapped in the "snare" of pride and high-mindedness (verse 17, above).
>
> Next, in verses 19–23, the Prophet is given specific instructions that he is to carry out. First, a home is to be provided for President Williams and his family.

19 Now, verily I say unto you, let there be a place provided, as soon as it is possible, for the family of thy counselor and scribe, even Frederick G. Williams.

20 And let mine aged servant, Joseph Smith, Sen. [*sixty-one years old at this time*], **continue with his family upon the place where he now lives**; and let it not be sold until the mouth of the Lord shall name.

21 And let my counselor, even Sidney Rigdon, remain where he now resides until the mouth of the Lord shall name.

22 And let the bishop [*Newel K. Whitney*] **search diligently to obtain an agent** [*to assist with managing the temporal affairs and needs of the Church in Ohio and the surrounding areas*], and **let him be a man who has got riches in store** [*he needs to be a man with considerable wealth available to him*]— **a man of God, and of strong faith**—

23 That thereby he may be enabled to discharge [*pay*] **every debt**; that the storehouse of the Lord [*the bishop's storehouse*] may not be brought into disrepute before the eyes of the people.

24 Search diligently, pray always, and be believing, and all things shall work together for your good, if ye walk uprightly and remember the covenant [*to live the law of consecration*] wherewith ye have covenanted one with another.

> In order to understand verse 25, next, we must know the context. Otherwise, we would think that the Lord is telling us to limit our families to very few children. First, the verse:

25 Let your families be small, especially mine aged servant Joseph Smith's, Sen., as pertaining to those who do not belong to your families;

The last phrase of verse 25, above, is a clue as to the meaning of "let your families be small." Because of the large numbers of Saints gathering in the Kirtland area at this time in history, it was common for a number of families to move in temporarily with other families, thus overloading the capability of the host families to care for all under their roof.

The generosity of the Prophet's father was apparently taking a heavy toll on him and his family, therefore, he was counseled to place tighter limits on the number of people he invited to live with him and his family.

Also, as we look at verse 26, next, we see a hint that some of the "guests" may have been taking advantage of the situation.

26 That those things that are provided for you, to bring to pass my work, be not taken from you and given to those that are not worthy—

27 And thereby you be hindered in accomplishing those things which I have commanded you.

Specific instructions are given to the Prophet in verses 28–31 regarding Sister Vienna Jaques. She had recently traveled alone from Boston to Kirtland at the age of forty-three after having glanced through the Book of Mormon and becoming convinced by a vision that it was worth reading.

After meeting the Prophet and being taught further by him, she was baptized. She returned to Boston, converted many family members, and returned to Kirtland with her valuables, which included $1,400 in savings that she consecrated to the Church on March 8, 1833, the day of this revelation to the Prophet.

By the way, she remained faithful despite going through all the Missouri persecutions of the Saints. At age sixty, she drove her own team and wagon across the plains, arriving in the Salt Lake Valley on October 2, 1847. She died at age ninety-six in her own home in Salt Lake City.

28 And again, verily I say unto you, **it is my will that my handmaid Vienna Jaques should receive money to bear her expenses, and go up unto the land of Zion** [*she is to be given sufficient money back from what she consecrated to the Church to enable her to go to Jackson County, Missouri, and settle with the Saints there*];

29 And **the residue of the money** [*the remainder of the $1,400 plus, which she consecrated to the Church in Kirtland*] **may be consecrated unto me, and she be rewarded in mine own due time.**

30 Verily I say unto you, that **it is**

meet in mine eyes [*it is the Lord's will*] **that she should go up unto the land of Zion, and receive an inheritance from the hand of the bishop** [*she is to be given land and supplies by Bishop Partridge when she arrives in Zion*];

31 **That she may settle down in peace inasmuch as she is faithful, and not be idle** [*a major principle in living the law of consecration*] **in her days from thenceforth.**

Verses 32–33 hint that some members in Missouri were complaining and grumbling because Joseph Smith was still living in Kirtland, and they felt that he was ignoring them by not coming to Missouri to live and help build up Zion.

32 And behold, verily I say unto you, that ye shall **write this commandment, and say unto your brethren in Zion, in love greeting** [*in kindness and gentleness*], **that I have called you also to preside over Zion in mine own due time** [*in other words, tell the brethren in Zion that I will have you come to Missouri when the time is right*].

33 Therefore, **let them cease wearying me concerning this matter.**

Verse 34, next, informs us that the attitude on the part of many in Missouri is improving. Still, verse 35 tells us of specific concerns dealing with William E. McLellin (see sections 66 and 67), Sidney Gilbert (the bishop's agent and assistant in Zion), and Bishop Edward Partridge (who was told in D&C 85:8 that he must stop trying to "steady the ark" by refusing to issue written deeds to those living the law of consecration—D&C 51:4–5—among other things).

34 Behold, I say unto you [*Joseph Smith*] that **your brethren in Zion begin to repent, and the angels rejoice over them.**

35 **Nevertheless, I am not well pleased with many things**; and **I am not well pleased with my servant William E. McLellin**, neither with my servant **Sidney Gilbert**; and **the bishop** [*Edward Partridge*] **also**, and **others have many things to repent of.**

36 But verily I say unto you, that **I, the Lord, will contend** [*will continue to work*] **with Zion, and plead with her strong ones** [*the local leaders of the Church in Missouri at this time*], **and chasten her until she overcomes and is clean before me.**

37 For **she shall not be removed out of her place** [*the city of Zion, New Jerusalem, and the temple will yet be built, as prophesied, in*

Independence, Missouri; see D&C 84:3–5]. **I, the Lord, have spoken it. Amen.**

SECTION 91

Background

This revelation was given through the Prophet Joseph Smith on March 9, 1833, in Kirtland, Ohio.

As you can see in the heading to section 91 in your Doctrine and Covenants, the Prophet was working on the inspired translation of the Bible, more particularly on the revising and correcting of the Old Testament at this time. The question came up as to whether or not he should translate the Apocrypha.

The Old Testament Apocrypha consists of fifteen ancient texts that were not included in the Hebrew Bible but that were included in the Greek Old Testament referred to as the Septuagint. They were considered scripture by some but not by others.

They ultimately became part of the Christian Bible until Martin Luther came along and placed them in a different section in the Bible referred to as the "Apocrypha." They are of questionable value and validity and are contained in some editions of the Bible but not in others today. The King James version of the Bible used by Joseph Smith in his inspired translation of the Bible contained the Apocrypha, located between the Old Testament and the New Testament. Thus, his question to the Lord as to whether or not he should translate it.

They are books in addition to the thirty-nine books of the Old Testament. These apocryphal books are

1. The First Book of Esdras
2. The Second Book of Esdras
3. Tobit
4. Judith
5. The Rest of the Chapters of the Book of Esther
6. The Wisdom of Solomon
7. Ecclesiasticus or the Wisdom of Jesus son of Sirach
8. Baruch
9. A Letter of Jeremiah
10. The Song of the Three
11. Daniel and Susanna
12. Daniel, Bel, and the Snake
13. The Prayer of Manasseh
14. The First Book of the Maccabees
15. The Second Book of the Maccabees

The Lord's answer is found next in section 91.

SECTION 92

1 VERILY, thus saith the Lord unto you concerning the Apocrypha—**There are many things contained therein that are true, and it is mostly translated correctly;**

2 **There are many things contained therein that are not true,** which are interpolations by the hands of men.

3 Verily, I say unto you, that **it is not needful that the Apocrypha should be translated** [*in other words, you don't need to include the Apocrypha in your JST work on the Bible*].

4 Therefore, **whoso readeth it, let him understand, for the Spirit manifesteth truth;**

5 And **whoso is enlightened by the Spirit shall obtain benefit therefrom;**

6 And **whoso receiveth not by the Spirit, cannot be benefited. Therefore it is not needful that it should be translated.** Amen.

SECTION 92

Background

This revelation was given to the Prophet Joseph Smith on March 15, 1833, in Kirtland, Ohio. It was given to Frederick G. Williams regarding his duties in the United Firm in Kirtland (see heading to section 92 in the 2013 edition of the Doctrine and Covenants).

Frederick G. Williams had recently been called to be a counselor in the First Presidency, to serve with Joseph Smith and Sidney Rigdon (see D&C 81:1).

Although this revelation consists of just two verses, it contains at least two messages that apply to all of us. They are that each of us should "be a lively member" in the Church (verse 2), and that by keeping the commandments we have been given, we qualify for eternal blessings (verse 2).

1 VERILY, thus saith the Lord, **I give unto the united order** [*the formal organization of those in the Ohio area who were living the law of consecration*], organized agreeable to the commandment previously given, **a revelation and commandment concerning my servant Frederick G. Williams, that ye shall receive him into the order** [*the United Firm. See background notes for section 82 in this study guide*]. **What I say unto one I say unto all.**

Verse 2 is specifically addressed to President Williams, recently appointed as a counselor in the First Presidency.

2 And again, I say unto you my

servant Frederick G. Williams, **you shall be a lively member** in this order; and **inasmuch as you are faithful in keeping all former commandments you shall be blessed forever.** Amen.

SECTION 93

Background

This revelation was given through the Prophet Joseph Smith in Kirtland, Ohio, on May 6, 1833. It is a powerful revelation about our potential to become like our Heavenly Father. It is a "high mountain" revelation in the sense that it takes us up into a "high mountain," as it were (compare to Nephi's experience in 1 Nephi 11:1), and lets us see things as the Lord does, thus giving us knowledge and perspective that enable us to make better decisions and draw closer to the Lord in our daily living, especially when we are faced with opposition. (See notes about "high mountain experiences" in the background for section 88.)

At this time, opposition to the Church and the faithful members was mounting, both in Missouri and in Kirtland. This revelation provided additional strength and perspective for enduring the increasing opposition from within and from outside the Church.

In early April, a mob of about three hundred men had gathered in Missouri and attempted to organize to drive the Saints from their land. Also, some members of the Church had apostatized in both Ohio and Missouri and were a source of persecution against the Saints.

The Prophet provided information about the mob in Missouri as follows:

"In the month of April, the first regular mob rushed together, in Independence, to consult upon a plan, for the removal, or immediate destruction, of the Church in Jackson county. The number of the mob was about three hundred. A few of the first Elders met in secret, and prayed to Him who said to the wind, 'Be still,' to frustrate them in their wicked designs. The mob, therefore, after spending the day in a fruitless endeavor to unite upon a general scheme for 'moving the Mormons out of their diggings' (as they asserted), became a little the worse for liquor and broke up in a regular Missouri 'row,' showing a determined resolution that every man would 'carry his own head'" (*History of the Church*, 1:342).

In this revelation, we will be given many doctrines and insights that can help us maintain a steady course on the covenant path toward exaltation.

First, in verses 1–5, the Savior bears witness of His existence, and the fact that the faithful can know, without doubt, that He exists.

1 VERILY, thus saith the Lord: It shall come to pass that **every soul who forsaketh his sins** and **cometh unto me,** and **calleth on my name** [*both by praying and by making covenants in the name of Jesus Christ and keeping them*], and **obeyeth my voice,** and **keepeth my commandments, shall see my face and know that I am;**

> Regarding the privilege of literally seeing the Savior, D&C 88:68 reminds us that it will be "in his own time, and in his own way, and according to his own will." Thus, it could be during this life or in the next.
>
> The most powerful witness of all that the Savior exists comes not by literally seeing Him but rather through the witness of the Holy Ghost. Thus, all who fulfill the requirements spelled out in verse 1, above, can "see" the Savior and "know" now by the power of the Holy Ghost that He is.
>
> Next, the Master reminds us that everyone born on earth is blessed with a conscience and has the Light of Christ to guide and direct them in every aspect of living. You may wish to refer back to D&C 88:6–13 to gain further insights as to the powerful influence of the Light of Christ. As you will see, it is much more than a conscience.

Doctrine, verse 2

Everyone has a conscience plus much more because of the Light of Christ.

2 And that **I am the true light that lighteth every man that cometh into the world;**

> Next, the Savior teaches us that He and His Father work together in perfect harmony with each other.

3 And that **I am in the Father, and the Father in me, and the Father and I are one—**

> We see much of symbolism, next, as Jesus explains how He is both the "Father" and the "Son." You may wish to read Mosiah 15:1–5 before going on. In effect, Jesus is the "Father" of our salvation. He is the "Father" of our being "born again." We are His "children" symbolically (see Mosiah 5:7) because He is the "Father of our salvation," because He carried out the Atonement in our behalf. He is the Father of our salvation in the same sense that George Washington is the "father" of our country.
>
> He is the "Son" because He is literally the Son of God the Father.

4 **The Father** [*of our salvation*] **because he** [*Heavenly Father*] **gave me of his fulness** [*because the Father gave Him all power and authority to be our Redeemer*], and **the Son**

because I was in the world and made flesh my tabernacle, and dwelt among the sons of men.

Next, in verse 5, Jesus teaches, in effect, that He came on earth to live in order to teach about His Father, and that the Father's love and mercy are plainly shown by the plan of salvation.

5 **I was in the world** [*Jesus came to earth to perform His mortal mission*] **and received of my Father** [*received all that was needed from the Father in order to carry out His mission*]**, and the works of him** [*the Father*] **were plainly manifest.**

John the Baptist kept a record, but we do not have it in the Bible. Someday we will get it (see verses 6 and 18). In the meantime, verses 6–18, next, give us excerpts from his record. This is an example of the restoration of an ancient record through pure revelation and is similar to the Book of Moses in the Pearl of Great Price.

As we study these verses, you will get a better feeling for the greatness of John the Baptist. In fact, Jesus said, "Among them that are born of women there hath not risen a greater than John the Baptist" (Matthew 11:11). It is hoped that you will feel the greatness of his testimony by the power of the Holy Ghost.

6 And **John** [*the Baptist*] **saw and bore record of the fulness of my glory**, and the fulness of John's record [*the complete record kept by John the Baptist*] is hereafter to be revealed.

7 And **he bore record, saying: I saw his** [*Christ's*] **glory, that he was in the beginning, before the world was;**

8 Therefore, **in the beginning the Word** [*Jesus Christ*] **was,** for **he was the Word, even the messenger of salvation—**

9 **The light and the Redeemer of the world; the Spirit of truth,** who came into the world, because **the world was made by him, and in him was the life of men and the light of men.**

10 **The worlds** [*worlds without number—compare with Moses 1:33*] **were made by him; men were made by him; all things were made by him, and through him, and of him.**

11 And **I, John, bear record that I beheld his glory, as the glory of the Only Begotten of the Father, full of grace and truth, even the Spirit of truth, which came and dwelt in the flesh, and dwelt among us.**

Next, in verses 12–13, John the Baptist teaches us, in effect, that

Jesus began with the veil and learned and grew as part of His mortal experience.

12 And I, John, saw that he received not of the fulness at the first, but received grace for grace;

13 And he received not of the fulness at first, but continued from grace to grace, until he received a fulness;

Apostle James E. Talmage taught that Jesus had the veil over the memory of His premortal life when He began His mortal life on earth, just as we do. He said:

"Over His mind had fallen the veil of forgetfulness common to all who are born to earth, by which the remembrance of primeval existence is shut off. The Child grew, and with growth there came to Him expansion of mind, development of faculties, and progression in power and understanding. His advancement was from one grace to another, not from gracelessness to grace; from good to greater good, not from evil to good, from favor with God to greater favor, not from estrangement because of sin to reconciliation through repentance and propitiation" (*Jesus the Christ*, 111).

On this same subject, President Lorenzo Snow taught:

"When Jesus lay in the manger, a helpless infant, He knew not that He was the Son of God, and that formerly He created the earth. When the edict of Herod was issued, He knew nothing of it; He had not power to save Himself; and His father and mother had to take Him and fly into Egypt to preserve Him from the effects of that edict. Well, He grew up to manhood, and during His progress it was revealed unto Him who He was, and for what purpose He was in the world. The glory and power He possessed before He came into the world was made known unto Him" (In Conference Report, April 1901, 3.)

14 And thus he was called the Son of God, because he received not of the fulness at the first.

Next, in verse 15, John the Baptist tells us about the marvelous witness given to him at the time he baptized the Savior.

15 And I, John, bear record, and lo, the heavens were opened, and the Holy Ghost descended upon him in the form of a dove, and sat upon him, and there came a voice out of heaven saying: This is my beloved Son.

We learn from the teachings of Joseph Smith that the phrase "in the form of a dove," as given in verse 15, above, is symbolic rather than literal. The dove represented the fact that the Holy Ghost was present and came upon the Savior. The

Prophet Joseph Smith, speaking of John the Baptist, taught (**bold** added for emphasis):

"He was entrusted with the important mission, and it was required at his hands, to baptize the Son of Man. Whoever had the honor of doing that? Whoever had so great a privilege and glory? Whoever led the Son of God into the waters of baptism, and had the privilege of **beholding the Holy Ghost descend in the form of a dove, or rather in the *sign* of the dove**, in witness of that administration? The sign of the dove was instituted before the creation of the world, a witness for the Holy Ghost, and the devil cannot come in the sign of a dove. **The Holy Ghost is a personage, and is in the form of a personage. It does not confine itself to the *form* of the dove, but in *sign* of the dove. The Holy Ghost cannot be transformed into a dove**; but the sign of a dove was given to John to signify the truth of the deed, as the dove is an emblem or token of truth and innocence (*Teachings of the Prophet Joseph Smith*, 275–76).

16 And **I, John, bear record that he received a fulness of the glory of the Father**;

17 And **he received all power, both in heaven and on earth, and the glory of the Father was with him**, for he dwelt in him.

In verse 18, next, the Savior informs us that we will yet be given the full record kept by John the Baptist if we are faithful.

18 And **it shall come to pass, that if you are faithful you shall receive the fulness of the record of John.**

Perhaps you have noticed that the majority of those in the world who believe in God do not know what they worship. Consequently, they do not really know how to worship, nor do they realize that they can become like God.

Next, in verse 19, the Savior tells us why He revealed John the Baptist's teachings and testimony to us (given above), as well as why He gives us the teachings in verses 20–39, next.

19 **I give unto you these sayings that you may understand and know how to worship, and know what you worship, that you may come unto the Father in my name, and in due time receive of his fulness** [*become like the Father—in other words, receive exaltation in celestial glory*].

20 For **if you keep my commandments you shall receive of his fulness** [*will be exalted*], **and be glorified in me as I am in the Father**; therefore, I say unto you, **you shall receive grace for grace**

[*this will come step by step, with the help (the grace) of God*].

21 And now, verily I say unto you, **I was in the beginning with the Father, and am the Firstborn** [*Jesus is the firstborn of all the Father's spirit children; see Colossians 1:13–15*];

22 And **all those who are begotten through me** [*who are "born again" through the Atonement of Christ*] **are partakers of the glory of the same** [*receive exaltation*], **and are the church of the Firstborn** [*another term for exaltation; see D&C 76:58, 94*].

23 **Ye were also in the beginning with the Father**; that which is Spirit, even the Spirit of truth [*we will do more with this when we get to verse 29*];

> Next, the Savior defines pure truth.

24 And **truth is knowledge of things as they are, and as they were, and as they are to come**;

25 And **whatsoever is more or less than this is the spirit of that wicked one** [*the devil*] **who was a liar from the beginning.**

26 **The Spirit of truth is of God. I am the Spirit of truth** [*compare with D&C 88:6–13*], and **John bore record of me, saying: He received a fulness of truth, yea, even of all truth**;

27 And **no man receiveth a fulness** [*no one receives all the Father has to give—exaltation*] **unless he keepeth his commandments.**

> Next, in verses 28–29, the Savior teaches us that gaining exaltation is a step-by-step process that began in our premortal existence. As we obeyed the commandments of God back then, and as we obey them now, we gradually and definitely progress toward exaltation.
>
> In fact, in the context of this lesson from the Master Teacher, "intelligence" will be defined as the behavior of forsaking "that evil one" (verse 37)—in other words, avoiding evil and following the light brought by the gospel of Jesus Christ.

28 **He that keepeth his commandments receiveth truth and light, until he is glorified in truth and knoweth all things** [*has become a god*].

29 **Man was also in the beginning with God. Intelligence, or the light of truth, was not created or made, neither indeed can be.**

> Verse 29, above, is an important doctrine of the plan of salvation. It teaches us that we have always

existed. The basic part of us, intelligence, "was not created or made." The Prophet Joseph Smith explained this. He said:

"Is it logical to say that the intelligence of spirits is immortal, and yet that it has a beginning? The intelligence of spirits had no beginning, neither will it have an end" (*History of the Church,* 6:311).

30 **All truth is independent in that sphere in which God has placed it, to act for itself, as all intelligence also** [*in other words, we had agency in premortality also; see D&C 29:36*]; otherwise there is no existence.

31 Behold, **here is the agency of man,** and **here is the condemnation of man** [*here is how man gets himself in trouble*]; because **that** [*the truths of the gospel*] **which was from the beginning is plainly manifest unto them, and they receive not the light** [*they reject the gospel*].

32 And **every man whose spirit receiveth not the light is under condemnation** [*is accountable and is thus being slowed or stopped in his progress*].

Doctrine, verses 33–34

We cannot have the highest satisfaction and joy until our spirit and body are permanently joined in exaltation.

33 For man is spirit. The elements are eternal, and **spirit and element, inseparably connected, receive a fulness of joy** [*the only way to receive the highest joy and happiness—in other words, the "fulness" (verse 27) of the Father—is to be resurrected into a celestial body (D&C 88:28–29) and to enter into exaltation*];

34 And **when separated** [*without resurrection*], **man cannot receive a fulness of joy.**

Next, we are reminded that we are a "temple" in which the Spirit of God can reside. We must keep our "temple" clean.

35 **The elements are the tabernacle of God** [*the Father has a resurrected body of "flesh and bones, as tangible as man's"; see D&C 130:22*]; yea, **man is the tabernacle of God, even temples; and whatsoever temple is defiled, God shall destroy that temple.**

Verses 36 and 37, next, go together. They teach that true "intelligence" is the behavior of forsaking evil. We are empowered to forsake evil by the "light and truth" that we accept from God. (In this context, "intelligence" has nothing to do with IQ.)

Doctrine, verses 36–37

True intelligence, in the eternal, spiritual sense, is the behavior of forsaking evil.

36 The glory of God is intelligence, or, in other words, light and truth.

37 Light and truth forsake that evil one [*Satan and his temptations*].

As you will see, when we get to verse 39, the devil's major goal and focus is to take "light and truth" away from us.

But first there are important and interesting doctrines taught in verse 38, next.

38 Every spirit of man was innocent in the beginning [*we all started out innocent as spirits in premortality*]; **and God having redeemed man from the fall, men became again, in their infant state, innocent before God** [*we all became innocent again when we were born into mortality*].

As we study the implications of what is taught in verse 38, above, we conclude that since we were "innocent" when we were born as spirit children of Heavenly Parents (we know we have "parents" in heaven because it is so stated in "The Family: A Proclamation to the World"; see *Ensign* or *Liahona*, Nov. 2010, 129), and since we became "again" innocent upon mortal birth, then we must not have remained "innocent" throughout our premortal education as spirits.

That this was the case is evident from the War in Heaven. This, then, brings up the question as to whether we could sin, repent, be forgiven and thus progress during our premortal probation. In other words, did the Atonement of Christ work for us there? The answer is "yes." We will provide two quotes in support of this answer.

The first quote is from the 1979 New Testament student manual, *The Life and Teachings of Jesus and His Apostles*, used by the institutes of religion of the Church. We read (**bold** added for emphasis):

"Some accounts that we have of the premortal life teach that we 'were on the same standing' (Alma 13:5), and that we were 'innocent' in the beginning (D&C 93:38). **We were given laws and agency, and commandments to have faith and repent from the wrongs that we could do there. '... Man could and did in many instances, sin before he was born.'** (Smith, *The Way to Perfection*, 44.)

"'God gave his children their agency even in the spirit world, by which the individual spirits had the privilege, just as men have here, of choosing the good and rejecting the evil, or partaking of the evil to suffer the consequences of their sins. . . . Some even there were more faithful than others in keeping the commandments of the Lord. . . .

"'The spirits of men . . . had an equal start, and we know they were all innocent in the beginning; but the right of free agency which was given to them enabled some to outstrip others, and thus, through the eons of immortal existence, to become more intelligent, more faithful, for they were free to act for themselves, to think for themselves, to receive the truth or rebel against it.' (Smith, *Doctrines of Salvation,* 1:58–59.)" (Quoted in *Life and Teachings of Jesus and His Apostles,* 336.)

The second quote is from Elder Jeffrey R. Holland. He said:

"We could remember that even in the Grand Council of Heaven [in the premortal realm] He loved us and was wonderfully strong, that we triumphed even there by the power of Christ and our faith in the blood of the Lamb" ("'This Do in Remembrance of Me,'" *Ensign,* November 1995, 68).

Revelation 12:11 teaches the same doctrine.

Revelation 12:11

11 And **they** [*premortal spirits*] **overcame him** [*the devil*] **by the blood of the Lamb** [*the Atonement of Christ*]**, and by the word of their testimony; and they** [*righteous mortals who applied the Atonement to their lives on earth*] **loved not their lives unto the death.**

Verse 39, next, summarizes the efforts of the adversary to take light and truth—in other words, "intelligence" (verses 36–37, above), away from us.

39 And **that wicked one** [*Satan*] cometh and **taketh away light and truth, through disobedience, from the children of men** [*people*]**, and because of the tradition of their fathers.**

There is a transition now, and in verses 40–53, the Savior gives instructions to the Prophet and others. He reproves some of the leaders for not taking proper care in teaching their children and setting their own houses in order. There is good counsel for all parents here.

40 But **I have commanded you to bring up your children in light and truth.**

41 **But verily I say unto you, my servant Frederick G. Williams** [*a counselor to the Prophet in the First Presidency*]**, you have continued under this condemnation;**

42 **You have not taught your children light and truth, according to the commandments; and that wicked one hath power, as yet, over you, and this is the cause of your affliction.**

43 And now a commandment I give unto you—**if you will be delivered you shall set in order your own house**, for there are many things that are not right in your house.

44 Verily, **I say unto my servant Sidney Rigdon, that in some things he hath not kept the commandments concerning his children**; therefore, **first set in order thy house.**

45 Verily, I say unto my servant Joseph Smith, Jun., or in other words, **I will call you friends, for you are my friends**, and **ye shall have an inheritance with me** [this is very encouraging and gives hope during this time of being called to repentance]—

46 I called you servants for the world's sake, and **ye are their servants for my sake**—

47 **And now, verily I say unto Joseph Smith, Jun.—You have not kept the commandments, and must needs stand rebuked before the Lord;**

48 **Your family must needs repent and forsake some things, and give more earnest heed unto your sayings**, or be removed out of their place.

As mentioned above, the advice given to specific brethren above can apply to all of us.

49 **What I say unto one I say unto all; pray always lest that wicked one have power in you, and remove you out of your place** [in the kingdom of God].

50 My servant **Newel K. Whitney** [the bishop in Kirtland] also, a bishop of my church, **hath need to be chastened, and set in order his family, and see that they are more diligent and concerned at home, and pray always**, or they shall be removed out of their place.

51 Now, I say unto you, **my friends, let my servant Sidney Rigdon go on his journey**, and make haste, and also proclaim the acceptable year of the Lord [a phrase meaning to preach the gospel of Christ], and the gospel of salvation, as I shall give him utterance; **and by your prayer of faith with one consent I will uphold him.**

Did you notice at the end of verse 51, above, that the Lord says that our prayers in behalf of others have an effect on the blessings they receive?

Sidney Rigdon had been the main scribe, assisting the Prophet with the translation of the Bible (the JST). With him gone on a preaching journey, Frederick G. Williams was to take over as scribe. You can see from verses 52–53, next, that the Lord is anxious for them to continue with the translation of the Bible and with the School of the Prophets (see D&C 88:118–41).

52 And **let my servants Joseph Smith, Jun., and Frederick G. Williams make haste also** [*in the work of translating the Bible*]**, and it shall be given them even according to the prayer of faith; and inasmuch as you keep my sayings you shall not be confounded in this world, nor in the world to come.**

53 **And, verily I say unto you, that it is my will that you should hasten to translate my scriptures** [*The JST*]**, and to obtain a knowledge of history, and of countries, and of kingdoms, of laws of God and man** [*in the school of the prophets*]**, and all this for the salvation of Zion.** Amen.

The Joseph Smith Papers, Documents, Volume 3: February 1833–March 1834, 166, tells us that they diligently finished the translation of the Bible (the JST) on July 2, 1833, a short two months after verses 52 and 53, above, were given them by the Lord.

Sources

Anderson, Richard Lloyd. *Investigating the Book of Mormon Witnesses*. Salt Lake City: Deseret Book, 1981.

Barrett, Ivan J. *Joseph Smith and the Restoration*. Provo, UT: Brigham Young University, 1982.

Black, Susan Easton. *Who's Who in the Doctrine and Covenants*. Salt Lake City: Bookcraft, 1997.

Book of Mormon Student Manual. Salt Lake City: The Church of Jesus Christ of Latter-day Saints (Institutes of Religion), 1982.

Cannon, George Q. *Life of Joseph Smith the Prophet*. Good Press, 1888.

———. *Life of Joseph Smith the Prophet*. Salt Lake City: Deseret News Press, 1907.

Church History in the Fulness of Times. Salt Lake City: The Church of Jesus Christ of Latter-day Saints (Institutes of Religion), 1989, 2003.

Clark, James R. (Compiler.) *Messages of the First Presidency of The Church of Jesus Christ of Latter-day Saints*. 6 vols. Salt Lake City: Bookcraft, 1965–75.

Conference Reports of The Church of Jesus Christ of Latter-day Saints. Salt Lake City: The Church of Jesus Christ of Latter-day Saints, 1898 to the present.

Cowley, Matthias F. *Wilford Woodruff: History of His Life and Labors*. 2d ed. Salt Lake City: Bookcraft, 1964.

Doctrine and Covenants Student Manual. Salt Lake City: The Church of Jesus Christ of Latter-day Saints (Institutes of Religion), 1981, 2018.

Doctrines of the Gospel Student Manual. Salt Lake City: The Church of Jesus Christ of Latter-day Saints (Institutes of Religion), 1981.

Doxey, Roy W. (Compiler.) *Latter-day Prophets and the Doctrine and Covenants*. Salt Lake City: Deseret Book, 1978.

"The Family: A Proclamation to the World." *Ensign or Liahona*, Nov. 2010, 129.

Hancock, Levi Ward. Autobiography. Typescript. L. Tom Perry Special Collections, Harold B. Lee Library, Brigham Young University, Provo, Utah.

Hinckley, Bryant S. *Sermons and Missionary Services of Melvin J. Ballard*. Salt Lake City: Deseret Book, 1949.

Joseph Smith Papers, The. Salt Lake City: Church Historian's Press. See also josephsmithpapers.org. (These books consist of several volumes now [2020] and will consist of more than 30 volumes when they are complete.)

Journal of Discourses. 26 vols. London: Latter-day Saints' Book Depot, 1854–86.

Kimball, Spencer W. *The Teachings of Spencer W. Kimball.* Edited by Edward L. Kimball. Salt Lake City: Bookcraft, 1982.

Lang, W. *History of Seneca County [Ohio], from the Close of the Revolutionary War to July, 1880.* Woburn, MA: Unigraphic, 1973.

Latter-day Saints' Millennial Star, The. Manchester, Liverpool, and London, England: The Church of Jesus Christ of Latter-day Saints, 1840–1970.

Life and Teachings of Jesus and His Apostles: New Testament Student Manual, The. Salt Lake City: The Church of Jesus Christ of Latter-day Saints, 1979.

Ludlow, Daniel H. *Encyclopedia of Mormonism.* Edited by Daniel H. Ludlow. 5 vols. New York: Macmillan, 1992.

Lundwall, N. B. *Temples of the Most High.* Salt Lake City: Bookcraft, 1971.

Matthews, Robert J. *A Plainer Translation: Joseph Smith's Translation of the Bible—A History and Commentary.* Provo, Utah: Brigham Young University Press, 1975.

McConkie, Bruce R. *Doctrinal New Testament Commentary.* 3 vols. Salt Lake City: Bookcraft, 1965–73.

———. *The Millennial Messiah: The Second Coming of the Son of Man.* Salt Lake City: Deseret Book, 1982.

———. *Mormon Doctrine.* 2d ed. Salt Lake City: Bookcraft, 1966.

———. *The Mortal Messiah: From Bethlehem to Calgary.* 4 vols. Salt Lake City: Deseret Book, 1979–81.

———. *The Promised Messiah: The First Coming of Christ.* Salt Lake City: Deseret Book, 1978.

McGavin, Cecil E. *Historical Background of the Doctrine and Covenants.* Salt Lake City: Literary Licensing, 2011.

Otten, L. G. *Historical Background and Setting for each section of the Doctrine and Covenants.* Privately published, 1970.

Pratt, Parley P. *Autobiography of Parley P. Pratt.* Salt Lake City: Deseret Book, 1938–1985.

Proctor, Scott and Maurine. *The Revised and Enhanced History of Joseph Smith by His Mother.* Salt Lake City: Bookcraft, 1996.

Revelations in Context. Edited by Matthew McBride and James Goldberg (2016). See history.lds.org.

Roberts, B. H. *A Comprehensive History of The Church of Jesus Christ of Latter-day Saints, Century One.* 6 vols. Salt Lake City: Deseret Press, 1930.

Smith, Hyrum M. and Janne M. Sjodahl. *Doctrine and Covenants Commentary.* Salt Lake City: Deseret Book, 1951.

SOURCES

Smith, Joseph. *History of The Church of Jesus Christ of Latter-day Saints.* Edited by B. H. Roberts. 2d ed. rev., 7 vols. Salt Lake City: The Church of Jesus Christ of Latter-day Saints, 1932–51.

———. *Teachings of the Prophet Joseph Smith.* Selected by Joseph Fielding Smith. Salt Lake City: Deseret Book, 1976.

Smith, Joseph F. *Gospel Doctrine.* Salt Lake City: Deseret Book, 1939.

Smith, Joseph Fielding. *Answers to Gospel Questions.* Compiled by Joseph Fielding Smith Jr. 5 vols. Salt Lake City: Deseret Book, 1957–66.

———. *Church History and Modern Revelation—A Course Study for Melchizedek Priesthood Quorums.* Salt Lake City: The Council of the Twelve Apostles of The Church of Jesus Christ of Latter-day Saints, 1946.

———. *Doctrines of Salvation.* Compiled by Bruce R. McConkie. 3 vols. Salt Lake City: Bookcraft, 1954–56.

———. *Way to Perfection.* Salt Lake City: Deseret Book, 1975.

Smith, Lucy Mack. *History of Joseph Smith by His Mother, Lucy Mack Smith.* Salt Lake City: Bookcraft, 1958.

Talmage, James E. *The Articles of Faith.* Salt Lake City: Deseret Book, 1984.

Talmage, James E. *Jesus the Christ.* Salt Lake City: Deseret Book, 1977.

Teachings of Presidents of the Church—Wilford Woodruff. Salt Lake City: The Church of Jesus Christ of Latter-day Saints, 2004.

———. *Jesus the Christ.* Salt Lake City: Deseret Book, 1977.

Times and Seasons. Commerce (later Nauvoo), Illinois, 1839–46.

Widtsoe, John A. *Evidences and Reconciliations.* Salt Lake City: Bookcraft, 1943.

———. *The Message of the Doctrine and Covenants.* Salt Lake City: Bookcraft, 1978.

———. *The Word of Wisdom: A Modern Interpretation.* Salt Lake City: Deseret Book, 1938.

Young, Brigham. *Discourses of Brigham Young.* Selected by John A. Widtsoe. Salt Lake City: Deseret Book, 1954.

Additional sources for the notes given in this work are as follows:

- The Standard Works of The Church of Jesus Christ of Latter-day Saints.
- Footnotes in the Latter-day Saint version of the King James Bible.
- The Joseph Smith Translation of the Bible.

SOURCES

- The Bible Dictionary in the back of the Latter-day Saint version of the King James Bible.
- Various dictionaries.
- Various student manuals provided for our institutes of religion.
- Other sources as noted in the text.

About the Author

David J. Ridges was raised in southeastern Nevada until his family moved to North Salt Lake City, Utah, when he was in fifth grade. He is the second of eight children.

Brother Ridges graduated from Bountiful High, served a two-and-a-half-year German-speaking mission to Austria, attended the University of Utah and BYU, and then graduated from BYU with a major in German and a physics minor. He later received a master's degree in educational psychology with a Church History minor from BYU.

He taught seminary and institute of religion as his chosen career for thirty-five years. He taught BYU Campus Education Week, Especially for Youth, Adult Religion, and Know Your Religion classes for over twenty-five years.

ABOUT THE AUTHOR

Brother Ridges has served as a Sunday School and seminary curriculum writer. He has had many callings, including Gospel Doctrine teacher, bishop, stake president, and patriarch. He and Sister Ridges have served two full-time, eighteen-month CES missions. He has written over forty books, which include several study guides for the standard works, Isaiah, Revelation, and many doctrinal publications on gospel topics such as the signs of the times, plan of salvation, and temples.

Brother and Sister Ridges met at the University of Utah. They were married in the Salt Lake Temple, are the parents of six children, and have sixteen grandchildren and one great-granddaughter so far. They make their home in Springville, Utah.

Scan to visit

www.davidjridges.com

Notes

Notes

Notes

Notes

Notes

Notes